W9-CZO-483

Books by David Madden

FICTION:

On the Big Wind (1980)
Pleasure-Dome (1979)
The Suicide's Wife (1978)
Bijou (1974)
Brothers in Confidence (1972)
The Shadow Knows (stories) (1970)
Cassandra Singing (1969)
The Beautiful Greed (1961)

NONFICTION

Harlequin's Stick, Charlie's Cane (1975)
James M. Cain (1970)
The Poetic Image in Six Genres (1969)
Wright Morris (1964)

EDITED WORKS

Nathanael West: The Cheaters and the Cheated (1973)
Contemporary Literary Scene (co-editor) (1974)
Rediscoveries (1971)
American Dreams, American Nightmares (1970)
Tough Guy Writers of the Thirties (1968)
Proletarian Writers of the Thirties (1968)

TEXTBOOKS

Studies in the Short Story (co-editor) (1979)
Creative Choices (short story) (1975)
The Popular Culture Explosion (co-editor) (1972)

A PRIMER OF THE NOVEL: *FOR READERS & WRITERS*

by

David Madden

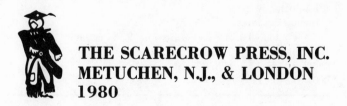

THE SCARECROW PRESS, INC.
METUCHEN, N.J., & LONDON
1980

Permission to use excerpts from the following works has been granted by the publishers: A. Camus, *The Stranger*, copyright © 1942 by Alfred A. Knopf; T. Capote, *Other Voices, Other Rooms*, copyright © 1948 by Random House, Inc.; J. Conrad, *Victory*, copyright © 1915, 1921 by Doubleday & Co., Inc.; © 1915 by Joseph Conrad; W. Faulkner, *The Sound and the Fury*, copyright © 1929 by Random House, Inc.; F. Scott Fitzgerald, *The Great Gatsby*, copyright © 1925 by Charles Scribner's Sons; also by The Bodley Head; G. García Márquez, *One Hundred Years of Solitude*, by Harper & Row; J. Heller, *Catch-22*, copyright © 1961 by Simon & Schuster; E. Hemingway, *The Sun Also Rises*, copyright © 1926 by Charles Scribner's Sons; and with the title, *Fiesta*, by Jonathan Cape, Ltd.; with thanks to the Executors of the Ernest Hemingway Estate; J. Joyce, *Portrait of the Artist as a Young Man*, copyright © 1916 by The Viking Press, Inc.; and thanks also to The Society of Authors, representing the Estate of James Joyce; J. Joyce, *Ulysses*, copyright © 1934 by Random House, Inc.; D. H. Lawrence, *The Rainbow*, copyright © 1915 by The Viking Press, Inc.; thanks also to Laurence Pollinger, Ltd., and to the Estate of the late Frieda Lawrence Ravagli; C. McCullers, *The Heart Is a Lonely Hunter*, copyright © 1940 by Houghton Mifflin Co.; © 1967 by Carson McCullers; S. Maugham, *Of Human Bondage*, copyright © 1915 by Doubleday & Co., Inc.; thanks to A. P. Watt, Ltd., and to the Estate of the late W. Somerset Maugham; J. C. Oates, *With Shuddering Fall*, copyright © 1964 by Joyce Carol Oates, published by Vanguard Press, Inc.; M. Proust, *Remembrance of Things Past*, copyright © 1934 by Random House, Inc.; V. Woolf, *To the Lighthouse*, by Harcourt Brace Jovanovich, Inc., and by The Hogarth Press, Ltd.

Library of Congress Cataloging in Publication Data

Madden, David, 1933–
  A primer of the novel.

  Bibliography: p.
  Includes indexes.
  1. Fiction—History and criticism. 2. Fiction
—Technique. I. Title.
PN3353.M25   808.3'3   79-21881
ISBN 0-8108-1265-7

For my students and my teachers

ACKNOWLEDGMENTS

I am grateful for invaluable editorial assistance that only Peggy Bach could have given.

I want to thank Joyce Carol Oates for suggesting this project. Charlene Clark prepared an early version of the chronology. My wife Robbie offered many good suggestions in the early drafts, as did Larry Shaffer, Maureen Trobec, and Martha Hall.

I wish to thank the following publishers for allowing me to reprint material: Frank Magill, *Collier's Encyclopedia*, Scott-Foresman, Holt, Rinehart, and Winston, Southern Illinois University Press, and Crown; and the following magazines: *The English Record, Renaissance, Literature and Psychology,* and *Ohio University Review*.

CONTENTS

viii / Contents

x / Contents

PREFACE

As writer, student, teacher, critic, and reader, I've often felt the need of a book such as *A Primer of the Novel;* forced to work without one for many years, I finally decided to put one together myself. I have done the job as much in the role of a novelist and reader as critic and teacher. Although most of the book is as objective as I could make it, personal opinions do flare up. And although I have drawn primarily upon existing knowledge and critical concepts, I have invented a few variations (especially on terms for types), and formulated several critical concepts, such as "the charged image." Because I think I have done work that will be useful to me, I imagine this book will have various uses for other fiction writers, teachers, students, critics, and general readers.

The book is organized so that it may be read from cover to cover, but I want to suggest to casual users some of its uses:

If you're interested only in reading a discussion of a particular technique—point of view, for instance—simply consult the table of contents under techniques, or consult the techniques index, which will tell you not only where to find the general discussion of point of view but also references to it throughout the book.

If you wish to read about a type—the historical novel, for instance—consult either the table of contents under types or the types index.

Following your own interests, you may wish to read sections out of order; for instance, you may begin with the essays in the "Close Analyses" section.

Suppose you're reading Dickens's *Bleak House* and you wonder what other novels were published in England or around the world in the same year or decade. Consult the chronology.

Or suppose you're reading *Bleak House* and you want to know more about Dickens's technique: consult the authors and titles index.

If you're a teacher, you may want to put together a course consisting of American novels of the thirties. See the chronology.

If you're in a creative writing workshop, you may wish to make use mainly of Part II, Techniques.

If you're studying short fiction, most of the material in this book applies as well to short stories and novellas (some novellas are discussed; for instance, Camus' *The Stranger*).

Here and there, critics are cited briefly. For fuller publication data, consult the selective bibliography of criticism of the novel (which also provides, by the way, an outline of critical approaches).

If you want to see how several technical concepts apply to a single work, read one of the essays in the "Close Analyses" section.

If you want to know the birth and death dates of an author and do not know the year of publication of any of his books, consult the index, where a "C" will indicate the page of the chronology on which that information is first given. Outside the chronology, publication dates for novels are given only in Part I, Types (dates would have cluttered Part II, Techniques unnecessarily).

If you want to know the nationality of an author, consult the chronology. Nationalities are *usually* given also in Part I, Types *only* if the author is neither American nor English, on the assumption that American and English writers are better known to most English speaking readers; nationalities are much less relevant in Part II, Techniques.

If what you seek is a history of the novel, this book will not directly serve your purpose; a kind of history emerges indirectly, especially from Part I, Types where I have *roughly* grouped types historically.

The organization of I and II is not inevitable; I have dealt with types and techniques in an order that *feels* most effective.

I should stress again that I have conceived this primer not for a single kind of reader—not, for instance, solely for critics. As a fiction writer, I have one use for it; as a general reader another; as a teacher another; as a critic another; and I only wish that as a student I had had access to such a book. Scholars, critics, and teachers may disagree with some of my emphases and concepts and the use to which I put common knowledge; and some students in creative writing workshops may disagree with some of my pontifications about technique. But the fiction writer in me wants this book to be first of all suggestive, in the richest sense (to provoke thought by both agreement and disagreement), not just authoritative, in the driest objective sense.

David Madden

Baton Rouge, Louisiana

INTRODUCTION

The novel is the most difficult literary form to define. Most critics settle
for a simple definition based on length. But many works called short stories
(Conrad's "The Secret Sharer") are also called novellas and many novellas
are also called novels (F. Scott Fitzgerald's *The Great Gatsby* and Albert
Camus' *The Stranger*).

A controversy continues over whether to perpetuate the historical divorce between the early long fiction called romance (from the French *roman,* a term still used for the novel in most European countries) and the
newer fiction called novel (from the Italian novella, or "little new thing").
Most literary scholars today agree that the term "novel" should be reserved
for those works that present a realistic picture of life contemporary to the
author and his readers; works that relate invented, more imaginary adventures, usually set in the past, with exotic locales, should be called "romances."

One solution is to make the distinction as long as it is historically valid
and drop it at that point in literary history (about the turn of the twentieth
century) when the proliferation of types made a strict distinction arbitrary.
It is clear, however, that a too careful, or narrow and limiting definition
would be unbecoming so venturesome a genre.

Despite rumors of the death of the novel, the debate continues as to
whether ours is the age of fiction or non-fiction (see Norman Podhortez,
"The Article as Art"). Traditionally, the distinction between fiction and non-
fiction has been that each in its use of facts and other aspects of reality
strives to present a different kind of truth. Although the boundaries between
the two forms are becoming blurred, perhaps they differ less in subject matter than in the way they use style and technique to negotiate the relationship between writer and reader; the result is two different kinds of experience. In *The Nature of Narrative*, Robert Scholes and Robert Kellogg argue
that a greater interest in all narrative forms, fictional and nonfictional,
should replace our exaggerated interest in the novel as we have known it for
two centuries. (For complete data on each critic cited in the text, see
"Selective Bibliography of Criticism of the Novel.")

APPROACHES

"The House of fiction has... not one window," said Henry James, "but a million." There are many approaches to the house of fiction. Most readers experience no division between form and content, theme and subject, vision and raw material, technique and structure, style and expression. But there is a difference between simply reading a novel and studying the novel as a form. The novel may be studied in two general ways: in terms of types or techniques.

Since the days of Homer's epics, during both the oral and the written phases, literature has been considered an institution. Eventually, that institution produced scholars, then critics, dedicated to preserving traditions. Although the many, often contradictory, critical approaches have always tended to impose rules or precepts upon literature, each kind of critical emphasis has been encouraged by fictions which stress one or more of its many possibilities. (See "Selective Bibliography of Criticism of the Novel" for a long note on types of critical approaches.)

The novel is new. The youngest of the major forms of literary expression, it is only about 200 years old. Its newness as a type of narrative derives from its departure from characteristics of the Greek *epic* poem (Homer, *The Odyssey,* c850 B.C.) and the prose-poem *romances* of the Middle Ages (*The Romance of the Rose,* c1235; 1280) and other ancient narratives in poetry and prose. But further back, oral narrative, which was mainly poetic, set patterns that evolved into the novel we read today. Like poetry and the drama, the early prose narratives, comic and heroic, were written mainly by and for the aristrocracy.

The novelties of the novel have always attracted readers, but the historical development of the form is marked by the influence of other narrative forms (epic, drama, poetry, cinema) and other arts (painting, music, dance, architecture) and other kinds of knowledge (science, philosophy, psychology, history). The novel utilizes all characteristics of earlier oral and written forms of narrative and discourse: essay, character sketch, biography, autobiography, philosophical treatise, travel, folk tale, fable, fairy tale, anecdote, myth, legend, ballad, romance. The novel has also incorporated aspects of new forms: the newspaper, the magazine, advertising. These and other elements have been fused into types of narration.

Nearly every type and every technique came into use early in the history of the form; each can be traced to the present. For instance, the epistolary novel became popular with Samuel Richardson's *Pamela* (1740) and the protagonist's letter writing figures prominently in Saul Bellow's *Herzog*

(1964). Various countries, east and west, have contributed types and techniques, from oral to written, from poetic to prose. The novel today is an amalgam of many kinds and a great variety of narrative elements. The author's originality arises from the way he transforms his universal material through traditional techniques; experimentation is a re-structuring of tradition and convention.

EARLY NARRATIVES

The earliest types of narrative reveal a magical view of nature. Ceres and Proserpina is one of many Greek allegories of fertility and death. Classical legends and myths out of the folk tradition formed the basis of early recorded stories: Cadmus, Jason, and Hercules. Homer's narratives of heroic deeds, *The Iliad* and *The Odyssey*, were composed of poetic formulas; through his epic poems the gods and heroes of ancient times were perpetuated in the living traditions of Greek civilization for centuries. Denmark's Johannes V. Jensen, the Nobel Prize winner, wrote a cultural epic depicting the progress of man from the Ice Age to the twentieth century, in *The Long Journey* (1923-24). Many modern novels have a mythic dimension, William Golding's *Lord of the Flies* (1954), for instance, a fable about human nature. Some elements of the Homeric poems contributed to the comic epics of Henry Fielding, as in *Tom Jones* (1794). *Beowulf* (1000), author unknown, is one of many legends which the English perpetuated in the Homeric tradition.

In the middle ages, from the eleventh to the thirteenth century, many Scandinavian, German, and Frankish national epics that were dying out in the oral tradition were preserved in written literature. The Norse Prose Edda, an Icelandic family saga, was transcribed by Snorri Sturluson, an Icelandic bard and chief; a German version of this Volsung saga, *Song of the Nibelungenlied* was transcribed about 1200; it told of the heroic deeds of Siegfried and other heroes. Sturluson also transcribed the *Heimskringla,* an historical chronicle about Norwegian Kings. Other Icelandic or Norse sagas, transcribed a few centuries later, are *Grettir the Strong* and *The Story of Burnt Nijal;* true to political and social history, and written in a clear style, these adventure romances were full of action.

The term "saga" ("tell") is now used to describe large cycle, or series novels, or trilogies, that chronicle the experiences of a family from generation to generation against a larger historical or economic background: John Galsworthy's *The Forsyte Saga* (1906-1921), George Duhamel's *Salavin* (1920-1932), Riccardo Bacchelli's *The Mill on the Po* (1938-1940), and Icelandic Gunnar Gunnarsson's *Guest the One-Eyed* (1912-14).

Most of the national epics transcribed in the eleventh and twelfth centuries, were episodic: The Irish *Finn Cycle*, a ballad-like series of tales about a romantic, third century Irish hero similar to Robin Hood or King Arthur; the Welsh *Mabinogion* (*Red Book of Hergest*), best representative of Celtic culture, a series of heroic romances; the Spanish *Poem of the Cid* (Lord) based on Rodrigo Diaz de Bivar, an historical figure.

The national novel depicts the history and development of a nation newly emerging into modern civilization or newly created, with an attempt to capture the spirit and articulate the purpose of the author's country. In these novels, there is something of the *Volksgeist* (national mind or genius) that created oral epics. While no concept in other countries quite parallels the American aspiration to produce the Great American Novel, many other emerging nations take enthusiastically to the novel as though it were "new": South American, West Indian, and African countries. Ancient, dormant civilizations, reborn in the modern age, also take to the novel eagerly as a way of expressing new attitudes: India and Japan. These novels strongly emphasize what it means to be a native of the new or rejuvenated country, and their authors seem to want to show the world what life is like in their countries. Japan: Shohei Ooka, *Fires on the Plain* (1951); Bolivia: Adolfo Costa du Rels, *Bewitched Lands* (1940); Zion: Leon Uris, *Exodus* (1959); Biafra: Chinua Achebe, *Things Fall Apart* (1959).

ROMANCES

Romances, too, began with the Greeks. There were allegories (Greek: "to imply something else") of love, Cupid and Psyche, of grief, Orpheus, and pure romances such as Heliodorus' *Aethiopica* (second century A.D.), the strange story of Theagenes and Chariclea. But the love story is a universal phenomenon. In the ninth century, Arihara No Narihira wrote *Tales of Ise*, Japanese stories and poems of love. A century later, Lady Shikibu Murasaki wrote the courtly romance *The Tale of Genji* (c1004).

In the era of knighthood, romantic love and epic, heroic deeds produced the romance, first in verse, later in prose. These were tales about the adventures of a hero of chivalry. An early *chanson de geste* ("tale of deed") in verse was the French chivalric romance, *Huon de Bordeaux*, written in the early thirteenth century, author unknown. *The Song of Roland* (c. 1100) incorporates many Greek and German tales and bits of history and oriental lore, along with elements of the Hebrew testament, and of Virgil and Dante. A third French work, a song-story, or prose tale with verse passages, or *chante-fable*, the only one to survive, is *Aucassin and Nicolette* (14th c.), the masterpiece of chivalric romance. Through allegory, many of the romances conveyed such ethical and personality concepts as: chastity, courtly love, courtesy, contemplation, equity, constrained abstinence, grace, holiness, honor, *fides*, genius, fame, fortune, largesse, error, idleness, love, jealousy, hatred, disdain, fear, despair, danger, *ira*, beauty, shame, peace, time, the transfiguration, vice, sloth, prayer, remembrance, penance, youth, physics, reason, pride, sacrementalism, pity, virtue, pleasure, tribulations, sleep, poverty, stoicism; and personifications of the Gods, the Devil, Eve, the Graces, the Seven Deadly Sins, Venus, Seven Wise Men, Saturn. These qualities may strike the modern reader as too obvious, but in subtler forms they pervade most of the early novels and in still subtler ways dominate works right on up through Faulkner. Erotic love stories have survived also, such as *The Golden Lotus* and Li Yu's *Jou Pu Tuan* of the Ming Period.

The literature about King Arthur and the Knights of the Round Table is comprised of several sophisticated prose works. *Sir Gawain and the Green Knight* (1350–1400) is a Norman-French-Celtic tale attributed to the anonymous Pearl Poet. Sir Thomas Malory, an Englishman, wrote *Le Morte d'Arthur* in French during the last years of his wild and unchivalrous life; this episodic chronicle was published in 1485. *Robin Hood's Adventures* (c1490) combines elements of the chivalric romance with comic folk tales. The Spaniard, Fernando de Rojas, wrote *La Celestina* (1499) a tragi-comedy of idealistic love in dramatic dialog form. One of the most famous chivalric romances *Amadís de Gaul* (1508) written by a Portugese, Vasco de Lobeira.

The pastoral romance is another manifestation of the romantic narrative. Longus (second to fifth century A.D.) a product of Greece's decadent period, wrote one of the first, *Daphnis and Chloë*, a predecessor of the modern novel. Other pastoral novels are *Diana* (1559) by Jorge de Montemayor, a Portugese; *Pandosto* (1588) by Robert Greene and *Arcadia* (1590) by Sir Philip Sidney, both Englishman; centuries later a Norwegian, Björnstjerne Björnson wrote two pastoral allegories: *Arne* (1858) and *The Fisher Maiden* (1868); Felix Salten's *Bambi* (1923) depicted animals in human terms in his pastoral allegory, adapted in the next decade into one of Walt Disney's most famous animated feature cartoons. The Irish Renaissance or Celtic Twilight revived interest in the legendary romance, a good example of which is James Stephens' *Deidre* (1923).

In 1621, John Barclay wrote *Argenis*, a pseudo-classical heroic allegory set in the Hellenistic era in Sicily; written in Latin, it was a popular book for two centuries. A later development of the romance was Madeleine de Scudéry's *Artamène* (1646–53), full of noble sentiments, a little learning, and many qualities of escape literature. But another such romance, Madame de La Fayette's *The Princess of Clèves* (1678) anticipated the psychological novel and the *roman à clef* (novel based on well-known people); some say it is, according to the modern definition, among the first real novels.

In the sixteenth and seventeenth centuries, when there emerged types of fiction with which comparisons could be made, the romance was considered a story whose setting was exotic, whose incidents were remote from ordinary life, and whose purpose was escape. A century later, the romance was thought of as an "extravagant fiction" full of "wild and wanton exaggeration; a picturesque falsehood."

Attitudes toward fiction expressed by scholars and critics have remained influenced by the classical or neo-classical tradition to the present day. Classical concepts of literature are based on a study of Greek and Roman works and regard art as a search for and expression of absolutes. Past customs and traditions rather than the individual living in the present are the source of authority for attitudes about literature. The classical mind judges literature by such characteristics as balance, unity, proportion, restraint, simplicity, grandeur, correctness, decorum, majesty and magnitude (as in the epic), and by the author's sincerity and seriousness. These and other characteristics assume readers trained in the classical tradition who are receptive to them.

The traditional or classical forms are still with us in altered shapes, and many new forms are simply aspects of the old, exaggerated to achieve effects that better reflect our different world. For instance, out of two different emphases (social and psychological) upon the urge to realism come Honoré de Balzac's infatuation with objects and Alain Robbe-Grillet's terror of objects. The novel retains from its two main predecessors aspects of form and content: scope from the epic and imagination from the romance.

RISE OF THE NOVEL

The early romances were a product of the aristocracy. The middle-class modern realistic consciousness produced and read the novel; that the authors of this new form were supported not by the patronage of nobility but by publishers and readers was reflected in sales. Throughout much of its history, the novel has been regarded as a relatively inferior mode of expression. This attitude was partly influenced by the fact that so many women, regarded as second-class citizens, wrote novels, a great many of the worst of them and few of the finest.

In *The Rise of the Novel* (more specifically the English novel) Ian Watt discusses the forces that encouraged the growth of the form. Attitudes of individualism fostered by Puritanism encouraged a democratic spirit that, with the economic rise of the middle class, prevailed in many areas of human life, encouraging a literature that would describe individual experiences of real people. Secularization ameliorated the religious restrictiveness of Puritanism. So that even though religious and social attitudes forbade or disdained the reading of novels, too often written by women and read by girls to whom they were thought to be harmful, a growing worldliness excited interest in the lives of others as depicted in fiction.

Dualistic thinking in philosophy—analyzing the conflict between the individual ego and the external world—also prepared an intellectual atmosphere that would influence the writing and reception of the novel; the novel is uniquely suited to deal with the interaction between a character and his environment in empirical terms that appealed to the eighteenth century mind; the philosophers of the Enlightenment generally worked with problems best illustrated in the novel.

Urbanization created new subject matter for the writer, and the novel was best suited to deal with it; most of the readers of novels were concentrated in the cities, and they turned to the novel to describe to them their own private and public experiences and that part of which they were ignorant because of class distances. Urban women had more leisure to write and read novels.

With increased literacy and leisure and more efficient methods of printing, the middle class reading public as a cultural phenomenon arose. These readers read more for pleasure than anything else and welcomed the ease with which novels could be consumed. Unlike earlier forms of literature, the novel is almost entirely a creature of print.

And unlike poetry and drama, novels employ the gross materials of reality, just as the daily newspapers do. The expanding middle class wanted to know more about the wider world it was helping to create and in which it was rising in every sphere. The novel developed simultaneously with that other organ of middle class information: the newspaper. From the beginning, the novel competed with other media in the dissemination of facts that described the way things are. Newspapers portrayed the public life; novelists imagined the private life behind the news item. Many novelists were formerly journalists; not until recent years has this sequence been reversed, in the creative reporting of American novelists Truman Capote, Norman Mailer, and Jean Stafford. The novel is a more private means of conveying the news; it flourished in Japan just after the second world war as that country experienced great changes in its public and private spheres; the post-war experience in China and Taiwan is less private, more traditional, and thus we have seen no Chinese novels of consequence.

The novel has traditionally half-denied its own existence—or always proved its protean form—by pretending to be what it is not: documentary, Daniel Defoe's *Journal of the Plague Year* (1722); diary and journal, Tobias Smollett's *The Expedition of Humphrey Clinker* (1771); letters, Samuel Richardson's two major novels *Pamela* (1740) and *Clarissa* (1748); travel account, Jonathan Swift's *Gulliver's Travels* (1726); treatise, William Godwin's *Caleb Williams or Things as They Are* (1794). In the novel, these become mock or pseudo-forms. Still, the novel also satisfied a desire for transcendence of the ordinary. One of the first great English novels, therefore, Daniel Defoe's *Robinson Crusoe* (1719) depicted in very practical and realistic terms the everyday life of a man on a deserted island, thus fusing the commonplace and the exotic.

The prime purpose of the novel, as distinguished from other forms of narrative, is then, to depict reality, even when the novel is confined to subjective worlds. In a figurative sense, of course, all narratives are, in the end, realistic, for in reflecting the *actual* ideals of the people who read them, even the French romances were realistic. Franz Kafka's special realism in *The Trial*, for instance, is a means to the end of revealing aspects of human experience just as abstract as the allegorical personifications of French romances; and the gothic novel more overtly used elements employed in Kafka, one of whose novels is set in a castle (*The Castle*, 1926).

Not only would some critics and novelists distinguish the novel from the romance (Nathaniel Hawthorne made that distinction for his own work, calling *The House of the Seven Gables*, 1851, a romance—a form that allows a certain latitude), some would also make a distinction between the novel and forms such as prose satire, Swift's *Gulliver's Travels*, for instance. Graham Greene calls some of his fiction *entertainment* and other, more serious works, *novels*.

A DEFINITION

The novel has always been a genre in constant flux. Today there are a great many more types than in the eighteenth century, and the techniques of fiction are put to so many uses that we need either to limit the term even more and create new categories or allow it to embrace every prose work that is fictional and is over a certain length. But since the novel, as it has come to be defined (as distinct from earlier long narrative forms—the poetic epic and the romance), usually brings the news about the life of real people in the ordinary world, we may settle provisionally for a median definition: a prose fiction narrative that is not only longer than either a short story or a short novel (novelette) but that usually subjects the reader to an experience in more detail and depicts a greater variety of characters who are involved in a plot constituted of a multiplicity of episodes, with greater scope in time and space; and that is concerned with real people in "a stable society" (Northrop Frye) in the real world but is distinguished from nonfiction in being the product of a more inventive imagination and in being expressed in language and through a structure that is usually more carefully controlled to create effects in the reader.

PART I: TYPES

Each novel cited here as an example of a specific type will contain elements of several others, for no novel is a perfect example of a type. A novel cited to illustrate one type may serve as well to illustrate several others; thus, some novels are listed under as many as three or more type headings. Popular novels are also cited under various headings, and that broad type is itself discussed, along with several of its sub-types. Publication dates for each title are given each time it occurs. (Birth and death dates for the authors are not given here; see the chronology.) Often, the author's nationality is given; it is assumed that the nationalities of well-known American and British novelists need not be provided. A quotation from one novel of each type stating or suggesting the author's purpose is also included.

Characteristics of the types sometimes overlap; none of these types is pure; each type includes aspects of others. Each type emphasizes an element of fiction that is common to other types; for instance, the philosophical novel reminds us that most good and great novels are to some extent philosophical. But we may also say that some types, such as the philosophical, depart further than others from the novel as it is generally conceived. Few novelists set out to write within a type, although some may deliberately do so; certain types, such as the philosophical and the epistolary, lend themselves more than others to conscious attempts.

Among writers, general readers, reviewers, critics and scholars, and literary historians, there is little unanimity as to correct definitions of these types or even as to their usefulness. Some discussed here are not strict, formal types; at best those less-traditional terms share a quality that is characteristic of fiction itself, suggestibility. Discussion of all these types provide us with ways of talking about the nature and history of the novel, and of the short story and novella as well.

Some types emphasize technical, others emphasize subject matter aspects of the novel. Some terms used for types are also used to describe techniques. For instance, the term "epistolary" refers both to a type of novel and to a technique that may be employed in a novel.

The organization of Part I follows roughly a chronological or historical progression and a grouping of similar or significantly contrasting types. For instance, following the section on the Romantic novel, all types most closely related to it (Gothic, fantasy, historical, and so on) are discussed. The section on Realism follows the section on Naturalism.

THE PICARESQUE NOVEL

If Romances derive from myths, the picaresque novel derives much of its material from folklore. Myths are specialized, rarified distillations of legends out of folklore. On the other hand, folklore is composed of nonliterary tales, songs, sayings, fairy tales, ballads, proverbs, beast epics, jingles, incantations, and riddles that reveal the traditions, customs, and beliefs of a people. "Paul Bunyan" is a good example of a tall tale produced by the nonliterary folk culture. In a tale, the emphasis is on the story, with its interesting episodes, as in the picaresque, rather than on heroic character or noble ideals, as in the romance narrative. Although the brief folk tales are often about kings, events reduce them to the level of everyday human experience. In the picaresque novel, phantasy (or fancy), the source of imagination, is joined with reality to produce the cross-fertilized soil in which the realistic novel, with its emphasis on facts, was to grow. The novel's province is the ordinary mingled with the exceptional, the charm of common things mingled with the unusual and the remote. Folklore and picaresque novels render the trivial exotic; in the realistic novel, the trivial has a status of its own, adding to the illusion of reality.

A good example of the early tale is the third century Indian *Shilappadikaran (The Ankle Bracelet)* by Ilangô Adigal. In the fifteenth century, *The Arabian Nights* offered adventure romances as told by Shaharazad who, to save her life, entertained her king with tales, for a thousand and one nights, of such heroes as Sinbad (who is somewhat like Odysseus). P'u Sung-Ling's *Strange Stories from a Chinese Studio* (1766) is a collection of tales and legends. Danish Isak Dinesen (Karen Blixen), revived interest in the tale as a form with her *Seven Gothic Tales* (1934). One of the best examples of the African novel, *The Palm-Wine Drinkard* (1952) by Amos Tutuola, is a fantastic tale, full of folklore, in which the main character wanders over a nightmare landscape in search of his dead tapster.

In the monomyth that Joseph Campbell, in *The Hero with a Thousand Faces*, devised as the basic pattern for most myths and legends, the hero leaves his familiar home, wanders through strange regions of this world and the underworld, having adventures, and returns with some saving secret to bestow upon his people. There is a similar pattern in folk literature in the mock or pseudo-traveler's tale, which became a popular type of novel early in its history. If the narrator were the only person to have visited the remote place, the authenticity claimed for such a novel couldn't be verified.

Bringing back the news of other places was a prelude to presenting the news about the society one lived in and the way its various classes lived. One of the earliest pseudo-travel tales is the satirical fantasy, *The True History* (2nd C.), which is somewhat like the later work of Swift and Rabelais; it was written by a Syrian, Lucian. A very popular Japanese comic novel consisting of travel accounts was Jippensha-Ikku's *Hiza-Kurige (Shank's Mare)* (1802–1814).

The usual method of travel was by sea, and one type, now rather rare, the sea novel, was once so popular that the works of a writer like Joseph Conrad were labeled sea novels and thus, even though his novels transcended that special area of life, their deeper value was obscured. Herman Melville's novels, *Moby Dick* (1851), for instance, suffered the same fate for many years. The novels of Robert Louis Stevenson, *Kidnapped* (1886), for instance, came closer to deserving the label. The sea continues to fascinate readers, as Charles Bernard Nordhoff's and James Norman Hall's *Mutiny on the Bounty* (1932), Herman Wouk's *The Caine Mutiny* (1951), and David Madden's *The Beautiful Greed* (1961) testify. The sea novel also became a form of social protest in B. Traven's *The Death Ship* (1926), and an allegorical vehicle in Katherine Anne Porter's *Ship of Fools* (1962).

Some writers use the mock journey device to create a cross-section of characters who represent, sometimes allegorically, aspects of human nature or of a society the author is satirizing. Jonathan Swift's *Gulliver's Travels* (1726) satirizes in its very form the great mass of travel books popular in his time—a time of actual travel to places that had only recently been discovered. Another journey by sea, Edgar Allan Poe's *Narrative of Arthur Gordon Pym* (1838), takes the reader into the realm of the supernatural. Conrad's sea stories offer a serious and symbolic vision of life. In a good example of the rare antiquarian novel (usually used for satire), John Barth used the mock-travel journal device in *The Sot-Weed Factor* (1960).

A later revival of the kind of experience readers craved in the travel novel was the novel about the American West. Owen Wister visited the West and returned to tell about it in *The Virginian* (1902). Jack London worked in the gold fields of Canada and Alaska and wrote about them in *Call of the Wild* (1903). The road is another means of travel, made part of a religious quest in Hermann Hesse's *Siddhartha* (1922). In Geoffrey Chaucer's long poem, *The Canterbury Tales* (1393–1400), the religious pilgrimage is a pretext for a great variety of tales.

Irreverence for the traditional concept of the hero of myth, legends, and tales is seen in the mock-heroic passages in Henry Fielding's *Tom Jones* (1749), Laurence Sterne's *The Life and Opinions of Tristram Shandy, Gent.* (1759–67), and in James Joyce's *Ulysses* (1922), and *Finnegans Wake* (1939), in which the comparison between past and present becomes a critique of individual modern man's relative puniness.

The picaresque novel was one of the earliest types, beginning in Spain with *La Vida de Lazarillo de Tormes* (c1554, author unknown); an earlier picaresque romance was the Greek Lucius Apuleius' *The Golden Ass* (2nd C.), a fantastic, dimly allegorical, bawdy, realistic tale of the metamorphosis of the protagonist into an ass. The greatest Spanish picaresque romance was Miguel de Cervantes' *Don Quixote* (Part I, 1605, Part II, 1615).

> At this point they caught sight of thirty or forty windmills which were standing on the plain there, and no sooner had Don Quixote laid eyes upon them than he turned to his squire and said, "Fortune is guiding our affairs better than we could have wished; for you see there before you, friend Sancho Panza, some thirty or more lawless giants with whom I mean to do battle. I shall deprive them of their lives, and with the spoils from this encounter we shall begin to enrich ourselves; for this is righteous warfare, and it is a great service to God to remove so accursed a breed from the face of the earth."
>
> "What giants?" said Sancho Panza.

Even more popular was Mateo Alemán's *Larida y hechos del picaro Guzman de Alfarache* (1599-1604), the English title of which is *The Rogue*. Typically, the picaresque novel involves many characters, many episodes, many locales, a long time span. The usual picaresque tale is about a wandering *picaro* ("rogue") whose many adventures on the road involve him with a variety of stereotypes on every social level and realistically and satirically reveal the mores of a society in a particular era. Contrasted with the rogue's criminal code, respectable people are often seen to be hypocrites. The picaro usually tells his own (or her own, as in the case of Defoe's *Moll Flanders*) tale. Satire of society usually is the result of the picaro's movements on all social levels. Another Spanish picaresque novel, the satirical, witty *La Vida del Buscon (Life of the Great Rascal)* (c1660), was written by Quevedo (Francisco Gomez de Quevedo Villegas). In England, Thomas Nashe wrote *The Unfortunate Traveller* (1594), a combination of realism and romance. The only great German narrative of the seventeenth century, by H. J. C. Von Grimmelshausen, *Simplicissimus the Vagabond* (1669) is set during the Thrity Years War. A later Spanish example is José María de Pereda's *Pedro Sánchez* (1883).

In the twentieth century, the Spanish were still writing in a form they helped create; in a rather literary style, Ramón Pérez de Ayala wrote *La pata de la raposa (The Fox's Paw,* 1924), about a rake, an adventurer who encounters many ladies of the world. Swedish writer Selma Lagerlöf contributed *Gösta Berlings Saga* (1891). The picaresque has remained one of the most popular types.

Mark Twain's *The Adventures of Huckleberry Finn* (1884), using the river as the means of travel and using the story of youthful innocence to make bitter satire, is perhaps the finest example of the picaresque novel.

> I never felt easy till the raft was two mile below there and out in the middle of the Mississippi. Then we hung up our signal lantern, and judged that we was free and safe once more. I hadn't had a bite to eat since yesterday; so Jim he got out some corn-dodgers and buttermilk, and pork and cabbage, and greens—there ain't nothing in the world so good, when it's cooked right—and whilst I eat my supper we talked, and had a good time. I was powerful glad to get away from the feuds, and so was Jim to get away from the swamp. We said there warn't no home like a raft, after all. Other palces do seem so cramped up and smothery, but a raft don't. You feel mighty free and easy and comfortable on a raft. . . . Here is the way we put in the time. . . .

Other examples of this early type put to serious modern use are Louis-Ferdinand Céline's somber *Journey to the End of the Night* (1932), Saul Bellow's *The Adventures of Augie March* (1953), and Jack Kerouac's *On the Road* (1957).

THE COMIC NOVEL

Not all comic novels are, of course, basically picaresque. The comic novel, written out of a comic vision of human behavior, provides pure delight through the use of incongruity and other devices, and ends happily. As we laugh at the characters involved in extricating themselves from comic predicaments, we feel we are at least slightly superior to them; we feel scorn, and a little malice along with pure delight. When we recognize ourselves, to some extent, in these characters, we learn and gain insight, as in serious novels, but bypass one of the major experiences of the serious novel, empathy and compassion.

In the comic novel, as well as the closely-related picaresque, the Spanish were very adept. There is Pedro Antonio de Alarcón's *The Three-Cornered Hat* (1874), a comedy of intrigue. But the English handled the type best, as in Kingsley Amis' *Lucky Jim* (1953). The anglophile Irish-American J. P. Donleavy's *The Ginger Man* (1955) is considered one of the first black comedies. R. K. Narayan, a South Indian, imitates the British manner in *The Guide* (1958), a comedy of misunderstanding about a dreaming rogue, "Railway Raju," a tourist guide who becomes a bogus holy man. The American Gore Vidal created a black comic, almost farcical situation in *Myra Breckinridge* (1968), a story of a man who becomes a great movie love goddess.

Although "comedy" is a useful term for a type of drama, it becomes perhaps too broad when applied to the novel. Most novels contain comic elements or comic relief. (See Henri Bergson, George Meredith). The comic novel is to be distinguished from the satirical. The aim of pure comedy is to amuse through laughter without distressing the reader; the aim of satire is to criticize and correct, perhaps reform, man's follies through wit and ridicule. There are two few excellent examples of either type. Henry Fielding's *The History of Tom Jones* (1749), a comic epic, is perhaps the classic example of the comic.

Jones immediately interposing, a fierce contention arose, which soon proceeded to blows on both sides. And now Mrs. Waters (for we must confess she was in the same bed), being, I suppose, awakened from her sleep, and seeing two men fighting in her bedchamber, began to scream in the most violent manner, crying out Murder! robbery! and more frequently Rape! which last, some, perhaps, may wonder she should mention, who do not consider that these words of exclamation are used by ladies in a fright, as fa, la, la, ra, da, etc., are in music, only as the vehicles of sound, and without any fixed ideas.

Candide (1759) by Voltaire is a classic example of the satirical novel.

The terrified Candide stood weltering in blood and trembling with fear and confusion.
"If this is the best of all possible worlds," he said to himself, "what can the rest be like? Had it only been a matter of flogging, I should have not have questioned it, for I have had that before from the Bulgars. But when it comes to my dear Pangloss being hanged—the greatest of philosophers—I must know the reason why. And was it part of the scheme of things that my dear Anabaptist (the best of men!) should be drowned in sight of land? And Lady Cunegonde, that pearl amongst women! Was it really necessary for her to be disemboweled?"

Both types are usually loose in structure, told in the third person, allowing the author greater maneuverability and often a more direct commentary on the characters, mainly in the comic, and on the action, principally in the satirical novel. Satire is the use of irony, wit, humor and ridicule to expose human folly. Implicit in a true satirical novel is a vision of life that is superior to the target.

THE SATIRICAL NOVEL

The satirical novel ridicules mankind generally or an actual person, group, class, nation, system of thought, movement in art, or institution through a serious moral vision in a tone of gentle amusement and delight or with a pessimistic and ferocious moral indignation, the aim of which is to expose, to diminish, or to destroy the target so that the reader gains insight into specific human excesses, follies, and vices, and can thus, perhaps, correct them. With ironic humor and passionate wit, the author expresses scorn, contempt, even malice, giving himself and his reader a vantage point of laughing or sneering superiority upon the target. Satire is a difficult mode and the survival rate is very low. What saves great satire from topicality is that the author implies a greater scheme or vision of life simultaneously as he destroys the one he despises, as Swift does in *Gulliver's Travels*. Basically conservative, the satirist would restore the original vitality of withering institutions.

Many modern novels are misnamed satires because they merely mock, parody, lampoon, travesty, burlesque, caricature their targets, as Nathanael West does in *The Dream Life of Balso Snell* (1931) and *A Cool Million* (1934). Satire may use those elements, along with farce. Farce assaults the reader with every sort of low-comedy device: ridiculous and bizarre situations; fast, violent slapstick action; crude wit—to provoke gross laughter, with few demands upon the intelligence. In farce, characterization is broad, plot wildly improbable. The black humorists often fall into this trap; Kurt Vonnegut, Jr. and others mistake the ability to detect evil or corruption for a vision of life. One does not gain in stature by stepping on a cockroach. In too many instances, satire is merely the compliment that little minds pay trivial issues.

Satire, like other forms of comedy, is a basic element in most examples of that early type of novel, the picaresque. We see this element as early as the Italian Petronius' *Satyricon*. Of the many types of satire, here are a few: *El Periquillo Sarmiento (The Itching Parrot*, 1816–1830), by the Mexican J. J. Fernández de Lizardi, a picaresque satire; *All Men are Brothers* (14th C.), by the Chinese Shih Nai-an, a picaresque romance; *Tartarin of Tarascon* (1872), by Alphonse Daudet, a satirical romance about a braggart; *Zuleika Dobson* (1911), by the Englishman Max Beerbohm, a romantic satire; *Cream of the Jest* (1917), and *Jurgen* (1919), by James Branch Cabell, satirical fantasies; *Max Havelaar* (1860), by Multatuli; *Caesar or Nothing*

(1919), by Pío Baroja, a political satire; *El Senor Presidente* (1946), by Guatemalan Miguel Angel Asturias, which uses folklore and grotesque elements, but is aesthetically weak; *The Good Soldier Schweik* (1926), by Jaroslav Hasek of Czechoslovakia; *The Gods are Athirst* (1917), by Anatole France *Portnoy's Complaint* (1969), by Philip Roth, a realistic satire.

Some satires are simply humorous, often making satirical thrusts rather subtly, in the guise of the comic novel: *Handley Cross* (1843), by Robert Smith Surtees; *Huckleberry Finn* (1884), by Mark Twain; *You Know Me, Al* (1916), by Ring Lardner; *The Romantic Comedians* (1926), by Ellen Glasgow; *Mister Roberts* (1946), by Robert Heggen.

The social kind of satire, at which the English are most adept, embraces more novels than any other; the French, Russians, and Americans have also produced important social satires: *Nightmare Abbey* (1818), by Thomas Love Peacock; *Dead Souls* (1842), by Nikolai Gogol; *Vanity Fair* (1847–1848), by William Makepeace Thackeray; *Barchester Towers* (1857), by Anthony Trollope; *Tono-Bungay* (1909) by H. G. Wells; *The Unbearable Bassington* (1912), by Saki; *South Wind* (1917), by Norman Douglas; *Main Street* (1920) and *Babbitt* (1922), by Sinclair Lewis; *Decline and Fall* (1928), by Evelyn Waugh; *Brave New World* (1932), by Aldous Huxley; *Miss Lonelyhearts* (1933), by Nathanael West; *Wickford Point* (1939), by John P. Marquand; *The Groves of Academe* (1952), by Mary McCarthy; *Pictures from an Institution* (1954), by Randall Jarrell.

Parody and travesty are comparatively low forms of the imagination since they must feed directly on a target that, the work's premise must assert, is inferior. Parody imitates the distinctive and recognizable style of another novel for humorous effect, without invective. Henry Fielding wrote a parody of Richardson's *Pamela* called *Shamela* (1741). A travesty is a trivializing parody of a serious novel to insult the writer. Ernest Hemingway wrote a travesty of Sherwood Anderson's style in *The Torrents of Spring* (1926). Sometimes literary satires have a good deal of value in themselves, for instance, W. Somerset Maugham's *Cakes and Ale* (1930). A type rarer than literary travesty is the burlesque (Italian: "mockery") novel. A burlesque or caricature distorts a mere fault in a subject for amusement. This type includes two great classics that transcend the type, Cervantes' *Don Quixote*, a burlesque of medieval romances, and Frenchman François Rabelais' *The Lives, Heroic Deeds and Sayings of Gargantua and Pantegruel, His Son* (1533–1567), a burlesque romance, a mock-heroic chronicle of two giants.

> And so, I climbed up, the best way I could, and traveled a good two leagues over his tongue before entering his mouth....
> Going on from there, I made my way between the rocks, which were his teeth, and even climbed one of them, where I

found the prettiest spot in the world, with fine large tennis-courts, handsome promenades, beautiful meadows, many vineyards, and an endless number of Italian summer-houses, scattered through delightful fields.

Jane Austen wrote a burlesque of Gothic novels, *Northanger Abbey* (1818). Many comic or satirical novels contain passages that parody, travesty, burlesque, or lampoon a specific target within the larger comic or satirical range. For instance, James Joyce's *Ulysses* (1922). A lampoon is a malicious, satirical attack on a famous person or novel.

THE EPISTOLARY NOVEL

The epistolary novel is a narrative composed of an exchange of letters. It is understandable that what is now considered a rather unusual type of narrative was an early form of the novel. The early novelist, especially in England, sought many ways of claiming authenticity. Nothing could seem more genuine than a collection of letters exchanged between two people or among members of a group. The illusion of reality, however, is defied by the technique itself; no matter how justified by circumstances, very few people write such long and so many letters, detailing the events of nearly every day. In the Eighteenth century, both conversation and correspondence were an art, thus a favored form of first person narration in the novel was the epistolary, best exemplified in one of the earliest English novels of consequence, *Pamela* (1740), by Samuel Richardson. Pamela writes to her mother and father and we get their replies.

> O that I had never left my little bed in the loft, to be thus exposed to temptations on one hand, or disgusts on the other! How happy was I awhile ago! How contrary now!—Pity and pray for Your afflicted Pamela.

> My Dearest Child,
> Our Hearts bleed for your distress, and the temptations you are exposed to. You have our hourly prayers; and we would have you flee this evil great house and man, if you find he renews his attempts.

Other epistolary novels go beyond the family circle, for the novel was a reaching-out form in the early phases and letters were one such form of communicating. Smollett's *The Expedition of Humphrey Clinker* (1771), offers the letters of a variety of people, related through kinship or friendship. Pierre Choderlos de Laclos' *Les Liaisons Dangereuses* (1782), consists mainly of letters between an unscrupulous pair of lovers who corrupt other young people.

Among modern writers, Guido Piovene, an Italian, is notable for his *Letters of a Novice* (1941). Mark Harris uses the form in *Wake Up, Stupid* (1959). In Saul Bellow's *Herzog* (1964), the narrator talks directly to the reader, often quoting letters he writes to famous people but never mails.

THE NOVEL IN DIARY FORM

In the diary form of narration, the character usually speaks, as in the letter form, without the intervention of the author. But the diary is the opposite of the social form of communication, the letter, for the diary is private—a monologue, the character speaking directly to himself. Letters were written sometimes in the form of poetry, as if to be seen by the eyes of the world as well as the recipient. But few actual diaries have been published; one famous example is the diary (1825) of Samuel Pepys, which reads like social letters to the world of London.

The diary appears later than the epistolary in the history of the novel, related as it is to a later development in the attitude of the writer toward his characters—the stress is on private experience, and the character's own emotions are examined. Both Defoe's *Robinson Crusoe* (1719) and Goethe's *The Sorrows of Young Werther* (1774) are written partly in diary form. A modern example is André Gide's *Pastoral Symphony* (1919). Saul Bellow wrote *Dangling Man* (1944) and Jean-Paul Sartre wrote *Nausea* (1938) in this form.

Monday, 29 January, 1932:

> Something has happened to me, I can't doubt it any more. It came as an illness does, not like an ordinary certainty, not like anything evident. It came cunningly, little by little; I felt a little strange, a little put out, that's all. Once established it never moved, it stayed quiet, and I was able to persuade myself that nothing was the matter with me, that it was a false alarm. And now, it's blossoming.

The real diaries of Anaïs Nin are considered superior to her surrealistic fiction.

THE NOVEL IN JOURNAL FORM

The journal or notebook consists of a character's first person entries, not necessarily daily, related to a specific project he is involved in. Ostensibly, the journal is private, but sometimes a public or social use is foreseen, as in Daniel Keyes' *Flowers for Algernon* (1966). This type, more common than the diary, is used in Gide's masterpiece, *Les Faux Monnyeurs (The Counterfeiters*, 1926) and in Defoe's *A Journal of the Plague Year* (1722). Gide was himself keeper of one of the most readable journals any writer ever produced. Kenneth Patchen, a poet, created a surrealistic prose journal, *The Journal of Albion Moonlight* (1941). Parts of journals augment novels that are primarily of some other type: Stephen Dedalus' entries in his journal near the end of *Portrait of the Artist as a Young Man* (1916) by James Joyce.

> April 26. Mother is putting my new secondhand clothes in order. She prays now, she says, that I may learn in my own life and away from home and friends what the heart is and what it feels. Amen. So be it. Welcome, O life! I go to encounter for the millionth time the reality of experience and to forge in the smithy of my soul the uncreated conscience of my race.

THE MEMOIR NOVEL

A character keeps a journal almost day by day, but the memoir novel is a character's first person account of a significant period in his life that is usually well in the past. More public than a journal, a memoir is usually as much about one's society at a given time as about oneself. "Memoir" is another term for the first person narrative that has been in use since the beginning: Defoe's Moll Flanders tells the world about her worldly experiences; Richardson's Pamela tells only her parents. The author must live up to the narrator's claim that his story is worth hearing. "I only am escaped to tell thee," Ishmael quotes Job at the end of Herman Melville's *Moby Dick* (1851). Huckleberry Finn and Holden Caulfield (in Salinger's *Catcher in the Rye*) tell about the perils of trying to cope as a child in an adult's world. Holden says:

> If you really want to hear about it, the first thing you'll probably want to know is where I was born, and what my lousy childhood was like, and how my parents were occupied and all before they had me, and all that David Copperfield kind of crap, but I don't feel like going into it, if you want to know the truth. In the first place, my parents would have about two hemorrhages apiece if I told anything pretty personal about them. They're quite touchy about anything like that, especially my father. They're *nice* and all—I'm not saying that—but they're also touchy as hell. Besides, I'm not going to tell you my whole goddam autobiography or anything. I'll just tell you about this madman stuff that happened to

me around last Christmas just before I got pretty run-down and
had to come out here and take it easy.

Many first-person narratives, however, make no attempt to explain the occasion for the telling of the story; perhaps the character is telling it to a listener rather than to us as readers, and we overhear, as in William Faulkner's *Absalom, Absalom!* (1936).

Not all first-person narratives are memoirs; the emphasis is often on the
life of another character, as in F. Scott Fitzgerald's *The Great Gatsby*
(1925), narrated by Nick Carroway; Ken Kesey's *One Flew Over the Cuckoo's Nest* (1962), narrated by an American Indian, Chief Broom, in an insane asylum.

Some novels are announced as memoirs: *Hadrian's Memoirs* (1951), an
historical work by Marguerite Yourcenar and Walter de la Mare's *Memoirs
of a Midget* (1921) are good examples of the type.

THE AUTOBIOGRAPHICAL NOVEL

Another term for first person narrative is autobiography: a character
tells his life story, which is slightly different from a memoir in which the
character usually recounts only a major portion of his life.

An autobiograpical novel is based, unadmittedly in most instances, on
the author's own life, told in first or third person. The most famous example
is Marcel Proust's *A la Recherche du Temps Perdu (Remembrance of Things
Past)* (1913–1927); an interesting fabrication is his substitution of women
characters for the men Proust loved.

> "Mademoiselle Albertine has gone!" How much farther does an-
> guish penetrate in psychology than psychology itself! A moment
> ago, as I lay analysing my feelings, I had supposed that this separa-
> tion without a final meeting was precisely what I wished, and, as I
> compared the mediocrity of the pleasures that Albertine afforded
> me with the richness of the desires which she prevented me from
> realising, had felt that I was being subtle, had concluded that I did
> not wish to see her again, that I no longer loved her. But now
> these words: "Mademoiselle Albertine has gone!" had expressed
> themselves in my heart in the form of an anguish so keen that I
> would not be able to endure it for any length of time. And so what
> I had supposed to mean nothing to me was the only thing in my
> whole life. How ignorant we are of ourselves. The first thing to be
> done was to make my anguish cease at once.

Look Homeward Angel (1929) was the first of four massive novels recounting the life of Thomas Wolfe, who died at the age of 38. Wolfe is the artist as romantic cannibal, devouring life, swallowing it partially chewed; a vast body of raw material had a crippling effect on his novels as works of art. Henry Miller's works offer even more literal examples of the autonovel, for he is named as the narrator of his novels *Tropic of Cancer* (1931) and *Tropic of Capricorn* (1939); they are more a series of actual memoirs than novels. The imaginative quality resides not so much in events—real or fabricated—as in the poetic, vital language he forges.

The autobiographical element can take several forms: Laurence Sterne's *Sentimental Journey* (1768) is a novelized travel-autobiography; George Borrow's *Lavengro* (1851) and *The Romany Rye* (1857) are simulated autobiography; Swiss Gottfried Keller's *Der Grüne Heinrich* (1854-55) is an autobiographical romance; Chilean Eduardo Barrios' *Brother Ass* (1922) is a simulated autobiography, a mystic work, a rarity in South America; Japanese Dazai Osamu's (Shuji Tsushima) *No Longer Human* (1948) is a maudlin journal of a wild, suicidal buffoon, a travesty of autobiography; Canadian Malcolm Lowry's *Under the Volcano* (1947) is an allegorical, symbolic autobiographical novel that fails on the realistic level. A recent example is *The Autobiography of Miss Jane Pittman* (1971), by Ernest Gaines, a black writer.

THE PERSONAL HISTORY NOVEL

The personal history type is often pseudo or simulated autobiography, as is Defoe's *The Fortunes and Misfortunes of the Famous Moll Flanders* (1722).

> My true name is so well known in the records or registers at Newgate, and in the Old Bailey, and there are some things of such consequence still depending there, relating to my particular conduct, that it is not to be expected I should set my name or the account of my family to this work; perhaps, after my death, it may be better known; at present it would not be proper, no, not though a general pardon should be issued, even without exceptions and reserve of persons or crimes.

Again, the author wants to assure his middle-class readers that he is offering reality, not an idle work of fancy. This claim is made with more intricate irony in Laurence Sterne's *Tristram Shandy* (1760-67). And there is an even more complex irony in John Barth's *Giles Goat-Boy* (1966), in which a character pretends to be the editor of a journal, memoir, or confession entrusted to him by the main character and narrator. With such novels, the pretense is sometimes that the work is published posthumously.

THE CONFESSIONAL NOVEL

The confessional novel is narrated by a character moved by the compulsion to confess, to a crime against humanity or society, as in Italian Italo Svevo's *La Coscienza di Zeno (Confessions of Zeno,* 1924), a comic, pseudo-autobiography, written in an economical style, as in Yukio Mishima's *Confessions of a Mask* (1958), about a homosexual, and as in Vladimir Nabokov's *Lolita* (1955).

> "Lolita, or the Confession of a White Widowed Male," such were the two titles under which the writer of the present note received the strange pages it preambulates. "Humbert Humbert," their author, had died in legal captivity, of coronary thrombosis, on November 16, 1952, a few days before his trial was scheduled to start.
>
> .   .   .
>
> Lolita, light of my life, fire of my loins. My sin, my soul. Lo-lee-ta: the tip of the tongue taking a trip of three steps down the palate to tap, at three, on the teeth. Lo. Lee. Ta.
> She was Lo, plain Lo, in the morning, standing four feet ten in one sock. She was Lola in slacks. She was Dolly at school. She was Dolores on the dotted line. But in my arms she was always Lolita.

Actual confessions by St. Augustine, *Confessions* (397–401), Jean-Jacques Rousseau, *Confessions* (1784), and Thomas De Quincey's *Confessions of an English Opium Eater* (1822) inspired this fictional variant. Recently, a young Dutchman in *I, Jan Cramer* (1964) and a young American, Frank Conroy, in *Stop-time* (1967), wrote autobiographies with qualities of fiction.

THE LYRICAL NOVEL

Some poets have written autobiographical novels: e. e. cummings' *The Enormous Room* (1922), Kenneth Rexroth's *An Autobiographical Novel* (1966). One might even refine this type further and designate some novels lyrical, whether obviously autobiographical or not, for the author, Emily Brontë in *Wuthering Heights* (1847), for instance, may project herself into *two* characters, Catherine and Heathcliff. The lyrical novel is an expression of the author's own feelings, as in a lyric poem, overtly or projected through other characters. Lyrical qualities are usually joined with other elements, blending the inner private with the outer public world (see Ralph Freedman in *The Novel*, edited by Davis). The lyric novel is carefully compressed, impressionistic, and expresses a poetic vision of human experience. The following may be considered lyrical novels: Goethe's *The Sorrows of Young Werther* (1774); Djuna Barnes' *Nightwood* (1936); Friedrich Hölderlin's *Hyperion, or The Hermit in Greece* (1797899); Novalis' *Heinrich von Ofterdingen* (1802); Rainer Maria Rilke's *The Notebooks of Malte Laurids Brigge* (1910); André Gide's *Nourritures Terrestres (Fruits of the Earth* 1897), composed of loosely related images; Virginia Woolf's *The Waves* (1931); and William Goyen's *House of Breath* (1950).

> Open the rusted iron gate and step across the stickerburrs blooming in the grass, go round past the rotted tire where the speckled canna used to live and turn towards the cisternwheel that does not turn. See the cistern, rusted and hollow and no water in it, and the wheel of the windmill wrecked and fallen and rats playing over the ruin. The wheel is like an enormous metal flower blighted by rust. Bend down to touch the fallen petals and, bending, hear the grinding groan of the wheel that begins to turn again in your brain of childhood, rasping the overtone of loneliness and moaning the undertone of wonder. Remember how it rose up on long legs out of the round, deep, lidded stock tub, and remember once when the lid was left off how the child of a Negro washwoman (recall her poking, head wrapped in a scrap of red bandanna, the steaming black iron pot full of Starnes and Ganchion clothes) climbed up and fell into the tub and was drowned and how the cows come to drink bellowed to find its corpse.

THE BIOGRAPHICAL NOVEL

The overtly biographical novel is an entirely opposite type. The author deliberately and clearly claims to have fictionalized the life of a famous person, as in Dmitri Merejkowski's *The Romance of Leonardo da Vinci* (1902). The justifications for writing a fictional rather than a factual life of a real person are so weak that only a masterful writer can get away with it. Fact-fiction hybrids, combining elements of the historical novel, are often popular successes but seldom artistic achievements. The form began with such works as Xenophon's *Cyropaedia* (4th C., B.C.). In *The Moon and Sixpence* (1919), W. Somerset Maugham offered genuine insight into the life of the French artist Paul Gauguin.

> When so much has been written about Charles Strickland, it may seem unnecessary that I should write more. A painter's monument is his work. It is true I knew him more intimately than most: I met

him first before ever he became a painter, and I saw him not in-
frequently during the difficult years he spent in Paris; but I do not
suppose I should ever have set down my recollections if the
hazards of the war had not taken me to Tahiti. There, as is notori-
ous, he spent the last years of his life; and there I came across persons who were familiar with him. I find myself in a position to
throw light on just that part of his tragic career which has remained most obscure. If they who believe in Strickland's greatness
are right, the personal narratives of such as knew him in the flesh
can hardly be superfluous. What would we not give for the re-
miniscences of someone who had been as intimately acquainted
with El Greco as I was with Strickland?

In *Lust for Life* (1934), the life of Van Gogh, Irving Stone did not succeed
so well. In this vein, Stone has written several other best-sellers, *The Agony
and the Ecstasy* (1961), on Michelangelo, and *The Passions of the Mind*
(1971), on Freud.

Three pretended or simulated biographies are John P. Marquand's *The
Late George Apley* (1937); Carl Van Vechten's *Peter Whiffle* (1922); and Ste-
ven Millhauser's *Edwin Mullhouse: The Life and Death of an American
Writer, 1943–1954 by Jeffrey Cartwright* (1972).

Few great works fall into the category of the overtly biographical novel;
the implicit contradiction of genres is too strong; the reader cannot sustain
belief in such a hybrid form.

A novel loosely *based* on a famous person becomes a somewhat different matter; it is similar to the autobiographical novel, since through the
faculty of imagination, more of the author himself comes into play. The historical and the biographical novel pose similar problems, which serious
novelists are tempted, now and then, to solve. One of the most imaginative
examples of the loosely biographical and historical—perhaps also lyrical—
novel is Virginia Woolf's *Orlando* (1928), a biographical fantasy, a strange
story of a man born in the Elizabethan age whom we follow into the 1920's
as he metamorphoses into a woman, part Virginia Woolf, part Victoria
Sackville-West, her friend.

THE ROMAN À CLEF

The *roman à clef* differs somewhat from the autobiographical or biographical novel in that the author has tried to conceal, but unsuccessfully,
the identities of real people, usually famous, on whom he has based his
characters. A well-known example is Ernest Hemingway's *The Sun Also*

Rises (1926); his characters were quickly recognized by their real life coun-
terparts, their friends, and their public.

> Robert Cohn was once middleweight boxing champion of
> Princeton. Do not think that I am very much impressed by that as
> a boxing title, but it meant a lot to Cohn. He cared nothing for
> boxing, in fact he disliked it, but he learned it painfully and
> thoroughly to counteract the feeling of inferiority and shyness he
> had felt on being treated as a Jew at Princeton. There was a cer-
> tain inner comfort in knowing he could knock down anybody who
> was snooty to him, although, being very shy and a thoroughly nice
> boy, he never fought except in the gym. He was Spider Kelly's
> star pupil. Spider Kelly taught all his young gentlemen to box like
> featherweights, no matter whether they weighed one hundred and
> five or two hundred and five pounds. But it seemed to fit Cohn.
> He was really very fast. He was so good that Spider promptly
> overmatched him and got his nose permanently flattened. This in-
> creased Cohn's distaste for boxing, but it gave him a certain satis-
> faction of some strange sort, and it certainly improved his nose. In
> his last year at Princeton he read too much and took to wearing
> spectacles. I never met any one of his class who remembered him.
> They did not even remember that he was middleweight boxing
> champion.

This type can become a cheap, commercially exploitable product as in such
best-sellers as Harold Robbins' *The Carpetbaggers* (1961), an inside-dope
exposé of Howard Hughes.

BILDUNGSROMAN

As the name suggests, the *Bildungsroman* is mainly a German type, beginning with Goethe's *The Sorrows of Young Werther* (1774) and *The Appren-
ticeship of Wilhelm Meister* (1795–96). This type shows the "formation" in
relation to society of a young man who is typical of his time and place. A
modern example is Thomas Mann's *Der Zauberberg (The Magic Mountain)*
(1924); a young man confined to a mountain-top tuberculosis sanitarium is
schooled in philosophy, psychology, sex, etc., by the other inmates, most of
whom are older men and women.

The Germans also have a name for a type that is a variant on the *Bildungsroman,* the *Erziehungsroman* or "upbringing" or education or initiation novel. Good examples are Charles Dickens' *David Copperfield* (1849–
50), Samuel Butler's *The Way of All Flesh* (1903), and George Meredith's
The Ordeal of Richard Feverel (1859).

It was now, as Sir Austin had written it down, The Magnetic Age: the Age of violent attractions; when to hear mention of Love is dangerous, and see it, a communication of the disease. People at Raynham were put on their guard by the Baronet, and his reputation for wisdom was severely criticized in consequence of the injunctions he thought fit to issue through butler and housekeeper down to the lower household, for the preservation of his son from any visible symptom of the passion. A footmen and two housemaids are believed to have been dismissed on the report of Heavy Benson that they were in, or inclining to, the state; upon which an under-cook and a dairymaid voluntarily threw up their places, averring that "they did not want no young men, but to have their sex spied after by an old wretch like that," indicating the ponderous butler, "was a little too much for a Christian woman," and then they were ungenerous enough to glance at Benson's well-known marital calamity, hinting that some men met their deserts. So intolerable did Heavy Benson's espionage become, that Raynham would have grown depopulated of its womankind, had not Adrian interfered, who pointed out to the Baronet what a fearful arm his butler was wielding. Sir Austin acknowledged it despondently. "It only shows," said he, with a fine spirit of justice, "how all but impossible it is to legislate where there are women!"

This type differs from the novel of subjective adolescent perception that burgeoned in the 1940's and 1950's in America. Carson McCullers' *A Member of the Wedding* (1946) and J. D. Salinger's *A Catcher in the Rye* (1951) emphasized the psychological traumas of growing up; that element is also involved in the education type.

THE NOVEL OF CHARACTER

The novel of character has always been a major type. It shows the formation and operation of character through interaction with other characters and with a stable society. The concept of "character" is basically optimistic: any man can willfully achieve good character and function usefully in society. A type practiced mainly by the English, the novel of character predominated in the Victorian era. Characters are regarded primarily as social types, rather than as universal or ideal types or as individuals; human nature is depicted as basically good and unchanging; the aim of such novels was generally to profit the reader by instruction and pleasure; indeed for such sensibilities there was pleasure, or at least delight, in instruction.

The eighteenth century was a period of transition; the late nineteenth and twentieth centuries have been periods of disintegration. Novels of character become less numerous the more heterogeneous society becomes. They are based on fixed assumptions about human nature, morality, the intellect, and society; the serious undermining or destructions of these assumptions makes the novel of character difficult to write. It has been replaced by the novel of consciousness, or the subjective novel of psychological analysis. Events in which characters come into conflict with each other within the social framework are replaced by conflicts within the character himself. The eighteenth and nineteenth century concept of character assumes that external forces, and the individual's choices in response to them within a social framework, form and reveal qualities of character. In the twentieth century man is seen mainly as a victim; his humanity diminished by external forces, he is wracked to suicide by doubts produced by introversion. *Little Women* (1868) by Louisa May Alcott and *The Mill on the Floss* (1860) by George Eliot are studies in character.

> It may be surprising that Maggie, among whose many imperfections an excessive delight in admiration and acknowledged supremacy were not absent now, any more than when she was instructing the gypsies with a view towards achieving a royal position among them, was not more elated on a day when she had had the tribute of so many looks and smiles, together with that satisfactory consciousness which had necessarily come from being taken before Lucy's cheval-glass, and made to look at the full length of her tall beauty, crowned by the night of her massy hair. Maggie had smiled at herself then, and for the moment had forgotten everything in the sense of her own beauty. If that state of mind could have lasted, her choice would have been to have Stephen Guest at her feet, offering her a life filled with all luxuries, with daily incense of adoration near and distant, and with all possibilities of culture at her command. But there were things in her stronger than vanity—passion, and affection, and long deep memories of early discipline and effort, of early claims on her love and pity; and the stream of vanity was soon swept along and mingled imperceptibly with that wider current which was at its highest force to-day, under the double urgency of the events and inward impulses brought by the last week.

Charles Dickens wrote novels of character, although many are full of characters who are almost caricatures. The adroit handling of stock or stereotype characters (or flat characters, as E. M. Forster calls them) is more difficult than the creation of caricature; deliberate caricature is not as frequent as accidental, for the novel demands that the author create a total, real world, one in which caricatures do not breathe well. A good author sometimes unintentionally creates a caricature out of his own previous, well-realized characters, as Hemingway did with Colonel Cantwell in *Across the River and Into the Trees* (1950).

The didactic element is often stressed in novels of character, such as John Lyly's *Euphues, The Anatomy of Wit* (1579), whose main contribution to literature was a carefully polished style that, in the hands of other writers, came to be called euphuistic. Other didactic romances are: Mrs. Alpha Behn's *Oroonoko* (1688); and Thomas Day's *Sandford and Merton* (1783–89), which shows nature as a beneficent influence on character.

THE NOVEL OF MANNERS

Closely related to the novel of character is the novel of manners, best exemplified in the works of Jane Austen, as in *Pride and Prejudice* (1813); the very title suggests aspects of character, and the man and woman who exemplify them work out their conflict in a society of manners.

> Darcy mentioned his letter. "Did it," said he, "did it *soon* make you think better of me? Did you, on reading it, give any credit to its contents?"
> She explained what its effect on her had been, and how gradually all her former prejudices had been removed.
>
> . . .
>
> "I have been a selfish being all my life, in practice, though not in principle. As a child, I was taught what was *right;* but I was not taught to correct my temper. I was given good principles, but left to follow them in pride and conceit."

If the concept of manners is widened, one can say that even a novel about beatniks, Jack Kerouac's *On the Road* (1958), is a novel of manners, since it depicts the way people within a clearly defined, small and narrow, culture relate to one another. Many American southern fictions are novels of manners. In this broader context, then, most novels have been novels of manners (see Lionel Trilling). Samuel Richardson's *Pamela* (1740) and *Clarissa* (1747–48), are novels of manners in the epistolary mode. Others are Anthony Trollope's *Barchester Towers* (1857); William Dean Howells' *A Hazard of New Fortunes* (1890); the French novel, *Marianne* (1731–1741), by Pierre Carlet de Chamblain de Marivaux; John P. Marquand's *The Late George Apley* (1937); Henry James' social morality novel *The Spoils of Poynton* (1897).

A study of character and manners in society is bound to produce comic results. A classic work of humorous sensibility is Laurence Sterne's *Tristram Shandy*. Other social comedies or comedies of manners, all English, are: the novels of Jane Austen, including *Emma* (1815) and *Persuasion* (1818); Thomas Love Peacock's *Crotchet Castle* (1831); Mrs. Elizabeth Gaskell's *Cranford* (1853); E. M. Forster's *A Room with a View* (1908); and Joyce Cary's *Herself Surprised* (1941).

THE SENTIMENTAL NOVEL

The sentimental novel (or novel of sensibility) depicts the behavior of resolutely moral, honorable, and somewhat humorless heroes and heroines whose compassionate and benevolent temperaments prompt them to weep at spectacles of sin and suffering. Merely to express feeling proves that one has breeding, virtue, and a kind soul. Such virtue is its own reward. These novels also demonstrate that villains can reform. A phenomenon of the late eighteenth century, these fictions appealed to the new middle classes, especially in England, and reflected their values. Again, in Richardson's *Pamela* (1740), a sentimental romance, the heroine's struggle to retain her virtue got the reader's sympathy. Henry Mackenzie's *The Man of Feeling* (1771) and Oliver Goldsmith's *The Vicar of Wakefield* (1766), are two major novels of sentiment.

It were to be wished then that power, instead of contriving new laws to punish vice, instead of drawing hard the cords of society till a convulsion come to burst them, instead of cutting away wretches as useless before we have tried their utility, instead of converting correction into vengeance, it were to be wished that we tried the restrictive arts of government, and made law the protector but not the tyrant of the people. We should then find that creatures whose souls are held as dross only wanted the hand of a refiner; we should then find that wretches, now stuck up for long tortures lest luxury should feel a momentary pang, might, if properly treated, serve to sinew the state in times of danger; that as their faces are like ours, their hearts are so too; that few minds are so base as that perseverance cannot amend. . . .

Sentimental romances are not confined to English literature. There are the Japanese Ibara Saikaku's *Five Women Who Loved Love* (c. 1685); Madeleine de Scudéry's *Artamène* (1646–1653); Madame de La Fayette's *The Princess of Clèves* (1678); Abbé Prévost's *Manon Lescaut* (1731); Goethe's *The Sorrows of Werther* (1774); Fanny Burney's *Cecilia* (1782), a sentimental novel of manners; Americans Harriet Beecher Stowe's *Uncle*

Tom's Cabin, or Life Among the Lowly (1852) and John Esten Cooke's belated example, *The Virginia Comedians* (1854).

Today, the terms "sensibility" and "sentimentality" have very different meanings. "Sensibility" suggests restrained emotional responses and highly refined intellectual acumen and aesthetic appreciation. The person of sensibility is quick to ridicule sentimentality, defined as "emotion in excess of the occasion." Everyone is sentimental about something, but sentimentality is a tendency to be influenced excessively by thoughts and feelings rather than reason. Some authors deliberately play upon a reader's inclinations toward sentimentality; others deliberately avoid it and often treat it ironically or satirically. When our reason tells us that the cause of a character's feelings is trivial and his response excessive, we may conclude that he is being too sentimental. Today we find sentimentality in such popular novels, of varying quality, as Betty Smith's *A Tree Grows in Brooklyn* (1943), Kathleen Norris' *Mother* (1911), or Faith Baldwin's *The Heart Remembers* (1941); but there are strains of sentimentality even in the melodrama of John Steinbeck's *Of Mice and Men* (1937). Modern sentimental novels such as Erich Segal's *Love Story* (1970) are often called tear-jerkers. Tears, some writers and critics believe, drown the aesthetic elements in an artistic novel.

THE DIDACTIC NOVEL

Closely related to the novel of manners and of sentiment is the didactic (to teach) novel. The didactic novel manipulates narrative and exemplary characters who embody various virtues and vices to demonstrate explicitly a particular religious, moral, political, or philosophical doctrine. The context may be the circumstances of everyday life or allegory, fable, parable, even fantasy, and devices such as symbolism and personification may be utilized. Novels of character, manners, and of sensibility were often didactic, but pure examples of this domestic type are rare, especially today.

One of the original major purposes of fiction was to instruct. We see this function in the short allegorical tales called *fables* ("narrative," "plot") which illustrate a moral, often tacked on at the end. The *Fables* (6th c. B.C.), of the Greek Aesop, which originated more than fourteen centuries before Christ, were *didactic*. There are also the Indian fables, *Panchatantra* (in Sanskrit), about 300–500 A.D. Collections of stories in which animals enact human foibles were called *beast* epics; as examples, there are *Reynard the Fox* (12th century) in which folk comedy becomes subtle satire of the institutions of the Middle Ages, and later, the *Brer Rabbit* tales (1880) by Joel Chandler Harris, and Rudyard Kipling's *The Jungle Book* (1894), which also includes an Indian boy as innocent and natural as the animals.

Two major ways of actuating the didactic impulse are illustrative (through symbolism or allegory or personification, ancient devices) and representational (through imitation of reality); one is a clearly allegorical world, the other a world true to fact. In John Bunyan's *Pilgrim's Progress* (1678), a young man named Christian is subjected to every typical test of faith and virtue by characters personifying the qualities that give them their names: Mr. Worldly Wiseman, Mr. Great-Heart, Lady Feigning; in such places as the City of Destruction, the Celestial City, the Slough of Despond, and Vanity Fair. These are called exemplary figures because they embody certain vices and virtues. Many have argued that the book is so packed with didacticism that it shouldn't be called a novel at all.

> Then I saw in my dream that when they were got out of the wilderness, they presently saw a town before them, and the name of that town is Vanity; and at the town there is a fair kept, called Vanity Fair; it is kept all the year long; it beareth the name of Vanity Fair, because the town where it is kept is lighter than vanity; and also because all that is there sold, or that cometh thither, is vanity. As is the saying of the wise, "all that cometh is vanity."

James Branch Cabell's *Jurgen* (1919) uses similar devices.

Exemplary characters function in non-allegorical novels, too. Richardson's *Clarissa* is an exemplary but not an allegorical figure; "I thought the story might tend to promote the cause of religion and virtue," said Richardson. Clarissa is very real and her world is full of realistic domestic detail. However, the quality of moral sensibility is exaggerated in this realistic setting. Clarissa is too good to be true. So, too, are the later male characters in *Tom Brown's School Days* (1857) by Thomas Hughes and in the novels of Horatio Alger: *Work and Win, Do and Dare, Try and Trust, Bound to Rise, or Up the Ladder* (1873), illustrating the Puritan ethic of work and virtue; his characters existed only to set a moral example for boys, as he suggests in his introduction.

> Harry Walton and Luke Harris were two country boys who had the same opportunities to achieve success. Harry Walton by his efforts succeeded, and Luke Harris's life was a failure. Read this story and you will see what qualities in the one brought about his success, and what in the other caused his downfall.

Harold Bell Wright, an ex-minister, performed the same function for adults in such novels as *The Winning of Barbara Worth* (1911).

In a time when many charged that novels had a corrupting influence on young girls, Anthony Trollope swore that "no girl has risen from the reading of my pages less modest than she was before." Oscar Wilde later said, "There is no such thing as a moral or an immoral book. Books are well written or badly written."

In setting out to depict the world as it is, the best novelists have not presumed to teach or instruct, only to expose or reveal (two very different aims). The didactic novel teaches, said Thomas Hardy, "nothing but the impossibility of tampering with natural truth to advance dogmatic opinions." Even though Henry James wrote what might be called a moral allegory in *The Turn of the Screw* (1898), he once said that there are only bad and good, interesting and uninteresting novels. A novel infused with a moral vision, such as Leo Tolstoy's *The Resurrection* (1899), does not necessarily set out overtly to teach.

The compulsion of some writers to expose and criticize the corruptions of society today comes out of a didactic attitude that is revealed only implicitly. Today, a strong element of didacticism is frowned upon, while a cruder form of moral assertion is considered sophisticated: that is, attacking evil or hypocrisy in social institutions, from the radical and proletarian novels of the 1910's and the Thirties to such novels as Norman Mailer's *Why Are We in Vietnam?* (1967) in the Sixties.

THE RELIGIOUS NOVEL

Pilgrim's Progress is a religious allegory. A comparable modern work is William Faulkner's *A Fable* (1954). A strong element of religion—usually Protestant—has characterized most novels that instruct. Many novels are about religion itself, from novels about the clergy to novels about the individual's quest for salvation. One view of history sees the coming of Christ as the major event in the story of man, but few novels are embued with such a vision, and although there have been prophetic novelists—Thomas Mann, Franz Kafka, D. H. Lawrence—their works do not deal primarily with religion. Still, Christianity pervades most of Western literature, in negative terms as a reaction (hypocrisy, the anti-christ, salvation on earth, the resurrection of the body in a kind of paganized Christianity) and in positive terms (God in man, poetized religion in allegories of human greatness, in the spirit of knowledge). (See Ellmann, *The Modern Tradition*.)

Although most so-called serious novels that deal at all with religion satirize it or treat it comically, especially novels about the clergy, many novels are directly about religion itself. There are novels in which the hero quests for spiritual enlightenment, such as Hermann Hesse's *Siddhartha* (1922); novels that depict the individual's search for salvation or redemption.

> But he, Siddhartha, where did he belong? Whose life would he share? Whose language would he speak?
>   At that moment, when the world around him melted away, when he stood alone like a star in the heavens, he was overwhelmed by a feeling of icy despair, but he was more firmly himself than ever. That was the last shudder of his awakening, the last pains of birth. Immediately he moved on again and began to walk quickly and impatiently, no longer homewards, no longer to his father, no longer looking backwards.

Other good examples are: Graham Greene's *The Heart of the Matter* (1948); the Spanish Carmen Laforet's *Nada (Andrea*, 1945), about spiritual desolation; Benito Pérez Galdós' *Doña Perfecta* (1876), a popular Spanish tragedy of religion in which modern ideas clash with bigotry and prejudice in a small Andalusian town; Franz Kafka's *The Castle* (1926); the French Catholic François Mauriac's *Thérèse* (1927), about sin and guilt; William Gaddis' *The Recognitions* (1955), a modern Divine comedy; and Eugene Vale's *The Thirteenth Apostle* (1959). Italian Antonio Fogazzaro's *The Saint* (1905), a trilogy, is a religious romance.

The religious novel is a minor popular type. There are the popular religious chronicles or historicals: Polish Henryk Sienkiewicz's *Quo Vadis* (1896); American Lew Wallace's *Ben Hur* (1880), a tale of the Christ; Sholem Asch's *The Nazarene* (1939) and *The Apostle* (1943); Franz Werfel's *The Song of Bernadette* (1941); and Lloyd C. Douglas' *The Robe* (1942).

There are mystical works, such as French Remy de Gourmont's *A Night in the Luxembourg* (1906); Booth Tarkington's *The Magnificent Ambersons* (1929); T. F. Powys' *Mr. Weston's Good Wine* (1927); and the poetic mysticism of Hermann Broch's *The Death of Virgil* (1945).

THE ROMANTIC NOVEL

Rising above these fable-like novels and far more numerous are the romantic novels. (The love novel, a very different type, will be discussed later.) The romantic novelists reacted against the realistic fiction of the early nineteenth century and revived some elements of romance narratives—heroes, idealized heroines, exotic places of antiquity, the wonderful, the marvelous—adding the bizarre and the grotesque. The romantic novel satisfied a relatively new type of sensibility—the man of romantic temperament, totally self-centered, thoroughly subjective, sometimes with an ironic self-awareness, melancholy, suicidal, who lived to the hilt, with an emphasis on spontaneous emotion, suffering, loving in the extreme—in conflict with most of his fellow men, who pursue lesser goals of mind and spirit, in love with a

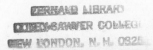

woman who epitomizes his higher, spiritual, aesthetic ideals or their opposites; a person who sees nature, even in its destructive moods, as a mirror
of his own soul. Goethe's phrase "storm and stress" (*Sturm und Drang*) describes romantics well.

In *The Birth of Tragedy* (1872), the German philosopher Friedrich
Nietzsche spoke of the two major kinds of artists: the Apollonian—classical,
balanced, harmonious, clear, traditional—and the Dionysian—wild, irrational, anarchic, obscure, experimental, visionary, romantic. The romantic
sometimes fought the injustices of society. In his conflict with society, the
romantic artist, when young, conceives of human behavior as essentially
tragic and experiences romantic agony; older, disillusioned, he experiences
romantic irony. In their imaginative encounter with problems of technique
and style, classical writers discover the shapes and significance of their raw
material. The romantic, fascinated by the scope and complexity of life, attempts to project massive chunks of relatively unprocessed raw material,
expressing everything through the self, in a rich language.

Byron, Shelley, Keats, Blake, Wordsworth, and Coleridge exemplified
the romantic spirit in poetry in the late eighteenth century and early
nineteenth century, and most romantics display strains of all six. Another
romantic was Sir Walter Scott, some of whose novels, *The Heart of Midlothian* (1818), for instance, showed the social concern of Shelley, who fought
for liberal causes. The totally self-centered romantic, such as Keats, is rare
in fiction. Keats was solitary and sickly and thoroughly subjective, lyrical;
Byron was cynical beneath his romantic aura, exhibiting the element of
romantic irony, for he did not take himself as seriously as Shelley, for instance. Goethe's *The Sorrows of Young Werther* (1774) is a famous example
of romantic agony and melancholy—with suicide as the climax (many of the
novel's young readers identified so deeply with Werther that they, too, killed themselves).

The romantic lived in a world of fact, but built a fantastic world of the
imagination into which he could escape. The romantic protagonist is very
different from the hero of medieval romances whose life was almost entirely
external and oriented to the church, a pure woman, and society, in realms
of the ideal. Unlike Beowulf or King Arthur, the romantic hero does not
perform deeds, he strikes attitudes of defiance and self-love, hoping to force
entry into new realms of thought and feeling by colossal wishfulness as opposed to physical willfulness. However, the upsurge of the historical novel
came during the romantic period and the use of the hero in that type is a
combination of one strain of the new romantic attitude and the old chivalric
code. Cervantes' *Don Quixote* (1605–15) was at once a critique of the excesses of the old Chivalric romances and an assertion of the Byronic sort of
world view—live as if dreams are reality, with dire consequences, for one-

self, as it usually turned out, and for others not so powerfully romantic. Gustave Flaubert's *Madame Bovary* (1856) is Don Quixote later on, but without his means to action, and his ironic distance on himself. The irony is all between reader and writer.

The romantic temperament had a resurgence in Thomas Wolfe's four gargantuan novels; the last one, *The Web and the Rock* (1939), showed a Byronic self-awareness. Henry Miller is another ironic, Byronic novelist. Miller's friend, Lawrence Durrell in his *Alexandria Quartet* (1957–1960) revived the romantic novel once again; these are very strange, fascinating, interrelated novels, employing a lush style, psychological approaches to character, and experimental techniques.

While romanticism was essentially a rebellion against realism, some romantics, such as Joseph Conrad, tried to create a realism still embued with romanticism; he faced up to life, but only so he could transform life. "We only suffer reality to suggest," said Charlotte Brontë, "never to dictate." For the romantic individualist, reality is open to personal interpretation and—perhaps—to re-creation. Goethe's *Werther* and a similar work, Gottfried Keller's *Der Grüne Heinrich* (1879), like Goethe's, an autobiographical romance and an education novel, dramatize the ways in which the romantic sensibility tries to transform fact into fiction—with less drastic results for Heinrich than for Werther.

Sensitivity and subjectivity are major traits in the romantic temperament, combined with a seemingly paradoxical, aggressive theatricality, as seen in two psychological romances, Charlotte Brontë's *Jane Eyre* (1847) and Alain-Fournier's *Le Grand Méaulnes* (*The Wanderer*, 1913). The romantic writer thinks of himself and thus of his usually autobiographical work as a unique product of personality and spontaneity. In asserting himself as a personality (as opposed to the earlier concept of character) the romantic as artist and as a protagonist alienates himself from middle class society. Some claim that alienation has always been a threat to the novel, which is essentially a social art form.

In his conflict with society, the romantic artist conceives of human behavior as essentially tragic: Spanish Fernando de Rojas' *Celestina* (1499), a novel in dialogue, dramatic form, divided into acts; Madame de Staël's *Delphine* (1802); Prosper Mérimée's *Carmen* (1845); Thomas Hardy's *Return of the Native* (1878) and *The Woodlanders* (1887); Bulgarian Ivan Vazov's *Under the Yoke* (1893); and Mexican Ignacio Manuel Altamirano's *El Zarco* (1901).

For the romantic, art and nature are inseparable; the romantic brought nature, literally, into the novel. François-René de Chateaubriand's *Atala*

(1801) and *René* (1802), philosophical romances, are set in an imagined New World, where nature is supreme.

The romantic work of art is the product not of society but of the individual idea; the romantic triumphs not only over himself and society, but over obstacles that would prevent him from recreating the world in his own image. The romantic is the artist as hero. His weapons are inspiration, intuition, imagination (fancy was an older term), and enthusiasm, and what they express are themselves, as processes and as pure sensations. George Eliot claims to have been possessed; she abandoned herself to "the inspiration of the moment." The Italian aesthetician Croce said: "to intuit is to express."

There are impressionistic romances: Pierre Loti's (Julian Viaud) *An Iceland Fisherman* (1886); Arthur Machen's *Hill of Dreams* (1907); and Emily Brontë's *Wuthering Heights* (1847).

> "Don't torture me till I am as mad as yourself," cried he [Heathcliff], wrenching his head free, and grinding his teeth.
> The two, to a cool spectator, made a strange and fearful picture. Well might Catherine deem that heaven would be a land of exiles to her, unless with her mortal body she cast away her moral character also. Her present countenance had a wild vindictiveness in its white cheek, and a bloodless lip and scintillating eye; and she retained in her closed fingers a portion of the locks she had been grasping. As to her companion, while raising himself with one hand, he had taken her arm with the other: and so inadequate was his stock of gentleness to the requirements of her condition, that on his letting go I saw four distinct impressions left blue in the colourless skin.
> "Are you possessed with a devil," he pursued savagely, "to talk in that manner to me when you are dying?"

"The exceptional gains our wonder," said Longinus. The romantics brought to the novel a wonder new to it. Before, most novelists put great stock in the probable, but the romantic was obsessed with the marvelous. The exotic is experienced in Lafcadio Hearn's *Chita: A Memory of Last Island* (1889); Joris-Karl Huysmans' *À Rebours (Against the Grain,* 1884); Donn Byrne's *Messer Marco Polo* (1921); Frederic Prokosch's *Seven Who Fled* (1937). There are the adventure romances: Robert Montgomery Bird's *Nick of the Woods* (1837); Robert Louis Stevenson's *Kidnapped* (1886); Rudyard Kipling's *Captains Courageous* (1897) and *Kim* (1901); H. Rider Haggard's *King Solomon's Mines* (1886); and Jack London's *The Sea Wolf* (1904).

The American poet T. S. Eliot has said that "in the seventeenth century a dissociation of sensibility set in"—thought and emotion, fused in the classic writers, split, and one can see the emphasis in the Romantic era upon the emotions. Even allegory and symbolism are suffused with emotional sense, rather than intellectual: William Beckford's *The History of the Caliph Vathek* (1786); Herman Melville's *Moby Dick* (1851); D. H. Lawrence's *The Plumed Serpent* (1926); and Ernest Hemingway's *The Old Man and the Sea* (1952).

The romantic artist focuses upon emotions that were once only partial experiences in novels. The reader feels a pervading sense of sadness or melancholy. Plato called poets divinely mad, inspired by the gods, and the idea of poetic madness has persisted; Thomas Mann wrote several stories about the artist as a diseased person. In their public behavior and writings, the romantic poets and novelists revived that image of the literary artist. To be possessed by the Muses is to be mad, said Plato, and the controlled poet is not divinely inspired. Thus while the irrational is an element in most art, the romantics began to explore the irrational for its own sake; society condemned their images then, but today the boundaries between the rational and the irrational are less defined. The romantic offers his readers extravagance in a Puritan society. He sometimes deliberately sets out to bring off a *tour de force*, sharing his exhilaration with the reader. Byron's *Don Juan* is a good example in poetry and Durrell's *Alexandria Quartet* in fiction. The romantic's over-reaching often ends in melodramatic effect, but that is sometimes what we go to the romantics for. The classic writer strains to avoid the false; the romantic is willing to risk seeming false by classical standards to achieve his own new, special effects. The romantic painter is well depicted in Joyce Cary's *The Horse's Mouth* (1944), a picaresque romance, and the proletarian romantic in Nikos Kazantzakis's *Zorba, the Greek* (1946).

The romantic is capable of many attitudes, including humor: Hungarian Kálmán Mikszáth, *St. Peter's Umbrella* (1895); Booth Tarkington, *Seventeen* (1916), reflecting romantic attitudinizing in an American midwestern boy. There are the sentimental mystery romance, Dickens' *Martin Chuzzlewit* (1843–44); the domestic romance, Scott's *The Antiquary* (1816); and even the sporting romance, George J. Whyte-Melville's *Market Harborough* (1861).

During the Victorian Era, the romantic novel went underground, although elements appeared in other types, especially in the adventure tale set in romantic places; a resurgence of romanticism, neo-romanticism, came when writers once again looked inward, inspired by the writings of Sigmund Freud and other psychologists. In poetry, it took the form of symbolism, inspired in part by the American Gothic romanticist, Edgar Allan Poe.

Romanticism came late to America. Thomas Wolfe is the arch American romanticist; in England D. H. Lawrence, a very different sort, wrote out of a romantic concept of sex as salvation, as religion, as blood power—physical sex, as opposed to the Platonic love of the heroes of French romances or the unspoken sex of English and German romantics. Here is a passage from Wolfe's *Look Homeward, Angel* (1929).

> He cared nothing for the practical need of the world. He dared to say the strange and marvelous thing that had bloomed so darkly in him.
>
> "Laura," he said, hearing his low voice sound over the great plain of the moon, "let's always love each other as we do now. Let's never get married. I want you to wait for me and to love me forever. I am going all over the world. I shall go away for years at a time; I shall become famous, but I shall always come back to you. You shall live in a house away in the mountains, you shall wait for me, and keep yourself for me. Will you?" he said, asking for her life as calmly as for an hour of her time.
>
> "Yes, dear," said Laura in the moonlight. "I will wait for you forever."

THE GOTHIC NOVEL

The gothic novel is an early, special manifestation of the romantic world view. The gothic novel depicts the perverse, sometimes fantastic and terrible behavior of an introverted and decayed aristocracy at a time (usually the eighteenth and nineteenth centuries) when the old social order and political norms have been destroyed and is usually set in the ruins of castles built in the time of chivalry. The chivalric knight fought demons for his lady-love in the name of the Virgin Mary, according to a Christian code; the gothic figure is obsessed by a demon within; consequently, a beautiful lady, as in some of the stories of Edgar Allan Poe, suffers. The ambience is supernatural, the mode of behavior perverse. The romantic, said Victor Hugo, mingles the grotesque, once mainly the province of satire, with the sublime, as he did in his historical romance *The Hunchback of Notre Dame* (1831); the ugly, even the obscene, may be aspects of the divine in nature; the supernatural may be an extension of the natural. The most famous classic examples of the gothic romance are Horace Walpole, *The Castle of Otranto* (1764); Mrs. Ann Radcliffe, *The Mysteries of Udolpho,* (1794); Matthew Gregory Lewis, *The Monk* (1795); American Charles Brockden Brown, *Wieland* (1798); Irishman Charles Maturin, *Melmoth the Wanderer* (1820). Then came the gothic fantasy, Robert Louis Stevenson's *Dr. Jekyll and Mr. Hyde* (1886), and the horror romance, Bram Stoker's *Dracula* (1897).

The mystery novel creates suspense in a romantic atmosphere, another manifestation of the gothic romance. Examples are Eugène Sue, *The Wandering Jew* (1844-45); Charles Dickens, *Great Expectations* (1860-61); Wilkie Collins, *The Woman in White* (1860).

Charlotte Brontë's *Jane Eyre* (1847) was the first great gothic romance. With the publication of a modern gothic romance, *Rebecca* (1938), by Daphne du Maurier, a revival of that type began; it is now extremely popular in America. It is interesting to compare *Jane Eyre* with *Rebecca*.

> I looked with timorous joy towards a stately house: I saw a blackened ruin.
> No need to cower behind a gate-post, indeed!—to peep up at chamber lattices, fearing life was astir behind them! No need to listen for doors opening—to fancy steps on the pavement or the gravel-walk! The lawn, the grounds were trodden and waste: the portal yawned void. The front was, as I had once seen it in a dream, but a shell-like wall, very high and very fragile-looking, perforated with paneless windows: no roof, no battlements, no chimneys—all had crashed in.
> And there was the silence of death about it: the solitude of a lonesome wild. No wonder that letters addressed to people here had never received an answer: as well despatch epistles to a vault in a church aisle. The grim blackness of the stones told by what fate the Hall had fallen—by conflagration: but how kindled? What story belonged to this disaster?
>
> .   .   .
>
> A cloud, hitherto unseen, came upon the moon, and hovered an instant like a dark hand before a face. The illusion went with it, and the lights in the windows were extinguished. I looked upon a desolate shell, soulless at last, unhaunted, with no whisper of the past about its staring walls.
> The house was a sepulchre, our fear and suffering lay buried in the ruins.

Two best-selling examples are Victoria Holt's *Bride of Pendoric* (1963) and Mary Stewart's *Nine Coaches Waiting* (1958), whose locale is an old French chateau where "a strange terror lay coiled behind its brooding elegance." Other contemporary gothic writers are: Emilie Loring, Grace Livingston Hill, Georgette Heyer, Charlotte Armstrong, Josephine Edgar, and, far above these in quality, Margaret Millar, whose *Beast in View* (1956), is an excellent psychological study. (See Popular, p.45; see Love, p.56.)

SOUTHERN GOTHIC AND GROTESQUE NOVELS

Some critics maintain that gothic and grotesque novels are in the mainstream of American fiction. The southern gothic novel (with its northern variants) is a rebirth of the spirit of the classic gothic novel. But the emphasis is less on descriptions of bizarre settings and weird actions than on Freudian perversions and psychoses growing out of the traumatic changes in the South after the Civil War; southern aristocrats going mad in decaying mansions in small towns certainly seemed both gothic and grotesque to northern and even to many southern readers.

The *grotesque* is a strong element in the gothic novel. But some distinction should be made. Both elements grew out of the American phase of romanticism. The grotesque deals with characters who are mentally and/or physically stunted or deformed, as in the stories and novels of Sherwood Anderson and Wright Morris. *Winesburg, Ohio* (1919), composed of interrelated stories, by Sherwood Anderson, begins with "The Book of the Grotesque." In the gothic novel, the style is usually ornate, echoing the lyricism of the romantics and the rhetorical flourishes of the early gothic writers; in the grotesque, the style is plain, as in a tale, for there is no indulgence in the romantic agony of being different for its own sake. The gothic character is often an aristocrat in decay; the grotesque character is a common man deformed by small town life or urban industrialism.

The typical modern gothic character is weak, afraid, impotent, trapped in a compulsive, self-destructive narcissism, and afflicted with a monstrous self love. For him (the protagonist is as often male as female), a neurotic, antagonistic, authoritarian family is a microcosm of the hostile environment beyond. He flees the nightmares of the real world into a dream world. Physically and mentally, he languishes in a claustrophobic, haunted room, insulated against outer nightmares by inner dreams. When the room is invaded, the self violated, he is forced to make journeys, sometimes pursued, into the "dark forests" of the real world, which proves to be full of distorting mirrors. Seeking but fearing love, unable to communicate with others, he finds only a grotesque reflection of his own disintegrating self. He flounders in a vicious circle. The tensions between social reality and private fantasy often erupt in violence. (See Irving Malin, *New American Gothic*, and William Van O'Connor, *The Grotesque: An American Genre*.)

The gothic and the grotesque are found in these southern novels: William Faulkner, *Sanctuary* (1931); Carson McCullers, *The Heart Is a Lonely Hunter* (1940) and *Reflections in a Golden Eye* (1941); Davis Grubb, *Night of the Hunter* (1953); Flannery O'Connor, *The Violent Bear It Away* (1960); and Truman Capote, *Other Voices, Other Rooms* (1948).

Miss Wisteria stood so near he could smell the rancid wetness of her shriveled silk; her curls had uncoiled, the little crown had slipped awry, her yellow sash was fading its color on the floor. "Little boy," she said, swerving her flashlight over the bent, broken walls where her midget image mingled with the shadows of things in flight. "Little boy," she said, the resignation of her voice intensifying its pathos. But he dared not show himself, for what she wanted he could not give: his love was in the earth, shattered and still, dried flowers where eyes should be, and moss upon the lips, his love was faraway feeding on the rain, lilies frothing from its ruin. Withdrawing, she went up the stairs, and Joel, who listened to her footfalls overhead as she in her need of him searched the jungle of rooms, felt for himself ferocious contempt: what was his terror compared with Miss Wisteria's? He owned a room, he had a bed, any minute now he would run from here, go to them. But for Miss Wisteria, weeping because little boys must grow tall, there would always be this journey through dying rooms until some lonely day she found her hidden one, the smiler with the knife.

Some of the same elements are found in these novels by writers of the north: James Purdy, *Malcolm* (1959); John Hawkes, *The Lime Twig* (1961); Joyce Carol Oates, *A Garden of Earthly Delights* (1967).

THE FANTASY NOVEL

Romanticism manifested itself early in man's history in fantasy and the fairy tale. The origin of fairy tales—short stories in which something magical or supernatural occurs—and the manner in which they are diffused among different cultures is unknown; over 500 distinct types of plots have been catalogued. Most are short, but John Ruskin wrote a long heroic adventure, *The King of the Golden River* (1851), in fairy tale form. Unlike fairy tales, fantasies may end unhappily. They can become highly sophisticated. The fantasy novel that doesn't use fantasy for a serious purpose is rare, though fantasy of any kind is rare enough. Several seemingly written for children appeal even more to adults. J. R. R. Tolkien's three-volume *The Lord of the Rings* (1954–55) is a revival in the atomic age of interest in the fairy tale and in fantasy.

> *Thirdly and finally,* he said, *I wish to make an* ANNOUNCEMENT. He spoke this last word so loudly and suddenly that everyone sat up who still could. *I regret to announce that— though, as I said, eleventy-one years is far too short a time to*

spend among you—this is the END. I am going. I am leaving
NOW. GOOD-BYE! ·

He stepped down and vanished. There was a blinding flash of
light, and the guests all blinked. When they opened their eyes
Bilbo was nowhere to be seen. One hundred and forty-four flab-
bergasted hobbits sat back speechless. Old Odo Proudfoot removed
his feet from the table and stamped. Then there was a dead silence, until suddenly, after several deep breaths, every Baggins,
Boffin, Took, Brandybuck, Grubb, Chubb, Burrows, Bolger,
Bracegirdle, Brockhouse, Goodbody, Hornblower, and Proudfoot·
began to talk at once.

Fantasy deals with incredible, magical, exotic, supernatural, monstrous
characters and events, and is often written in a very ornamental, lyrical, or
witty style. Usually, our pleasure derives from the comparison of the totally
created fantasy world, which has its own consistent reality, with our everyday world; but in many fantasies incidents occur within a context of everyday reality.

Other fantasies are: the satiric fantasy—Chinese Wu Ch'eng-ên's
Monkey (16th C.); Norwegian Ludwig Holberg's fantastic *Journey of Niels*
Klim to the World Underground (1741); Lewis Carroll's *Alice in Wonderland*
and *Through the Looking Glass* (1871); Oscar Wilde's *The Picture of Dorian*
Gray (1891); W. H. Hudson's *Green Mansions* (1904); the fantasy allegory of
Kenneth Grahame, *The Wind in the Willows* (1908); Franz Kafka's *The Trial*
(1914), which objectifies universal guilt in terms of ordinary situations and
relationships; David Garnett's *Lady into Fox* (1922); Andrew Sinclair's *Gog*
(1967); Richard Adams' *Watership Down* (1974). (See Science Fiction, p. 54.)

THE OCCULT NOVEL

A type of fantasy novel that is currently very popular is the occult.
These novels dramatize spectacularly and with suspense the workings of
evil, or of good against human evil, through supernatural agencies. Major
examples are William Blatty's *The Exorcist* (1971), second all-time fiction
best seller; Ira Levin's *Rosemary's Baby* (1967); Thomas Tryon's *The Other*
(1971); and Stephen King's *Carrie* (1974), all of which were best sellers and
made into big box office movies.

She paused on the lower step, looking at the flocks of people
streaming toward the center of town. Animals. Let them burn,
then. Let the streets be filled with the smell of their sacrifice. Let
this place be called racca, ichabod, wormwood.
Flex.

And power transformers atop lightpoles bloomed into nacreous purple light, spitting catherine-wheel sparks. High-tension wires fell into the streets in pick-up-sticks tangles and some of them ran, and that was bad for them because now the whole street was littered with wires and the stink began, the burning began. People began to scream and back away and some touched the cables and went into jerky electrical dances. Some had already slumped into the street their robes and pajamas smoldering.

Carrie turned back and looked fixedly at the church she had just left. The heavy door suddenly swung shut, as if in a hurricane wind.

THE HISTORICAL NOVEL

Another type related to the romantic vision is the historical novel. With his *Waverley* novels (1814), Sir Walter Scott made the historical novel a world-famous genre.

It was up the course of this last stream what Waverly, like a knight of romance, was conducted by the fair Highland damsel, his silent guide. . . .

While gazing at this pass of peril, which crossed, like a single black line, the small portion of blue sky not intercepted by the projecting rocks on either side, it was with a sensation of horror that Waverly beheld Flora and her attendant appear, like inhabitants of another region, propped, as it were, in mid air, upon this trembling structure. She stopped upon observing him below, and, with an air of graceful ease, which made him shudder, waved her handkerchief to him by way of signal.

Related to the saga, this type has had a long early history, from the Alexander romances that combined history with fiction, and the Japanese feudal romances, such as Kyôden Santô, *Inazuma-Byôshi* (1806) to the Chinese historical romance of Lo Kuan-Chung, *Romance of the Three Kingdoms* (14th C.) and Fêng Mêng-Lung, *Lieh Kuo Chih* (early 17th C.). There is a stage in most civilizations when no strict distinction is made between myth, legend, and historical events. With a scientific attitude comes the split between myth and history, and the imagination of writers then re-mythicizes the historical past in fiction of varying quality.

The historical novel projects its characters back into an era of the recent or distant past to achieve a serious illumination of, or an entertaining distraction from, the present. Serious historical novelists attempt to preserve a spirit of the past, striving for a sense of reality as authentic as that of contemporary novels. Some depict great moments of historical conflict to show men enacting man's destiny.

Here are examples of historical or period romances, both serious and popular: Italian Alessandro Manzoni's *The Betrothed* (1826); Edward Bulwer-Lytton's *The Last Days of Pompeii* (1834); Flemish Hendrik Conscience's *The Lion of Flanders* (1838); James Fenimore Cooper's *The Deerslayer* (1841); Alexandre Dumas' *The Count of Monte Cristo* (1844); Charles Kingsley's *Westward Ho!* (1855); Charles Reade's *The Cloister and the Hearth* (1861); Flemish Charles de Coster's *The Legend of Tyl Ulenspiegel* (1867); Ouida's *Under Two Flags* (1867); Leo Tolstoy's *War and Peace* (1865–1869); Anthony Hope's *The Prisoner of Zenda* (1894); Booth Tarkington's *Monsieur Beaucaire* (1900); Mary Johnston's *To Have and to Hold* (1900); Winston Churchill's *The Crisis* (1901); Russian Stefan Zeromski's *Ashes* (1904); Joseph Hergesheimer's *Java Head* (1919) and *Three Black Pennies* (1917); Sigrid Undset's *Kristin Lavransdatter* (1920–22); Hervey Allen's *Anthony Adverse* (1933); Stark Young's *So Red the Rose* (1934); Kenneth Roberts' *Northwest Passage* (1937); Italian Riccardo Bacchelli's *The Mill on the Po* (1938–40); Brazilian Jorge Amado's *The Violent Land* (1954); Alfred Duggan's *Leopards and Lilies* (1954) and *The Cunning of the Dove* (1960); Mary Renault's (Mary Challans's) *The Last of the Wine* (1956); T. H. White's *The Once and Future King* (1958); David Stacton's *A Dancer in Darkness* (1960); Cecelia Holland's *Rokóssy* (1966). One might also include John Erskine's witty *Private Life of Helen of Troy* (1925); James Joyce's surrealistic cycle of history *Finnegans Wake* (1939); and two historical philosophical romances Robert Penn Warren's *World Enough and Time* (1950) and H. L. Davis' *Harp of a Thousand Strings* (1947).

As in the movies, spectacle (a minor element in Aristotle's definition of tragedy) is a major element in historical fiction. Too often, the historical novel degenerates into melodrama in a context of well-researched detail that lacks a convincing quality of imagination and of the spirit of the era being recaptured. With a few notable exceptions, this type is regarded today as mainly a mediocre form of entertainment, a vestige of shallow romanticism, less serious than science fiction in its aims and possibilities.

In the thirties and forties, the popular historical romance flourished with Margaret Mitchell's *Gone with the Wind* (1936), Kathleen Winsor's *Forever Amber* (1944), and Frank Yerby's *Foxes of Harrow* (1946), then languished in the late fifties, the sixties, and early seventies. Today, the historical romance is a very popular commercial success. The titles suggest why: Rosemary Rogers, *Wicked Loving Lies;* Barbara Cartland, *The Sheik* (new version); Kathleen Woodiwiss, *Shanna*; Kyle Onstott, *Drum* and *Mandingo;* Laurie McBain, *Devil's Desire;* Joyce Verrette, *Dawn of Desire;* Sergeanne Golon, *Angelique;* Georgette Heyer, *Royal Escape;* Philippa Carr, *Lament for a Lost Lover;* Fiona Hill, *The Love Child;* Olivia O'Neill, *Indigo Nights:* (See Popular, below; see also Georg Lukács, *The Historical Novel.*)

THE CHRONICLE NOVEL

A variation on the historical novel is the novel that chronicles the life of a family or of a town. Chinese Tsao Hsüeh-chin's *Dream of the Red Chamber* (1792), a domestic chronical, is a good example.

The chronicle novel, another variant, attempts a detailed panorama of a time and place, with a multiplicity and great variety of representative characters, locales, and episodes that illustrate facets of the social and economic stratification. Often, there is no one hero, as is the case with John Dos Passos' *U. S. A.* (1937), which is related to the "history of our times" series novels of the Frenchmen Duhamel, du Gard, Aragon, and Aymé.

> U. S. A. is the slice of a continent. U. S. A. is a group of holding companies, some aggregations of trade unions, a set of laws bound in calf, a radio network, a chain of moving picture theatres, a column of stock-quotations rubbed out and written in by a Western Union boy on a blackboard, a public library full of old newspapers and dogeared historybooks with protests scrawled on the margins in pencil. U. S. A. is the world's greatest rivervalley fringed with mountains and hills, U. S. A. is a set of bigmouthed officials with too many bankaccounts. U. S. A. is a lot of men buried in their uniforms in Arlington Cemetery. U. S. A. is the letters at the end of an address when you are away from home. But mostly U. S. A. is the speech of the people.

Other social and historical chronicles are: Italian Ippolito Nievo, *The Castle of Fratta* (1867); Mexican Mariano Azuela, *The Underdogs* (1915); and Jules Romains' (Louis Farigoule's) ten-volume *Les Hommes de Bonne Volonté* (*Men of Good Will,* 1932–1946).

THE POPULAR NOVEL

The classical writers considered one of the ends of art to be recreation. In popular fiction, that basic purpose has come to be called "escape" or mere play. Popular fiction is simply fiction found in mass-circulation magazines (*Redbook, Playboy, Harper's*) or on the best-seller list or in special publications that reach a large number of like-minded people. Popular novels are usually written out of commercial motives for a specialized or general mass readership for the purpose of entertainment. Sex (or romance) and violence and an emphasis on stereotyped characters and plots written by an often-proven formula are among the salient characteristics of the commerical or popular novel. While all "literature is the art of playing on the minds of others" (Valéry), popular fiction exploits and manipulates famil iar emotions and attitudes, accepted moral and social concepts, and strives to excite its readers without leaving them profoundly stimulated or disturbed. It is simple and easy to read. It is above all, as Stephen King, author of *Carrie* (1974), has said, "accessible."

The reader of popular fiction approaches a new novel with rather clear expectations, determined mainly by response to a clearly identifiable subjec matter (exorcism, sharks, the Mafia) or by a predisposition based on taste to a distinct type or genre of fiction: westerns, crime, science-fiction, or love stories. Mass advertising announces and hypes up those *given* appeal factors. The product is conceived to appeal to the tastes of the so-called general reader.

The popular novel is dominated by its subjects, as the names of the types suggest: western, detective, tough guy, science fiction; love or romance, historical, neo-gothic, hospital, sex, pornographic; war, sea, and other adventure types; religious; inside dope or exposé (of advertising, show business, politics, hotel, automobile, aviation businesses). Two of the most popular types appealing to general audiences are the detective and the western; they seldom reach the best-seller list; they are consumed as a type rather than as individual titles; historical novels, on the other hand, seem to make their impact individually. Until recently, best-seller lists seldom accounted for cheap editions and paperbacks—the domain of mysteries and westerns; earlier, they appeared most often in a line of pulp magazines, with crude ink drawings. Most of these types include, as does the best-seller list, serious novels: western, Walter Van Tilburg Clark, *The Ox-Bow Incident* (1940); detective, Friedrich Dürrenmatt, *The Pledge* (1959); love, D. H. Lawrence, *Lady Chatterley's Lover* (1928).

A mid-nineteenth century innovation, the dime novel offered strongly but improbably and melodramatically plotted tales, featuring superhuman heroes, based often on famous people, sometimes outlaws (Jesse James), and printed on pulp paper for mass distribution on newsstands. Example: *Buffalo Bill's Fair Square Deal, or the Duke of Dagger's Deadlock.*

With the new line of paperbacks, Penguin, Bantam, and Pocket Books, in the 1930's and 1940's, these and many other types of novels, including classics, were given a new life ("every movie is first run until you've seen it"); a book published in the 1920's, then forgotten, was received by the new paperback audience, often unused to hard-cover books even in libraries, as if they were new.

Here is a list, representing the major types (except westerns), crime, science fiction, love and others, of twenty-five all-time bestselling novels, hardcover and paperback combined, from 1895 through 1975.

1. *The Godfather*, Mario Puzo, 1969
2. *The Exorcist*, William Blatty, 1971
3. *To Kill a Mockingbird*, Harper Lee, 1960
4. *Peyton Place*, Grace Metalious, 1956
5. *Love Story*, Erich Segal, 1970
6. *Valley of the Dolls*, Jacqueline Susann, 1966
7. *Jaws*, Peter Benchley, 1974
8. *Jonathan Livingston Seagull*, Richard Bach, 1970
9. *Gone with the Wind*, Margaret Mitchell, 1936
10. *God's Little Acre*, Erskine Caldwell, 1933
11. *1984*, George Orwell, 1949
12. *In His Steps*, Charles Monroe Sheldon, 1897
13. *The Carpetbaggers*, Harold Robbins, 1961
14. *Animal Farm*, George Orwell, 1946
15. *Lady Chatterley's Lover*, D. H. Lawrence, 1932
16. *Catch-22*, Joseph Heller, 1961
17. *I, the Jury*, Mickey Spillane, 1947
18. *The Great Gatsby*, F. Scott Fitzgerald, 1925
19. *The Catcher in the Rye*, J. D. Salinger, 1951
20. *The Big Kill*, Mickey Spillane, 1951
21. *Rich Man, Poor Man*, Irwin Shaw, 1970
22. *Airport*, Arthur Hailey, 1968
23. *Exodus*, Leon Uris, 1968
24. *My Gun Is Quick*, Mickey Spillane, 1950
25. *One Lonely Night*, Mickey Spillane, 1951

Bestselling western novels are Niven Busch, *Duel in the Sun* (1944); Max Brand, *Singing Guns* (1938); Zane Grey, *Nevada* (1928) and *Riders of the Purple Sage* (1912). Note that on the above list numbers 11, 14 (both science fiction), 15 (love), 16 (war), 18 (love), and 19 (a novel of adolescence) are so-called serious novels.

By temperament or by conscious strategy, the commercial writer strives for immediate effect, knowing most of his readers are looking for a "good story" that will provide instant gratification of an already passing desire for diversion, entertainment, or escape. He has fixed assumptions about his likely readers and manipulates as immediately and effectively as he can their attitudes and expectations. He accosts the reader with a tug at his sleeve as he passes. While the serious writer may think less consciously of *who* his readers may be, he does take great care to create effects (as in his use of symbolism, for instance) to which he expects attentive readers to respond.

He assumes that his reader is an intelligent, sensitive, imaginative collaborator in the creative process, who expects, even insists, that the author make demands; and who expects to derive, perhaps through several readings, a lasting intellectual, spiritual, and aesthetic pleasure from every aspect of the experience the author has created. In a sense, then, every writer is a "con man" who calculates an effect upon his "mark," the reader; but unlike the con man, he knows he must "pay off" in the end.

The terms "commercial" or "popular" and "serious" run the risk all labels do of distorting. They are used here to describe, not to make judgments. It is best, perhaps, when studying fiction, to think of serious fiction as being different from, not necessarily better than commercial fiction. If in our evaluation of both types, we consider what each sets out to achieve, we may see that the master craftsman of the commercial story and the fine serious writer meet in the neutral realm of excellence. Even the reader with a well-developed critical mind and discriminating tastes can benefit from a study of commercial fiction, just as writers themselves do. Albert Camus, a great philosophical writer, has said he used *The Postman Always Rings Twice* (1934) by James M. Cain, a master craftsman of commercial fiction, as a basis for his masterpiece *The Stranger* (1942). Both novels open with "narrative hooks" (a device associated with commercial fiction): "They threw me off the hay truck about noon" (*Postman*); "Mother died today. Or, maybe, yesterday; I can't be sure" (*The Stranger*). The subtle techniques of highbrow literature may be studied in cruder form in popular fiction.

The Penny Dreadfuls and the Dime Novels reflect the spirit of the times just as accurately as do the serious novels of their era. Distortion of truth and fact are common to both popular and serious novels; the popular novel caters to the ideals and prejudices of the masses; and serious fiction caters to its readers in subtler ways. Once the extent to which these two kinds of literature share certain processes is fully understood, we can better understand the psychology of reading. The best place to start is with popular fiction, since its elements are often more obviously manipulated to appeal to the readers for whom it was devised.

Discussions of the novel have traditionally treated it as if it were solely a "serious" artistic form; the novels read by most people in a given culture at a given time have, supposedly, no relevance to the history and forms of the novel; on the contrary, recent studies show that many popular types of novels have influenced serious novelists, especially avant garde, and the process works the other direction as well. Popular novels often keep alive elements of serious works, and are sometimes forerunners. (See Nye, *The Unembarrassed Muse;* Hart, *The Popular Book;* Hackett, *Eighty Years of Best Sellers, 1985–1975;* Goodstone, *The Pulps, Fifty Years of American Pop Culture.*)

THE POP NOVEL

The same literary mind which rejects the popular fiction of the masses often resurrects it when the masses have buried it. The "pop" or "camp" novel is a recent phenomenon and demonstrates the effect on the novel of popular mass culture. The pop novel is one aspect of the popular culture avant garde collusion: L. J. Davis, *Cowboys Don't Cry* (1969); Robert Mayer, *Superfolk* (1977); Donald Barthelme, *Snow White* (1967).

> "*Which prince?*" Snow White wondered brushing her teeth. "Which prince will come? Will it be Prince Andrey? Prince Igor? Prince Alf? Prince Alphonso? Prince Malcolm? Prince Donalbain? Prince Fernando? Prince Siegfried? Prince Philip? Prince Albert? Prince Paul? Prince Akihito? Prince Rainier? Prince Porus? Prince Myshkin? Prince Rupert? Prince Pericles? Prince Karl? Prince Clarence? Prince George? Prince Hal? Prince John? Prince Mamillius? Prince Florizel? Prince Kropotkin? Prince Humphrey? Prince Charlie? Prince Matchabelli? Prince Escalus? Prince Valiant? Prince Fortinbras?" Then Snow White pulled herself together. "Well it is terrific to be anticipating a prince—to be waiting and knowing that what you are waiting for is a prince, packed with grace—but it is still waiting, and waiting as a mode of existence is, as Brack has noted, a darksome mode. . . . I wonder if he will have the Hapsburg Lip?"

Susan Sontag's essay "Notes on 'Camp'" in the *Partisan Review* in 1964 stimulated an interest in "camp." She defined it as the product of an aesthetic sensibility that: responds more to an artificial style than to content; transforms everyday experience; is partial to eighteenth century gothic and to *Art Nouveau;* is wilfully innocent and naive; loves extravagance; adores the wildly bad but not the mediocre; cherishes "failed seriousness" and "the theatricalization of experience"; is antiserious, mainly comic; appreciates vulgarity; inclines toward dandyism; reveres Oscar Wilde; appreciates, doesn't judge; and has a love of human nature. "It's good *because* it's awful." Max Beerbohm's *Zuleika Dobson* (1911) and the novels of Ronald Firbank, for instance. "One cheats oneself as a human being," says critic-novelist Sontag, "if one has *respect* only for the style of high culture." (See Sontag, *Against Interpretation.*) George Eliot would disagree: "And bad literature of the sort called amusing is spiritual gin." S. J. Perelman said, "Easy writing makes hard reading."

Still, the authors of serious novels that criticize Western materialistic culture are themselves products of mass communication, and the pop novel, conceived in nostalgia and executed with satirical purpose, shows the extent to which a so-called inferior form of human expression can shape attitudes and predispose responses. Still, like most exaggerations of a single facet of the novel, which is basically a conventional form, the pop novel has not caught on, any more than the ideological novel of the Thirties did. Universal affection for Bugs Bunny cannot in itself sustain a reader's interest, any more than another universal, sex.

THE WESTERN NOVEL

The western novel is based on the history of the cowboy, featuring cattle-rustlers, stage and train robbers, Indian battles, and heroes who ride into predicaments alone and ride out alone. Authentic or pseudo-authentic details about costume, setting, firearms appeal to many readers. Once a major popular type, the western, one of the few types indigenous to America, is now less prevalent than Science Fiction. The first great wester was Owen Wister's *The Virginian* (1902).

> It was now the Virginian's turn to bet, or leave the game, an he did not speak at once.
> Therefore Trampas spoke. "Your bet, you son-of-a—."
> The Virginian's pistol came out, and his hand lay on the table holding it unaimed. And with a voice as gentle as ever, the voice that sounded almost like a caress, but drawling a very little more than usual, so that there was almost a space between each word, he issued his orders to the man Trampas:—
> "When you call me that, *smile!*" And he looked at Trampas across the table.

Others are: Clarence E. Mulford, *Hopalong Cassidy* (1910); Zane Grey, *Light of Western Stars* (1914); Emerson Hough, *The Covered Wagon* (1922 Max Brand, *Destry Rides Again* (1930); William MacLeod Raine, *Bucky Fe lows a Cold Trail* (1937); Luke Short, *Hardcase* (1942); Ernest Haycox, *Alder Gulch* (1942); A. B. Guthrie, *The Big Sky* (1947), Jack Schaefer, *Shane* (1949); Louis L'Amour, *Radigan* (1958). Here are a few other notab writers of westerns: James B. Hendryz, Frank Gruber, Will Ermine, Will James, Charles Russell, W. C. Tuttle, Eugene Manlove Rhodes, Stewart Edward White, Vardis Fisher, John Cunningham, Will Henry (Clay Fishe H. H. Knibbs, Bliss Lomax, Peter Field, James Warner Bellah. (See Popu lar, p. 45. See Cawelti, *The Six-Gun Mystique*.)

THE DETECTIVE NOVEL

The detective novel, a major popular genre, delineates the detection clues and the solution of a crime. Begun by the French, made famous and popular by American poet Edgar Allan Poe in short story form, it was take over by the English, and practiced with variations by Americans, who introduced sex and violence into it. The all-time best seller (in which, however, the emphasis is upon detection, with very little sex and violence) is Erle Stanley Gardner's *The Case of the Sulky Girl* (1933).

> "And isn't it a fact," thundered Perry Mason, extending his rigid forefinger, so that it pointed directly at Judge Purley, "that now the matter has been called to your attention, and your recollection has had an opportunity to check over the circumstances of what happened upon that fateful night of the murder, that you *now* realize that the voice which called down to you from that second story window on the night of the test, was the same voice which had called down from that window on the night of the murder?"
>
> Tense, dramatic silence gripped the courtroom.

Other examples: Wilkie Collins, *The Moonstone* (1868); Émile Gaboriau, *Monsieur Lecoq* (1869); Sir Arthur Conan Doyle, *The Hound of the Baskervilles* (1902); Mary Roberts Rinehart, *The Circular Staircase* (1908); G. K. Chesterton, *The Innocence of Father Brown* (1911); E. C. Bentley, *Trent's Last Case* (1913); Agatha Christie, *The Murder of Roger Ackroyd* (1926); S. S. Van Dine, *The Canary Murder Case* (1927); Ellery Queen, *The Roman Hat Mystery* (1927); Georges Simenon, *The Patience of Maigret* (1940); Robert Traver, *Anatomy of a Murder* (1958); Ross Macdonald, *The Underground Man* (1971). Other major writers of traditional whodunits are: Nicholas Blake, A. C. Bailey, Frances Iles (Anthony Berkeley), Margery Allingham, Mabel Seeley, Dorothy Sayers, Freeman Wills Crofts, Cornell Woolrich, Craig Rice, Brett Halliday, Kenneth Fearing, Edgar Wallace, Dickson Carr (Carter Dickson), Earl Derr Biggers, Michael Innes, Rex Stout, Ngaio Marsh, Mignon Eberhart, Leslie Ford, I. A. Fair, Philip MacDonald, John Latimer, Leslie Ford, Frank Gruber, Charlotte Armstrong, Leslie Charteris, August Derleth, Stanley Ellin, A. A. Fair, Dick Francis, Richard Lockridge, Ed McBain, E. Phillips Oppenheim, Roderick Thorp, Nero Wolfe, Donald Westlake. (See Popular, p. 45.)

THE SPY NOVEL

Related to the detective novel is the spy or espionage novel, the most famous practitioner of which is Ian Fleming, with *Thunderball* (1965) and others in the James Bond series, all of which are on the all-time best seller list.

> Bond got a foot against a lump of coral and, with this to give him impetus, flung himself forward. The man had no time to de-

fend himself. Bond's spear caught him in the side and hurled him against the next man in line. Bond thrust and wrenched sickeningly. The man dropped his gun and bent double, clutching his side. Bond bored on into the mass of naked men now scattering in all directions, with their jet packs accelerated. Another man went down in front of him, clawing at his face. A chance thrust of Bond's hand had smashed the glass of his mask. He threshed his way up toward the surface, kicking Bond in the face as he went. A spear ripped into the rubber protecting Bond's stomach and Bond felt pain and wetness that might be blood or sea water. He dodged another flash of metal and a gun butt hit him hard on the head, but with most of its force spent against the cushion of water. It knocked him silly and he clung for a moment to a niggerhead to get his bearings while the black tide of his men swept past him and individual fights filled the water with black puffs of blood.

Other spy novelists are Eric Ambler, John Creasey, E. Howard Hunt, John Le Carré, John Buchan, Helen MacInnes, Frederick Forsyth, Graham Greene, W. Somerset Maugham. (See Popular, p. 45. See Science Fiction, p. 54. See Cawelti, *Adventure, Mystery, and Romance;* Nevins, *The Mystery Writer's Craft.*)

THE TOUGH GUY NOVEL

The tough guy or hard-boiled novel is a variant of the detective, sometimes featuring a private eye and a loose plot structure (some of Dashiell Hammett's and Raymond Chandler's best novels were forced combinations of scattered short stories). But the *pure* tough guy novel had no link to the detective novel except violence. The tough guy novel depicts the down-and-out, the disinherited, who develop a hard-boiled attitude that enables them to maintain a granite-like dignity against hostile forces. An unusually tough era turned out the early hard-boiled hero. The traumatic wrench of the Depression caused a violent reaction in him. He is strategically placed to detect lies and hypocrisy in our institutions. In his actions, he takes revenge upon the forces that shaped and ultimately destroy him. Even his attitudes seem acts of aggression. Usually, he tells his own story, and the brutal formula of his language is: style as action. The tough guy's attitudes and the style in which he expresses them derive in part from Ernest Hemingway.

For the French, American tough or hard-boiled novels of Horace McCoy, *They Shoot Horses, Don't They?* (1935), Dashiell Hammett, *The Maltese Falcon* (1930), James M. Cain's novels, and Raymond Chandler,

The Big Sleep (1939), had serious, even existential implications and aesthetic qualities.

> Outside the bright gardens had a haunted look as though small wild eyes were watching me from behind the bushes, as though the sunshine itself had a mysterious something in its light. I got into my car and drove off down the hill.
>
> What did it matter where you lay once you were dead? In a dirty sump or in a marble tower on top of a high hill? You were dead, you were sleeping the big sleep, you were not bothered by things like that. Oil and water were the same as wind and air to you. You just slept the big sleep, not caring about the nastiness of how you died or where you fell. Me, I was part of the nastiness now. Far more a part of it than Rusty Regan was. But the old man didn't have to be. He could lie quiet in his canopied bed, with his bloodless hands folded on the sheet, waiting. His heart was a brief, uncertain murmur. His thoughts were as gray as ashes. And in a little while he too, like Rusty Regan, would be sleeping the big sleep.

In their use of violence as a reaction against social conditions, tough and proletarian writers have much in common, though the social purpose of tough novels is implicit while it is explicit in proletarian novels. (See Proletarian, p. 81.) The French detective writer Georges Simenon (Georges Sim) writes a conventional detective series featuring inspector Maigret, but he also writes serious novels, such as *The Snow Was Black* (1950). Graham Greene writes serious novels, but he also writes what he once called "entertainments," or mystery thrillers, such as *This Gun for Hire* (1936).

Among the best tough-guy novels are: B. Traven, *The Treasure of Sierra Madre* (1927); W. R. Burnett, *Little Caesar* (1929); John O'Hara, *Appointment in Samarra* (1934); Benjamin Appel, *Brain Guy* (1937); Graham Greene, *Brighton Rock* (1938); James Hadley Chase, *No Orchids for Miss Blandish* (1942); Mickey Spillane, *I, the Jury* (1947); John D. MacDonald, *The Damned* (1952); Jim Thompson, *The Killer Inside Me* (1952); Jay Dratler, *The Judas Kiss* (1955). These writers, along with Hammett and Chandler, appeared in the famous pulp magazine *Black Mask:* Lester Dent, Raoul Whitfield, Frederick Nebel, John K. Butler, Norbert Davis, George Harmon Coxe, Paul Cain, Carroll John Daly. Other tough guy writers of note are: Donald Henderson Clark, Charles Gorham, Richard Sale, William Lindsay Gresham, Richard Hallas, Irving Shulman, Joseph Wambaugh, John Latimer, Frank Gruber, Joe Gores, Richard Stark, Richard S. Prather, David Morrell. (See Detective, p. 45. Popular, p. 50. Madden *Tough Guy Writers of the Thirties.*)

SCIENCE FICTION

Science fiction is to be distinguished from pure fantasy in that it utilizes present scientific achievements as a basis for imagining scientific discoveries in the future, usually enabling man to explore, colonize, settle, and govern other worlds in space. The outer spaces of science fiction remind one of the wide open spaces of the old west, but the two types seem to appeal to very different, though basically romantic, temperaments. Science fiction is to the Atomic Age what the western was to the late Industrial Revolution at the turn of the century. With their indulgence in the imagination as it takes flight into the historical past or the prophetic future from a basis in fact, both types are essentially romantic. Psychological analysis and supernatural speculation characterize some of these novels. As the projections of early science fiction novelists become everyday realities and as novelists working in this type today use visions of the future to make serious comments on social and political problems of the present, this major popular type is being read more seriously.

The range of this type is quite broad. Mary Shelley's *Frankenstein* (1816) is a Gothic variant that anticipates science fiction. Some of the early classics extrapolate as logically and, as it has turned out, as prophetically as possible from actual scientific knowledge to probable future developments: Jules Verne, *A Trip to the Moon* (1865) and H. G. Wells, *The War of the Worlds* (1898).

No one would have believed in the last years of the nineteenth century that this world was being watched keenly and closely by intelligences greater than man's and yet as mortal as his own; that as men busied themselves about their various concerns they were scrutinized and studied, perhaps almost as narrowly as a man with a microscope might scrutinize the transient creatures that swarm and multiply in a drop of water. With infinite complacency men went to and fro over this globe about their little affairs, serene in their assurance of their empire over matter. It is possible that the infusoria under the microscope do the same. No one gave a thought to the older worlds of space as sources of human danger, or thought of them only to dismiss the idea of life upon them as impossible or improbable. It is curious to recall some of the mental habits of those departed days. At most, terrestrial men fancied there might be other men upon Mars, perhaps inferior to themselves and ready to welcome a missionary enterprise. Yet across the gulf of space, minds that are to our minds as ours are to those of the beasts that perish, intellects vast and cool and unsympathetic, regarded this earth with envious eyes, and slowly and surely drew their plans against us. And early in the twentieth century came the great disillusionment.

Some writers combine conventional elements of fantasy and romance and depict the nearly impossible; some writers use science fiction as a basis for psychological studies or excursions into the supernatural.

Regarded until recently as a sub-literary genre, often lurid and overly spectacular, full of clichés in style, stereotyped characters and stock situations, the science fiction novel has, along with the occult, recently achieved a kind of respectability, even in universities. The various types of science fiction can be used as bases for serious comment on the actual world. Social and political problems are implicit in science fiction. George Orwell's *1984* (1949) combines elements of proletarian fiction with anti-Utopian futurism; it may be termed more a prophetic than a science fiction novel of the usual sort. Aldous Huxley's *Brave New World* (1932) is a somber satire of utopias; Anthony Burgess's *A Clockwork Orange* (1962) and Kurt Vonnegut's *Slaughterhouse Five* (1970) and *Cat's Cradle* (1963) are black humor satires.

> "I am thinking, young man, about the final sentence for *The Books of Bokonon*. The time for the final sentence has come."
> "Any luck?"
> He shrugged and handed me a piece of paper.
> This is what I read:
> If I were a younger man, I would write a history of human stupidity; and I would climb to the top of Mount McCabe and lie down on my back with my history for a pillow; and I would take from the ground some of the blue-white poison that makes statues of men; and I would make a statue of myself, lying on my back, grinning horribly, and thumbing my nose at You Know Who.

Other fine examples of the science fiction novel are: Karel Čapek, *War with the Newts* (1937); C. S. Lewis, *Out of the Silent Planet* (1938); Ray Bradbury, *The Martian Chronicles* (1950); Walter M. Miller, Jr., *A Canticle for Leibowitz* (1959); Robert Heinlein, *Stranger in a Strange Land* (1961); Frank Herbert, *Dune* (1965); Walter Tevis, *The Man Who Fell to Earth* (1963); Ursula Le Guin, *The Left Hand of Darkness* (1969). Other important science fiction writers are: Isaac Asimov, Robert Bloch, James Lish, Poul Anderson, August Derleth, H. P. Lovecraft, Frederick Pohl, G. Stanley Weinbaum, Theodore Sturgeon, Harlan Ellison, A. E. Van Gogt, Robert Silverberg. (See Fantasy, p. 41. Popular, p. 45. See Sam Moscowitz, *Seekers of Tomorrow* and Kingsley Amis, *New Maps of Hell.*)

THE LOVE NOVEL

Obviously in the line of descent from the medieval French romances and from the Romantic era and related to the historical romances and the neo-gothic romances are the love novels, with their Madame Bovary readers. At present perhaps the major popular type, the love novel, quite simply, caters to assumptions its readers, mostly women, have about love. The top best seller of this type is *Love Story* (1970) by Erich Segal.

> I stood there at the bottom of the steps, afraid to ask how long she had been sitting, knowing only that I had wronged her terribly.
> "Jenny, I'm sorry—"
> "Stop!" She cut off my apology, then said very quietly, "Love means not ever having to say you're sorry."

Among other all-time best selling love novels are: *The Sheik,* E. M. Hull (1921); *Butterfield 8,* John O'Hara (1935); *Leave Her to Heaven,* Ben Ames Williams (1944); *So Well Remembered,* James Hilton (1945); *Not as a Stranger,* Morton Thompson (1954); *The Arrangement,* Elia Kazan (1967); *Valley of the Dolls,* Jacqueline Susann (1966); *The Summer of '42,* Herman Raucher (1971); *The Other Side of Midnight,* Sidney Sheldon (1973); *Fear of Flying,* Erica Jong (1973). Other effective practitioners of this type are: Faith Baldwin, Katherine Brush, Vicki Baum, Fannie Hurst, Kathleen Norris, Mary Burchell, Fiona Hill, Philippa Carr, Rose Franken, Emilie Loring, Margaret Culkin Banning, Helen Topping Miller, Olive Higgins Prouty, Betty Smith, Ethel Vance, A. J. Cronin, Gladys Hasty Carroll, Barbara Cartland. The biggest seller of paperback romances (2,300 titles) is the Harlequin series, one of whose 140 authors is Janet Dailey, author of *No Quarter Asked* and 32 other titles. (See Popular, p. 45; Gothic, p. 38; Historical, p. 43.)

THE ANTIQUARIAN NOVEL

A very rare, but interesting, type is the antiquarian novel, which either exploits or utilizes for more serious purposes some type that has ceased to be used. When it is successful, this type offers a peculiar pleasure; for instance, John Fowles' *The French Lieutenant's Woman* (1969) is written in the style of the Victorian novel. One chapter ends this way:

> Who is Sarah?
> Out of what shadow does she come?

The next chapter begins:

13

For the drift of the Maker is dark, an Isis hid by the veil...
Tennyson, *Maud* (1855)

I do not know. This story I am telling is all imagination.
These characters I create never existed outside my own mind. If I
have pretended until now to know my characters' minds and inner-
most thoughts, it is because I am writing in (just as I assumed some of
the vocabulary and "voice of) a convention universally accepted at
the time of my story: that the novelist stands next to God. He may
not know all, yet he tries to pretend that he does. But I live in the
age of Alain Robbe-Grillet and Roland Barthes; if this is a novel, it
cannot be a novel in the modern sense of the word.

The Sicilian Giuseppe Tomasi di Lampedusa's *The Leopard* (1958), an historical family chronicle, is unconsciously antiquarian in its method of presentation. Some say the series of novels by scientist C. P. Snow, *Strangers
and Brothers*, (1940), are antiquarian. John Seelye wrote a modern, "unex-
purgated," version of Twain's novel in *The True Adventures of Huckleberry
Finn* (1970).

THE NATURALISTIC NOVEL

At the opposite pole from romanticism is naturalism. The early romantic rejected the oncoming Industrial Revolution and immersed himself in nature to find his true self; the naturalist shows how nature, or at least human
nature, changes in an industrial setting. There is some dispute among literary historians as to whether periods or movements in literature are real or
simply conveniences for critics. But naturalism is clearly one of the first important, concerted, programmatic movements in the novel. According to
Émile Zola, its pioneers were Honoré de Balzac, Gustave Flaubert, and
Stendhal; its precursors were Edmond and Jules Goncourt, whose novels
were called "slices of life" because they turned the microscope on one seg-
ment of social injustice: *Charles Demailly* (1860), *Manette Salomon* (1867),
and, their best, *Renée Mauperin* (1864).

The naturalistic novel is the logical end-development of the novel's
original impulse to provide the news. Its ultimate goal is truth about man's
immediate environment, based on a scientific understanding of heredity and
other biological factors. The thinking of Herbert Spencer and Charles Dar-
win on evolution and on natural selection encouraged the biologically determined view of man. Determinism is the "philosophical doctrine that
every event, act, decision is the inevitable consequence" of physical,
psychological, or environmental conditions and that the human will in nature is ineffectual. A positive variation on this vision of life is organicism, a
joyous sense of being one with all other living organisms. "Naturalistic de-

terminism" sees man as a "natural mechanism" and presents him with "clin ical realism"; the novel becomes a branch of "social science." (See Ellmann Modern Tradition)

The first great exponent and theorist of this type of novel was Emile Zola, whose main purpose was to delineate dramatically, but clinically, the effect of biology and environment—slums, etc.,—upon his characters. "An experimental novel, [Balzac's] Cousine Bette, for example, is simply the repor of the experiment that the novelist conducts before the eyes of the public," said Zola. "In fact, the whole operation consists in taking facts from nature, then in studying the mechanism of these facts, acting upon them, by the modification of circumstance and surrounding without deviating from the laws of nature. Finally, you possess knowledge of the man, scientific knowl edge of him, in both his individual and social relations." "Observation indi cates and experiment teaches" (Zola, "The Experimental Novel").

Earlier novels stressed conflicts between characters produced by social institutions who are defeated by or victorious over other people and estab lished forces. In the naturalistic novel, the fall of a person is determined n so much by a flaw in character as by biological factors and economic condi tions beyond his control. Prostitution defeats Nana (1880), hard work wears out Gervaise in L'Assomoir (The Dram Shop) 1877.

> Nana was left alone, her face turned upwards in the candle-
> light. It was a charnel-house, a mass of matter and blood, a shovel
> ful of putrid flesh, thrown there on the cushion. The pustules had
> invaded the entire face, one touching the other; and, faded, sunk
> in, with the greyish aspect of mud, they already seemed like a
> mouldiness of the earth on that shapeless pulp, in which the fea-
> tures were no longer recognizable. One of the eyes, the left one,
> had completely disappeared amidst the eruption of the purulence;
> the other, half open, looked like a black and stained hole. The
> nose still continued to suppurate. A reddish crust starting from on
> of the cheeks, invaded the mouth, which it distorted in an abo-
> minable laugh; and on this horrible and grotesque mask of noth-
> ingness, the hair, that beautiful hair, retained its sun-like fire, fell
> in a stream of gold. Venus was decomposing. It seemed as if the
> virus gathered by her in the gutters, from the tolerated carrion—
> that the ferment with which she had poisoned a people—had as-
> cended to her face and rotted it.
> The room was deserted. A strong breath of despair mounted
> from the Boulevard, and swelled the curtain.

The naturalists, then, set out to compete with science as a source of infor mation and truth, to popularize its findings, and by giving an extremely accurate picture, to persuade people to act. Because their novels portrayed the ugly (an element banished from art in Plato's *Republic*), naturalists were often accused of mere sensationalism. "We are looking for the causes of social evil," said Zola. "We study the anatomy of classes and individuals to explain the derangements which are produced in society and in man. This often necessitates our working on tainted subjects, our descending into the midst of human follies and miseries."

Maxim Gorki's *Mother* (1907) is a lyrical, visionary novel, but a good example also of Russian naturalism. Two English works are George Moore's *Esther Waters* (1894) and Arnold Bennett's *The Old Wives' Tale* (1908). V. Blasco-Ibáñez is a kind of Spanish Zola, as seen in *Blood and Sand* (1908) and *The Four Horsemen of the Apocalypse* (1916). Giovanni Verga's *Mastro Don Gesnaldo* (1889) and Camilo José Cela's *The Family of Pascual Duarte* (1942) are two Spanish examples. A later naturalism is seen in Alberto Moravia's *Woman of Rome* (1947).

Industrialization, based partly on the findings of science, promised so much—all over the western world, people left the farms and went to the cities—that the disillusionment was grim and dramatic. Science opened up a new "multiverse" governed by a mechanical force in which some found a new joy; physics was seen to have a shaping influence on human character; truth was seen as pluralistic, pragmatic, instrumental; and thought itself was regarded as a "natural event." Uncertainty came with the death of tradition. (See Ellmann, *Modern Tradition*) The scientific method that produced these conditions was then used to describe them.

In America, especially, the contrast between the dream and the reality was shocking, because the cities were filled with immigrants who fled the European nightmare. Naturalism had a resurgence in the United States in the muck-raking journalistic novels of Upton Sinclair, whose *The Jungle* (1906) was instrumental in getting the pure food and drug act passed. Another naturalist—though not strictly—was Frank Norris. Let's look at the railroads, he said, in *The Octopus* (1901), and see what they really did to America; let's look at wheat, he said, in *The Pit* (1903). Theodore Dreiser looked at young women coming to work in the cities (*Sister Carrie*, 1900); at young men trying to rise in the world (*An American Tragedy*, 1925); and at financiers and artists. Another American with a somewhat deterministic world-view is John Steinbeck, especially in *The Grapes of Wrath* 1939). The proletarian novelists of his time pictured the predicament of the working man as black only to propose in the end some way of shedding light on it. But Steinbeck's world-view did not permit programmatic solutions, even though he alleviated a pessimistic determinism with sentimentality. Another good example of American naturalism is John O'Hara's *Appointment in*

Samarra (1934). The novels of Joyce Carol Oates are seen as belonging to this tradition, especially *them* (1969).

The novel has always tended to focus upon negative experience: violence, death, hardships, murder; but it was the naturalists who fostered the notion, still strong, that fiction which tells the truth deals primarily with the poor and the criminal element, while novels about well-to-do or middle-class people aren't really about reality, aren't even, perhaps, honest. Among some novelists and some serious readers then, a novel dealing with the poor is credited with a serious purpose: to give a factual picture of life the way it really is. That this attitude is just as unreal, by virtue of its one sidedness, as the so-called popular fiction view of life, which distorts reality and glamorizes heroes and heroines in unlikely situations, has never been realized fully enough.

But the purely naturalistic novel was short-lived; it came to be regarded as a kind of fad and the concept was regarded as a fallacy: fiction cannot be judged primarily by its fidelity to fact or by its aim. The compulsion to tell the truth is only one aspect of the novelistic impulse, and when it is carried to an extreme, as it was in this type, it suffers from one sidedness, because another powerful compulsion is to use language, analyze character, exercise imagination, tell a story for their own sakes. The other arts have always claimed a *primary* self-justification: music, painting, poetry, drama, etc. But the novel has been plagued by self-defense; it continues to live on the assumption that it is good for something beyond itself: as an instrument, somehow, of practical value. (See Ellmann, *Modern Tradition*)

THE NOVEL OF REALISM

Realism is a much broader term than naturalism, embracing many more and many different kinds of novels. The term is sometimes used interchangeably with naturalism, but it *includes* naturalism, with some elements of determinism. The concept of modernity in literature has always meant some *new* form of realism. The realist is usually more selective than the naturalist. All literature is both general and particular; the realist emphasizes the particular to evoke the general; unlike the naturalist, he does not feel the compulsion to amass detailed evidence to support a thesis about man and society; he simply selects details that are true to life. Endeavoring to avoid improbability (a classic taboo), romanticism, and falsification, he strives for plausibility, credibility, and, above all, verisimilitude. He remains objective, avoiding a special philosophy about or a remedy for the problems he dramatizes. He assumes that there is a human desire to see life as it is and he satisfies his own need to dramatize an honest picture. Like the naturalist, he often thinks that that means a picture of the slums. *Verism* is the doctrine that novels should include the sordid in their depiction of reality. Scholes and Kellogg state that "the connection between the fictional world and the real can be either *representational* or *illustrative*"; the novel recreates a "replica of actuality" or merely reminds us "of an aspect of reality." The realists strive to achieve the former. (See Scholes, *The Nature of Narrative*.)

The realist is more interested in historical determinism than in social science. Thus, the French authors of series novels show how history determines the fate of families, groups, individuals; heredity has less an effect than history. The realist may turn more to socialism or Marxism than to science for a basis of proceeding. This is seen most simply in Soviet realism, which reduces man to a collective creature, historically determined to act out his role in a mass revolution and the reconstruction of society to be headed by the state rather than monarchs or rich individuals. We see this type of realism in Boris Pilnyak's *The Naked Year* (1922) and in Mikhail Zoshchenko's *Restored Youth* (1933), a comic approach. An example of German social realism is Gustav Freytag, *Debit and Credit* (1855). Edith Wharton dealt with the moneyed class in *The Age of Innocence* (1920); Spanish Ramon Sender depicted war with a restrained, objective realism in *The King and the Queen* (1948); Elio Vittorini in *The Red Carnation* (1948) and *In Sicily* (1949); and Vasco Pratolini in *A Hero of Our Time* (1949) showed the decadence of Fascism and of post WW II in Italy with an Italian version of realism, "verismo"; Nelson Algren revealed the life of dope addicts in the Chicago slums with an ethnic lyrical realism in *The Man with the Golden Arm* (1949); Juan Goytisolo in *The Party's Over* (1962) and *Island of Women* (1962) is a Spanish "angry young man" whose novels are nihilistic, written in the "tremendismo" Spanish style of realism, similar to Baroja and Cela.

Another sort of realism attempts, without being directly didactic, to give an ethical, humanistic, and prophetic but not politically doctrinaire picture of man among his fellow men; the purpose is to warn and/or guide man to a better life. André Malraux's *La Condition Humaine (Man's Fate*, 1933), is a good example of that sort of realism.

> ... ideas were not to be thought, but lived. Kyo had chosen action, in a grave and premeditated way, as others choose a military career, or the sea; he left his father, lived in Canton, in Tientsin, the life of day-laborers and coolies, in order to organize the syndicates. Ch'en—his uncle, taken as hostage at the capture of Swatow, and unable to pay his ransom, had been executed—had found himself without money, provided only with worthless diplomas, with his twenty-four years and with China before him. He was a truck-driver when the Northern routes were dangerous, then an assistant

chemist, then nothing. Everything had pushed him into political activity; the hope of a different world, the possibility of eating, though wretchedly (he was naturally austere, perhaps through pride), the gratification of his hatreds, his mind, his character. Th activity gave a meaning to his solitude.

THE NOVEL OF DOMESTIC REALISM

An interesting type of realistic novel, written mainly by Englishmen, the domestic, in which the moral vision of the writer is always felt and expressed. The domestic novel offers the story of a family in a domestic setting. Domestic realism, mainly English, gives a detailed picture of the everyday life of a family, over a time span of a day or even several generations. Three examples of English domestic realism are Henry Fielding's *Amelia* (1761); George Eliot's *The Mill on the Floss* (1860) and *Silas Marne* (1861). Other examples of domestic realism are: Norwegian Jonas Lie's *Th Family at Gilje* (1883) and *The Commander's Daughter* (1886); E. M. Forster's *Howard's End* (1910). William McFee's *Casuals of the Sea* (1916), realistically contrasts daily life at home with life at sea.

> In a few days, after Minnie had brought a wheezy, ill-strapp dressbasket and a paper bag containing her Sunday hat, and take up her quarters on a truckle bed which was hidden during the da under a yellow cover, she declared open war. In the first place, Minnie discovered with some surprise that the companionship of Mrs. Wilfley involved housework in all its branches, from washin dishes to cleaning hair-brushes with cloudy ammonia. Certainly t dishes were only breakfast dishes, and the latter task was begged from her as a favour, but the vertical furrow in the girl's forehead deepened for all that.

. . .

> Engrossed in his work of laying the breakfast-table the next morning, Hannibal did not hear the door leading to the Chief's room open; the roar of the coal pouring from the up-ended truck into the empty hold, the tramp of feet overhead, the soft slither ropes and hissing of steam, overpowered all minor sounds. He turned and found a sharp-eyed lady looking him over.

Mazo de la Roche's *Jalna* (1927) and Austrialian Christina Stead's *The Man Who Loved Children* (1940) are two more examples of domestic realism. There are also domestic tragedies: Prussian Theodor Fontane, *Effi Briest* (1895); English Gerald Griffin, *The Collegians* (1828); and Polish Isaac Bashevis Singer, *The Family Moskat* (1966).

THE NOVEL OF FORMAL REALISM

Another type is formal realism, or realistic formalism. A recent approach is propounded by French Alain Robbe-Grillet who argues that true realism depicts our relationships with the actual physical objects in our everyday environment. In ways that we intuitively sense and respond to, these objects are hostile or benevolent; they witness our gradual disintegration or even conspire with chance to destroy us. His best novels are *Jealousy* (1957) and *The Voyeur* (1955). To depict a man's feelings, one describes the objects around him.

> Along dark hallways lined with closed doors, up narrow stairways leading to failure after failure, he lost himself again among his specters. At one end of a filthy landing he knocked with his ring at a door with no knob which opened by itself. . . . The door swung open and a mistrustful face appeared in the opening—which was just wide enough for him to recognize the black and white tiles on the floor. . . . The large squares were of a uniform gray; the room he entered was not at all remarkable—except for an unmade bed with a red spread trailing on the floor. . . . There was no red bedspread, nor was there an unmade bed; no lambskin, no night table, no bed lamp; there was no blue pack of cigarettes, no flowered wallpaper, no painting on the wall. The room he had been directed to was only a kitchen where he put his suitcase flat on the big oval table in the middle. Then came the oilcloth, the pattern on the oilcloth, the click of copper-plated clasp, etc. . . .

The aesthetic trap here is that because such descriptions can be unendurably dull, the author is forced to create a melodramatic situation which the reader gradually perceives as a kind of reward for enduring the tedium. However, there is a very real fascination here, simply carried to an avant garde extreme, for from the beginning, the novel has been crowded with objects, as we see in Balzac and Dickens, and every other writer who catalogs objects among which the characters move; as only one element in his work, Wright Morris has described the effect on his characters of objects, which are inhabitated by the metaphysical essence of the characters and are therefore holy: *The Works of Love* (1952).

. . .

The great tradition in the American novel has been realism of one sort or another. Americans make a mystique of the real; our writers try to persuade us that they are men "who were there." They may have claimed to be something other than realists: Nathaniel Hawthorne called his novels romances; Mark Twain thought he was telling the tale of a boy but instead gave a realistic, sometimes satirical, dark vision of small-town western America in *The Adventures of Huckleberry Finn*. Stephen Crane took a somewhat naturalistic approach to *Maggie: A Girl of the Streets* (1893) and *George's Mother* (1896), but in *The Red Badge of Courage* (1894) he exemplifies selective, impressionistic realism, and uses a little symbolism. War is not heroics, the realist says; it is a natural fear.

Realism often debunks, reverses society's established platitudes about life. Thus, William Dean Howells, father of an American realism that looked at the middle-class, showed that the dream of America's better opportuniti in the city was false; in *A Hazard of New Fortunes* (1890), a novel of man- ners, and *The Rise of Silas Lapham* (1885), a domestic novel, Howells illus trated delusion and disillusionment in urban settings. One value of his realism was that he treated the middle-class rather than the poor. Sherwoo Anderson in *Poor White* (1920), F. Scott Fitzgerald in *The Great Gatsby* (1925), Ernest Hemingway in *The Sun Also Rises* (1926), and Willa Cather in *Death Comes for the Archbishop* (1927), were all realists. Later realists are Bernard Malamud in the ironic *The Natural* (1952) and Joyce Carol Oates (who is sometimes called a neo-naturalist) in *Expensive People* (1968)

Realism lies in the method of presentation. In this sense, Fitzgerald is not a realist, for a Byronic romantic aura hangs over his best work, even *The Great Gatsby*, which shows the nightmare consequences of the uncriti- cal American dream. Realism is as much a matter of style and technique as of purpose; the style is usually unadorned and the techniques are traditiona and simple. Most serious writers have intended to tell the truth, of one kin or another, even popular writers, sometimes in spite of themselves, particu larly the tough-guy writers of the Thirties, Dashiell Hammett, Horace McCoy, Raymond Chandler, and James M. Cain. Because it is associated with sticking to the facts and telling the truth—something for which wester civilization has great reverence—the term "realistic," like the term "aesthe tic," is too often used in an honorific sense. It should be applied descrip- tively.

THE PORNOGRAPHIC NOVEL

Novels have always been criticized for treating sex too frankly. In the name of higher realism, writers have always fought for greater and greater freedom to describe graphically sexual activity and human speech. Until the novel came along, obscenity of speech and sexuality posed problems almost exclusively in comic works of all genres; although Plato would censor poems that did not reflect proper standards of the Republic, censorship did not be come a problem until the novel reached its maturity, with Flaubert's *Madame Bovary* (1857) and works such as James Joyce's *Ulysses* (1922).

The pornographic novel, which concentrates on the depiction of every conceivable sexual act, has a long tradition and is sometimes written by respected writers, as one way of breaking out (though within a constricted circle of readers until recently) of conventional modes of expression. Great artists have painted pornographic, or at least overtly erotic pictures; Ruskin suppressed Turner's erotica. In language, the pornographic novel ranges from the wittiness of euphemism to naughty to bawdy to outright obscenity, and in intent from titillation to vicarious sexual gratification. Some of these novels have many qualities of works of art, for instance, Englishman John Cleland's *Fanny Hill, Memoirs of a Woman of Pleasure* (about 1749); others have serious philosophical or social or psychological implications: the French Marquis de Sade's massive *Justine* (1797). Some are satirical: Terry Southern's *Candy* (1959), is a critique of the society that produced negative sexual expression.

Some critics argue that so-called decent popular novels are hypocritically or piously pornographic, and regard more outright treatments as honest, true to life—realistic. Grace Metalious' *Peyton Place* (1956) is a recent example of "decent" pornography. In earlier decades, there were Vina Delmar's *Bad Girl* (1928); *The Glorious Pool* (1934) and *Topper Takes a Trip* (1932), the naughty novels of Thorne Smith; The rabelaisian Norman Lindsay tales, *The Cautious Amorist* (1932); the sophisticated sexuality of Tiffany Thayer novels, *Call Her Savage* (1931); and the cruder works of Jack Woodford, *Four Eves* (1935), and Donald Henderson Clark, *Millie's Daughter* (1939).

As a type, pornography may be fading out, for serious and popular novels, especially in paperback, more and more absorb the frank sexuality and coarse language that was once the exclusive province of pornographic novels. Here again, even among aesthetically inclined writers, we see the realistic impulse that formed the novel. A novel is good by virtue of its fidelity to life—now this aspect, now that: now the slums, now ideas, now drugs, now sex, etc.

In times when certain areas of human experience are taboo in literature, the writer is forced to get at them through his powers of suggestion (as Euripides got at the Gods in the golden age of Greek tragedy). Now that little is left to the reader's imagination, will the imagination atrophy? That is a problem for the future of the novel—one among many.

NOVELS OF THE SOIL

Naturalism and realism attempted primarily to expose or reveal the life of the worker in the city; and there has always been a type of novel that depicts life in the country: man's struggle against nature in a rural setting. Some glorify the farmer's way of life, some criticize it. Behind the novels of the soil is the romanticism of William Wordsworth's "The Solitary Reaper," for readers more than writers, are drawn to such novels less out of desire to see the life realistically depicted than to experience the natural man, noble savage concept that Jean-Jacques Rousseau made popular for centuries; this is a romantic expectation, little diminished by the truth such books as Knut Hamsun's *Growth of the Soil* (1917) depict.

The Europeans wrote about man and nature as one response to the new freedom of the novel as a new form. But Americans re-experienced the major patterns of European changes and their novels rediscovered the soil. Though the writers themselves fled to the city, they were seldom free of their past. Major American examples of the novels of the soil are: Ellen Glasgow, *Barren Ground* (1925); Pearl Buck, *The Good Earth* (1931), set in China; and O. E. Rölvaag, *Giants in the Earth* (1927).

> Bright, clear sky over a plain so wide that the rim of the heavens cut down on it around the entire horizon.... Bright, clear sky, to-day, to-morrow, and for all time to come.
> ... And Sun! And still more sun! It set the heavens afire every morning; it grew with the day to quivering golden light—then softened into all the shades of red and purple as evening fell.... Pure colour everywhere. A gust of wind, sweeping across the plain, threw into life waves of yellow and blue and green. Now and then a dead black wave would race over the scene... a cloud's gliding shadow... now and then....
> It was late afternoon. A small caravan was pushing its way through the tall grass. The track that it left behind was like the wake of a boat—except that instead of widening out astern it closed in again.

THE REGIONAL NOVEL

The first major example of the regional novel was *Castle Rackrent* (1800) by Maria Edgeworth. American regional literature—in the strict use of the term—was created in the period from the Civil War through Reconstruction to 1900. Among the forces determining the identity of a region are: historical, cultural, economic, political, and, most important, geographical (climate and topography). Geographical isolation can cause economic and cultural isolation and stagnation. The purely regional writer said, "Reconsider your attitude toward this region; look at these people and where and how they live—they *are* different; listen to these people—they talk differently." Regionalism depicts faithfully ordinary ways of life or life styles—

the manners, customs, mores, local idioms of speech, and social organization of common people, mostly villagers and country folk, of a vanishing or vanished past. One thinks of the New England villager, the southern black plantation laborer, the New Orleans Creole, the California prospector. These phrases, negative and positive, describe most regional writing: exploitation of a narrow range of material; sentimentality; charm; nostalgia; simplicity; purity; the unique; the curious; the quaint. Many regionalists wrote self-consciously, in a discursive prose that was leisurely in pace; they stressed the picturesque for its own sake. To present day readers, most regional novels give off the odor of pressed flowers.

Regional novels seem to take two opposing approaches: some exhibit a romanticized re-creation of the past and some a realistic exposé of the past. Modern critical opinion on the value of regional writing is sharply divided: it is useful as a social and cultural art; it confuses social and creative impulses, and so falsifies both. But writing out of a "democratic regionalist tradition," some of these writers helped Americans to look at evidence that variety is an important characteristic of the American identity. When studying regional novels, one might ask these questions: How does the region see itself? How do outsiders see the region? How do the region's writers— regionalist writer or not—see the region? How do people in the region view the works of these writers? How do readers *outside* the region view those writings? (See Spiller, *Literary History of the United States.*)

Here, separated by region, are some salient examples of the "pure" regional novel in America, New England: Mary E. Wilkins Freeman *A New England Nun* (1891); Sarah Orne Jewett, most distinguished of all regional writers, *A Country Doctor* (1884):

> . . . Mrs. Jake asked about the candles, which gave a clear light. "Be they the last you run?" she inquired, but was answered to the contrary, and a brisk conversation followed upon the proper proportions of tallow and bayberry wax, and the dangers of the newfangled oils which the village shop-keepers were attempting to introduce. Sperm oil was growing more and more dear in price and worthless in quality, and the old-fashioned lamps were reported to be past their usefulness.
> "I must own I set most by good candle light," said Mrs. Martin.

From the South we have: William Gilmore Simms, *Yamassee* (1835); George W. Cable, *The Grandissimes* (1880); Charles Egbert Craddock, *In the Clouds* (1887); Charles Waddell Chesnutt, a black writer, *Conjure Woman* (1899). From the Midwest: Edward Eggleston, *A Hoosier Schoolmaster* (1871); E. E. Howe, *The Story of a Country Town* (1883); Booth Tar-

kington, *The Gentleman from Indiana* (1899). From the West: Helen Hunt
Jackson, *Ramona* (1884) and Owen Wister, *The Virginian* (1902).

One should make a distinction between regionalism in the traditional
and generally negative sense, and the positive function of region in fiction
more universal scope. The best examples of the pure regional novel already
cited succeed on the level of universality, as do novels produced by regions
in the twentieth century listed by region below. The North: Elsie Singmas-
ter, *A Boy at Gettysburg* (1913). The South: Thomas Wolfe, *Look Homeward,
Angel* (1929); James Still, *River of Earth* (1940); Eudora Welty, *Delta Wedding*
(1946); Harriette Arnow, *Hunter's Horn* (1949); David Madden, *Cassandra
Singing* (1969). The Midwest: Willa Cather, *O Pioneers* (1913) and *My Án-
tonia* (1918); Glenway Wescott, *The Grandmothers* (1927); Ross Lockridge,
Jr., *Raintree County* (1948); Wright Morris, *The Home Place* (1948) and *The
World in the Attic* (1949). The West: Walter Van Tilburg Clark, *The
Ox-Bow Incident* (1940); Wallace Stegner, *The Big Rock Candy Mountain*
(1943).

Here are several European examples of the regional novel: *Sotileza*
(1884) by José María de Pereda, Spanish; *The Naked Year* (1922) by Boris
Pilnyak, Russian; *A Nest of Gentle Folk* (1933) by Seán O'Faoláin, Irish.

Many countries have produced regional romances, endowed with a dis-
tinctively lyrical imaginative element: *The Copperhead* (1893) by Harold
Frederic and *Trail of the Lonesome Pine* (1908) by John Fox, America;
Maria Chapdelaine (1916) by Louis Hémon, Canada; *Black Valley* (1918) by
Hugo Wast (Gustavo Martínez Zuviría), Argentina; *Porgy* (1925) by DuBose
Heyward, America; *Precious Bane* (1924) by Mary Webb, England; *Don
Segundo Sombra* (1926) by Ricardo Güiraldes, Argentina; *Doña Barbara*
(1929) by Rómulo Gallegos, Venezuela; *When the Mountain Fell* (1935) by
Charles Ferdinand Ramuz, French Switzerland; *Taps for Private Tussie*
(1943) by Jesse Stuart, America.

THE NOVEL OF SMALL TOWN LIFE

A type that is almost indistinguishable from the regional novel is what
we might call the novel of small town life. Most American writers have rejected the narrow provincialism of the small town: One example is Sherwood Anderson's *Poor White* (1920).

> Hugh McVey was born in a little hole of a town stuck on a
> mud bank on the western shore of the Mississippi River in the
> state of Missouri. It was a miserable place in which to be born.
> With the exception of a narrow strip of black mud along the river,
> the land for ten miles back from the town—called in derision by

river men "Mudcat Landing"—was almost entirely worthless and unproductive. The soil, yellow, shallow and stony, was tilled, in Hugh's time, by a race of long gaunt men who seemed as exhausted and no-account as the land on which they lived. They were chronically discouraged, and the merchants and artisans of the town were in the same state. The merchants, who ran their stores—poor tumble-down ramshackle affairs—on the credit system, could not get pay for the goods they handed out over their counters and the artisans, the shoemakers, carpenters and harnessmakers, could not get pay for the work they did. Only the town's two saloons prospered.

Several other examples are: Ruth Suckow, *The Folks* (1934); Sinclair Lewis *Main Street* (1920) and *Babbitt* (1922); Edgar Lee Masters, *Kit O'Brien* (1927) and *Mitch Miller* (1920). Other small town novels are Gustav Flaubert's *Madame Bovary* (1856), France; Pío Baroja y Nessi's *The Restlessness of Shanti Andia* (1930), Spain; and two novels of India, Kamala Markandaya's *Nectar in a Sieve* (1954), about a woman's battle against nature, changing times, and poverty, and Khushwant Singh's *Mano Majra* (*Train to Pakistan,* 1956), a love story set amidst a war of religious strife in a small village.

THE LOCAL COLOR NOVEL

Both the regional and the local color novel depict life in a distinctly remote or isolated area of a country, in either a rural or small town setting. But the local color novel differs from the regional and the small town novel by exploiting quaintness rather than giving a balanced picture. The regional novelist does not deliberately set out to be regional, although he may have a compulsion to describe his region to the rest of the country; the local colorist, however, deliberately attempts to attract readers to the odd details of the distinctively different region he describes; almost subordinate to their quirks, people become caricatures. The local color novel is to the regional novel what the superficial historical novel (*Gone with the Wind*) is to the serious historical novel (*World Enough and Time*). But when we use the term "local color fiction" in its most positive sense, the tales of Sarah Orne Jewett, Bret Harte, Kate Chopin, George W. Cable, Joel Chandler Harris, Hamlin Garland, Mark Twain come to mind, and, of course, many novels make use of that element to some extent.

THE ETHNIC NOVEL

Though its characters may live in a special place, the ethnic novel deals with a speciality of people, a minority group, rather than a place. The minority novel is a kind of off-shoot of the urban and the rural realistic novel; it deals with immigrants, Jews, Negroes, Indians, and other minority groups. In ethnic novels, the author often attempts to understand himself in relation to his ethnic group, then to society at large, and his purpose is also to explain his people to themselves and to the majority.

The Armenians in William Saroyan's *The Human Comedy* (1943) are lovable. *Children of the Ghetto* (1892) by Englishman Israel Zangwill is a realistic ethnocentric novel, and Abraham Cahan's *The Rise of David Lavinsky* (1917) is an excellent example of the American Jewish immigrant novel.

> Sometimes, when I think of my past in a superficial, casual way, the metamorphosis I have gone through strikes me as nothing short of a miracle. I was born and reared in the lowest depths of poverty and I arrived in America—in 1885—with four cents in my pocket. I am now worth more than two million dollars and recognized as one of the two or three leading men in the cloak-and-suit trade in the United States. And yet when I take a look at my inner identity it impresses me as being precisely the same as it was thirty or forty years ago. My present station, power, the amount of worldly happiness at my command, and the rest of it, seem to be devoid of significance.

Jews Without Money (1930) tells of life in the New York Jewish ghetto. There was a great upsurge of creativity in the Jewish novel in the 1940's, 50's and 60's: Norman Mailer, Bernard Malamud, Saul Bellow, Philip Roth, Edward Wallant.

In the 1960's and 70's the black novel has emerged. One of the first important novels about the Negro was *Porgy* (1925), by a white man, DuBose Heyward, and in 1967 appeared William Styron's controversial *The Confessions of Nat Turner*. Major novels by black writers are *Cane* (1923) by Jean Toomer; *Native Son* (1940), by Richard Wright; *Go Tell It on the Mountain* (1953), by James Baldwin; *The System of Dante's Hell* (1965), by LeRoi Jones; *Song of Solomon* (1977), by Toni Morrison; and *Invisible Man* (1952), by Ralph Ellison, once more:

> I am an invisible man. No, I am not a spook like those who haunted Edgar Allan Poe; nor am I one of your Hollywood-movie ectoplasms. I am a man of substance, of flesh and bone, fiber and liquids—and I might even be said to possess a mind. I am invisible, understand, simply because people refuse to see me. Like the bodiless heads you see sometimes in circus sideshows, it is as though I have been surrounded by mirrors of hard, distorting

glass. When they approach me they see only my surroundings, themselves, or figments of their imagination—indeed, everything and anything except me.

Suppressed minority groups of all kinds have always found ways to deal with their problems. Thus, Frank Yerby, the best-selling historical novelist, subtly argued the black man's cause in *The Foxes of Harrow* (1946), and in *Knock on Any Door* (1947) Willard Motley masked his exposé of the effects of Chicago's slums by creating an Italian hero instead of a black.

It is expected that more novels by American Indians (native Americans) and Mexican-Americans will appear in the future. In 1968, an American Indian, N. Scott Momaday, won the Pulitzer prize with *House Made of Dawn* (1968), his lyrical story of the struggle of a young Indian who feels alien to both whites and Indians.

> At dusk he met with the other hunters in the plain. San Juanito, too, had got an eagle, but it was an aged male and poor by comparison. They gathered around the old eagle and spoke to it, bidding it return with their good will and sorrow to the eagles of the crags. They fixed a prayer plume to its leg and let it go. He watched it back away and stoop, flaring its wings on the ground, glowering, full of fear and suspicion. Then it took leave of the ground and beat upward, clattering through the still shadows of the valley.... He felt the great weight of the bird which he held in the sack. The dusk was fading quickly into night, and the others could not see that his eyes were filled with tears.

Winter in the Blood (1973) by James Welch was also well received. Two novels about Indians in other parts of the world are *Broad and Alien Is the World* (1941), by Ciro Alegría, which argues justice for Peruvian Indians, and *Ashini* (1960), by Yves Thériault, which makes a plea for Indians in French Canada.

Mexican-American novelists have also made a powerful impression, with *The Plum, Plum Pickers* (1972), by Raymond Barrio; *Bless Me, Ultima* (1972), by Rudolfo A. Anaya; *Macho!* (1973), by Edmund Villasenor; *Rabbit Boss* (1973), by Thomas Sanchez; and *Chicano* (1970), by Richard Vasquez.

> ... "God did not bring me back. I escaped. I am now a deserter from the Mexican Army. They'll be looking for me in the morning, to make an example of me."
> Before his mother could begin wailing, Hector Sandoval took command. "All right. All of you listen. Neftali knows what we must

do. He and I have talked it over before when we were alone working with the burros. We leave. Now. To go north. Quick. No talk. Pack our things. Neftali and I will go get the burros. We have six. We should be able to take everything and be a long way from here before another night."

Except for the boy, the others were stunned. "But, where . . .

"To los Estados Unidos. Where there will no more of all that makes us suffer. Hurry now. You women wrap up everything and bring it out here. We can leave within an hour. Or the lieutenant might return for Neftali."

THE PHILOSOPHICAL NOVEL

Related to the novels of instruction are the novels of enlightenment or philosophical novels. The philosophical novel demonstrates an intellectual proposition or a generally philosophical approach to life. Action is minimal, erudite dialogs among characters in search of enlightenment are frequent. A great number of novels devote much space to discourse that is closer to the imaginative or lyrical essay than to fiction. An early example is Swift's *Gulliver's Travels* (1726). Oscar Wilde's *The Picture of Dorian Gray* (1891), inspired by J.-K. Huysmans' *Against the Grain* (1884), analyzes the phenomena of the senses and the qualities of the aesthetic experience as often as they depict or describe them.

The novelist has often struggled with two contrary impulses, to tell about life in generalities or to render the qualities of experience in particularities. As Aristotle said, our first knowledge comes from imitating; the novelist comes to know life by imitating particulars, but he also feels the impulse to draw his knowledge together into a kind of philosophical system. We want the novel to tell the truth about life, to convey its meaning; some novelists satisfy that interest—which most serious novels elicit—more directly than others by an overt philosophical approach that satisfies our intellectual hunger; but so, in another context, do detective novels that set up riddles to be solved by the reader as the detective's partner. Thomas Mann wrote perhaps the greatest of the philosophical chronicles: *Doctor Faustus* (1947); *The Confessions of Felix Krull* (1954), dealing with the artist as con man, the con man as artist; and *The Magic Mountain* (1924).

On the contrary, Naptha hastened to say. Disease was very human indeed. For to be man was to be ailing. Man was essentially ailing, his state of unhealthiness was what made him man. There were those who wanted to make him "healthy," to make him "go back to nature," when the truth was, he never had been "natural." All the propaganda carried on today by the prophets of

> nature, the experiments in re-generation, the uncooked food, fresh-air cures, sun-bathing, and so on, the whole Rousseauian paraphernalia, had as its goal nothing but the dehumanization, the animalizing of man. They talked of "humanity," of nobility—but it was the spirit alone that distinguished man, as a creature largely divorced from nature, largely opposed to her in feeling, from all other forms of organic life. In man's spirit, then, resided his true nobility and his merit—in his state of disease, as it were; in a word, the more ailing he was, by so much was he the man. The genius of disease was more human than the genius of health. . . . Had not the normal, since the time of man, lived on the achievements of the abnormal?

But Mann's characters are far more than representative of philosophical concepts, because he is also interested in psychological analysis.

Most of the philosophical novels have been German: Goethe's *Elective Affinities* (1808), a philosophical romance; Hermann Broch's *Die Schlafwandler* (*The Sleepwalkers*, 1930–32). Many have been French: Jean-Jacques Rousseau's *The New Héloïse* (1760), an example of philosophical realism; Honoré de Balzac's *The Wild Ass's Skin* (1830); André Gide's *Theseus* (1946); Simone de Beauvoir's *Les Mandarins* (1954). The English are well-represented with Samuel Johnson's philosophical romance *Rasselas* (1759); Joseph Henry Shorthouse's historical philosophical romance *John Inglesant* (1881); Walter Pater's philosophical romance *Marius the Epicurean* (1885); Thomas Hardy's philosophical realism *Jude the Obscure* (1894); George Gissing's reflective romance *The Private Papers of Henry Ryecroft* (1903); and Iris Murdoch's *A Severed Head* (1961). Fewer Americans have used the form: Herman Melville's philosophical tragedy *Pierre, or the Ambiguities* (1852); Thornton Wilder's philosophical romance *The Bridge of San Luis Rey* (1927); Robert Penn Warren's philosophical romance *World Enough and Time* (1950). In Ayn Rand's *The Fountainhead* (1943) and *Atlas Shrugged* (1957), creative individuals reject the altruism of society; each of her many characters and situations illustrate a facet of her objectivist philosophy. Other countries have produced even fewer philosophical novels: from Russia, Mikhail Artsybashev's *Sanin* (1907); from Spain, Joaquim Maria Machado de Assís' *Epitaph of a Small Winner* (1880).

Another term for the philosophical novel is the *novel of ideas*, but the latter term is more embrasive, including novels that emphasize investigations into areas not strictly philosophical, though basically intellectual: the social and Utopian, for instance. American examples of novels of ideas are Saul Bellow's *Herzog* (1964), Susan Sontag's *The Benefactor* (1963), and *Mr. Sammler's Planet* (1970), philosophical comedies; and Walker Percy's *Love in the Ruins: the Adventures of a Bad Catholic at a Time Near the End of the World* (1971). "Intellectual" might be a more apt term for writers such as John Barth, whose *End of the Road* (1958) features a super-intellectual narrator. Unlike Jean-Paul Sartre in his trilogy *Roads to Freedom* (1945–49), such writers present no coherent philosophical view of life; the "intellectual" novelist reveals an attitude, as Sartre does in an earlier novel, *La Nausée* (*Nausea*, 1938), and as Albert Camus does in *The Fall* (1956) and *The Plague* (1947).

While most of the great novels are often studied for their philosophical implications, the philosophical novelist always runs the risk of having to justify arguing his ideas in fiction rather than in a book of philosophy. On the other hand, the philosophers who have most influenced the writers of fiction have—with the exception of Descartes, Locke, Hegel, Kant, and Marx—been near-poets themselves: Kierkegaard, Nietzsche, Bergson.

The philosophical type of novel is limited because its thematic content demands that its characters be intellectual and its action be relatively obvious in illustrating abstract ideas. "The chief defect of the novel of ideas is that you must write about people who have ideas to express—which excludes all but about .01 percent of the human race," said Aldous Huxley, whose *Point Counter Point* (1928), is as much philosophy as social criticism. Ezra Pound said to the Imagist poets, "Go in fear of abstractions."

THE THESIS NOVEL

The thesis novel is different from the philosophical in that it illustrates a rather simple proposition and advocates, at least, by implication, a solution to a problem. The resources of the novel are used to elicit sympathy for an idea about people and institutions and disapproval of conditions that need changing. In *Emile*, Jean-Jacques Rousseau wrote:

> Even if I considered that education was wise in its aims, how could I view without indignation those poor wretches subjected to an intolerable slavery and condemned like galley-slaves to endless toil. . . . ? The age of harmless mirth is spent in tears, punishments, threats, and slavery. You torment the poor thing for his good; you fail to see that you are calling Death to snatch him from these gloomy surroundings.

. . .

> When our natural tendencies have not been interfered with by human prejudice and human institutions, the happiness alike of children and men consists in the enjoyment of their liberty.

The writer can influence society only if he has himself first been influenced by society. The writer appeals to known empirical processes and his novel in turn affects those processes. All literature affects the beliefs and behavior of its readers, but the various kinds of thesis novels deliberately set out either to inform and instruct readers to change their picture of man in society and in history or to shock them into corrective acts. These novels satisfy the ancient utilitarian criterion with a vengeance. Providing programs of action, they are useful to political and sociological movements and to individuals. This is generally an inferior type for it stifles the imagination, dealing, as it must, with what is given. Corrado Alvaro's *Man Is Strong* (1938) and Ayi Kwei Armah's *The Beautiful Ones Are Not Yet Born* (1968) are two good examples. (See Naturalism, Problem, Philosophical, Social Criticism, Socialist.)

THE SOCIAL CHRONICLE NOVEL

The social chronicle, a broad type of thesis novel, provides a kind of cultural or social history, revealing an idealism about the individual's potential for self-realization of spirit, if history is understood as a process enabling man to achieve self-knowledge. The social chronicle reveals patterns of repetition, the organic logic of history, even, on a higher plane, the concept of the eternal recurrence. The author's historical imagination reveals the symbolic reality of historical events and the novel becomes, at its best, a kind of triumph of art over history. (See Ellmann, *Modern Tradition*).

Victor Hugo's *Les Misérables* (1862) was one of the first great social chronicles.

> Jean Valjean, at that very moment, was a prey to a frightful uprising. All the gulfs were reopened within him. He also, like Paris, was shuddering on the threshold of a formidable and obscure revolution. A few hours had sufficed. His destiny and his conscience were suddenly covered with shadow. Of him also, as of Paris, we might say: the two principles are face to face. The angel of light and the angel of darkness are to wrestle on the bridge of the abyss. Which of the two shall hurl down the other? which shall sweep him away?

Then came Benito Pérez Galdós' four-volume *Fortunata and Jacinta* (1886–87); Thomas Mann's *Buddenbrooks* (1901); Polish Wladislaw Reymont's *The Peasants* (1902–09); Romain Rolland's ten-volume *Jean Christophe* (1904–12); Mexican Mariano Azuela's *Los de Abajo (The Underdogs,* 1915); Norwegian Knut Hamsun's *Growth of the Soil* (1917); Dutch Johanna Van Ammers-Küller's *The Rebel Generation* (1925); Austrian Vicki Baum's

Grand Hotel (1930); Icelandic Halldór Laxness's *Independent People* (1934-35); Polish Israel Joshua Singer's *The Brothers Ashkenazi* (1936); Fannie Hurst's *Back Street* (1931); Henry Bellamann's *King's Row* (1940); Hamilto Basso's *The View from Pompey's Head* (1953).

In the 1920's and 30's a number of multi-volume novels appeared. Thi series of novels shows how history determines the fate of families, groups, individuals, nations. A species of realistic novel that stresses historical determinism more than the findings of social science, this type included Norwegian Olav Dunn, *The People of Juvik* (1918-1923), six volumes; Georges Duhamel, *Vie et Aventures de Salvin* (*Salavin*, 1920-1932), five volumes; Ford Madox Ford, *Parade's End* (1924-26), three volumes; Austr lian Henry Handel Richardson (Ethel Florence Richardson Robertson), *Th Fortunes of Richard Mahony* (1917-25-29); John Dos Passos, *U.S.A.* (1937) Roger Martin du Gard, *Les Thibaults* (*The World of the Thibaults*) (1922-29), eight volumes.

THE PROBLEM NOVEL

The thesis novel is sometimes called the problem novel. For instance, many of the novels of Upton Sinclair—*The Jungle* (1906) is one—dramatize a specific social problem and report on it in journalistic detail, often in editorializing language.

> There were the men in the pickle-rooms, for instance, where old Antanas had gotten his death; scarce a one of these that had not some spot of horror on his person. Let a man so much as scrape his finger pushing a truck in the pickle-rooms, and he migl have a sore that would put him out of the world; all the joints of his fingers might be eaten by the acid, one by one. Of the butchers and floorsmen, the beefboners and trimmers, and all those wh used knives, you could scarcely find a person who had the use of his thumb; time and time again the base of it had been slashed, ti it was a mere lump of flesh against which the man pressed the knife to hold it. The hands of these men would be criss-crossed with cuts, until you could no longer pretend to count them or to trace them. They would have no nails—they had worn them off pulling hides; their knuckles were swollen so that their fingers spread out like a fan. There were men who worked in the cooking-rooms, in the midst of steam and sickening odours, by art ficial light; in these rooms the germs of tuberculosis might live for two years, but the supply was renewed every hour.

Other examples are: South African Olive Schreiner, *The Story of an African Farm* (1883), an early plea for women's rights; American Harold Frederic, *The Damnation of Theron Ware* (1896), abuses in training of the clergy; Ivan Bunin (Alexeiyevich), *The Village* (1910), landlord abuses; Brazilian José Lins do Rêgo, *Dead Fires* (1943), misuse of power by landowners; Lillian Smith, *Strange Fruit* (1944), racial discrimination in the American South; South African Alan Paton, *Cry the Beloved Country* (1948), racial discrimination; American John Hersey, *The Wall* (1950), Jews in German concentration camps; Ghanaian Ayi Kwei Armah, *The Beautiful Ones Are Not Yet Born* (1969), a parable of exploited people; Italian Corrado Alvaro, *Man Is Strong* (1938), intellectual freedom. Too often the problem novelist is so certain of the rightness of his attitude about the problem that he rigs all events and characterizations so that they strike the reader as too predictable. There is little room for the imagination to expand or characters to break out of the strait-jacket of high purpose. The reader must revel in exposé—usually sordid, shocking, sensational details.

THE PROPAGANDA NOVEL

Another example within the thesis type is the propaganda or polemical novel. The author selects characters and situations to preach a limited point of view, such as a political doctrine. This type is a little more blatantly rhetorical in the handling of its various elements, and too often its appeal can be only to the already converted, and thus its purpose may be defeated. The most famous and artistically successful example of this type, and indeed one of the most widely read novels in the history of literature, is Harriet Beecher Stowe's *Uncle Tom's Cabin* (1852).

> If any of our refined and Christian readers object to the society into which this scene introduces them, let us beg them to begin and conquer their prejudices in time. The catching business, we beg to remind them, is rising to the dignity of a lawful and patriotic profession. If all the broad land between the Mississippi and the Pacific becomes one great market for bodies and souls, and human property retains the locomotive tendencies of this nineteenth century, the trader and catcher may yet be among our aristocracy.

Two other examples are Ecuadorian Jorge Icaza's *Huasipungo* (1934), about the enslavement of Indians, and African Bloke Modisane's *Blame Me on History* (1963), a traditional, historical panorama about apartheid. Serious readers are offended by this type, for its methods are employed on the assumption that the reader has little intelligence of his own and can be manipulated to adopt the point of view the author represents. Fortunately, no great audience on any level will tolerate any but the best examples of this sort of novel. Still, many good novels contain an element of propaganda.

THE NOVEL OF SOCIAL CRITICISM

The novel of social criticism attempts to show the way our social environment shapes us. The shapes are usually ugly. Portuguese Eça de Queiroz's Os Maias (1888), depicted in romantic, melodramatic fashion the decadence of upper classes in Lisbon. Two studies of the Russian aristocracy are Ivan Goncharov's Oblomov (1858) and Leo Tolstoy's Anna Karenina (1873–77); Fëdor Sologub's The Petty Demon (1907) is about a paranoid school teacher. American James T. Farrell in his trilogy Studs Lonigan (1932–35) and Williard Motley in Knock on Any Door (1947) depicted the way the slums turn young men into criminals. Nigerian Alex La Guma's A Walk in the Night (1962) demonstrates the relation between criminality and communality; E. W. Howe exposed marital betrayal and loneliness in frontier town life in Story of a Country Town (1883); Erskine Caldwell presents social melodrama in rural settings in God's Little Acre (1933) and Tobacco Road (1932).

> "I reckon old Jeeter had the best thing happen to him," Lov said. "He was killing himself worrying all the time about the raising of a crop. That was all he wanted in this life—growing cotton was better than anything else to him. There ain't many more like him left, I reckon. Most of the people now don't care about nothing except getting a job in a cotton mill somewhere. But can't all of them work in the mills, and they'll have to stay here like Jeeter until they get taken away too. There ain't no sense in them raising crops. They can't make no money at it, not even a living. If they do make some cotton, somebody comes along and cheats them out of it. It looks like the Lord don't care about crops being raised no more like He used to, or He would be more helpful to the poor. He could make the rich people lend out their money, and stop holding it up. I can't figure out how they got hold of all the money in the country, anyhow. Looks like it ought to be spread out among everybody."

War is criticized in Irwin Shaw's The Young Lions (1948), humorously in Mac Hyman's No Time for Sergeants (1953); the Spanish civil war is depicted in José María Gironella's The Cypresses Believe in God (1953). Unlike China, modern Japan has produced many fine novels; Shohei Ooka's Fires on the Plain (1951) is considered the best Japanese novel of the war; it is a fable-like work, resembling William Golding's Lord of the Flies (1954). South African James Ngugi's Chocolates for my Wife, Slices of My Life

(1961) examines natives of the professional middle-class. Edna Ferber depicts in *So Big* (1924) women in the business world and Dutch Louis Maria Anne Couperus shows how a woman is hounded by gossip in *The Book of Small Souls* (1901–1903).

In this type of novel, criticism of society may be implicit or explicit. Any type of novel can be handled with skill and the sociological novel often is. Still, it is, like the thesis novel, an inferior form in that it stifles the imagination. Ironically, the tyranny of fact subverts as art many novels that set out to expose tyranny of any kind in society.

THE UTOPIAN NOVEL

The utopian novel depicts an ideal society, using a combination of fantasy, science fiction, philosophy, and prophecy to conjecture ways of solving problems posed by other types of thesis novels. The Utopian novel depicts an ideal society. One of the First was a non-fiction Utopian proposal that claimed to be a true report: Thomas More's *Utopia* (1516), inspired by Plato's *Republic;* another Englishman, Francis Bacon conjured another non-fiction vision *The New Atlantis* (1627). There are both Utopian and anti-Utopian elements in *Gulliver's Travels.* (Utopia is Greek for "nowhere.")

> Ingratitude is among them a capital crime, as we read it to have been in some other countries; for they reason thus, that whoever makes ill returns to his benefactor, must needs be a common enemy to the rest of mankind, from whom he hath received no obligation, and therefore such a man is not fit to live.

.   .   .

> After this preface he gave me a particular account of the Struldbruggs among them. He said they commonly acted like mortals, till about thirty years old, after which by degrees they grew melancholy and dejected, increasing in both till they came to fourscore. This he learned from their own confession, for otherwise there not being above two or three of that species born in an age, they were too few to form a general observation by. When they came to fourscore years, which is reckoned the extremity of living in this country, they had not only all the follies and infirmities of other old men, but many more which arose from the dreadful prospect of never dying. They were not only opinionative, peevish, covetous, morose, vain, talkative, but uncapable of friendship, and dead to all natural affection, which never descended below their grandchildren.

Other Utopian works, mostly English, are: American Edward Bellamy's *Looking Backward* (1888), a Utopian romance; William Morris' *News from Nowhere* (1890); H. G. Wells' *A Modern Utopia* (1905); James Hilton's *Lost Horizon* (1933), an adventure romance about Shangri-la; Herbert Read's *Th Green Child* (1935); Austin Tappan Wright's *Islandia* (1942); and B. F. Skinner's *Walden Two* (1948), a scientific Utopia based on behavioral psychology.

THE ANTI-UTOPIAN NOVEL

The anti-Utopian novel satirically posits an opposing, sceptical view to that of the optimistic Utopian novels. Examples are: Samuel Butler's *Erewhon* (1872), which carries a title that is an anagram of "nowhere"; Anatole France's *L'Ile des Pinguoins (Penguin Island,* 1908); Russian Yevgeny Zamyatin's *We* (written 1920–21); Aldous Huxley's *Brave New World;* and George Orwell's *Animal Farm* (1945) and *Nineteen Eighty-Four* (1949).

The voice from the telescreen was still pouring forth its tale of prisoners and booty and slaughter, but the shouting outside had died down a little. The waiters were turning back to their work. One of them approached with the gin bottle. Winston, sitting in a blissful dream, paid no attention as his glass was filled up. He was not running or cheering any longer. He was back in the Ministry of Love, with everything forgiven, his soul white as snow. He was in the public dock, confessing everything, implicating everybody. He was walking down the white-tiled corridor, with the feeling of walking in sunlight, and an armed guard at his back. The long-hoped-for bullet was entering his brain.

He gazed up at the enormous face. Forty years it had taken him to learn what kind of smile was hidden beneath the dark mustache. O cruel, needless misunderstanding! O stubborn, self-willed exile from the loving breast! Two gin-scented tears trickled down the sides of his nose. But it was all right, everything was all right, the struggle was finished. He had won the victory over himself. He loved Big Brother.

Conformity in the name of the greater good proves to be just as tyrannical and dehumanizing as, for instance, conformity to a corrupt, capital society. The emphasis is usually on a rebelling individual, who refuses to conform to the kind of group eulogized in the Utopian novel; or on a cre *unable* to conform.

THE RADICAL NOVEL

The radical novel embraces works by communists, socialists, anarchists, and authors of other persuasions whose heroes advocate radical solutions to social and political problems. (See Daniel Aaron and Walter Rideout.) An "historical determinism" operates behind human affairs; society is seen as an "historical organism," art as an "historical product," and man as the "creator of history." (See Ellmann, *Modern Tradition*.) A Frenchman, Louis Aragon, offers an example of a Marxist novel, *Les Communistes* (1949). One critical approach to literature in general is the Marxian. (See Caudwell.)

THE SOCIALIST NOVEL

The socialist novel, a species of radical novel, illustrates the arguments of socialism and usually brings its characters and situations to the dawn of a socialistic era of reform. (It can go no further without becoming Utopian science fiction.) It is a sociological novel with a solution—socialism. Economics is seen as the source of consciousness in author and hero, and fiction is a weapon in the class struggle; its end is to show "historical truth." (See Ellmann, *Modern Tradition*.) Few radical, socialist novels are aesthetic achievements. An Italian example is Edmondo de Amicis' *The Romance of a Schoolmaster* (1876). A few other examples are: Isaac Kahn Friedman, *The Radical* (1907); Jack London, *The Iron Heel* (1907); Susan Glaspell, *The Visioning* (1911); Albert Maltz, *The Underground Stream* (1940); Howard Fast, *The Unvanquished* (1942); Ruth McKenney, *Jake Home* (1943); Joseph Freeman, *Never Call Retreat* (1943); Isidor Schneider, *The Judas Time* (1947); and Norman Mailer, *Barbary Shore* (1951). Jack London's *The Iron Heel*:

> And through it all moved the Iron Heel, impassive and deliberate, shaking up the whole fabric of the social structure in its search for the comrades, combing out the Mercenaries, the labor castes, and all its secret services, punishing without mercy and without malice, suffering in silence all retaliations that were made upon it, and filling the gaps in its fighting line as fast as they appeared. And hand in hand with this, Ernest and the other leaders were hard at work reorganizing the forces of the Revolution.

THE PROLETARIAN OR PROTEST NOVEL

The proletarian or protest novel (a term rejected by most socialist novelists) was mainly an American phenomenon of the 1930's. These novels depict social and economic injustices, reflect a Marxist viewpoint, attempt to make the worker class-conscious, and often end with a violent uprising of the workers. Fiction is used as a weapon in the class war. Few Americans, and, ironically, few workers read these novels. Here is a representative list the titles of which are quite descriptive: Edward Dahlberg, *Bottom Dogs* (1930); Edwin Seaver, *The Company* (1930); Mary Heaton Vorse, *Strike!* (1930); Maxwell Bodenheim, *Run, Sheep, Run: A Novel* (1932); Catherine Brody, *Nobody Starves* (1932); Grace Lumpkin, *To Make My Bread* (1932); Jack Conroy, *The Disinherited* (1933); Arnold B. Armstrong, *Parched Earth* (1934); Robert Cantwell, *The Land of Plenty* (1934); Albert Halper, *The Foundry* (1934); Edward Newhouse, *You Can't Sleep Here* (1934); Daniel Fuchs, *Williamsburg Trilogy* (1934-37); Fielding Burke, (Olive Tilford Dargan), *A. Stone Came Rolling* (1935); Tom Kromer, *Waiting for Nothing* (1935); Henry Roth, *Call It Sleep* (1934); Clara Weatherwax, *Marching! Marching!* (1935); James T. Farrell, *A World I Never Made* (1936); Josephine Johnson, *Jordanstown* (1937); Dalton Trumbo, *Johnny Got His Gun* (1939); Richard Wright, *Native Son* (1940); and Michael Gold, *Jews Without Money* (1930).

> And I worked. And my father and mother grew sadder and older. It went on for years. I don't want to remember it all; the years of my adolescence. Yet I was only one among a million others.
>
> A man on an East Side soap-box, one night, proclaimed that out of the despair, melancholy and helpless rage of millions, a world movement had been born to abolish poverty.
>
> I listened to him.
>
> O workers' Revolution, you brought hope to me, a lonely suicidal boy. You are the true Messiah. You will destroy the East Side when you come, and build there a garden for the human spirit.
>
> O Revolution, that forced me to think, to struggle and to live.
>
> O great Beginning!

A recent example from Senegal is Sembène Ousmane's *God's Bits of Wood* (1960). (See Madden, *Proletarian Writers.*)

THE POLITICAL NOVEL

A type that is more embrasive than the proletarian is the political novel, which may criticize or simply describe a system or situation and may advocate any number of political solutions, or none. Benito Pérez Gáldos' *Angel Guerra* (1890-91) is a political and religious tragedy. Benjamin Disraeli's *Coningsby* (1844), Anthony Trollope's *Phineas Finn* (1869), and Alphonse Daudet's *Kings in Exile* (1879) are political romances. Examples of political realism are Ignazio Silone's *Fontamara* (1933) and *Bread and Wine* (1936); South Indian Raja Rao's mythical, folk-epic, *Kanthapura* (1937), about the coming of Gandhi's struggle to a typical village; Mexican Agustin Yáñez's *Al Filo del Aqua* (1947), another story of small town politics; Anglo-Hungarian Arthur Koestler, *Darkness at Noon* (1941), about communist betrayals.

> "You have heard the accusation and plead guilty."
> Rubashov tried to look into his face. He could not, and had to shut his eyes again. He had had a biting answer on his tongue; instead he said, so quietly that the thin secretary had to stretch out her head to hear:
> "I plead guilty to not having understood the fatal compulsion behind the policy of the Government, and to have therefore held oppositional views. I plead guilty to having followed sentimental impulses, and in so doing to have been led into contradiction with historical necessity. I have lent my ear to the laments of the sacrificed, and thus became deaf to the arguments which proved the necessity to sacrifice them. I plead guilty to having rated the question of guilt and innocence higher than that of utility and harmfulness. Finally, I plead guilty to having placed the idea of man above the idea of mankind. . . .

Other examples are: Yugoslavian Ivo Andric, *The Bridge on the Drina* (1945), a part of a Bosnian trilogy; Gerald Green, *The Last Angry Man* (1957); Allen Drury, *Advise and Consent* (1959); Lagosian Cyprian Ekwensi, *People of the City* (1963), depicting facets of African urban life; South African Peter Abrahams, *A Night of Their Own* (1965); Nigerian Chinua Achebe, *A Man of the People* (1966). Many novels describe politics without being dominated by the subject. Robert Penn Warren's *All the King's Men* (1946) transcends politics. The milieu depicted in many other novels exists as a consequence of political corruption, as in Norman Mailer's *Why Are We in Vietnam?: A Novel* (1967).

"Politics in a work of literature," said Stendhal, "are like a pistolshot in the middle of a concert." (See Irving Howe, *The Political Novel*.)

THE TOPICAL NOVEL

Most novels that deal with a current problem or phenomenon are fated to oblivion once the problem is solved. These are called topical novels. Eugene Burdick and William L. Lederer wrote an obvious example, *The Ugly American* (1958).

It is not orthodox to append a factual epilogue to a work of fiction. However, we would not wish any reader to put down our book thinking that what he has read is wholly imaginary. For it is not; it is based on fact. It is our purpose here to give our reasons and our sources.

Although the characters are indeed imaginary and Sarkhan is fiction, each of the small and sometimes tragic events we have described has happened... many times. Too many times. We believe that if such things continue to happen they will multiply into a pattern of disaster.

. . .

The authors have taken part in the events in Southeast Asia which have inspired this book, and in both the records and in the field we have studied the Communist way to power. As writers, we have sought to dramatize what we have seen of the Americans who represent us in the struggle.

Closely related to the topical is the journalistic; sometimes called the documentary novel, it sets out to report, in fictional terms, on a current or recent situation. One of the first of these was *The Journal of the Plague Year* (1722). There are many American examples, one of which is Laura Z. Hobson's *Gentleman's Agreement* (1947), about discrimination against Jews in the United States.

. . .

The purpose of the thesis (social chronicle, problem, propaganda, sociological, Utopian, anti-Utopian, radical, proletarian, topical) novel is similar to that of early novels—to instruct; but in later novels the purpose is, in some instances, to incite, outrage, shock into action. While instructing, most early novels attempted also to delight; many of the types just named do not. But it is implicit in the nature of fiction that no matter how grim the didactic quality, other elements will offer some possibility of entertainment or delight.

All these types, and many others, suffer from what might be called the fallacy of subject dominance. That is, the writer is so overwhelmed by the timeliness, the controversy, the strangeness, the supposed importance of his subject, which may be an idea or a thesis, or something more spectacular, such as sex, dope, or war, that he is blind to the problems of craft that must be solved if the novel is to be a work of the imagination, a work of art.

Overwhelmed by his vision of reform or his awareness of his reader's *given* interest in his subject, he neglects the art of handling that subject in novelistic terms. While any type of novel can become subject-dominated, these types are especially vulnerable. (See Madden, *The Poetic Image.*)

THE NONFICTION NOVEL

The impulse that produces theses novels has resulted in a new type today called the nonfiction novel; one of the first examples was produced by a novelist of great skill and imagination, Truman Capote in *In Cold Blood* (1966), a true account of a multiple murder and its consequences. Norman Mailer wrote *The Armies of the Night: History as a Novel, The Novel as History* (1968).

> It is on this particular confrontation that the conceit one is writing a history must be relinquished. Doubtless it has been hardly possible to ignore that this work resides in two enclaves, the first entitled *History as a Novel*, the second here before us called *The Novel as History*. No one familiar with husking the ambiguities of English will be much mystified by the titles. It is obvious the first book is a history in the guise or dress or manifest of a novel, and the second is a real or true novel—no less!—presented in the style of a history. ... the novel must replace history at precisely that point where experience is sufficiently emotional, spiritual, psychical, moral, existential, or supernatural to expose the fact that the historian in pursuing the experience would be obliged to quit the clearly demarcated limits of historic inquiry. So these limits are now relinquished. The collective novel which follows, while still written in the cloak of an historic style, and, therefore, continuously attempting to be scrupulous to the welter of a hundred confusing and opposed facts, will now unashamedly enter that world of strange lights and intuitive speculation which is the novel.

These nonfiction works use some of the devices of fiction, especially a strong personal quality in the narrative, and offer subjective insights; one feels the emotions, the working intellect, the tone of voice of the author more intensely than is usually true of either fiction or nonfiction. We have always had such books, certainly many novels that verged on nonfiction. And it must be remembered that it was a sort of nonfiction impulse that produced the first novels (Defoe again): the marriage of fact and fiction, a marriage currently in peril of annulment after 200 years. (See Norman Podhoretz, "The Article as Art.")

THE PSYCHOLOGICAL NOVEL

In contrast to those novels that deal with a character who is typical of his class and who develops in the external context of his social world, the psychological novel analyzes the subjective life of the individual. Even if h is a very ordinary individual, the psychological approach, based on the insights of Freud and Jung, can make him as interesting as the hero of the romance. Often the character is the author himself. Flaubert's *Madame Bovary* (1856) and Stendhal's *The Red and the Black* (1830) are combinations of psychological and character novels and the novel of manners. The purely psychological novel began with Henry James, Marcel Proust, Jame: Joyce, Virginia Woolf, and Ford Madox Ford.

The new psychology of Sigmund Freud, James Frazer's *Golden Boug* (1890), a study of primitive religion, and the experiments of the French Symbolist poets influenced the psychological and mythical approach to fiction. Writers felt freed by insights into primitive thinking and the social psychology of myth; they saw a special imaginative validity in the form of mythical thought. Carl Jung's concept of the collective unconscious of the race appealed to critics and writers as a way of transcending everyday real ity, of cutting through traditions. Jung's concept of archetypes and their psychological function in our daily lives gave writers a new way of shaping character and event. Psychoanalysis indicated that each man relives the myths of his race (as in the Oedipus complex); thus, a modern mythology evolved in fiction, new imaginative types; myth became modern man's memory, and works like Oswald Spengler's visionary interpretation of history, *The Decline of the West* (1918–22) became possible. Joseph Conrad and other novelists showed that the primitive survives in the civilized man the pre-human and the savage in human beings today give all life in the metropolis a sense of archaic mystery. Thus, "reason and unreason," "energy and reason," "will and knowledge," war in man's consciousness; th demoniac element in man breaks through repression. The dadaists and sur realists tried to liberate the unconscious. (See Ellmann, *Modern Tradition*.

Frederick Hoffmann in *Freudianism and the Literary Mind* (1945) shows how Freud's concepts are illustrated in works that precede Freud a in many that follow him. Psychological fiction explicitly shows the force of the *Id*, our basic drives, as revealed in dreams and in neuroses. The Id, ac cording to the pleasure principle, must seek some outlet for the instincts while keeping the conflict between itself and the ego and superego in balance; an imbalance causes the anxiety we so often see depicted in modern literature. The ego is made up of both conscious and available unconscious thought patterns that make up one's visible personality; the reality principl compliments the pleasure principle in that it mediates between the conscious ego and the demanding superego, which is the conscience trained b society through parents and institutions. An understanding of the workings of the libido—source of sexual energy, a kind of psychic energy—liberated writers in their way of handling sex and its importance in human behavior. We also see many examples in fiction of sublimation, an expression of censored sexual drives in expenditures of nonsexual psychic energy.

The modern writer is fascinated by the way the mind works. The preconscious, through which we receive perceptions every moment, is at work in the interior monologue technique, first used by Edouard Dujardin in *We'll to the Woods No More* (1887) and perfected by Joyce in *Ulysses* (1922). Faulkner in *As I Lay Dying* (1930) and in *The Sound and the Fury* (1929) and Conrad Aiken in *Blue Voyage* (1927) found ways of expressing the subconscious.

Modern literature is full of examples of psychological mechanisms which help maintain the pleasure principle while cushioning the impact of the reality principle, thus averting neuroses or psychoses. Projection is the transference of an affect from one object to another by substitution—a form of rationalization; transference is the process whereby a patient loves or hates his analyst intensely, as seen in Fitzgerald's *Tender Is the Night* (1934) and satirized in Rose Macaulay's *Dangerous Ages* (1921); the opposite of this mechanism is resistance. The unconscious is full of latent thoughts that the mind's superego censor may let rise to consciousness, and of taboo desires that must remain suppressed or repressed.

The content of the unconscious is expressed or manifested in dreams which have a language of their own; dreams do a special work for the psyche: forbidden wishes are fulfilled, latent thoughts expressed; meaning is masked by a symbolism that many writers find appealing. The writer, like the analyst, must interpret these symbols, as we see in Conrad Aiken's *Great Circle* (1933). Many mechanisms are at work in dreams: condensation, whereby materials are combined in images, puns, pormanteau words; displacement, which disfigures, distorts, and disguises material from the censor; inversion, whereby last things in a conventional scheme of priorities are put first. We see all these dream mechanisms at work in Joyce's *Finnegans Wake* (1939).

A major influence on writers is the concept of repression whereby unconscious impulses or drives are kept out of the consciousness, forcing the expression of self in disguises. The cause of such repressions may be a sudden physical and/or psychological shock or trauma or a complex (negative behavior pattern) slowly built up since childhood. Especially appealing to the writer is the compulsion neurosis, the desire to enact taboos, one of which is incest, as developed in Dorothy Baker's *Cassandra at the Wedding* (1962). Another, more frequently depicted, is homosexuality: André Gide's *The Immoralist* (1902); Radcliffe Hall's *The Well of Loneliness* (1928); Djuna

Barnes' *Nightwood* (1937); Gore Vidal's *The City and the Pillar* (1948);
Japanese Yukio Mishima's *Confessions of a Mask* (1958).

Thomas Mann was fascinated in many of his short works, as well as in
The Magic Mountain (1924) and *The Confessions of Felix Krull, Confidenc*
Man (1954), by the way the artist or genius expresses certain affinities wit
disease; an alien from society (which must pretend always to a general stat
of health) he understands disease, mental or physical; he is even inspired
it and often takes it as his subject.

The modern novel began with an interest in private, subjective exper
ence, (Richardson's *Pamela*, 1740); Marcel Proust and others made a new
start. Novel reading itself is a private experience, intensified when one rea
psychological analyses of private experience. The extreme expression of thi
impulse in fiction is an unconscious art that is closer to myth and magic, a
is thus more public, than to realistic depiction of behavior: this art is irrational, emotional, spontaneous, and feeds on unfettered memory and imag
nation. And the form it takes resembles the processes of the mind itself: a
psychological form.

THE PSYCHOLOGICAL ROMANCE

A number of psychological romances anticipated the more conscious
explorations of psychology in novels of the twentieth century: there were
Boccaccio, *L'Amorosa Fiametta* (1340–1345); Benjamin Constant, *Adolphe*
(1815); Augustin Charles Sainte-Beuve, *Volupté* (1832); Nathaniel Hawthorne, *The Scarlet Letter* (1850); Eugène Fromentin, *Dominique* (1862);
Gabriele D'Annunzio, *The Triumph of Death* (1894); Alain-Fournier, *The*
Wanderer (1913); Joseph Conrad, *Victory* (1915) Hermann Hesse, *Der Ste*
penwolf (1927); Mikhail Yurievich Lermontov, *A Hero of Our Time* (1839)

> I learned not long ago that Pechorin had died on his way back
> from Persia. This news gladdened me very much, it gave me the
> right to publish these notes. ...
>
> .   .   .
>
> While reading over these notes, I became convinced of the
> sincerity of this man who so mercilessly exhibited his own failings
> and vices. The history of a human soul, be it even the meanest
> soul, can hardly be less curious or less instructive than the history
> of an entire nation—especially when it is the result of self-
> observation on the part of a mature mind, and when it is written
> without the ambitious desire to provoke sympathy or amazement.

And the impressionistic romance uses various psychological processes: Emily Brontë's *Wuthering Heights* (1847) and Jean Giono's *Song of the World* (1934). The psychological melodrama is another type: Liam O'Flaherty, *The Informer* (1926); Faulkner's *Sanctuary* (1931); Graham Greene's *The Ministry of Fear* (1943); and Charles Jackson's *The Lost Weekend* (1944).

THE NOVEL OF PSYCHOLOGICAL REALISM

Realism is what most psychological novels strive for: Pierre Choderlos de Laclos' *Les Liaisons Dangereuses* (*Dangerous Acquaintances*, 1782); Dostoyevsky's *Crime and Punishment* (1866), *The Possessed* (1867), and *The Idiot* (1866–69); Ivan Turgenev, *Fathers and Sons* (1862); Spanish Juan Valera, *Pepita Jimenez* (1874); Henry James, *The Ambassadors* (1903); Luigi Pirandello, *The Late Mattia Pascal* (1904); Marcel Proust, *À La Recherche du Temps Perdu* (*Remembrance of Things Past*, 1913–1927); Ford Madox Ford, *The Good Soldier* (1915); French Sidonie Gabrielle Colette, *Cheri* (1920); James Joyce, *Portrait of the Artist as a Young Man* (1916); Italian Grazia Deledda, *The Mother* (1920); André Gide, *Les Faux Monnayeurs* (*The Counterfeiters*, 1927); François Mauriac, *Thérèse* (1927); Julien Green, *Leviathan* (*The Dark Journey*, 1929); Antoine de Saint-Exupéry, *Night Flight* (1931); Elizabeth Bowen, *Death of the Heart* (1938); George Bernanos, *The Diary of a Country Priest* (1937); William Styron, *Lie Down in Darkness* (1951); John Updike, *Rabbit, Run* (1960); Japanese Jun-ichiro Tanizaki, *The Key* (tr. 1961); and Virginia Woolf, *To the Lighthouse* (1927).

> No, she thought, putting together some of the pictures he had cut out—a refrigerator, a mowing machine, a gentleman in evening dress—children never forget. For this reason, it was so important what one said, and what one did, and it was a relief when they went to bed. For now she need not think about anybody. She could be herself, by herself. And that was what now she often felt the need of—to think; well, not even to think. To be silent; to be alone. All the being and the doing, expansive, glittering, vocal, evaporated; and one shrunk, with a sense of solemnity, to being oneself, a wedge-shaped core of darkness, something invisible to others.

THE NOVEL OF CONSCIOUSNESS

Another term for the psychological novel is novel of consciousness; the reader experiences a sense of how the mind and emotions function and the ways in which the characters experience consciousness of themselves; the senses are brought into full play, stimulated as much by memory as by pre-

sent events. We are given impressions rather than realistic reconstructions
actual life. Henri Bergson's concept of time and metaphysics was a strong
influence. (See Edel; Humphrey.)

The novel of consciousness took the reader into the immediate mental
processes of its characters, achieving a psychic intimacy. With a new self-
consciousness in the characters, what was striven for were self-realizations
and ultimately revelations that transcend self. When writers examined the
relation between the conscious self and reality, it was seen that with all
its inconsistencies, the self is a living field of consciousness; it has centers
of focus, moves like a stream, and has a quality of duration that makes it a
special kind of entity, enabling one to recapture oneself.

One method of showing forth the consciousness of the self was
expressionism—a means of expressing outwardly in an exaggerated image on
an action what the character feels inwardly. One way of developing and exploring the consciousness was to stimulate the senses; J.-K. Huysmans in
Against the Grain (1884) makes his character investigate natural sensations
and then he creates artificial ones, as another way of knowing one's mind
and body and the world outside them. It is a simultaneous process: self-
awareness causes awareness of the external reality, and the novelist tries to
convey these experiences of consciousness in a special moment (*epiphany*)
or flow of moments. This type of novel is composed of a series of *Gestalts*
that become compressed into a single *Gestalt* in the reader's own mind.
"The mind receives a myriad impressions—trivial, fantastic, evanescent, or
engraved with the sharpness of steel," says Virginia Woolf; "life is a luminous halo, a semi-transparent envelope surrounding us." The proper effect
such art is a kind of *vitalism* that heightens our feeling for life. A value of
this and other types of psychological novel is that it reveals to the reader
ways in which not just his social behavior but his mental processes makes
him akin to all men. "The novel is the highest example of subtle inter-
relatedness that man has discovered," said D. H. Lawrence.

The novel of consciousness offers impressions of reality: Dostoyevsky's
The Brothers Karamazov (1880); Norwegian Knut Hamsun's *Hunger* (1890);
Stephen Crane's *The Red Badge of Courage* (1895); John Dos Passos' *Man-
hattan Transfer* (1925); Hemingway's *A Farewell to Arms* (1929); Thomas
Wolfe's *Look Homeward, Angel* (1929) and *Of Time and the River* (1935); L
A. G. Strong's *The Garden* (1931); Albert Camus' *The Plague* (1947); and
Carson McCullers' *The Heart Is a Lonely Hunter* (1941).

> The hot afternoon passed slowly and Mick still sat on the step
> by herself. This fellow Motsart's music was in her mind again. It
> was funny, but Mister Singer reminded her of this music. She
> wished there was some place where she could go to hum it out

loud. Some kind of music was too private to sing in a house cram
full of people. It was funny, too, how lonesome a person could be
in a crowded house. Mick tried to think of some good private place
where she could go and be by herself and study about this music.
But though she thought about this a long time she knew in the beginning that there was no good place.

THE NOVEL OF PSYCHOLOGICAL FANTASY

Explorations of the subconscious produced psychological fantasies:
German Ernst Theodor Amadeus Hoffman, *Devil's Elixir* (1815); Spanish
Miguel de Unamuno, *Mist* (1928), a Pirandello-like novel in which the
characters confront their author, as characters do in Pirandello's play *Six
Characters in Search of an Author*; Mexican Juan Rulfo, *Pedro Paramo*
(1955); Jean Cocteau, *Les Enfants Terribles* (*The Holy Terrors*, 1929).

He was sinking. He was ebbing out towards Elisabeth, towards the snow, the Game, the Room, their childhood. Still by a
single thread of light the Maiden Goddess holds him out of darkness; his stone body is still penetrated by one last all-pervading
thought of life. Still his eyes held his sister; but she was nothing
more than a tall shape without identity, calling his name. For still
her finger on the trigger, like one clasped with her lover in the act
of love, Elisabeth watched and waited on his pleasure, cried out to
him to hasten to his mortal spasm, to accompany her into the final
moment of mutual rapture and possession, mutual death.

. . .

The Room has flown; all that remains is the foul breath of poison
and one small stranded figure, the figure of some woman, dwindl-
ing, fading, disappearing in the distance.

THE SYMBOLIC, ALLEGORICAL NOVEL

The novel had employed symbolism before the advent of psychology,
but mingled with psychological significance, symbolism took on new dimensions and possibilities. Among early symbolic allegories are Melville's *Mardi*
(1849) and *Moby Dick* (1851).

. . . . He was intent on an audacious, immitigable, and supernatural
revenge.
Here, then, was this gray-headed, ungodly old man, chasing

with curses a Job's whale round the world, at the head of a crew,
too, chiefly made up of mongrel renegades, and castaways, and
cannibals—morally enfeebled also, by the incompetence of mere
unaided virtue or rightmindedness in Starbuck, the invulnerable
jollity of indifference and recklessness in Stubb, and the pervading
mediocrity in Flask. Such a crew, so officered, seemed specially
picked and packed by some infernal fatality to help him to his
monomaniac revenge. How it was that they so aboundingly re-
sponded to the old man's ire—by what evil magic their souls were
possessed, that at times his hate seemed almost theirs; the White
Whale as much their insufferable foe as his; how all this came to
be—what the White Whale was to them, or how to their unconscious understandings, also, in some dim, unsuspected way, he
might have seemed the gliding great demon of the seas of life—all
this to explain, would be to dive deeper than Ishmael can go. The
subterranean miner that works in us all, how can one tell whither
leads his shaft by the evershifting, muffled sound of his pick?
Who does not feel the irresistible arm drag? What skiff in tow of a
seventy-four can stand still? For one, I gave myself up to the
abandonment of the time and the place; but while yet all a-rush to
encounter the whale, could see naught in that brute but the dead-
liest ill.

Friedrich de la Motte-Fouqué wrote *Undine* in 1811, and G. K. Chesterton
The Man Who Was Thursday in 1908. Then came Virginia Woolf's *Between
the Acts* (1941), Walter Van Tilburg Clark's *The Track of the Cat* (1949),
and Ernest Hemingway's *The Old Man and the Sea* (1952). Melville's *Billy
Budd,* first published in 1924, is an excellent example of symbolic tragedy.
A good example of realistic tragedy is Swedish Pär Fabian Lagerkvist's
Barabbas (1950). The symbolic novel overtly uses patterns of major and
minor symbols to create a more richly expressive context for realistic experience.

THE ANTI-HERO NOVEL

The chaos and relativism of psychological introspection in the novel of
consciousness, combined with the breakdown of social, religious, cultural,
and political institutions and absolutes, produced the anti-hero of existentialism. His predicament is dramatized in cataclysmic world events and in
instances of social injustice. Heroes are possible only in a world of relatively
stable concepts of character and patterns of behavior. Thus, we speak today
not of protagonists in conflict with antagonists, but of nonpersons dehumanized by psychological and cultural determinism, unjustly manipulated
by external forces or pathetically acting as their own antagonists. One might

even speak of the alienated novelist himself as the reader's antagonist, as in the novels of Céline, who says, "A style is an emotion"; that emotion is sometimes directed against the reader.

Self-scrutiny, combined with rapid changes in the outer environment, often produces an identity crisis. In striving for freedom, the characters of many contemporary novels often must first indulge themselves in and then attempt to overcome a perverse, alienated, divided selfhood through ironic self-consciousness; it may conceal the necessity for contrition. Some writers depict these "fractured selves" through a fractured structure and a capricious style. The self expresses itself indirectly, through masks. An extreme reaction to the "divided selfhood" is the cultivation of anti-selfhood. (See Ellmann, *Modern Tradition*.) The anti-hero novel depicts the psychological and physical agonies of a character at the mercy of his own pathetic weaknesses and a phalanx of dehumanizing social pressures.

The existential novel is a revival in France in the 1930's and 40's of the philosophical novel, based on the insights of Sartre and Camus (who rejected the term "existential," substituting the "absurd."). The existential philosophy rejects every type of orthodoxy, especially those based on absolutes; in this world of absurd freedom, man discovers faith in man by virtue of a common condition—existence in a world without God, without absolute meanings. The state of anxiety and dread of death, after which there is nothing, can result in faith in man, producing the will to communicate with other men in terms of basic concepts as opposed to absolute precepts. Existential writers found meaning in meaninglessness by basing their values on the nature of man's existence itself, on existence made up of moments of authentic being, of choices in the midst of absurdity. Thus, men may become committed to this world, engaged in its problems, a world in which existence precedes any kind of essence.

The anti-hero results from a recognition by serious writers, themselves alienated from bourgeois society, that the heroic character is an anachronism; he is the ideal of the middle class, which insists, even today, on reading novels about improbably heroic figures. Unable to believe in heroes, these writers have embraced the anti-hero with a perverse fervor that matches the masses' resolute belief that heroes are still possible. The anti-hero is the dominant figure in serious twentieth century literature. (See Kaufmann, *Existentialism* and Barrett, *Irrational Man*.) There are signs, however, that with the unconscious complicity of the mass media, the anti-hero view is slowly becoming, among all kinds of readers, a mere convention.

Here are only a few examples of the existential, anti-hero novel: Dostoyevsky, *Notes From Underground*, (1864); Jules Romains *Death of a Nobody* (1911); Franz Kafka, *The Trial* (1925); Louis-Ferdinand Céline, *Jour-*

ney to the End of the Night (1932); Jean-Paul Sartre, *Nausea* (1938); J. P.
Donleavy, *The Ginger Man* (1955); Simone de Beauvoir, *The Mandarins*
(1954); Samuel Beckett, *Malone Dies* (1956); Iris Murdoch, *A Severed
Head* (1961); Richard Farina, *Been Down So Long It Looks Like Up to Me*
(1966); and Albert Camus, *The Stranger* (1942).

Then he tried to change the subject by asking me why I
hadn't once addressed him as "Father," seeing that he was a
priest. That irritated me still more, and I told him he wasn't my
father; quite the contrary, he was on the others' side.

"No, no, my son," he said, laying his hand on my shoulder.
"I'm on *your* side, though you don't realize it—because your heart
is hardened. But I shall pray for you."

Then, I don't know how it was, but something seemed to
break inside me, and I started yelling at the top of my voice. I
hurled insults at him, I told him not to waste his rotten prayers on
me; it was better to burn than to disappear. I'd taken him by the
neckband of his cassock, and, in a sort of ecstasy of joy and rage, I
poured out on him all the thoughts that had been simmering in my
brain. He seemed so cocksure, you see. And yet none of his certainties was worth one strand of a woman's hair. Living as he did,
like a corpse, he couldn't even be sure of being alive. It might look
as if my hands were empty. Actually, I was sure of myself, sure
about everything, far surer than he; sure of my present life and of
the death that was coming. That, no doubt, was all I had; but at
least that certainty was something I could get my teeth into—just
as it had got its teeth into me. I'd been right, I was still right, I
was always right. I'd passed my life in a certain way, and I might
have passed it in a different way, if I'd felt like it. I'd acted thus,
and I hadn't acted otherwise; I hadn't done x, whereas I had done
y or z. And what did that mean? That, all the time, I'd been waiting for this present moment, for that dawn, tomorrow's or another
day's, which was to justify me. Nothing, nothing had the least importance, and I knew quite well why. He, too, knew why. From
the dark horizon of my future a sort of slow, persistent breeze had
been blowing toward me, all my life long, from the years that were
to come. And on its way that breeze had leveled out all the ideas
that people tried to foist on me in the equally unreal years I then
was living through. What difference could they make to me, the
deaths of others, or a mother's love, or his God; or the way a man
decides to live, the fate he thinks he chooses, since one and the
same fate was bound to "choose" not only me but thousands of mil
lions of privileged people who, like him, called themselves my
brothers. Surely, surely he must see that? Every man alive was
privileged; there was only one class of men, the privileged class.

All alike would be condemned to die on day; his turn, too, would come like the others. And what difference could it make if, after being charged with murder, he were executed because he didn't weep at his mother's funeral, since it all came to the same thing in the end?

KUNSTLERROMAN

The *Kunstlerroman* is a German type of novel that shows the development from childhood to young manhood of the artist; but the finest example is the work of an Irishman, James Joyce: *Portrait of the Artist as a Young Man* (1916). Another good example is Samuel Butler's *The Way of All Flesh* (1903).

It was after dinner, however, that he completed the conquest of his aunt. She then discovered that, like herself, he was passionately fond of music, and that, too, of the highest class. He knew, and hummed or whistled to her all sorts of pieces out of the works of the great masters, which a boy of his age could hardly be expected to know, and it was evident that this was purely instinctive, inasmuch as music received no kind of encouragement at Roughborough. There was no boy in the school as fond of music as he was. He picked up his knowledge, he said, from the organist of St. Michael's Church, who used to practice sometimes on a weekday afternoon. Ernst had heard the organ booming away as he was passing outside the church and had sneaked inside and up into the organ loft. In the course of time the organist became accustomed to him as a familiar visitant, and the pair became friends.

It was this which decided Alethea that the boy was worth taking pains with. "He likes the best music," she thought, "and he hates Dr. Skinner. This is a very fair beginning." When she sent him away at night with a sovereign in his pocket (and he had only hoped to get five shillings) she felt as though she had had a good deal more than her money's worth for her money.

This type follows a new development in the novel itself and a new attitude of the bourgeoise toward it: the novel as a work of art, the novelist himself as solely an artist, a concept that became contagious after Flaubert, who did not himself write a novel about the formation of an artist.

THE PURE NOVEL—A NOT-YET-REALIZED TYPE

Two kinds of writers have written about two general types of artists. In *The Birth of Tragedy,* Nietzsche describes two kinds of "art-drives": 1) "the

Apollonian," which represents culture, civilization, classicism, reason, the artificial in art, but a kind of healing vision; and 2) "the Dionysian," which represents anarchy, primitive instincts, unleashed psychic energy, nature, the senses, ecstasy, orgiastic outpourings, intoxication, narcosis, romanticism. A third type of art tries to achieve a synthesis of this dichotomy. The spectacle of the Dionysians has inspired the belief even among artists that the will to art is unnatural; certain Apollonians argue that art is more artifice than "real" experience.

Although some writers and critics see the imagination and nature in conflict, most argue an interaction; too much stress on the role of nature in artistic creation has caused periods of revolt against nature. The relation between imagination and thought reflects Nietzsche's dichotomy: art should produce doubt not certainty; it should draw no conclusions; some even argue that it should not transmit ideas. Keats proposed a "negative capability." There has been a perpetual argument over the importance of style as opposed to subject, and whether style should be simple or magnificent; the Apollonian insists that the style should be appropriate to the subject; thought and expression should be harmonious with each other. *Vorticism* was a classical revival in poetry by T. E. Hulme in 1914 that affected attitudes about fiction.

The two kinds of artists argue about rules, laws, precepts, principles, the Apollonian insisting that rules set limitations which free the artist and that classical works are the source of these rules; the Dionysian rebels against all rules as unnatural inhibitors of freedom and decries slavish limitation of the classics. Romantics follow nature, not rules. Georges de Scudéry argues for rules: "The works of the spirit are too significant to be left to chance; and I had rather be accused of having failed consciously, than of having succeeded without knowing what I was about. . . . " Discipline more than inspiration produces great art. The Apollonian knows that, as novelist Séan O'Faoláin says, "the art of writing is rewriting." He knows that all art is by its nature artificial, that what seems to be natural today will appear artificial in the future; a work of art is an artifice by definition. But the Dionysian declares that any kind of artifice destroys the illusion of reality, whether it is internal or external. To the romantic, formal excellence is no criterion for art; in opposition to the classic demand for balance, he may strive for deliberate imbalance. The classicist would strive for purgation of all impure feelings and thoughts; the romantic immerses himself in such elements and absorbs them into his being. To the classicist, excellence of expression is sublime; but the romantic reaches back and forth across the spectrum from the sublime to the ridiculous. He strives not to arrange aesthetic pleasure for a spectator, but rather to engage a reader so fully as a co-creator that he experiences aesthetic joy rather than repose.

The desire to create a pure novel is a classical or Apollonian impulse. The pure novel strives to create a world as constricted as a lyrical poem. Flaubert aspired to write a novel with no people in it. A product of the art for art's sake sensibility, the pure novel depends as little as possible on any carry-over into the real world; it tries to contain every aspect of the experience within the work itself: "... the pure novel (and in art, as in everything else, purity is the only thing I care about)," says Gide's writer-hero in *Les Faux Monnayeurs (The Counterfeiters,* 1925). The French popular novelist, Georges Simenon, whom Gide admired, said, "I would like to carve my novel in a piece of wood." Simenon continues:

> The "pure" novel will do only what the novel can do. I mean that it doesn't have to do any teaching or any work of journalism. In a pure novel you wouldn't take sixty pages to describe the South or Arizona. ... Just the drama, with only what is absolutely part of this drama. What I think about novels today is almost a translation of "the rules of tragedy into the novel."

Simenon believes that the novel, like tragedy, should be short enough to enable a reader to absorb it in one sitting. It should be, one might add, as brief as a movie and as unified in its effects and impressions as a poem.

The novels of James M. Cain suggest that the novel should raise and answer its own necessary questions and depend as little as possible upon anything beyond the bounds of its own immediacy. All fictive elements should effect one clean, simple thrust, as do the first twenty-three pages of *The Postman Always Rings Twice,* Cain's nearest realization of the "pure" novel. Like a piece of music, a "pure" novel should be an experience that has rhythm, tempo, style, movement, pattern, motif; it is generated by time or pace, following (to use a term from drama) a "spine."

While the novelist, by the very nature of his medium, cannot entirely avoid making moral and social value judgments, writers in one tradition have tried since Flaubert, Valéry, and Verlaine to make the novel or the poem as "pure" a work of art as a statue. For instance, in Rodin's sculpture we find subject and treatment; but form and space provide the most exciting aspects of the experience. Stephen quotes Aquinas in Joyce's *Portrait of the Artist as a Young Man:* "That is beautiful the apprehension of which pleases." Necessary to aesthetic stasis are wholeness, harmony, and radiance. Is it possible for a novel to possess any of these qualitites to the extent that the plastic arts—and also those forms devoid of apparent subject matter, music and architecture—do? Stephen argues that "art necessarily divides itself into three forms, progressing from one to the next"—the lyrical, the epical, and the dramatic, "the form wherein [the artist] presents his image in immediate relation to others." It is to this last, and finest, form that the "pure" novel belongs. "Pure" means to the novel what "nonobjective" means to painting. To paraphrase Archibald MacLeish, a pure novel should not *mean* but *be*. The serious reader returns to Cain's *The Postman* not for its meaning, or even for its characters, but to experience *again* an aesthetic emotion. He regards thought and content as seriously as he would if he were looking at a loaded gun on a table.

The artistic novelist sometimes tries to achieve parallels or analogies with other arts. "All art," said Walter Pater, "aspires to the condition of music." Artistic success often proves to be in areas common to all or most arts anyway; what is called musical structure in certain novels is really a property of literature itself, simply used more deliberately. "What I should like to do is something like the art of fugue writing," said Gide's author-character in *Les Faux Monnayeurs*. "And I can't see why what was possible in music should be impossible in literature. ..." Painting, drama, and poetry also have provided forms that enhanced the artistic novel.

The poetic novel is mainly a use of language and imagery as concentrate as poetry: Lautréamont (Isidore Lucien Ducasse) *Maldoror* (1868–69). Man novelists have wanted most of all to be poets (Thomas Hardy, Thomas Wolfe while few poets have wanted to be novelists, several poets have written good nvoels: e. e. cummings, *The Enormous Room* (1922), an autobiographical work; Conrad Aiken, *The Great Circle* (1933); William Carlos Williams, *White Mule* (1937); Lawrence Ferlinghetti, *Her* (1960). Tennesse Williams—primarily a playwright, but also a novelist—has written many short stories but only two novels, *The Roman Spring of Mrs. Stone* (1950) and *Moise and the World of Reason* (1975). Some novelists have written works with the care and precision of the best modern poetry: Virginia Woolf, *The Waves* (1931). And Flaubert saw affinities between his classical sort of fiction artist and the scientist; the novel should become as objective and precise as science.

Ever since the English poet Swinburne defiantly and proudly asserted the importance of "art for art's sake," there has been a misunderstanding about this phrase—even though few writers ever repeated it approvingly. The popular image became that of the artist in his garret or Ivory tower. Swinburne was mainly arguing against the prevailing insistence that literature convey a moral; Baudelaire called this moral imperative "the heresy of didacticism." Both Dionysian and Apollonian writers have taken this attitud about art: that it is something that has a value in itself. For the classicist, ar is an objective artifact, impersonal, held in stasis; for the romantic, it is the product of individual, personal, subjective, spontaneous expression of one's inner being.

Few novelists have thought of themselves as aesthetes. Oscar Wilde did, and he has expressed the art-for-art's-sake philosophy best: "Art never expresses anything but itself." "The only beautiful things are the things that do not concern us." "Life imitates Art far more than Art imitates Life." "Lying, the telling of beautiful untrue things, is the proper aim of Art."

Art-for-Art's-sake, the image of the aesthete writing from an ivory tower (or a grimy garret), disdainful of any audience but himself, and possibly his friends, expresses a hostility to conscious art as it if were a threat to life itself. But if life is superior, why read at all? Some writers have considered style as absolute; they are not far from primitive conceptions of creation or from the Christian "in the beginning was the Word." Many people feel that a work of fiction must justify its existence by being something more than a pleasure achieved through hard work by both creator and perceiver; it must perform some utilitarian function, from bearing ideas about the "real" world to providing escape from it. Reacting against this demand, some writers have tried to achieve pure poetry, pure fiction, with as few extensions beyond itself as possible—a self-contained experience, like non-objective painting. But unlike geometrical shapes and colors, words are not pure abstractions.

A little more acceptable is the conviction that art transforms the world into a greater reality. Poems, says poet Marianne Moore, are "imaginary gardens with real toads in them." Gatsby—Fitzgerald's creation—is larger than all his real-life models put together; he transcends mortality and will live forever in Fitzgerald's work of art, *The Great Gatsby* (1925); so will Huck Finn; and not just characters, but places: Joyce's Dublin, Dickens' London, Faulkner's Mississippi. And moments such as Don Quixote attacking the windmills; Gatsby's reunion with Daisy; Meursault confronting the Arab; Jake Barnes fishing at Burgette; Heathcliff at Cathy's deathbed. Man's ability to make things makes him human; his ability to transform things makes his potential for transcendence palpable.

From this attitude evolved a kind of "aesthetic mysticism," the notion of art as an aristocratic mystery. (See Ellmann, *Modern Tradition*.) Flaubert said to despondent Guy de Maupassant, "Sacrifice everything to Art." Some call this attitude, at its worst, snobbery; the writer writes for himself and/or perhaps for a small knowing group who are better than the average reader, the vulgar public; serious writing versus commercial writing; and the snob takes pleasure in being one of the elite. The classical writers pictured the ideal, or proposed at least a reaching for it, and they created a love of the ideal itself as art embodied it; the romantic yearned to achieve an ideal state of consciousness and express it in all its frenzy. Perfection, though perhaps unattainable, was the end of learning, and the purpose of literature, said the classicist, is to show perfection of character. Out of this attitude was bound to come the concept of the autonomy of art, of purity, of the nondidactic, and of the notion of the permanence of art and the aesthetic principles that produced it and of the true and the good portrayed in it; a work's likelihood to have permanence was a sign of greatness. Though they longed for some sort of spiritual transcendence, the romantics were just as concerned with the imperfect and the transient.

Around the turn of the century, for both Apollonian and Dionysian, art became a modern absolute. Aesthetic quality came to have a moral dimension after all, for we judge artistic fiction good if its authors or characters revere the aesthetic experience and if the book is aesthetically fine. For art transforms life and such a transformation is a moral act improving life. It is art that establishes certain values. Art is an ethical experience; perhaps even a religious experience; certainly, some writers seem to have been prophets. (See Ellmann, *Modern Tradition.*) "To be hopeful in an artistic sense," said Conrad, "it is not necessary to think that the world is good."

PART II: TECHNIQUES

Henry James said that we must grant the writer his *donnee,* that is, the basic materials he starts with and the technical approach he takes. We may quarrel only with the way he handles the elements he has chosen. James implies, rightly, that any form, any content is admissable to the house of fiction, within its million windows. Few critics seriously disagree. Critics only *seem*—to each other as well as to their readers—to be prescriptive in their theories. There are conventional techniques (once experimental, now assimilated into the tradition of the novel) and there are experimental or special techniques. The two often intermingle in today's novels, as in Thomas Pynchon's *Gravity's Rainbow,* John Barth's *Giles Goat-Boy,* and David Madden's *Bijou.* Eclecticism, a fusion of diverse techniques, less than tradition or experimentalism, characterizes fiction today.

A study of techniques entails a study of all the other arts, for techniques and terms from one are often appropriated by others. The novel is so lacking in terms of its own origination that, more than any other art form, it draws heavily on others for devices to create and words to describe its own processes. And because, more than any other form, all life is its province, some assert that the novel cannot, in fact, be an art, except in isolated instances—for instance, a short novel such as *The Great Gatsby.* The novel, they maintain, is some other kind of experience, not inferior to art forms—simply different. But let us continue to speak of the novel as an art form.

A technique is any method a writer uses, consciously or unconsciously, to stimulate a response in his reader. In the broadest sense, technique is the combination of methods a writer uses to present his raw material. "Literature," said the French symbolist poet Paul Valéry, "is the art of playing on the minds of others." On that assumption, Wayne C. Booth wrote one of the great works of fiction theory, *The Rhetoric of Fiction.* The rhetoric of fiction is a congeries of techniques that enable the writer to persuade his reader to accept the world he is creating and to respond to it in the way he wishes, with the purpose of achieving maximum effects on all levels of the experience.

The term *style* is sometimes used to include technique; one hears of a particular writer's style in this sense more often than his technique. Style

differs somewhat from technique in that style, the arrangement of words f
specific effects, is the medium through which techniques are employed.
Style is one aspect of the larger realm of technique. But if style is taken to
mean the author's handling of words, and technique to mean his handling
all facets of the work, then style is included in the concept of technique.

Novelist-critic Mark Schorer said, in "Technique as Discovery,"
perhaps the single most influential essay in modern criticism: "When we
speak of technique, then, we speak of nearly everything. For technique . .
is the only means" the writer "has of discovering, exploring, developing h
subject, of conveying its meaning, and, finally, of evaluating it." Dostoyevsky recognized his own limitations in that respect: "Yes, that was and
ever is my greatest torment—I never can control my material . . . I have
allowed myself to be transported by poetic enthusiasm." Philip Rahv ("Fic
tion and the Criticism of Fiction") expresses a point of view in opposition
Schorer's and to all New Critics. Dostoyevsky's greatness, he says, lies not
in his style but in his scenes, in the kind of life-experiences that revitalized
narrative fiction in the early realistic phases of the development of the
novel. What matters, he says, is realistic detail more than aesthetic form,
which is too often discussed in terms of poetry, thus impeding our understanding of the nature of fiction. What is most important in Proust is sensi
bility, not a learned technique. There is too much emphasis on interpretation, on locating symbols, which some seem to think demonstrates excellence in a work, says Rahv; the life forces in a novel, which encourage con
trary reactions, are neglected because aesthetic elements lend themselves
more readily to critical analysis.

It is true that discussions of technique predicate, to some extent at
least, the viability of aesthetic constants, values, rules, and norms out of
great traditions, and of criteria in relation, as Booth says, to author, reader
and the work itself. But that point did come when *someone* devised a few
concepts, deriving them in part from the Classical tradition that nurtured
him: ". . . I am, in reality, the founder of a new province of writing," said
Henry Fielding, "so I am at liberty to make what laws I please therein."
Some of the criteria that have evolved are appropriateness, consistency,
simplicity (or complexity, depending on other factors), subtlety; whether to
tell in narrative summaries or to *show* in dramatic scenes; the importance
avoiding anachronisms and antiquarianisms. There are many ways to see
techniques at work in a novel; one might begin by reading the author himself as he discusses the germination and development of his own work. (Se
Novelists on the Novel, Allott, ed.)

As a demi-god creating a world, the writer must exert *control* over all
the elements of his creation. To most writers, this control means being crit

cally conscious at some crucial stage in the process of composing the novel. "Interest in the technicalities of his art can alone prevent the mind dulling, the imagination losing power," said Graham Greene ("Fiction," *The Spectator*). Other writers regard control as dishonest, unnatural; in their own way, they are being true to fact, that is, to life as it is lived; the other kind of writer is being true to art, an artificer in his own right, not an unconscious mirror or an ape of god.

Some writers mistake the notion of control for lack of freedom; for them freedom is, or ought to be, the natural state of man; therefore, to write out of this freedom is to depict man as he *is*, deep down, or should be once again—a natural man, feeling what comes naturally. Such writers must pretend that they are not using mechanical symbols, such as words, as the essence of their creation, and that they are free of the influence of everything they have ever read that works differently from their own writing. The conscious artist, on the other hand, does not deny influences, nor even that imitation contributes to his formation (Faulkner admitted the influence of Conrad and Thomas Wolfe); he is in control because he knows what he creates, and he creates deliberately. He does not mistake self-discipline for externally-imposed discipline, or self control for external control. Freedom lies in being able to control whatever creation one chooses to become engaged in. "Be always faithful to the conception of a limit," said T. E. Hulme.

The writer takes no risks when he thinks of himself as totally free. And it is only in taking risks within a context of self-imposed control that one sees all the possibilities of one's material and avoids missing opportunities for creating effects that reveal the deepest essence of one's subject. Such a writer shares with the reader his pleasure in skillfully executing his mastery. In wilfully choosing not to be in control, a writer becomes a slave to chance—sometimes with very interesting results, it must be admitted; and the controlled artist may sometimes end in controlling only a robot. But generally when we examine a good novel, we find that what is good in it is the result of control.

Technique enables a writer to discover possibilities in his raw material that would otherwise remain submerged in it. *Raw material* is the subject matter the writer processes through imagination, conception, and *technique* into a story. "By raw material," says Wright Morris, "I mean that comparatively crude ore that has not yet been processed by the imagination—what we refer to as *life*, or as experience, in contrast to art. By technique I mean the way the artist smelts this material down for human consumption. ... Technique and raw material are dramatized at the moment that the shaping imagination is aware of itself"(*The Territory Ahead*). Specific techniques may be most naturally appropriate for transforming a particular kind of raw material. In *The Field of Vision*, Morris used a multiple point of view technique to transform the fragments of his raw material.

The raw materials of a work are drawn from nature and society; the author must be true to nature and to life in his society even as he reconceives and recreates it in his imagination, which is a recombining agent that makes a new perspective or vision occur (Melville, and, recently, Gabriel Márquez). Even when it must operate within the strictest externally or internally imposed limitations, what holds a reader is the author's imagination and his techniques for conceptualizing those elements he expects will make us feel his imagination at work. "The materials have to take the place of God," said Sherwood Anderson.

It is not enough to be in control of the elements of one's creation; one must also achieve a *conception* about the entire body of raw material out of which one creates. Content with random effects and sensations and bizarre images, the spontaneous writer never strives for a conception. While it is true that "there is nothing in the intellect that is not first in the senses" (Aristotle), it is also true that "Feeling does not make poetry" (Flaubert). Conception is a willed act of intelligence wedded to imagination.

The opposite of a conception is a *notion*, the kind of clever premise that comes often and easily to the inventive mind. A notion can usually be formulated in the question: "What would happen if. . . ?" A notion is a launching pad. Most stories begin with a notion; many never transcend notion into the realm of conception.

A genuine conception offers the reader a different kind of experience. An intuitive fusion of emotion and idea produces a conception. A conception is a total, *gestalt*-like grasp of the story that enables the author to control the development of the situation, the characters, theme, plot, style, and technique, so that in the end they cohere, as in a single charged image. A concept orders, interprets, and gives form to the raw material of the story and infuses it with vision and meaning. Notion-mongering freezes the imagination and many opportunities are missed; a conception frees it to explore all possibilities. This fusion of raw material, imagination, and conception is best seen today in the 19 novels of Wright Morris. His concept of the hero and the witness is at work not only in his own novel, *The Field of Vision*, but also in *Don Quixote, Moby Dick, Lord Jim, The Great Gatsby, A the King's Men, The Heart Is a Lonely Hunter, A Separate Peace,* and *One Flew Over the Cuckoo's Nest*. In the conceptualizing process, intuition remains important, as expressed by F. Scott Fitzgerald: "All good writing is swimming under water and holding your breath."

The kind and degree of *distance* between the writer and his raw material and between the reader and the experience the novel offers determine a great deal. There are several kinds of distance: perceptual, conceptual, psychic, aesthetic, authorial, tonal, time and space, social, moral and emotional. A novel may suffer if the distance is too near, or too far.

The author's attitude determines the distance he has from his material. A writer's attitude toward his *raw material* or his subject is revealed in the *tone* of his narrative voice. "Everything is in the tone," said Sherwood Anderson, whose own was generally that of the old-fashioned teller of tales. The pervasive tone of a work can be tragic, comic, ironic, skeptical, pessimistic, compassionate, sentimental, and so on. The author's distance in relation to his story affects his tone. It is important that the tone be appropriate to the kind of experience a writer is trying to create. Compare the satirical with the lyrical attitude: the one is relatively cold, far, and formal; the other warm, near, and intimate. A writer can hardly create a tragedy if he is too close to his characters; intimacy may produce pathos, or even bathos, instead of tragedy. Distance is greater in the comic than in the serious novel.

Aesthetic (or psychic) distance is a theatrical term that refers to the degree of objectivity audience and writer have toward the characters and the action. Paradoxically, by being removed, we are able to experience more intensely, but without losing our ability to see the action in some larger perspective. Some writers want to destroy this distance and immerse the reader; some want to widen it even further with alienation effects to achieve didactic aims. Aesthetic distance (a tautology since "aesthetic" originally meant distance) is achieved through the techniques of art as perceived, intellectually and emotionally, by the reader.

Flaubert argued that the master writer, as a pure creative force, must, like the architect and the composer, achieve an impersonal relation to his creation. "The less one feels a thing, the more likely one is to express it as it really is." Joyce put this attitude of detachment into an epigram: "The artist, like the God of creation, remains within or behind or beyond or above his handiwork, invisible, refined out of existence, indifferent, paring his fingernails." The writer's field of consciousness may be narrow, constricted (Joyce's *Portrait of the Artist as a Young Man*) or extensive (Joyce's *Ulysses*), promoting subjectivity or objectivity; the degree will produce different kinds of work. In the 1830's, the French Parnassians Victor Hugo, Alfred de Vigny, Alphonse de Lamartine, Théophile Gautier insisted on an objectivity that would produce poetry as impersonal as sculpture; the English Parnassians Algernon Swinburne and Edmund Gosse of the 1870's kept this attitude in force, and it affected some fiction writers.

Every writer is stretched on a rack, some on the rack of their own su
jectivity, others on a rack especially designed by them to produce a transcendent agony. The subjectivity rack produces the *inspiration fallacy* or
conviction that the writer is able to plug into the Muses' Switchboard and
receive inspiration from a divine power source. Such writers often seem o
sessed with what Plato called "poetic madness." Although Wordsworth
spoke of "emotion recollected in tranquility," the Romantics made frequen
use of the Muses' Switchboard. On the me-rack, writers, especially young
writers, sacrifice themselves to the two-headed god subjectivity/self-
expression. The *hysterical discovery of the obvious* fallacy follows from the
conviction that the axis of the universe is the author's own navel. And on
broader plane, me-rack writings produce the *fallacy of expressive form*, th
conviction that if the writer's feelings are sufficiently intense their reflecti
in the work will be a true expression of those feelings. Readers often disto
a novel or poem by insisting that such and such is the poet's *real* intentio
Writers themselves sometimes work out of mistaken intentions. The compulsion to report on actual events results in the *it-really-happened* fallacy.
There is an even greater suffocation of imagination in the *it-really-
happened-to-ME* fallacy.

The writer who places great value on intuition or inspiration as oppos
to the rational working out of a novel belongs to a category that includes
many fine novelists (Thomas Wolfe, Henry Miller, Louis-Ferdinand Célin
Certainly most novelists write their first drafts spontaneously, in response
intuition. Many finished novels include bursts of lyricism, stretches of
seemingly spontaneous writing and the effect is dramatic immediacy, whic
creates and sustains the illusion of reality: the author, or the character, is
really, right now, feeling this way. "The sudden gut joy of beer when the
visions of great words in rhythmic order all in one giant archangel book go
roaring thru my brains" (Jack Kerouac, *The Subterraneans*). But the write
who is primarily lyrical or subjective places great value on *spontaneity*, as
sign of sincerity, as opposed to fabrication or calculation; he refuses to alte
the product of that spontaneous process. In a few cases, that process produces some fine, though limited, writers. The reader's interest, however,
less aesthetic than biographical: he wants to see what Jack Kerouac or
Thomas Wolfe is really like, through exposure to the uninhibited action of
naked consciousness. Or the reader simply enjoys the sensation of seeing
sensitive person's emotions reacting to life's erratic events.

The notion of spontaneous creation as a virtue and a value is restricte
almost entirely to certain modern types of painting, dance, sculpture,
poetry, and fiction. (The illusion of spontaneity is too labored in a play or
concert, which must be rehearsed.) Few people want to live in a spontane
ously built house or sit on a spontaneous chair or fly in a spontaneous
airplane. But they like to feel that there is some area of human experience

where spontaneity is possible and viable. Writers and readers sometimes make a cult of spontaneity and attempt to carry it over into a life-style; they often make the discovery that life is where it works best, and give up writing and reading altogether. Ken Kesey stopped writing after his second novel *Sometimes a Great Notion* (1964). The charge is often made that this sort of creation is self-indulgent, a form of daydreaming, a charge few young writers seldom make, however, engaged as they are in the that sort of writing. For the uninitiated reader, the result of self-indulgence is obscurity and irrelevance. The author of free writing claims an unearned relevance to the lives of others; in the Sixties, nothing was considered more relevant than freedom of expression itself, regardless of content or excellence. But other writers claim that the best moments of literature are the product of self-imposed discipline in solving problems posed by externally and self-imposed limitations; the result is freedom of a different sort.

Lack of control often produces ambiguity. Ambiguity occurs in a novel when an element (statement, action, or symbol, for instance) lends itself to more than one interpretation. Ambiguity is the result of unresolved conflicts between one possibility and another, as in the endings of *A High Wind in Jamaica, or The Innocent Voyage* by Richard Hughes and *Lord of the Flies* by William Golding. Sometimes a style may be characterized as frequently ambiguous, unintentionally, if the writer is unaware of what he is doing and lacks control; deliberately, if he wants the reader to explore possibilities and experience the tensions among them, causing a deeper involvement in the story and thus a more lucid revelation perhaps at the end (Faulkner's *Light in August*). Unintentional ambiguity results in obscurity; it is often the result of confusion in the author's mind as to the meaning of his ideas or of inability to express his ideas clearly. Uncontrolled ambiguity promotes a kind of subjectivity in the reader by encouraging him to merge with the author (usually subjectively involved himself) and the characters (usually self-reflective).

Sometimes the writer lacks *distance* on his material because the *subject* itself overwhelms him. When the artist or the hack is so bemused by the timeliness, the controversy, the strangeness, the importance, the subjective relevance of his raw material that he neglects the mysterious dictates of art, he is in the act of writing a *subject-dominated novel* (Madden, *Poetic Image in Six Genres*). The writer is so overwhelmed by his subject, which may be an idea or a thesis, or something more spectacular, such as sex, war, or dope, that he is blind to the problems of craft that must be solved if the novel is to be a work of the imagination, a work of art. Overwhelmed by his vision of a reform or his awareness of his reader's given interest in his subject, he neglects the art of handling that subject in novelistic terms. The *naturalists* fostered the notion that the writer's function is to reproduce "a slice of life." The *imitation fallacy* assumes that art and life are synonymous.

The process is, however, marvelously reciprocal, for life imitates art quite frequently, and sometimes quite terrifyingly. The writer who is a creator does not praise his work because it is "just like life," but because it heightens our awareness of ordinary life; he does not claim that the events in his novel "really happened," but that they "really happened in my imagination." In Ralph Ellison's *Invisible Man*, one of the most successful novel about blacks in the North and the South, outrage has been refined into art Ezra Pound said, "Literature is news that *stays* news." A sensational subje matter is not enough.

With or without the effects of aesthetic distance, every novel provides perspective on life, and some achieve a larger dimension by creating some context of myth, religion, philosophy, history (Scott's *Heart of Midlothian*) science, mysticism, or social significance (the naturalists). *Allusion* is one device that enables the writer to evoke an added dimension. An allusion is reference to a person, event, or aspect of culture which a writer assumes most of his readers will recognize. A literary allusion may evoke a familiar line from a poem, or a character from a novel or play. Some of the effects the novels of Cocteau and Joyce, Camus' *The Fall*, Walker Percy's *The Moviegoer*, depend upon such allusions. "No, I am not a spook like those who haunted Edgar Allan Poe," says the narrator of Ralph Ellison's *Invisib Man*. Fiction casts a spell most intensely when the reader feels that the ill sion which fiction seeks to create and the larger dimensions that emanate from it come from a master faculty or dominant psychic state, which we sense, for instance, in Faulkner, but not in Truman Capote. Most successf works of the imagination, however, do succeed at least in giving us a sense of mystery, wonder, exhilaration, and in satisfying the curiosity they stimu late in the reader. And the kind, quality, and degree of all these elements are determined by varieties of distance.

Let us look at some of the techniques writers have at their command. Techniques are used, of course, in combinations; thus a novel cited to illus trate one technique may serve just as well for others. No novel embodies techniques to the same degree or in the same way; some are emphasized more in one novel than in another; not every novel utilizes them all.

A study of technique has the same general usefulness for the reader a for the writer—it provides a guide to understanding what makes a novel e press what it does. Each reader, each writer, must make his own use of these techniques, in his own way.

Most of the techniques discussed apply to other forms of writing, and in different ways to other art media. And most of the techniques apply jus as well to a study of the short story—both for readers and writers—as they do to a study of the novel. Some of the concepts discussed here—conflict, characterization, theme—are elements of fiction rather than techniques, but they are best examined in the process of talking about techniques.

POINT OF VIEW

The reader responds to the voice of a creator, surrenders himself to an authority. Where does that authority, the author, stand in relation to his work? The writer uses many techniques that are artificial, but their purpose is to create an illusion of reality. The writer must make technical choices. And the technique that most directly affects the choice and use of all others is *point-of-view*. Everything in a novel is told through a certain point-of-view from which the writer decides to tell the story.

There are three major types of point-of-view: 1) Omniscient; 2) first person; and 3) third person/central intelligence. The omniscient author is godlike; the author sees, hears, feels, knows all; he moves anywhere he wishes, in time and space, giving us objective views of his characters' actions, or subjective views of their thoughts. The omniscient author tells us his story in the third person. Tolstoy's *Anna Karenina:*

> Happy families are all alike; every unhappy family is unhappy in its own way.
> Everything was in confusion in the Oblonsky household. The wife had discovered that the husband was carrying on an affair with their former French governess, and she had announced to her husband that she could not go on living in the same house with him. This situation had now lasted three days, and not only the husband and wife, but also all the members of their family and household, were painfully conscious of it. Every person in the house felt that there was no sense in their living together, and that people who met by chance in any inn had more in common with one another than they, the members of the Oblonsky family and household. The wife did not leave her own room; the husband had not been home for three days. The children ran wild all over the house; the English governess quarreled with the housekeeper, and wrote to a friend asking her to look out for a new position for her; the chef had walked out the day before just at dinnertime; the servants' cook and the coachman had given notice.

Other examples of novels using the omniscient point of view are: Henry Fielding, *Tom Jones;* Laurence Sterne, *Tristram Shandy;* William Thackeray, *Vanity Fair;* Anthony Trollope, *Barchester Towers;* Nikolai Gogol, *Dead Souls;* Honoré de Balzac, *Père Goriot;* Charles Dickens, *A Tale of Two Cities;* George Eliot, *Mill on the Floss;* George Meredith, *The Ordeal* of *Richard Feverel;* Ivan Turgenev, *Fathers and Sons;* Sherwood Anderson *Poor White;* E. M. Forster, *Howard's End;* John O'Hara, *Appointment in Samarra.*

2) First person: the author surrenders part of his control over the elements of the story by allowing one of the characters to tell it. We experience only what that character sees, hears, feels, knows, while the author works in the background. The character-narrator combines his own subjective thoughts and feelings with his role as omniscient story-teller. Hemingway's *The Sun Also Rises:*

> "Don't be sentimental."
> "You make me ill."
> We kissed good night and Brett shivered. "I'd better go," she said. "Good night, darling."
> "You don't have to go."
> "Yes."
> We kissed again on the stairs and as I called for the cordon the concierge muttered something behind her door. I went back upstairs and from the open window watched Brett walking up the street to the big limousine drawn up to the curb under the arclight. She got in and it started off. I turned around. On the table was an empty glass and a glass half-full of brandy and soda. took them both out to the kitchen and poured the half-full glass down the sink. I turned off the gas in the dining-room, kicked off my slippers sitting on the bed, and got into bed. This was Brett, that I had felt like crying about. Then I thought of her walking up the street and stepping into the car, as I had last seen her, and of course in a little while I felt like hell again. It is awfully easy to b hard-boiled about everything in the daytime, but at night it is another thing.

Other examples of first person point of view are: F. Scott Fitzgerald, *The Great Gatsby;* Ford Madox Ford, *The Good Soldier;* Defoe, *Moll Flanders* Twain, *Huckleberry Finn;* W. Somerset Maugham, *The Razor's Edge* (in which Maugham is not only the narrator but a character, under his own name, as well). As a means of controlling (and thus releasing) the tremendous romantic-demonic energy of Heathcliff and Cathy, Emily Brontë uses two other characters as first person narrators. A male voice, Mr. Lockwood's, frames the story, most of which Nellie Dean tells. Brontë moves from Lockwood's to Nellie's voice in this passage from *Wuthering Heights:*

> She returned presently, bringing a smoking basin, and a basket of work; and, having placed the former on the hob, drew in her seat, evidently pleased to find me so companionable.

> Before I came to live here, she commenced—waiting no further invitation to her story—I was almost always at Wuthering Heights. ...

3) Third person/central intelligence: A combination of omniscient and first person, this point-of-view technique allows the reader to experience everything from inside a single character, but the story is told in the third person; all the elements are filtered through a single character (the central intelligence), revealing his personality. James Joyce, *Portrait of the Artist as a Young Man:*

> It was not thought nor vision though he knew vaguely that her figure was passing homeward through the city. Vaguely first and then more sharply he smelt her body. A conscious unrest seethed in his blood. Yes, it was her body he smelt: a wild and languid smell: the tepid limbs over which his music had flowed desirously and secret soft linen upon which her flesh distilled odour and a dew.
>
> A louse crawled over the nape of his neck and, putting his thumb and forefinger deftly beneath his loose collar, he caught it. He rolled its body, tender yet brittle as a grain of rice, between thumb and finger for an instant before he let it fall from him and wondered would it live or die. There came to his mind a curious phrase from Cornelius a Lapide which said that the lice born of human sweat were not created by God with the other animals on the sixth day. But the tickling of the skin of his neck made his mind raw and red. The life of his body, ill clad, ill fed, louse eaten, made him close his eyelids in a sudden spasm of despair: and in the darkness he saw the brittle bright bodies of lice falling from the air and turning often as they fell. Yes; and it was not darkness that fell from the air. It was brightness.
> *Brightness falls from the air.*

Other examples of third person/central intelligence: Henry James, *The Ambassadors;* John Cheever, *Falconer;* Truman Capote, *Other Rooms, Other Voices;* Graham Greene, *The Heart of the Matter* (with a few shifts to other characters for contrast); Frederick Buechner, *A Long Day's Dying.*

In the last two points of view, the author works outward from inside the character; it is through that character's perspective that the elements of the story are worked out.

In many novels, several point-of-view techniques are used in combination: Charles Dickens, *Bleak House;* Faulkner, *The Sound and the Fury;* Wright Morris, *The Huge Season* and *Cause for Wonder.*

Because it most directly affects the choice and use of all other elements, point of view is the most important technique. In the creative process, a writer may ask himself: is this the best point of view for the story I want to tell? Does the choice itself mean something or is it arbitrary? What are the consequences of this choice, affecting character creation, character relationships, what the reader sees and feels, the style, and so on? What is the psychological effect of telling this story in the third person as opposed to letting a character tell it in his own voice? What are other possible points of view and their effects? The student of fiction may ask similar questions about the finished work.

The major fallacy from which all other fallacies spring is the point of view fallacy. If the writer uses poor judgment in his choice of the point of view through which the elements of his story are presented or if he mishandles the one he chooses, he sets up a chain-reaction that demolishes most of his carefully prepared intentions and effects. The reader may commit a similar fallacy if he fails to identify and follow the workings and implications of the author's point-of-view technique.

The writer who is in control of his material strives to make the point of view consistent. He takes care not to attribute to a character things he couldn't know, think, or feel; nor does he attribute an unlikely vocabulary to his character (unless deliberately, for a special effect, as in Faulkner's *As I Lay Dying*). He avoids jumping from one character's mind to another's without careful transition or without re-orienting the reader. The writer does not allow the reader to become confused as to whose evaluation of events he is getting.

The writer may choose the third person omniscient, the first person, or the third person/central intelligence; these narrators may be active agents in the story or mere passive observers; but the reader must feel that the point of view through which the story is filtered is the *inevitable* one.

Each type of point of view allows the writer its own particular freedom and imposes its own particular limitations. Unless he intrudes in his own voice to make a pact with his reader that he is going to limit his vision, the *omniscient narrator* is obligated to tell all because he sees and knows all and can go anywhere. But he can so ingratiate himself with his reader that he is not reproached for withholding information or failing to render a scene which the reader knows he *can* render. The classic authors spoke directly to the reader. "Our doctrine is," said Trollope, "that the author and reader should move along together in full confidence with each other." The omniscient author may provide us with privileged information, though it can never be total. "It is hardly necessary that I should here give to the public any lengthened biography of Mr. Harding, up to the period of commencement of this tale" (Anthony Trollope, *Barchester Towers*).

The third person/central intelligence method provides us with inside views; the stream of consciousness technique provides the deepest view of the character's thoughts and feelings; the roving, omniscient narrator strives for balance between interior and exterior views of his characters.

The omniscient author intrudes to make explicit authorial comments, analyses, and judgments, manipulates the reader intellectually and emotionally, *telling* him in generalized commentaries instead of *showing* him in dramatic scenes, or the author may intrude his judgments with relative subtlety or even deviousness. The history of the novel reveals a pattern of emphasis on either telling (Leo Tolstoy, *Anna Karenina*) or showing (Hemingway, *The Sun Also Rises*), on rendering experiences in terms of scenes or on telling in passages of summary; the emphasis today is on dramatic narration, conveying a sense of events happening now, not told as having happened in the past. Wayne C. Booth would like to see more novels using a combination of scene and summary.

A distinction is also made between *story* and *plot*. A story is what happens; that is the conventional, rather mechanical notion of plot, also. But Ronald Crane argues that plot "is the particular temporal synthesis of the elements of action, character, and thought that constitute the matter of" the 'writer's invention. ... There are, thus, plots of action, plots of character, and plots of thought." Crane advocates "the more specific kind of criticism of a work that takes the form of the plot as its starting point and then inquires how far and in what way its peculiar power is maximized by the writer's invention and development of episodes... his handling of diction and imagery, and his decisions as to the order, method, scale, and point of view of his representation" ("The Concept of Plot").

Authorial intrusion can provide relief from dramatic pacing, and perform many other functions, such as enabling the author to cover a great deal of important but nondramatic territory through generalization enlivened with the author's distinctive first person voice. Until recently, modern writers, critics, readers, generally objected to the commentary approach because it shattered the illusion that real people are involved in a real event; unity also is shattered because a reader must re-orient himself each time a shift is made from dramatization to commentary. Wayne C. Booth argues that the narrating voices of Thackeray and Fielding, for example, must be taken as creations of the authors, just as Becky Sharp and Tom Jones are creations. A distinction must be made between the writer and his literary projection of himself; his voice is this second self. It is not the real-life voice

of Faulkner that the reader listens to; unconsciously, sometimes deliberately, the writer creates a persona, a mask, or second self, which determines the level or depth of the relationship between narrator and reader.
This voice provides the reader with perspectives on the story. There are
varying degrees of intimacy between reader and narrator, between the au
thor and his second self, and between the second self and his characters.

This implied author comes through in his technical choices, such as
point of view and style, if not in commentaries; the reader who experienc
the richer context of the actual and the implied authors, and the tensions
between them and himself, develops a deeper interest in the novel. The
reader himself becomes a different "mock reader" with each novel (even
each novel by the same author) he reads; we pretend to be some one else
response to the author's assumptions about his ideal reader.

Traditionally, either the first person (a character as narrator) or the o
niscient (the author as narrator) was used. In a way, the first person narra
has as much mobility and freedom and as much license to comment on th
action as the omniscient narrator. The omniscient point of view was most
appropriate and effective in times when the author might pretend to kno
all, to be the creator of the world he described, as Dickens could; today's
writers, feeling that to pretend to know all is an impertinence, specialize i
select areas, and use the mind of a single character through which to reve
this select area of experience to the reader. Thus, the first person is favor
today. William Gaddis in *The Recognitions* is one of the few contemporar
writers who can move from the mind of one character to another and also
give an omniscient, panoramic view of all history and the contemporary
scene as well.

The first person narrator may be a witness or a participant in the stor
he tells. He soliloquizes to a clearly identified or implied or ambiguous a
dience, which is usually physically present. "Really, *mon cher compatriot*
I am grateful to you for your curiosity. However, there is nothing extraor
nary about my story" (Albert Camus, *The Fall*). Or he writes his story, fo
readers generally: "So I'm in the death house, now, writing the last of thi
so Father McConnell can look it over. . . . If they get me, he's to take it a
see if he can find somebody to print it" (James M. Cain, *The Postman Always Rings Twice*).

James Joyce borrowed the interior monolog (daydream, reverie) tech
nique from Édouard Dujardin (*We'll to the Woods No More*, 1887), modifie
and perfected it in *Ulysses*.

> I'm going to have a splendid time. Now why is the stair carpet
> turned up at the corner here? A grey patch on the line of upwar

red, on the red strip looping up from step to step. Second storey; the door on the left. *Office*. I only hope he hasn't gone; no chance of running him to earth if he has. Oh well, in that case, I'd go for a stroll down the boulevard. No time to lose; in! The outer office. Where is Lucien Chavainne? The huge room ringed with chairs. There he is, leaning over the table; overcoat and hat on; he's arranging some papers with one of the clerks; seems in a hurry. Over there the library of blue files, rows of knotted tapes. I pause on the threshold. A great time I shall have telling him all about it! Chavainne looks up; he sees me. Hullo!

. . .

Mr Bloom entered and sat in the vacant place. He pulled the door to after him and slammed it tight till it shut tight. He passed an arm through the armstrap and looked seriously from the open carriage window at the lowered blinds of the avenue. One dragged aside: an old woman peeping. Nose whiteflattened against the pane. Thanking her stars she was passed over. Extraordinary the interest they take in a corpse. Glad to see us go we give them such trouble coming. Job seems to suit them. Huggermugger in corners. Slop about in slipperslappers for fear he'd wake. Then getting it ready. Laying it out. Molly and Mrs Fleming making the bed. Pull it more to your side. Our windingsheet. Never know who will touch you dead. Wash and shampoo. I believe they clip the nails and the hair. Keep a bit in an envelope. Grow all the same after. Unclean job.

The history of art is full of such instances; the innovator is obscure, while the man who best uses the discovery becomes famous. Another early practitioner was Dorothy Richardson *(Pilgrimage)*.

There is a difference between the stream-of-consciousness technique and the interior monolog. Pure instances of the stream-of-consciousness technique are few; Joyce's *Ulysses* is classic, particularly the Molly Bloom soliloquy at the end.

... a quarter after what an unearthly hour I suppose they're just getting up in China now combing out their pigtails for the day well soon have the nuns ring the angelus they've nobody coming in to spoil their sleep except an odd priest or two for his night office the alarm-clock next door at cockshout clattering the brains out of itself let me see if I can doze off 1 2 3 4 5 what kind of flowers are those they invented like the stars the wallpaper in Lombard street was much nicer the apron he gave me was like that something only I only wore it twice better lower this lamp and try again so I can get up early Ill go to Lambes there beside Findlaters and get them to send us some flowers to put about the place in case he brings him home tomorrow today I mean no no Fridays an unlucky day first I want to do the place up someway the dust grow in it I think while Im asleep then we can have music and cigarettes. . . .

The term was coined by William James to describe a psychological phenomenon. (For the distinction, see Humphrey's *Stream of Consciousness in the Modern Novel.*)

Stream-of-consciousness and interior monolog techniques are ways of getting at the character's subconscious; in a way, the reader feels that the writer is trying to tell him the news about the way the mind works (just as Defoe told in authentic detail the way a plague spreads). Another device for opening up the unconscious through free association (in this instance, the author's) is *automatic writing*, a random stream of words that come directly from the writer's own subconscious. Some of Gertrude Stein's writings seem to have been affected by her experiments in automatic writing. There are few instances of novels produced solely by automatic writing, though some may have started that way.

Each type of narration imposes limitations upon the writer, but he can sometimes turn those limitations to his advantage. For instance, the first person narrative is limited to those things the character has witnessed himself or that have been reported to him; he cannot get into the minds of other characters as the omniscient (god-like, all-knowing) narrator can. But his narration is dramatically immediate (as all quoted speech is) and thus has great authority: "And I only am escaped to tell thee," says Ishmael (quoting Job) in *Moby Dick.*

The author himself is most absent in the first-person narration, in which he impersonates one of his own characters, ventriloquizing his voice. The author may exit in other ways. Influenced by Henry James (*The Ambassadors*) and Flaubert (*Madame Bovary*), to some degree, a great many writers have favored the third person/central intelligence or center of consciousness method. In the language of his second self, the author paraphrases the narration from the mind of a main character; we see only what the character sees. To use James' phrase, the character is a reflection, not a straight teller of incident. The advantage of consistency of point-of-view is that we experience everything through the character's own mind and emotions with greater intimacy and intensity. But this method is dramatically weak because we cannot see the character himself in action; he is often a creative witness to an action involving characters more dramatic than himself; he remains physically passive and almost invisible. In *The Great Gatsby,* Nick Carroway is such a character:

> I wanted no more riotous excursions with privileged glimpses into the human heart. Only Gatsby, the man who gives his name to this book, was exempt from my reaction—Gatsby, who represented everything for which I have an unaffected scorn. If personality is an unbroken series of successful gestures, then there was something gorgeous about him, some heightened sensitivity to the promises of life.

"As to making known my own opinion about the characters I produce," said Flaubert, "no, no, a thousand times no!" The author must efface himself, he must be invisible and his voice must be neutral, silent, impartial, impersonal, disinterested; as much as is humanly possible, he must not take sides with one character against another and he must refuse to respond to and express attitudes about every passing controversy or social issue. "It is one of my principles that one must not write oneself into one's work." said Flaubert, "The artist must be in his work as God is in creation, invisible yet all-powerful; we must sense him everywhere but never see him." This camera-eye objectivity can never be total, of course. And the authorial silence may result in a dialog with the reader, based on the reader's on-going interrogation of the author's quietly implied attitudes.

The nature of fiction is to feign, to dissemble, create a figment. Still critics have always fought over the question of whether the writer should give himself free reign or impose restrictions. Involved with this question is the problem of sincerity as a criterion of excellence; again, some critics declare that the writer's personal sincerity does not matter; the work is what it is and the critic's criteria must determine only how good it is. Wayne C. Booth, in his major contribution to criticism, *The Rhetoric of Fiction,* raises the old question again. He feels that the modern over-use of the first person and the central intelligence method creates a fallacious, even immoral, ambiguity. A famous short story example is Ring Lardner's "Haircut." Too often the author's tone is misleading and the relationship between the character's perceptions and an implied reality is so heavily ironic that the reader can never know what the author's own true feelings are, and thus the reader is left without a frame of reference within which to evaluate the character's behavior. Other critics argue that in leaving moral issues unresolved, modern writers are being true to the spiritual, intellectual, and moral temper of our times, which is relativistic, situational, and, unlike that of the early novelists, non-absolute. Booth objects mainly to the *degree* of lack of control over the reader's moral responses, for surely the writer himself is not as undecided as his novel seems to be.

In novels in which several points of view are separately, and still objectively presented, the problem of unreliability (if it is indeed a problem) is improved or worsened to the extent that the writer is committed to a relativistic view. Aldous Huxley asks, why not let there be more than one or two implied novelists in a single novel? (See *Point Counter Point.*) While there are few examples of this multiplicity of authorial second selves, there are many novels in which objective and subjective points of view are presented along a continuum, with frequent shifts. A matrix of points of view is used in the works of Wright Morris, especially in *The Field of Vision*. He shuttles back and forth among five different characters, at least five times each, rendering their points of view in third person. The end of one character's vision impinges upon the beginning of the next, as in this exmaple. McKee's point of view ends: "'Well, here we are, Lois,' he said, opened the door, then just stood there, a smile on his face, waiting for what he knew she would say." Lois's point of view begins: "'If anything should happen to that boy—' she said, and saw his mouth pucker, like a hen's bottom." Other examples of novels that use a matrix of points of view are: Virginia Woolf, *To The Lighthouse* (quite similar to *The Field of Vision*); Faulkner, *The Sound and the Fury* (three very different first person narratives, ending with the author's omniscient point of view); Djuna Barnes, *Nightwood;* Carson McCullers, *The Heart Is a Lonely Hunter;* William March, *Company K* (a short novel that uses 113 points of view). (See Percy Lubbock, *The Craft of Fiction;* Norman Friedman, "Point of View in Fiction"; Wayne C. Booth, "Distance and Point-of-View"; Scholes and Kellogg, *The Nature of Narrative* Moffatt and McElheny, *Points of View;* Wallace Hildick, *Thirteen Types of Narrative*).

STORY

What is it that is being structured, controlled, and formed through the point-of-view technique? A story or plot of some kind, or a process (usually psychological). The traditional writer has a compulsion to tell a story in response to the universal plea, "Tell me a story." There is a primitive urge to respond to that craving, and the writer becomes conscious of his craft to tel a story well or many stories in many different ways. Isaac Singer *(The Slave)* is a recent writer for whom story telling is a compulsion. "The eager ness of a listener quickens the tongue of a narrator" (Brontë, *Jane Eyre*). Recently, the emphasis has been on a conscious desire to bring order to chaos; this impulse is natural in a time when the more technological progress we achieve the less social cohesion we experience. But from the start, the telling of stories has been a form of play, and the impulse to play has struggled continually with the compulsion to use the story for more "serious" purposes.

Stories first became stylized and serious with the *myths*, which are based on events far out of reach of memory, the original inspiration having been exaggerated out of all realistic context; the *tale* bears some resemblance to possibility. Myths are inspired partly by a religious impulse to embody in human action supernatural forces. Tales and legends answer to a desire to express the hope that man can become more than himself—physically, anyway—in his struggle against nature and other men in brute encounters. Modern novelists have tried to give their novels mythic and epic dimensions in various ways: by parallel, for satirical purposes (Joyce's *Ulysses*); by sheer size or scope (Tolstoy's epic *War and Peace*); by mythic patterns (Lockridge's *Raintree County*).

Many stories of the ancient past were tales. Americans and Russians returned the world to that stage because they re-enacted before the eyes of the world stages through which Europe had already passed. Tales remained the narrative form of ancient civilizations such as India, China, Japan, until they became forcibly westernized. In America, the tall-tale came into being, inspired by the mysteries of a new life in a new land; these were mixed with elements from the tales of kings and heroes of the old countries to form the tall-tales about Mike Fink, the personal tall-tales of Davy Crockett. The tale of Beowulf kept the community together with a code; the tall-tale's absurd, bitter humor, often black and irreverent, sustained the frontiersman living in isolation from communities.

The novel is the story of man in a way that history isn't; it is an affirmation of the everyday man in a way that the romance tale isn't. The novel tells the story of that which would seem to have no story. For a story was originally conceived as being the narrative of an extraordinary event as in myths, legends, tales. But there is nothing extraordinary about Pamela or Moll Flanders or Tom Jones, except that their creators managed to interest us in them quite as much as listeners of old were absorbed in the legendary exploits of Beowulf. The middleclasses are extremely narcissistic; novels that tell their story, favorably or not, seem to assert their importance in the face of evidence to the contrary.

The art of narrative has been part imitative, part inventive or fabricative from the beginning—in the oral tradition on up through the poetic to the dramatic to the prosaic (the cinematic is the present new stage). This is the way it happened to Beowulf, as retold by me, says the scop, even as he vows to tell it the way it was told to him.

Narrative is not a special characteristic of the novel; all other fictive and factual forms, and even the dance and fine arts, employ narrative. But the novel handles narrative in its own special way and each word used to delineate that narrative must, because of the high signative nature of words, with their several denotative and many connotative meanings, evaluate the narrative. The novel's words evaluate in a way that, compared with poetic narrative, is, apparently, straightforward. Poetic devices tend more obviously to embellish the narrative poem.

Some writers of fiction have managed to break out of the purely narrative thurst of words. There is something too nearly inevitable and fatalistic, maybe masochistic about stark narrative. "Story is the spoiled child of art," said Henry James. Writer and reader reach for a more human dimension in those techniques that allow for something more. "... what I should like to do is to write a book about nothing," said Flaubert, "a book which would have hardly any subject. ... That is why there are neither good nor bad subjects. ... from the point of view of pure art, there are none at all, style being itself alone an absolute way of looking at things." So stories aren't th;e only subjects of novels. "His childhood and youth alone is enough to provide a born novelist with an immense amount of literary nourishment," said François Mauriac.

There has always been debate about the subjects of narrative. The classical attitude is that some subjects are unworthy of treatment; there are important and there are trivial subjects, and the work is judged accordingly. But again, as James argued, "We must grant the artist his subject, his idea, his donnée; our criticism is applied only to what he makes of it." There has been a debate as to whether the events in a narrative should be credible, possible, probable, or whether the incredible should also be treated; the romance treats the latter occasionally, but the province of the novel is indeed the credible, sometimes made marvelous; the novelist strives for verisimilitude—a sense of reality, not necessarily an exact imitation of it.

CHARACTERS

The novel, more than other media (even the movies) offers a gallery of memorable characters, often seen in the titles: *Moll Flanders, Madame Bovary, Don Quixote, Gargantua, Tom Jones, Tristram Shandy, Young Werther, Sister Carrie, Studs Lonigan, Eugenie Grandet, Lord Jim, Huckleberry Finn, Augie March, Anna Karenina, Oliver Twist, The Great Gatsby, Steppenwolf, Daisy Miller, Emma.* And in other novels: Willie Stark (*All the King's Men*); Philip Marlowe (*The Big Sleep*); Scarlett O'Har (*Gone With the Wind*); Hester Prynne (*The Scarlet Letter*); Roskolnikov (*Crime and Punishment*); Jake Barnes (*The Sun Also Rises*); Eugene Gant (*Look Homeward, Angel*); Quentin Compson (*The Sound and the Fury*); Mersault (*The Stranger*).

It is upon characters that most stories concentrate. But in a good stor it is not what happens *to* a character or what he *does* that matters. Most important is what he *feels* and *thinks*, the effect upon him of what happens to him or of what he does or thinks; and more important is the ultimate meaning or implication of his problem. A character is revealed in action. "Character is action." Fitzgerald hung that statement on the wall in the room where he wrote. In a good novel action and character are so interrelated that the character *is* action—neither means much without the other.

But action need not be only physical—it may be psychological as well. Thus, we need to understand what motivates a character. The success of most stories depends upon the degree to which we are able to achieve *empathy* (put ourselves in his place) with the character. If we empathize with a character who is having a hard time, the effect may be pathos. We feel what he feels because for the moment we are the character for whom we have empathy.

First the writer, then the reader may ask: Is the main character well-developed; does he grow; does he experience some change in his circumstances, his attitude; do his personality and his actions affect others? Are any of the characters not fully enough explored? Are relationships among them clear? Hugo von Hofmannsthal said, "Characters without action are lame, action without characters blind."

In the early history of the novel, much attention was devoted to the study of characters and to the author's ability in characterization, his skill in conveying motivations for their behavior. Characterization is the creation of imaginary people through descriptions of physical appearance, actions, speech, thoughts, or what other characters say or think about them. The early heroes were exemplars, who taught by example. They personified such traits as are found in allegories: dignity, nobility, honor, patience. "Character is destiny" (Novalis, German romantic).

The traditional concept of character saw conflict mainly in terms of two different kinds of characters opposing each other: protagonist (hero) and antagonist (villain). Today all characters are guilty, no one is entirely innocent, so individuals are seldom one way or another, although recently the concept of the Establishment or the system has become so strong that anyone who represents the Establishment is a villain who victimizes the often passive main character. Conflict is dissolved into ways of coping with Systems managed by tainted people. But most often the main character is his own antagonist. He is caught up in a conflict of ideas or a conflict within his own psychological make-up. Hermann Hesse's *Steppenwolf*:

> There was once a man, Harry, called the Steppenwolf. He went on two legs, wore clothes and was a human being, but never-

theless he was in reality a wolf of the Steppes. He had learnt a
good deal of all that people of a good intelligence can, and was a
fairly clever fellow. What he had not learnt, however, was this: to
find contentment in himself and his own life. ... It might... be
possible that in his childhood he was a little wild and disobedient
and disorderly, and that those who brought him up had declared a
war of extinction against the beast in him. ...

W. J. Harvey in his essay "Character and the Context of Things" points out
that serious fiction tells us more about characters than we ever know of real
people or want known about ourselves, and this function of literature makes
some people uncomfortable—they turn to escape fiction. Fiction gives us
both intrinsic and contextual knowledge of people. Generally, the realistic
novel has dealt with typical characters who must seem natural to the reader;
naturalness is a criterion of quality in such works. Characters and their
backgrounds must be particularized, individualized while remaining typical.

E. M. Forster (who didn't really deal himself in protagonists and antagonists) thought in terms of flat and round characters. The flat characters
are there to help round out the more fully developed ones. The flat isn't the
same as the stock or the stereotyped character, which often destroys verisimilitude (similar to truth). Everything about them is *given*, has been
shaped in previous novels, good and bad. A stereotype is a character or
situation that has been overused in life or in fiction. The stereotype is cut to
a pattern or conforms to a formula that seldom varies. The shootout between the sheriff and the outlaw in front of a Western saloon is a stereotypical situation involving stereotyped characters. A stereotypical character is
like a cliché expression. The serious writer generally strives to create real,
complex people, not literary stereotypes. Of course, in modern fiction, the
alienated, super-sensitive character is a cliché, but the best writers present
him in a new light. Stock characters populate the popular novels in
stereotyped situations. A stock character is always in stock, available immediately to any writer on demand; the good writer resists the temptation
to take one out of stock; he tries to invent his own or re-imagine or resurrect stereotypes. The popular writer earns his royalties by satisfying his
mass reader's desire for the same characters and situations, depicted
through a set formula. With more and more people taking college English
courses, that approach to character is becoming less and less tolerated, although stereotyped characters remain useful in comedy and satire.

"Character types" is a different term. These may be found in any novel;
the question of stereotypes comes up when the types are handled unim-
aginatively, uninventively. Dickens was a master at handling a gallery of
character types and some of his combinations are with us today. *Bleak
House:*

The old gentleman is rusty to look at, but is reputed to have made good thrift out of aristocratic marriage settlements and aristocratic wills, and to be very rich. He is surrounded by a mysterious halo of family confidences; of which he is known to be the silent depository. There are noble mausoleums rooted for centuries in retired glades of parks, among the growing timber and the fern, which perhaps hold fewer noble secrets than walk abroad among men shut up in the breast of Mr. Tulkinghorn. He is of what is called the old school—a phrase generally meaning any school that seems never to have been young—and wears knee-breeches tied with ribbons, and gaiters or stockings. One peculiarity of his black clothes, and of his black stockings, be they silk or worsted, is, that they never shine. Mute, close, irresponsive to any glancing light, his dress is like himself. He never converses, when not professionally consulted. He is found sometimes, speechless but quite at home, at corners of dinnertables in great country houses, and near doors of drawingrooms, concerning which the fashionable intelligence is eloquent; where everybody knows him, and where half the Peerage stops to say "How do you do, Mr. Tulkinghorn?" he receives these salutations with gravity, and buries them along with the rest of his knowledge.

Ficelle is James' term for the confidante whose questions, as in a play, draw out the first-person/narrator or one whose own knowledge of events is limited; the omniscient author has less need of such a character. A *pawn* is a character whose only purpose is functionary; a *protatic* character is brought in only once for a specific use and then dropped. The *"card"* is an eccentric character who doesn't change; oddly enough he may be remembered more vividly than the hero—Dr. Pangloss more than Candide. A *"fragrant"* character is one whose influence is pervasively felt even though he may seldom appear directly. Gran'paw McDaniel dominates, unseen, in David Madden's *Cassandra Singing:*

> Then Momma turned to Lone. "Son, you just don't know what that old man's done to us *all* without even comin' near us. All those years Coot tried to make a farm to please his daddy, and then that hateful thing just went in the house when he saw who it was comin' up the path."
> "Well, you needn't git on that," said Coot.
> "You," she said, turning on Coot, "ain't never done a single thing in all your life without it somehow aimed to please your daddy. And knowin' how the old man hates the very sight of you."
> "It's not Gran'paw's fault, Momma!" Lone wanted to keep Gran'paw separate from Coot and Momma, and even from Cassie.
> "You don't know a thing about him—never even seen him."

"We used to dream up stuff about him all the time," said Cassie. "Want to hear my best song about him?"

"Least he stays up on Black Mountain," said Lone, "Where he don't bother and he ain't bothered." Lone knew that Gran'paw lived in a cove at the foot of Big Black Mountain, but he always thought of him as standing on the top—highest point in Kentucky—five thousand feet above Harmon.

Some modern novelists like to deal in archetypes. These are types of human roles that have always existed and are described by Jung as Mother, Father, Son, Daughter, Priest, Mentor, Authority Figure. By making his reader feel the presence, subtly at best, of archetypes, the writer gives his characters stature-by-association and expands the dimensions of his work. (See Northrop Frye, "The Archetypes of Literature.") D. H. Lawrence tried to present his characters in generalized somewhat archetypal terms but with other qualities. "You musn't look in my novel for the old stable ego of the character. There is another *ego*, according to whose action the individual is unrecognizable, and passes through, as it were, allotropic states. . . ."

The creation of character does not depend upon the writer's having a good memory of fascinating people he has known. "If I spoiled the portrait of old La Perouse," says Gide, "it was because I clung too closely to reality." "The difficult thing is inventing when you are encumbered by memory. . . ." Jean-Paul Sartre has argued that characters should be totally free of any of man's, even the author's, preconceived schemes of order, that the novels in which they thrive should seem to be natural objects, not planned artifices; the reader himself is just as free.

There is less emphasis today on the creation of characters who interact with each other out of something known as character. Personality, a relatively superficial quantity, is more often the focus. The novel attempts more now to render states of being, attitudes. Readers often wish they could know more fully the people who have these states of being. The novel becomes a graph of the author's, and at best the reader's, own state of being. As writers came more and more to feel that character was a protean phenomenon and that there was no such thing as human nature and that people behave irrationally as often as not, they began to de-emphasize the dramatization of *motive* and examine psychological processes instead. Jean-Paul Sartre's *Nausea:*

The thing which was waiting was on the alert, it has pounced on me, it flows through me, I am filled with it. It's nothing: I am the Thing. Existence, liberated, detached, floods over me. I exist.

I exist. It's sweet, so sweet, so slow. And light: you'd think it floated all by itself. It stirs. It brushes by me, melts and vanishes.

> Gently, gently. There is bubbling water in my mouth. I swallow.
> It slides down my throat, it caresses me—and now it comes up
> again into my mouth. Forever I shall have a little pool of whitish
> water in my mouth—lying now—grazing my tongue. And this pool
> is still me. And the tongue. And the throat is me.

Characters lost individual characteristics as the anti-hero came into
vogue; our interest was directed not so much to the formation of character
as to the deformation by environment of anonymous creatures with little
will or volition, moving about in a vaguely-defined world. Franz Kafka's K
in *The Trial*, is less real and less fully delineated than his predicament.
Often in such novels the main character is the only charactrer at all well-
defined; others merely reflect some facet of the main character, who very
gradually takes shape in the reader's mind. We gain insight into other
characters indirectly.

Early readers turned to the novel to learn why people behave as they
do, and to experience the behavior of people different from themselves. Today's reader knows far too much about psychology and sociology to depend
as much on the novel; the novel must present human behavior from radically
new perspectives, by ordering in various combinations the chaos of sensory
perception, for instance. Thus, motivations are not given or dramatized so
much as symbolically embodied or suggested or abstractly objectified,
through such techniques as impressionism and expressionism; juxtaposition
and montage of character and narrative fragments replace the sequential rendering of character in action (more about those terms later).

But the prevalent attitude, even today, is that characters should be
well-articulated, in terms of their idiocyncracies and eccentricities. The
reader is interested to know and to experience that character's motivations
for choosing—or refusing to choose. A character makes choices and thus so
must his creator, and the reader's interest lies in following the consequences
of those choices.

CONFLICT

In one form or another, conflict energizes every work of fiction. Traditionally, the conflict is between two people. But if a conflict is seen as a
struggle between two opposed forces, it may take many forms: a character
may have an external conflict with another character, a group, or with society or nature in general. Willard Motley's *Knock on Any Door:*

> Nick walked into the courtroom. His head was up, his shoul-
> ders back, his chin in, his long lashes drawn halfway down over his

> eyes. The crowd gawked. He enjoyed their staring eyes, their mouths held open a little, their silence and attention. He swaggered toward his chair at the counsel table. The news photographers started taking pictures of him. He grinned broadly.
>
> I didn't know I was such a big shot!

Or he may have an internal conflict within himself between two opposed attitudes. Graham Greene's *The Heart of the Matter:*

> But human beings were condemned to consequences. The responsibility as well as the guilt was his—he was not a Bagster: he knew what he was about. He had sworn to preserve Louise's happiness, and now he had accepted another and contradictory responsibility. He felt tired by all the lies he would sometime have to tell: he felt the wounds of those victims who had not yet bled. Lying back on the pillow he stared sleeplessly out towards the grey early morning tide. Somewhere on the face of those obscure waters moved the sense of yet another wrong and another victim, not Louise, not Helen. Away in the town the cocks began to crow for the false dawn.

Identification of the conflict helps the reader to comprehend everything else in a story. Minor conflicts may enhance the major conflict. As *complications* accumulate, these conflicts, usually in a story that has a *beginning* (introduction of the problem) *middle* (development of the problem through complications) and an *end (dénouement)* or climax, with interest further sustained by *suspense:* what happens next, will the hero survive, how will it all end? The climax of a story comes at that point when the complications of the *plot* are most fully developed and a resolution of the problem is in sight. Each episode or scene may have its own climax. When a story depends heavily upon suspense for its effects, the climax is especially intense. Some stories reach a quiet, subtle, almost submerged climax. Conflict, *tension*, and suspense are sometimes confused as being very much the same; they are not; they do, however, enhance each other.

Suspense for its own sake has come to be regarded as a cheap device for holding a reader, and is dependent upon a mechanical plot line. Suspense, allied with raw curiosity, is the province of popular fiction. Some writers deliberately destroy suspense to force the reader to pay attention to other values in the novel, such as the quality of experience for its own sake, rendered in a complex way, from which suspense would only distract the reader. Nevertheless, the psychological satisfaction of suspense has not been fully explored by critics or writers, while most readers go on hungering for it. It is still used as an attention-getter in serious works that deliberately omit other major elements, such as dramatic event or character development, as in, for instance, some of the French novels of the fifties and sixties.

Some readers are often less interested in the present moment, which the artist tries to arrest and present as fully as possible, than in plunging ahead into the future—to arrive at the denouement or resolution often is his goal, and the satisfaction of having all his anticipations consummated in the end is very great. As he brings the development of one episode to an end, a writer may introduce an element that anticipates an episode to come.

> You could not be upset about anything on a day like that.
> That was the last day before the fiesta.
>
> Chapter XV
>
> At noon of Sunday, the 6th of July, the fiesta exploded.
> (Ernest Hemingway, *The Sun Also Rises*)

The writer may satisfy that anticipation immediately or he may deliberately frustrate it for an even more interesting effect. "But before this could be done, an unexpected trouble fell upon her." New Chapter. "It was not unexpected entirely." (E. M. Forster, *Howard's End*). The reader then expects that a certain event or development will occur. Indications or suggestions of what is to come are often called "foreshadowings" or "plants." But in many recent novels a dramatic resolution may precede the opening of the novel, and subtler, more complex resolutions, ideological or aesthetic, may be striven for in the work, as in the novels of Wright Morris (*The Deep Sleep*, for instance). Just as the reader enjoys deviations from the mainline of developments, some writers delight in departing altogether from conventional expectations; and there are those readers who feel that the richer experiences are those that these deviations produce. But such novels are dependent upon the prior existence of conventional novels from which writer and reader collaborate in departing.

TIME-SPACE

Character relationships and conflicts occur in a time scheme and in a space pattern. The type of point of view used will determine the kinds of time and space patterns that emerge. Novelists pay little attention to the ancient quarrel in drama over the three unities (action, place, and time), but those three major elements are interwoven in different ways in fiction, and point of view is the dynamic medium in which a different unity is achieved; the mind of the narrator discovers relationships among all facets of those three elements. Each novel has its own spacial and temporal pattern or principle of organization; the possible varieties are infinite. Edwin Muir points out that in the dramatic novel time flies; we have a sense of time running out to the end. In the novel of character, time moves slowly; characters seem beyond time and change, deathless. (See Muir, *The Structure of the Novel.*)

In some of the finest modern novels, the characters achieve a deeper sense of self through their conscious involvement with time and space, as do Quentin in Faulkner's *Absalom, Absalom!* and *The Sound and the Fury;* Jack Burden in Robert Penn Warren's *All the King's Men;* Darley and Pursewarden in Lawrence Durrell's *Alexandria Quartet;* and Gerard in Jorge Semprun's *The Long Voyage.* Gerard speaks in the present tense most of the time; Semprun shifts to the past tense as he senses opportunities for emphasis; but the shift also has thematic relevance: all time is one in the consciousness that evaluates and shapes its own raw material.

> I try to realize that this is a unique moment, that we have tenaciously survived for this unique moment, when we could look at the camp from the outside. But I can't manage it. I can't manage to capture what is unique in this moment. I say to myself, look, friend, this is a unique moment. . . . I missed that unique moment.
>
> .   .   .
>
> As the years went by, I was sometimes assailed by memories, absolutely vivid memories that arose from the willful oblivion of this voyage with the polished perfection of diamonds that nothing can impair.

Durrell describes (in a note to the second novel, *Balthazar*) his intention:

> a four-decker novel whose form is based on the relativity proposition.
>
> Three sides of space and one of time constitute the soup-mix recipe of a continuum. The four novels follow this pattern.
>
> The three first parts, however, are to be deployed spatially . . . and are not linked in a serial form. They interlap, interweave, in a purely spatial relation. Time is stayed. The fourth part alone will represent time and be a true sequel.
>
> The subject-object relation is so important to relativity that I have tried to turn the novel through both subjective and objective modes.

"A story," said E. M. Forster, "is a narrative of events arranged in a time sequence." Time may be seen as a mechanical factor: how much time does it take the reader to finish a book, and what kind of time is it: intermittent, continuous?

In most novels, the tense is past. But A. A. Mendilow observes that the reader always translates past tense into present; the author's technique can facilitate this process to promote the illusion of immediacy (*Time and the Novel*). Very few novels can justify the use of the historical present. An example of effective use is Walker Percy's *The Moviegoer*.

> *Panic in the Streets* with Richard Widmark is playing on Tchoupitoulas Street. The movie was filmed in New Orleans. Richard Widmark is a public health inspector who learns that a culture of cholera bacilli has gotten loose in the city. Kate watches, lips parted and dry. She understands my moviegoing but in her own antic fashion. There is a scene which shows the very neighborhood of the theater. Kate gives me a look—it is understood that we do not speak during the movie.
> Afterwards in the street, she looks around the neighborhood. "Yes, it is certified now."
> She refers to a phenomenon of moviegoing which I have called certification.

Dialog always happens in the dramatic present. A source of pleasure to the reader is the tension between the immediacy of dialog and the past tense of narration. Denis Diderot's *Rameau's Nephew* is told almost entirely in dialog, and Ivy Compton Burnett's novels are unusually full of dialogs.

What is the chronological time scope of the novel, and how does the writer handle transitions? Sequential time governs in *War and Peace* and most other traditional novels.

Another mechanical use of time, though it may be handled subtly, is the movie device of *flashbacks*. Such time-shifts are most effective if the very fact of their occurrence contributes to the revelation of character and theme, as in the Benjy section of Faulkner's *The Sound and the Fury*. Bergson, among other philosophers, has influenced writers such as Joyce and Proust in their handling of time. Psychological time governs Virginia Woolf's *To the Lighthouse;* a middle section called "Time Passes" provides contrast. Past and present interact like a fugue in Wright Morris' *The Field of Vision*. Everything that happens during a bullfight in the present reminds each of the characters of events in the past. "Don't it take you back, Boyd?" asks McKee. Joyce's *Ulysses* takes place in Dublin in a single day (Bloomsday, Doomsday) but that day contains within it all Western time. Time rhythms—a day, a week, a moment (embodying a lifetime), a year, an hour, a decade, a day—are set up and the reader responds, perhaps more than to shifts from place to place. Responding to four different kinds of consciousness, types of narrators, the reader responds to four different kinds of time in Faulkner's *The Sound and the Fury.*

The old-fashioned way of conveying a sense of the time-space milieu of the characters was to present a block of description. Thomas Hardy's *Return of the Native:*

> A Saturday afternoon in November was approaching the time of twilight and the vast tract of unenclosed wild known as Egdon Heath embrowned itself moment by moment. Overhead the hollow stretch of whitish cloud shutting out the sky was as a tent which had the whole heath for its floor.
>
> The heaven being spread with this pallid screen and the earth with the darkest vegetation, their meeting-line at the horizon was clearly marked. In such contrast the heath wore the appearance of an instalment of night which had taken up its place before its astronomical hour was come: darkness had to a great extent arrived hereon, while day stood distinct in the sky.

Time and place are simple matters in Cain's *The Postman Always Rings Twice;* the time is the mid 1930's; the place is Los Angeles; and there's not much more to it. Modern techniques present time and place as filtered through the perceptions of characters, as in *Cassandra Singing* by David Madden.

> The backfiring of a motorcycle as it roared over the loose planks of the swinging bridge opened Lone's eyes. Through melting frost on the windowpane, he looked down the hollow and saw Boyd jounce off the bridge onto the highway in front of an overloaded coal truck.
>
> From the kitchen came the ringing clatter of a stove lid. Looking up past the catalpa tree, Lone watched Coot, followed by the snaking line of hounds, trudge up the ridge behind the barn, shotgun riding his shoulder.

A sense of place is a major part of the fictive experience in *Howard's End* by E. M. Forster.

Chapter I

One may as well begin with Helen's letter to her sister.

Howards End

Tuesday.

Dearest Meg,

It isn't going to be what we expected. It is old and little, and altogether delightful—red brick. We can scarcely pack in as it is, and the dear knows what will happen when Paul (younger son) arrives tomorrow. . . . Why did we settle that their house would be all gables and wiggles, and their garden all gamboge-coloured paths?

. . .

Howards End,
Sunday.

Dearest, dearest Meg,—I do not know what you will say: Paul and I are in love—the younger son who only came here Wednesday.

"Feelings are bound up in place," said Eudora Welty.

In Gabriel Márquez's *One Hundred Years of Solitude* place becomes a philosophical problem of space and time.

. . . he knew then that his fate was written in Melquiades' parchments. He found them intact among the prehistoric plants and steaming puddles and luminous insects that had removed all trace of man's passage on earth from their room. . . . he began to decipher them aloud. It was the history of the family, written by Melquiades, down to the most trivial details, one hundred years ahead of time.

Melquiades had not put events in the order of man's conventional time, but had concentrated a century of daily episodes in such a way that they coexisted in one instant. . . . impatient to know his own origin, Aureliano skipped ahead. Then the wind began, warm, incipient, full of voices from the past, the murmurs of ancient geraniums, sighs of disenchantment that preceded the most tenacious nostalgia. . . . he found the instant of his own conception among the scorpions and the yellow butterflies in a sunset bathroom where a mechanic satisfied his lust on a woman who was giving herself out of rebellion. He was so abssorbed that he did not feel the second surge of wind either as its cyclonic strength tore the doors and windows off their hinges, pulled off the roof of the east wing, and uprooted the foundations. . . . he began to decipher the instant that he was living, deciphering it as he lived it, prophesying himself in the act of deciphering the last page of the parchments, as if he were looking into a speaking mirror. Then he skipped again to anticipate the predictions and ascertain the date and circumstances of his death. Before reaching the final line, however, he had already understood that he would never leave that room, for it was foreseen that the city of mirrors (or mirages) would be wiped out by the wind and exiled from the memory of men at the precise moment when Aureliano Babilonia would finish deciphering the parchments, and that everything written on them was unrepeateable since time immemorial and forever more, because races condemned to one hundred years of solitude did not have a second opportunity on earth.

To shift time or place, the writer risks disorienting his reader; sometimes, for a particular effect, he deliberately disorients. He may delay telling where we are, letting us become gradually aware.

The *setting* of a story is the time and place in which the events occur. The time may mean the period (past, present, future) or the season or time of day in which a story is set. The place may be geographic (in a house, on a plane, in a city) or psychological (in a character's mind). An author may make time or place indeterminable. Settings can express something metaphorically about a character. Impressionistic or expressionistic description of setting can be one way of revealing character or a general climate of feeling, an atmosphere: In *Orlando,* Virginia Woolf depicts the story of Orlando over 500 years, during which we encounter various cultures and Orlando changes from a man to a woman. She evokes a sense of the Victorian era in her description of weather: "Damp swells the wood, furs the kettle, rusts the iron, rots the stone. So gradual is the process, that is not until we pick up some chest of drawers... and the whole thing drops to pieces in our hands, that we suspect even that the disease is at work." Setting can be significant because of the sense of history (Robert Penn Warren's *All the King's Men* and Faulkner's *Absalom, Absalom!*) or utter lack of it (Samuel Beckett's *The Unnamable* and Camus' *The Stranger*). The reader likes to be oriented securely in time and space, but disorientation can be another valid kind of experience. Sometimes the time scheme is jumbled to allow for juxtapositions of scenes and descriptions not otherwise possible, as in John Hawkes' *The Cannibal.*

More than in earlier kinds of narrative (tales, romances, etc.), people in novels live and die in particular places at particular times. Character and personality are shaped by environment; the novelist must therefore describe or evoke the landscape, the cityscape in detail, humanize it.

To test the degree to which setting affects all other elements in a novel, the reader might ask: Could the story be shifted, without serious effect, to another locale? In a fine novel, the answer is usually no. The writer reimagines real places so that, in fictive terms at least, the Brontës created, through consistency and passion of vision, the English moors; Thomas Hardy created the English small town; Faulkner created Mississippi; Bal -

zac, Paris; Sinclair Lewis, the midwestern small town; Willa Cather and
Wright Morris, rural Nebraska; William Styron and Ellen Glasgow, Virginia;
Twain, Missouri; Robert Penn Warren, Louisiana; Steinbeck, small town
California; Farrell and Algren, the slums of Chicago.

Setting is usually a matrix of place (geographic: a city, a nation; domestic: a house), time (of day, year, season), social context (class strata). Place
may be suggested by characters (quaint eccentrics); by common speech,
dress, ornamentation, manners, taboos, religion; by the researched details of
a period in the past. Setting may have the force of destiny, as in naturalistic
novels. Setting becomes a narrative element when description of the setting
is involved with the depiction of physical, emotional, mental action. Or setting may be mere backdrop, like a picture postcard, as in local color novels,
with their manipulation of clichés.

Out of a sense of obligation to describe a setting exhaustively, writers
often spend too much time setting the scene or they do it clumsily. Other
writers try to avoid describing the setting in a lump (dumping it all in the
first paragraph, although Conrad does that deliberately, with symbolic effect). They try to avoid excess (fullness is no criterion) or mere decoration,
or overemphasizing setting when it isn't really important; that can be dis-
tracting or misleading. However, setting usually *is* important. There are
subtle ways of describing setting, as in dialog, with the use of the curious
questioner. With restraint, with a selective use of detail, the best novelists
interweave setting and character in action.

Atmosphere is the mood or climate of a story. Sometimes writers feel
that mood or atmosphere is enough to sustain a story, but atmosphere is
more meaningful when it envelopes characters who have problems. An author establishes atmosphere by the objects he selects to describe, by how he
describes them, and by the setting in which he places them. The term atmosphere embraces setting and mood. We feel the author's tone of voice,
attitude, toward his material and his readers. Mood is an emotional ambience of sadness, gloom, decay, pessimism, gaiety. *Tone* expresses an attitude that creates degrees of distance. "In order to acquire the correct tone
I occasionally read a few pages of the Code Civil," said Stendhal of the writing of *The Charterhouse of Parma*. The pervasive tone may be tragic,
comic, ironic, skeptical, pessimistic, compassionate, sentimental; a variety of
these is possible within a single novel that has great scope and many shifts
in time and place. Atmosphere is a rather vague term and a difficult quality
in a novel to assess, but it is very important that we catch it and determine
its manifestations. "Her sudden appearance seemed to throw a trance across
the garden: a butterfly, poised on a dahlia stem, ceased winking wings, and
the rasping of bumblebees droned into nothing" (Truman Capote, *Other
Voices, Other Rooms*).

Style, more than anything else, conveys the writer's tone; he creates an atmosphere of tragedy, comedy, satire, melodrama, cynicism, optimism, or an elegiac mood. These three terms—tone, atmosphere, and mood—are similar but not quite the same. Tone suggests a voice, and the novelist's voice speaks more intimately to the reader than his devices for creating atmosphere and mood. Atmosphere suggests an emphasis on place, and mood an emphasis on character states. "I am an invisible man. No, I am not a spook like those that haunted Edgar Allan Poe. ... What did I do to be so blue? Bear with me" (Ralph Ellison, *Invisible Man*).

When two or more elements pull the reader simultaneously in different directions, the reader feels a *tension* that sustains emotional involvement in the story. The author may set up a tension between literal and metaphorical meaning; between characters; between techniques themselves. Tension derives partly from the interaction of tone, feeling, and mood that make up atmosphere. The reader's excitement comes partly from becoming involved in the development of the relationship between himself and the author, between the author and his material, and among certain elements dynamically interactive in the material itself—relationships between characters or between a character and society; but also the tension between the author's language and his subject-matter. Tension is the simultaneous existence of literal and metaphorical meaning organized in a novel, as in Carson McCullers' *The Heart Is a Lonely Hunter* and Conrad's *Victory*.

THEME

An overview of some of the major thematic concerns is just as useful as a survey of types, or genres and subjects, and techniques. The theme is the story's main idea or its underlying meaning. Sometimes "theme" is used to designate "subject matter," but not in this book. Characters and events express theme; but techniques, style, and form may also be expressive of theme.

"It is certain," said Novalis, "that my conviction gains infinitely the moment another soul will believe it." Part of the novelistic impulse is to persuade the reader to believe the illustrative or metaphysical truth of his work. The old term for this thought content was theme, replaced today by the search for meaning, and ultimately truth, about the characters and their predicament and ultimately about life. We try to discern the moral reference, purpose, attitude, or vision of the parts and the totality of the novel. A system of moral relationships is set up among the author, the fictive world he creates, and the reader. The traditional concept of moral or message was that it be positive, as the Bible is. Leslie Fiedler declares that the moral of ligation of today's novels is to be negative, to say "No in thunder," to wake people up to the true nature of life in our time.

Truth, like realism, is too often used as an honorific term as it relates to literature. Literature can be nonfactual and still convey a kind of truth that facts cannot convey: truths about the way men behave, think, feel, perceive. Aesthetic truths are self-proven, that is, it is *true* that readers experience aesthetic pleasure re-reading *The Great Gatsby* for the twentieth time. Science deals in different kinds of truth, based on observable or demonstrable facts. There are intrinsic or implicit and extrinsic or explicit truths; fiction mainly "proves" the former; at best, these kinds fuse.

How clear should the "truth" or "theme" be? Some novelists deliberately cause mystification for a special effect (Conrad's *Lord Jim*, and the novels of Thomas Pynchon, Joseph Heller, and Faulkner); in lesser writers it may cover certain shortcomings. Others create mystery as an end in itself. Beyond that there is willful obscurity, often on the premise that in trying to cope with obscurity, a diligent reader happens onto multiple and profound meanings not otherwise possible (Djuna Barnes' *Nightwood*, and some of the works of Joyce, Faulkner, and John Hawkes). Just as the writer experiences pleasure in making obscurities clear, he also enjoys providing the reader with occasions for doing that on his own. While most people enjoy solving a mystery or puzzle, readers often resent the feeling that the author has simply not bothered to make essential matters clear, or has sacrificed clarity for some other lesser value. But each of these negatives may be used positively.

Related to meaning, theme, and truth is the question of *universality*. "The whole secret of fiction," said Thomas Hardy, "lies in the adjustment of things unusual to things eternal and universal." Universality is a very abstract notion, but it quickens to life as soon as a reader feels it in a novel; universality begins with the individual; thus, there is a quality of solitariness about it—the reader reading alone. We speak of universal meaning, predicaments, characters, feelings. There are private and universal dimensions to values; the novelist makes us feel simultaneously at both poles. Universal, also, is used as an honorific term. But what writer *can't* be universal?

There is in the teaching of literature today perhaps too much emphasis on *"theme-mongering,"* i.e., a search for complexities of meaning, with symbols as clues; theme is sometimes called a moral, even worse, a message. Obviously, every novel has a theme, but if it is a good novel, its theme is inseparable from its form and content, although it may be discussed apart. Some novels are obviously theme-dominated, but excessive theme-mongering can detract from other elements. Too often, form and technique are neglected, and the student is left with a course in philosophy. Although theme and content more often dictate form than the reverse, it is form and technique that enable the reader to *experience* meaning in the author's handling of the elements of fiction: character, scene, description, narrative.

In the romance narrative, the aim was illusion that revealed reality; in the novel, the aim is reality that reveals illusion. The grand theme of the novel—and most other arts—is the conflict between appearance and reality, often resulting in illusions and disillusions. And no wonder, since the essential medium and aim of fiction is illusion itself; thus, the novel's central subject and theme is its own nature. This conflict is reflected in the history of the novel itself, a conflict between an approach through reason as against an approach basically through unreason or the irrational, described in Nietzsche's concept of the Apollonian and the Dionysian attitude.

There are those writers who believe in the autonomy of a work of art—that it has no direct dependence upon a context outside itself—and those who see the work as part of the life process. But no matter what basic approach to form, all writers have dealt with similar themes. What follows is a representative sampling of those themes.

A theme (*a* because most novels are composed of more than one) that dominates the works of Henry James and Wright Morris is the relationship between life and literature, life and art, fact and fiction. Which influences which and how; is it a reciprocal process?

One facet of the life and literature theme is the concept of the artist as con man and the con man as artist, developed in Thomas Mann's *The Confessions of Felix Krull* and in David Madden's *Pleasure-Dome*. *Pilgrim's Progress* demonstrates the forces of good and evil in an allegorical, objective way; *The Brothers Karamazov* in more subjective ways, delving into the nature of good and evil (see especially the "Grand Inquisitor" chapter). Graham Greene (*The Power and the Glory*) and François Mauriac (*Viper's Tangle*) show the relationships between man and God, and the conflict between faith and doubt. Most writers deal in some way with the conflict between man's spiritual aspirations and his compulsions toward obsession with material things. On a more imaginative but perhaps less serious level, the supernatural has been one way of dealing with spiritual problems, as in James' *The Turn of the Screw* and Charles Williams' *All Hallow's Eve*.

Agnostic writers have raised doubts about man's religious quests, certainly about the effect of Christianity upon the individual, victimizing him he refuses to or cannot conform, as in Hawthorne's *The Scarlet Letter*. Atheist writers, such as Sartre, have argued the death of God. The hypoc risy of those who force Christianity upon the community is demonstrated in a great many novels, two of which are Samuel Butler's *The Way of All Flesh* and Sinclair Lewis' *Elmer Gantry*.

The conflict between orthodoxy and freedom in various spheres of human activity is dramatized in a majority of novels, with most writers advocating freedom. A few are conservative; for instance, James Gould Cozzens, in *The Just and the Unjust*, a realistic story of small town lawyers, written in a flat, matter-of-fact, though sometimes ornate style, rather intellectual in tone. And a few are anarchical: Jack Kerouac in *On the Road*. Stendhal's *The Red and the Black* is one of the first great psychological and realistic depictions of the rise of a young man in society (nineteenth century France); Julien's fall is tragic because he has a good mind that is directed only toward detecting the hypocrisies in a society so he can take advantage of them. Meursault in Camus' *The Stranger* is aware of shams almost as a second nature and doesn't even want to rise in society. The individual in conflict with society often has a compulsion to confess, as in Camus' *The Fall* and Dostoyevsky's *Crime and Punishment*.

The failure of society to satisfy the deepest needs of the individual is seen in the way national aspirations collapse; thus, in American fiction, one of the dominant themes is the conflict between American dreams and American nightmares, the promise and the reality, as in Fitzgerald's *The Great Gatsby* and Faulkner's *Absalom, Absalom!* (See Madden, *American Dreams, American Nightmares*.)

The failure of national ideals stems from the modern source of the ideals themselves: faith in science and technology to enable a nation to rise to less material levels. But the negative effect of technology on individuals and groups is the theme of many novels, as in Frank Norris's *The Octopus*. Cultural and social isolation is a prevalent theme, as in McCullers' *The Heart Is a Lonely Hunter*. Usually, the protagonist of a modern novel is a victim of society; he almost never wins, as in Saul Bellow's *The Victim*.

Some writers conceive of human experience in materialistic terms; others depict the negative results of a culture's emphasis on material things, to the neglect of spiritual values, as in John O'Hara's *Appointment in Samarra*. Characters belong to and are victims of mass society, whose values many writers abhor—understandably, since their medium, fiction, is itself a non-materialistic venture. The theme of dehumanization by mass technology dominates much modern literature, as in Harriette Arnow's *The Dollmaker*. Some novels depict the conflict between the individual and society: James T. Farrell, *The Studs Lonigan Trilogy*; others depict the group against society: Victor Hugo, *Germinal*. The plight of the individual caught up in the group

The modern concept of alienation is one of the major themes of fiction. Technology turns the individual into a mass man, and none of the social institutions provide him with the means of coping with his environment nor with his inner conflicts. He becomes alienated from society, because society pretends that nothing is wrong, that its tenets are sound even in the face of obvious contradictions: Hermann Hesse, *Steppenwolf.*

Even so, some writers believe that though man is originally estranged from nature and our human institutions are corrupt, the only alternative to suicide is to become engaged in the affairs of men, to be committed to something. This is possible in wartime, as in André Malraux's *Man's Fate* and *Man's Hope,* but difficult in peace, as in Camus' *The Plague.* To many writers, a falseness permeates man's life, and he must seek some kind of authenticity: Sartre's *Nausea.*

Another modern theme is the conflict between determinism and choice: Theodore Dreiser's *An American Tragedy* and Joyce Carol Oates' *them.* And there is the conflict between man and nature, individually and in groups: Rölvaag's *Giants in the Earth* and in Knut Hamsun's *Growth of the Soil.* Conrad and others have shown that the primitive still exists in modern man; his environment has changed more rapidly than his inner nature as an animal: *Victory* by Conrad and *Lord of the Flies* by William Golding. Nature is depicted as a struggle, as mechanical force, as organism; and some writers present thought as a natural rather than simply a human event: Nathalie Sarraute, *Tropisms.*

The novel deals with the author's present era, but often tries to recapture a sense of the past. Men "stand like giants immersed in time," said Proust. Jung's concepts of the collective unconscious have inspired writers to explore our primitive origins. Inhibited by modern social concepts, man suppresses his unconscious; many writers urge a liberation of the unconscious and a response to the blood: Lawrence in *Women in Love* and *The Rainbow.* Some writers examine the role of instincts in our lives, and depict efforts to break through social restraints: Nikos Kazantzakis, *Zorba the Greek.* An examination of man's dream life is one way to discover man's inner nature, for his outer relationships are corrupt and unfulfilling: the novels of Anaïs Nin, *A Spy in the House of Love.*

Man seeks reconciliation with himself and others as a social animal, and modern novels attempt to relate modern man to a larger scheme than history. Some novels present a mythic pattern as a way of giving a dimension and some significance to modern life: Joyce's *Ulysses,* Gide's *Theseus,* Faulkner's *The Bear,* Fitzgerald's *The Great Gatsby.* Other writers return to folk elements and origins and show their continuing relevance and effect

Chinua Achebe, *Things Fall Apart* and Amos Tutuola, *The Palm Wine Drinkard.*

Aware that in the nature of things, he must die, no matter what the outcome of his struggles within himself and in society, modern man experiences dread and anxiety. Mutability haunts many novels; characters, realizing they have no stake in eternity, attempt to live fully in the moment: Oscar Wilde, *The Picture of Dorian Gray*, J.-K. Huysmans, *Against Nature.*

Related to various perspectives on the reality versus illusion theme, the search for identity is perhaps the most important modern theme. Though society may force the individual to conform, as it fails to nourish him even physically, man turns inward; some writers deal with the theme of self-realization through self-consciousness. Psychological maladjustment within oneself and in relation to others is a frequent result: J. P. Donleavy, *The Ginger Man.* This maladjustment may be expressed in various forms of aggression—especially in this age of national aggressions: Thomas McGuane, *Ninety-two in the Shade.*

The theme of the divided self has fascinated many writers; if society is divided against itself, and individuals are alienated from it, and groups are in conflict with it, some characters find an inner conflict between one aspect and another of their natures. The dopplegänger (double) is a fascinating theme for many writers: Gerald Heard, *Dopplegängers.* Most often this divided self is perverse, as in the novels of Dostoyevsky: *The Brothers Karamazov.* Some characters deliberately set out to understand their divided natures, and one method is deliberate perversity or the cultivation of inconsistency as a way of making a break-through into self-revelation. The gratuitous act of Gide's characters *(Lafcadio's Adventures)* is double-edged; it enables the character to see himself in sharp relief and it is a deliberate act of alienation from society, so that he is forced to examine himself as an individual.

Sometimes this concentration upon oneself is depicted as an escape into oneself from the conflicts of society: J. D. Salinger, *A Catcher in the Rye.* Other characters go into a spiritual and physical exile, leaving their own society to move more easily within a foreign one in which they feel less involved and can therefore examine and cultivate their inner lives; usually, these are artists. Thus, the formation of the artist is another theme more modern than others; it is not found among the early novels: Joyce's *Portrait of the Artist as a Young Man.* We see his estrangement from the very society he depicts.

The artist's own failure to communicate with an indifferent bourgeois audience causes him to examine characters who are unable to communicate with each other on all levels of society. This problem is particularly acute for adolescents, who are neither children nor adults: Carson McCullers' *A Member of the Wedding*. The spiritual isolation of individuals is a larger variant of the failure to communicate: William Gaddis, *The Recognitions*.

Nor can people relate physically in a society that frowns upon sexual contact, and the psychotic effect of sexual mores on people is a major theme: Ludwig Lewisohn, *The Case of Mr. Crump*. As soon as the novel begins to deal with sex, individuality becomes more clearly defined; love can be handled in general terms, but not sexuality.

Thus estranged from society and from each other, some men come to see all life and its values as relative (another influence of science that transcends purely scientific matters and touches on the nature of man and his place in the universal scheme of things). Writers have always sensed this relativity, questioning values, abstractions, and notions, but today it has become a way of looking directly at *any* claim. In the novel today, attempts moral choices are beset with ambiguity; the moral quest almost always fail relativism triumphs. The claim is made either that it is the quest itself tha matters most or that the quest is intrinsically destructive, futile.

If everything is relative, all life is basically absurd: Camus is consequently optimistic *(The Stranger)* and Kafka is pessimistic *(The Trial)*. istentialism is a philosophy that attempts to put some order into this shatt ing concept, as in the novels of Sartre *(Nausea)* and Simone de Beauvior *(The Mandarins)*. The major question becomes one of *Being and Nothing-ness* (title of a philosophical work by Sartre), not one or the other, but the simultaneity of the two, and the tensions between.

The ancients declared: *Carpe Diem* ("seize the day"). Saul Bellow, in his novella *Seize the Day*, uses the term ironically, showing that modern man is incapable of acting on that philosophical attitude. The result is blac humor, victim psychology, and the only salvation seems to lie in man's capacity for compassion and imagination, as we see in the works of Wrigh Morris and in William Gaddis' *The Recognitions*.

Just as there exists polarities of artists (classic and romantic, makers a dreamers, Apollonian and Dionysian), there are polarities in visions of life as conducive to order and as intractable; there are attitudes basically of in tellect or of feeling, objective and subjective, public and private. And just there are writers, critics, and readers who take either single or pluralistic approaches to literature, there are writers whose visions of life may be se along a spectrum from narrow to pluralistic. The author's *vision* of man in the world, against a background of nothingness or of the divine, determines everything in his novel; technique helps him not only to focus but to discover what his vision is. When a writer achieves a vision of the "real" world that is sufficiently coherent, we begin to speak of "the world" of Conrad's novels or of Mann's, which is relatively not much more comprehensive than that world we individually speak of as ours, but which is charged more electrically with feeling, meaning, and power of perception, and perhaps of order.

The author's general vision may be mainly tragic or mainly comic, or, in rare instances, balanced: Charles Dickens, *Bleak House;* George Meredith, *The Ordeal of Richard Feverel;* and Faulkner, *Light in August.* The skeptical vision is usually productive of little, and paradoxical for two reasons: the true skeptic scorns any communication at all, and the partial skeptic, because he does speak, often makes his readers believers to some degree. The consistently cynical vision is even rarer, for cynicism stifles imagination (Céline, *Jouney to the End of the Night*). Pessimism is a dynamic combination of skepticism and cynicism that cannot finally make up its mind; nihilism is pessimism that *has* made up its mind, and there's an end to creation. The great writers achieve two things that transcend the raw materials of their own time: a universality of theme and a vision that is made unique by the author's imagination and technique (Dostoevsky's *The Brothers Karamazov;* Conrad's *Nostromo;* Thomas Mann's *The Magic Mountain;* Faulkner's *The Sound and the Fury*).

Allen Tate defines the *communication fallacy* (or the heresy of communication) as "the use of poetry to communicate ideas and feelings which should properly be conveyed by non-poetic discourse." This is sometimes called the propaganda or thesis or didactic or moral fallacy: the notion that the writer must communicate a moral or lesson, or an attitude about social evils. Most of the proletarian novels of the thirties are as dead as the headlines that inspired them; the works of the "tough guy" writers of that era are, on the other hand, still very much alive (Hammett, Chandler, Cain, McCoy, Traven). "For messages," said James M. Cain, "I use Western Union." Writers should not enlist or allow themselves to be conscripted as "celestial bellhops." Archibald MacLeish said, "A poem should not mean/ But be"—and then turned around and committed the communication fallacy himself during W.W. II.

A work of the imagination is first an experience, meaning-and-emotion fused in the instant of communication. The writer knows, or discovers, how that act is performed. Wimsatt and Beardsley talk about the *affective fallacy* as "a confusion between the poem and its results (what it is and what it does)." Too many writers today seem distracted by what they want their work to *do* thematically, and neglect what it *is*. Other writers strive to bring an imagined world into being, to make the word flesh.

Eventually, discussion of any element of fiction reveals some aspect of theme; theme should emerge from the reader's emotional and intellectual experience in reading the story. An over-preoccupation with the theme of individual novels will reveal very little about the nature of fiction. Joyce Cary said, "A novel should be an experience and convey an emotional truth rather than arguments." (See Ellmann, *Modern Tradition*.)

PLOT

Plot, a term Aristotle got going, is the arrangement of narrative events to demonstrate the development of an action involving characters. R. S. Crane argues a slightly more sophisticated approach: plot is the simultaneous ordering of all the elements, not just characters in action, in such a way as to produce a unified effect. A description of the plot sometimes traces the development of the story's meaning simultaneously with its storyline, for plot is an action that illustrates a basic idea.

In commercial fiction, plot means the skeleton of the story. For that very reason, some writers, horrified by the predictability of the movement of a plot, have abandoned plot altogether, either to achieve organic form or random effects. Even George Eliot referred to "the vulgar coercion of conventional plot." And later, Ivy Compton-Burnett said, "As regards plots, I find real life no help at all. Real life seems to have no plots. And as I think a plot desirable and almost necessary, I have this extra grudge against life." Elizabeth Bowen is more robust: "There must be combustion. Plot depends for its movement on internal combustion."

It has been said that there are only a few basic plots—the rest is variation and incidental inventiveness and imaginative enrichment. What appears to be plagiarism is often only the nature of fiction manifesting itself; "borrowing" and "imitation" are more apt words, frequently. What makes the difference is each individual writer's ability to invent and to imagine rich variations on the many kinds of plots.

Traditionally, a complete story has a beginning, middle, and end, each with perhaps three phases of development within itself. The main line of action is generated by some specific circumstance or act; we then become involved in the complications, or the entanglement or the tying of the knot. We follow "a rising action," a line of events more positive than negative. A the plot unfolds, the reader becomes aware of an enveloping action: the social background or the milieu in which events have preceded the action of the narrative and will continue once it ends. Walter O'Grady has suggested that many novels move from interior events to exterior incidents as changes occur, and the shifts create a rhythm that the reader enjoys ("On Plot"). The reader also delights in discovering how one event causes another, following cause-and-effect patterns throughout the novel, and in seeing the consequence in the plot of a character's choices. The plot reaches a turning point or a pivotal event, causing a reversal of fortune or situation for a character. There is a "falling action" toward a final solution. Then comes a crisis, climax, or catastrophe, followed by the denouement or resolution—or the unraveling of the complications, the untying of the knot. Character and plot developments should be so arranged as to make the ending seem inevitable.

There is satisfaction in a *resolution* or clarification at the end; the resolution (used interchangeably with denouement) follows the climax of the action; the mind dwells upon the bringing together of all loose ends, in the calm after the climax. Toward the end, the character may experience a discovery of the truth; this is sometimes called a moment of revelation or recognition, in which perhaps he understands himself and his relation with others. Elizabeth in Jane Austen's *Pride and Prejudice* finally recognizes faults based on prejudice. Jack Burden, the narrator of Robert Penn Warren's *All the King's Men,* realizes at the end that

> if you could not accept the past and its burden there was no future, for without one there cannot be the other, and if you could accept the past you might hope for the future, for only out of the past can you make the future. ... and soon now we shall go out of the house and go into the convulsion of the world, out of history into history and the awful responsibility of time.

The writer tries to avoid anti-climaxes: a sudden jolt in tone or attitude after the climax, or an ending that simply fades out (though the latter, done deliberately, may have a good effect, thus giving the term anticlimax a less negative connotation).

A plot may embrace a *subplot,* a double or multiple plots. A subplot or underplot is a story developed along with the main plot, enhancing it, but not strictly meshed with it, as with Levin's story in Tolstoy's *Anna Karenina.* Some novelists are frowned upon for concocting too many subplots, Dickens and George Eliot, in some instances, for they can distract from the main experience, all the more so if ineptly handled. The subplots in Dickens contribute to the sense of scope and richness; in the novels of Thomas Wolfe *(Look Homeward, Angel),* the subplots are justified because the basic premise is the very notion of the infinite richness of living in a world of many different kinds of people. Dickens designs most of his subplots so that they eventually mesh, as in *Bleak House;* Wolfe and others do not necessarily do that. Some current writers deliberately cultivate the subplot for special effects, to get at areas of experience not otherwise renderable. Camilo José Cela's *The Hive* describes many lives in Madrid; Dos Passos depicts many lives in New York in *Manhattan Transfer.* When subplots are part of an integrated vision of life, they cease, in the ordinary, in the negative sense, to be subplots.

A *double plot* is not the same thing as a subplot. In a double plot, the two may have almost equal value and are pursued simultaneously, as in Faulkner's *The Wild Palms* and Joyce's *Ulysses* (Stephen's and Bloom's narratives). A *multiple plot* is another thing: a deliberate presentation of three or more stories alternately, with varying degrees of final coherence (John Dos Passos, *U.S.A.,* Irwin Shaw, *The Young Lions*). Readers delight in such plot variety (as offered also by epics and romances). A story-within-a-story is not, strictly speaking, the same as subplot. A famous example is the Grand Inquisitor's story in *The Brothers Karamazov;* it illuminates the main story, coming in the straight stream of the main story, transcribed in first person, by Ivan. A later example is Jack's story of Cass Mastern in *All the King's Men* by Robert Penn Warren.

As the plot develops, the writer may use various devices to hold reader interest and enhance the main elements. He may foreshadow what is to come, as Anna Karenina's suicide at the end is foreshadowed by the accidental death of a man at the railroad station early in the novel. Dickens often stimulates the reader to anticipate that something will happen, then satisfies or frustrates, or manipulates that anticipation; he sometimes delays it, or reverses it with a surprise. A writer may present a key moment, an incident endowed with meaning for everything presented so far, as when Meursault shoots the Arab at the exact center of Camus' *The Stranger.* Accidents and *coincidences* are frowned upon in serious fiction, but they can be presented in such a way as to suggest a vision of life. In Wright Morris' *Ceremony in Lone Tree,* events cause McKee to conclude that "in more cases than he cared to remember what was described as an accident was the most important event of a man's life. ... the accident made sense." And in Morris' *One Day:* "It is one of Cowie's notions that meaningful events are accidents." One of the major experiences for the reader (more than for the characters) is the perception of patterns of coincidences in William Gaddis's *The Recognitions* and Joyce's *Ulysses.*

Later writers depart in various ways from basic plot formulas, realizing that life does not develop or resolve in patterned ways. One writer imitates the natural chaos of actual life, adding one episode and detail to another (William Gaddis, *JR*). Another writer imposes an aesthetic pattern, the product of his own unique mind and intelligence, producing a sensation of beauty for the reader in the form itself, while leaving the lives of the characters perhaps still in flux (Joyce, *Ulysses*).

STRUCTURE

The arrangement or organization or structure of the elements of a novel determines its power, force, charm, and excellence. Structure and plot are rather mechanical concepts, but they are not quite the same. A writer structures a plot, and there is usually variety in the way he does so. Some episodes are long, some short, some detailed, some general. (See O'Grady, "On Plot.") E. M. Forster sees a difference between the structure of a story and a plot: story is "a narrative of events arranged in their time-sequence"; plot is a narrative also, but with the "emphasis falling on causality."

The structure of a novel reflects the way an author's mind works, his vision of life, and the world around him. Structure is also partially dictated by the type of story being told, the theme, characters, and plot concept. The structure of a narratively intricate novel (D. H. Lawrence's *The Rainbow*) will differ greatly from that of a novel that renders psychological processes (Virginia Woolf, *To the Lighthouse*). Even novels that pretend to imitate chaos have structure, derived from the repetition of certain elements, ideas, sensations, types of characters (Julio Cortazar, *Hopscotch*); no novel, told in words that signify, no matter how hard a writer tries to make them meaningless, can contain chaos; it's a contradiction. A novel by virtue of its existence is a denial of chaos. Sometimes chaos can be felt best when presented in a highly controlled and artificial manner (Jerzy Kosinski, *Steps*). Randomness is not the same as chaos; a novel can give an impression of randomness by being spontaneous (William Burroughs, *Nova Express* or Steve Katz, *The Exaggerations of Peter Prince*). The structure of an historical or a chronical novel is dictated by type. Sometimes a realistic sequence of events in a character's life dictates the structure (Dickens, *David Copperfield* and Harriette Arnow, *The Dollmaker*). Some novels are composed of vignettes or episodes isolated in time and space, featuring characters whose relationship to each other is apparent more to the reader than to themselves (Virginia Woolf, *The Waves*).

Most novels are divided into chapters. Philip Stevik in "Fictional Chapters and Open Ends" observes that because chapters must end, they give the novel a quality of discontinuity, even though the reader knows that the novel will continue; this tension of contradiction is exciting to a reader, and some writers play off the starts-and-stops conventions for special effects. In *Tristram Shandy*, Laurence Sterne parodies the use of chapters. Philip Wylie uses sudden one-line chapters for shock effect: "I played bridge." Kurt Vonnegut in *Cat's Cradle*, Joan Didion in *Play It As It Lays*, and

Evan S. Connell in *Mrs. Bridge* make frequent use of chapters less than 3 pages long. Because of the *gestalt*-making tendency of readers, there is a need, especially in a long novel, to limit and control the span of concentration.

The writer must control the sequence of events, and of other elements; it is important to determine what comes when and what is to be stressed in sequence. *Beginnings* and *endings* are especially troublesome. A good novel begins where it has to. Ford Madox Ford often wondered whether he should have a dramatic or a reflective opening: "Openings are therefore of necessity always affairs of compromise." Some memorable opening lines: "This is the saddest story I have ever heard" (Ford Madox Ford, *The Good Soldier*). "Mother died today. Or, maybe, yesterday; I can't be sure" (Albert Camus, *The Stranger*). "Happy families are all alike; every unhappy family is unhappy in its own way" (Leo Tolstoy, *Anna Karenina*). Most writers try to get the novel's patterns started in the opening passages. "Beginnings are always troublesome," George Eliot observed. "Conclusions are the weak point of most authors, but some of the fault lies in the very nature of conclusion, which is at best a negation." Chekhov said, ". . . at the end of a novel. . . I must artfully concentrate for the reader an impression of the entire work. . . ." Virginia Woolf achieves that effect with the last line of *To the Lighthouse:* "It was done; it was finished. Yes, she thought, laying down her brush in extreme fatigue. I have had my vision."

A plot may be broken down into scenes, which are to be distinguished slightly from *episodes;* a scene usually has dialog, and is a term taken for that reason from the theater, while an episode may be pure narrative, as in Samuel Butler's *The Way of All Flesh* (which has very few dialog scenes).

> One morning he had gone out to attend some sales, leaving his wife perfectly well, as usual in good spirits, and looking very pretty. When he came back he found her sitting on a chair in the back parlour, with her hair over her face, sobbing and crying as though her heart would break. She said she had been frightened in the morning by a man who had pretended to be a customer, and had threatened her unless she gave him some things, and she had had to give them to him in order to save herself from violence; she had been in hysterics ever since the man had gone. This was her story, but her speech was so incoherent that it was not easy to make out what she said. Ernest knew she was with child, and thinking this might have something to do with the matter, would have sent for a doctor if Ellen had not begged him not to do so.

Some critics make an analogy between a scene in fiction and an image in a poem. The reader enjoys moving from scene to generalization, or *panorama*, as Percy Lubbock calls it: an authorial overview of a stretch of time or of a character's general state of mind, followed by scenes of varying length. (See Lubbock, *The Craft of Fiction*.) Some novels are episodic in structure: *Tom Jones*, *Huckleberry Finn*, Saul Bellow's *Adventures of Augie March*, and Céline's *Journey to the End of the Night*.

Emphasis and stress is achieved through the scenic or the panoramic picture method. The scenic method may be either objective (like a play or a movie), relying heavily on dialog, or there may be some rendering of the thoughts of the characters; in any case, the scenic method is the most immediate. The "panorama" is an omniscient view at some distance, giving a general "picture" through "narrative summary" (Lubbock, *Craft of Fiction*). W. Somerset Maugham's *Of Human Bondage:*

> For the next three months Philip worked on subjects which were new to him. The unwieldy crowd which had entered the Medical School nearly two years before had thinned out: some had left the hospital, finding the examinations more difficult to pass than they expected, some had been taken away by parents who had not foreseen the expense of life in London, and some had drifted away to other callings. One youth whom Philip knew had devised an ingenious plan to make money; he had bought things at sales and pawned them. . . . the young man had gone out to bear the White Man's Burden overseas. The imagination of another, a lad who had never before been in a town at all, fell to the glamour of music-halls and bar parlours; he spent his time among racing-men, tipsters, and trainers, and now was become a book-maker's clerk. . . . A third, with a gift for singing and mimicry, who had achieved success at the smoking concerts of the Medical School by his imitation of notorious comedians, had abandoned the hospital for the chorus of a musical comedy. Still another, and he interested Philip because his uncouth manner and interjectional speech did not suggest that he was capable of any deep emotion, had felt himself stifle among the houses of London. He grew haggard in shut-in spaces, and the soul he knew not he possessed struggled like a sparrow held in the hand, with little frightened gasps and a quick palpitation of the heart: he yearned for the broad skies and the open, desolate places among which his childhood had been spent; and he walked off one day, without a word to anybody, between one lecture and another; and the next thing his friends heard was that he had thrown up medicine and was working on a farm.
>
> Philip attended now lectures on medicine and on surgery. On certain mornings in the week he practised bandaging on out-

patients glad to earn a little money, and he was taught ausculation and how to use the stethoscope.

If the writer is to create an illusion of reality, he must handle these two narrative techniques—scenic and panoramic—in skillful combinations, as do Henry James, Thomas Mann, George Eliot, Jane Austen, and Tolstoy.

The problem of which elements to stress comes up in the matter of *digressions*. Readers today are tolerant of episodic structure but especially impatient with digressions, such as Melville's long dissertations on the cetology of the whale in *Moby Dick*, Hugo's on politics in *Les Misérables* (which is otherwise remarkable for its narrative power, epic scope, dramatic scenes and smooth transitions); Faulkner's story of the three-legged race horse in *A Fable;* the numerous digressions in *Don Quixote;* Fielding's own digressions as the author in *Tom Jones.*

Usually, the episodic plot is the least effective. One feels that scenes or episodes are linked without enough regard for necessity or probability, as in many epics and romances. However, some fine novels deliberately violate this general rule: the surrealistic novel, such as William Burroughs' *Naked Lunch;* the sexually nightmarish but realistic *Steps* by Jerzy Kosinski; the philosophical *Hopscotch* by Julio Cortazar; William March's realistic war story *Company K;* Joaquim Machado de Assis' *Epitaph of a Small Winner;* Cesare Pavese's *The Moon and the Bonfires*, a personal, poetic, allusive book rendering the past in memory in terse five page chapters. One might say that the units of these novels are almost epigrammatic rather than episodic.

A *situation* is not the same as a scene or an episode, although it is partly presented in the form of a scene. A situation is a general predicamer the character is in. In *Great Expectations,* Pip's efforts to help Magwitch the convict escape is only one of the situations in which he becomes involved. Just as there are stock characters, there are stock situations, and, again, whether that is bad depends on how well they are handled. But eve in the best novels, when the girl goes home to mother after a fight with he husband, we wince, not only because we have experienced that before, bu we've had it too often, and the situation doesn't admit many variations. W will endure it once again only with the implicit promise of something more inventive coming up.

Frame is another structural concept. It is as mechanical as a frame around a window, though the best novels use it as a device along the way Time frame: Dreiser's *An American Tragedy* opens and closes with the sa scene, described in almost the same words, to emphasize the passing of time and the absence from the scene of Clyde Griffiths. Space frame:

William Styron's *Lie Down in Darkness* begins and ends with a train crossing the Virginia landscape and ends when it arrives in Port Warwick; the
novel's events are presented in flashback between these space images. Narrative frame: events on a single day, the 4th of July 1892, frame a series of
flashbacks that make up the body of Ross Lockridge's *Raintree County*.
Character frame: the story Rosa Coldfield tells Quentin Compson in Faulkner's *Absalom, Absalom!* is important mainly in its effect on the listener.
The effect is the same as with a frame around a painting: to set off, define
its best features, enhance its coloration and size.

The *pace* of a novel refers not only to the handling of action in mea-
sured doses, but to the rate of movement of all the novel's parts and it is set
by the nature of the other elements. (Some parts of a story may move at a
different rate than others.) An author may accelerate pace by using abrupt
transitions or short bits of dialog; the pace may be slowed by using narrative
description. The author's regulation of pace affects the reader's responses to
all the other elements in a story. Pace may contribute to the sense of inevitability we feel about the way the story turns out; pace may excite
psychological tension and sustain narrative tension.

One technique that most writers consider vital but that may slow down
the pace of a narrative is *exposition*. "It is the function of the exposition to
introduce the reader into an unfamiliar world," says Meir Sternberg (in her
essay "What is Exposition?"), "by providing him with the general and specific background information indispensable to the understanding of what
happens in it.... This expositional information the author is obliged to
communicate to the reader in one way or another." John Galsworthy's *The
Forsyte Saga:*

> On June 15, late in the eighties, about four of the afternoon,
> the observer who chanced to be present at the house of Jolyon
> Forsyte in Stanhope Gate, might have seen the highest efflores-
> cence of the Forsytes.
> This was the occasion of an 'at home' to celebrate the engage-
> ment of Miss June Forsyte, old Jolyon's granddaughter, to Mr.
> Philip Bosinney....
> When a Forsyte was engaged, married, or born, the Forsytes
> were present.

Most offer exposition in the beginning, some delay it, some concentrate it
all in one place, some distribute it piecemeal throughout; sometimes, it is
incidental, rather than crucial. "But the location and the form of exposition
are always worth inquiring into because they are usually indicative of and
often integral to the structure and compositional principles of the work as a
whole."

Pace and exposition, in very different ways, are time problems for the writer, and the way he solves the problem of exposition will affect pace. James M. Cain is a master of pace in the tough school of the Thirties but his best novel, *The Postman Always Rings Twice*, is not action-packed; however, the pace of the novel persuades the reader to believe that in 30 pages, Frank has met Cora and their passion for each other is so powerful they have decided to kill Cora's husband, Nick. (Compare with the pace of Camus' *The Stranger*, a philosophical novel modeled after *Postman*; compare also with another "existential" tough-guy novel, Horace McCoy's *They Shoot Horses, Don't They?*) The pace of Gide's short, simple, lucidly written novel *The Immortalist* is very slow; it is a meditative book. The pace of *All the King's Men* is varied, with alternating sections of action and meditation, and that is part of the reader's experience.

> So I had it after all the months. For nothing is lost, nothing is ever lost. There is always the clue, the canceled check, the smear of lipstick, the footprint in the canna bed, the condon on the park path, the twitch in the old wound, the baby shoes dipped in bronze, the taint in the blood stream. And all times are one time, and all those dead in the past never lived before our definition gives them life, and out of the shadow their eyes implore us.
>
> That is what all of us historical researchers believe.
>
> And we love truth.
>
> Chapter Six
>
> It was late March in 1937 when I went to see Miss Littlepaugh in the foul, fox-smelling lair in Memphis, and came to the end of my researches. I had been on the job almost seven months. But other things had happened during that period beside my researches. Tom Stark, a sophomore, had made quarterback c the mythical All Southern Eleven and had celebrated by wrappin, an expensive yellow sport job around a culvert on one of the numerous speedways which bore his father's name.

No matter how much action a novel offers, if the pace is wrong, the novel fails. Other masters of pace are Graham Greene *(The Heart of the Matter)* and Ivan Turgenev *(Fathers and Sons)*.

For some novels, a better term might be *rhythm*. E. M. Forster spea of rhythm as opposed to pattern (which is similar to plot), as in Forster's own novel, *A Room with a View*. What is being moved are the author's commentaries and the flow of blood through a living organism. The term *tempo* applies to the variable speed of the rhythm.

To facilitate pace, rhythm, and tempo, *transitions* must be handled e fectively. A transition is the point in a story when we move from one tim place, position, or idea to another. A transitional device is any method a writer uses to accomplish a transition. Transitions are often difficult to make because the writer must re-orient the reader and make a new start. Transitional devices enable the writer to make shifts in time and place without disturbing the reader's concentration. In some instances a subtle transition is most effective, in others an abrupt or jolting change may work best. Faulkner's complex methods—reorganization of time, shifts in space—require that he handle transitions effectively, as in the bewildering Benjy section of *The Sound and The Fury*.

> "They haven't started yet," Caddy said.

> *They getting ready to start, T. P. said.*

The shift in dialog in quotation marks to dialog in italics suggests a transition from one time to another. The similarity in what Caddy and T. P. say also signals a time shift. T. P.'s scene ends: "'Git on the box and see is they started.'" Faulkner then shifts back to Caddy's scene with: "'They haven't started because the band hasn't come yet,' Caddy said." Of course, most transitions are very simple. "I did not see Brett again until the night of the 24th of June. 'Did you hear from Cohn?'" (Hemingway's *The Sun Also Rises*) Some transitions are very carefully controlled. In *A Death in the Family*, James Agee moves at the end of Chapter 2, from the mother's point of view to that of the father at the start of Chapter 3:

> She was never to realize his intention of holding the warmth in for her; for that had sometime since departed from the bed.

> Chapter 3

> He imagined that by about now she would about be getting back and finding the bed. He smiled to think of her finding it.

Just as the reader delights in experiencing smooth or clever transitions, he also delights in unexpected *reversals* (this is the opposite of the operation of suspense, for here the reader knows what is happening and thus thinks he knows what will happen). When the reader is led to expect or anticipate a certain development and the reverse occurs, the surprise may delight him; if the reversal is contrived or forced, he may be resentful. A reversal may also deepen a reader's understanding of what he has experienced so far. A master of reversal is Henry James, as in *The Wings of the Dove* when Densher's and Kate's elaborate scheme against Milly misfires.

> Her memory's your love. You *want* no other."
> He heard her out in stillness, watching her face, but not moving. Then he only said: "I'll marry you, mind you, in an hour."

"As we were."

"As we were."

But she turned to the door, and her headshake was now the end. "We shall never be again as we were!"

Even when the narration is filtered through the mind of a character, mental processes need to be enhanced by the interplay of objects. T. S. Eliot, in describing metaphysical poetry, gave us a useful term: *"objective correlative."* The writer of fiction may describe an object or an action in such a way that we feel it correlates to a subjective experience of one of the characters. Much of Hemingway functions that way, as in the fishing scene at Burgette in *The Sun Also Rises*. Another term for this device is the poetic or the charged image.

A related technique of heightening mental experiences is the use of *contrasts*, a device used in all points-of-view strategies, but differently for each; for instance, the omniscient narrator may use a contrast of character types: Elizabeth's prejudice against Darcy's pride in Jane Austen's *Pride and Prejudice*. The first person narrator uses contrast to make us feel the reality of the narrator as more than a voice: The unnamed female narrator of Daphne du Maurier's *Rebecca*, contrasted with Miss Danvers. The central intelligence/point-of-view implies the contrast of illusion and reality: the reader perceives that the boy in Henry Roth's *Call It Sleep* understands very little of what he experiences.

The expressionistic device is an exaggeration of the use of contrasts and objective correlatives. *Expressionism*, a technique once used in avant-garde painting (Munch) and theater (Eugene O'Neill's *The Emperor Jones*) now thoroughly assimilated, even in Broadway musicals, is a deliberate distortion of the real to suggest an intense subjective reality. The device is used intermittently in some novels, as in Dickens' *Bleak House*. Tulkingham lies murdered under a dome where a Roman is depicted pointing his finger.

For many years, the persistent Roman has been pointing with no particular meaning from that ceiling. It is not likely that he has any new meaning in him to-night. Once pointing, always pointing—like any Roman, or even Briton, with a single idea. There he is, no doubt, in his impossible attitude, pointing, unavailingly, all night long. Moonlight, darkness, dawn, sunrise, day. There he is still, eagerly pointing, and no one minds him.

But, a little after the coming of the day, come people to clean the rooms. And either the Roman has some new meaning in him not expressed before, or the foremost of them goes wild; for, look ing up at his outstretched hand, and looking down at what is below it, that person shrieks and flies.

. . .

He is pointing at a table, with a bottle (nearly full of wine) and a glass upon it, and two candles that were blown out suddenly, soon after being lighted. He is pointing at an empty chair, and at a stain upon the ground before it that might be almost covered with a hand. These objects lie directly within his range. An excited imagination might suppose that there was something in them so terrific as to drive the rest of the composition, not only the attendant big-legged boys, but the clouds and flowers and pillars too—in short, the very body and soul of Allegory, and all the brains it has—stark mad. It happens surely, that every one who comes into the darkened room and looks at these things, looks up at the Roman, and that he is invested in all eyes with mystery and awe, as if he were a paralyzed dumb witness.

So, it shall happen surely, through many years to come, that ghostly stories shall be told of the stain upon the floor, so easy to be covered, so hard to be got out; and that the Roman, pointing from the ceiling, shall point, so long as dust and damp and spiders spare him, with far greater significance than he ever had in Mr. Tulkinghorn's time, and with a deadly meaning. For, Mr. Tulkinghorn's time is over for evermore; and the Roman pointed at the murderous hand uplifted against his life, and pointed helplessly at him, from night to morning, lying face downward on the floor, shot through the heart.

But very few novels use an expressionistic technique throughout. Words cannot function expressionistically in a work as long as a novel; the effect of exaggeration cannot be sustained that long. Another example is Faulkner's *Absalom, Absalom!*

> . . . and opposite Quentin, Miss Coldfield in the eternal black which she had worn for forty-three years now, whether for sister, father, or not husband none knew, sitting so bolt upright in the straight hard chair that was so tall for her that her legs hung straight and rigid as if she had iron shinbones and ankles, clear of the floor with that air of impotent and static rage like children's feet, and talking in that grim haggard amazed voice until at last listening would renege and hearing-sense self-confound and the long-dead object of her impotent yet indomitable frustration appear, as though by outraged recapitulation evoked, quiet inatten-

tive and harmless, out of the biding and dreamy and victorious dust.

Expressionistic devices might also be called *kinetic* because they act directly upon the senses, to shock, startle a reader into a breakthrough of some sort. Ideally, the reader has a physical sensation. One such kinetic technique is the collage, based on a principle somewhat like the montage. The author composes a sequence, using pieces of this and that, jamming them together in seeming chaos. William Burroughs has written an entire novel in this manner, throwing the pieces into the air and typing them as he picks them up at random *(Naked Lunch)*. Another novelist offers the reader a packet of loose pages which he may assemble any way he wishes. The pastiche novel, made up of pieces of other novels, is rare. Another possibility is the found-objects novel, made up of descriptions of events encountered accidentally from the moment one begins to the moment one ends the novel.

These and similar techniques are used by avant-garde theater groups (the Open Theater) composers (John Cage) and painters (Andy Warhol). Although few novels make exclusive use of any one, or a combination of these devices, a number of novels make incidental use of them for various effects: to shatter the illusion of reality; to thrust the reader suddenly into shifting realms of sensory experience; to ridicule traditional forms; to satirize institutions by satirizing first of all the forms of literature as an institution. The *dadaist* and *surrealist* movements initiated many of these techniques in the 1920's. (See Wallace Fowlie, *Age of Surrealism*, and back issues of *transition*.)

Quite different from kinetic devices, although some effects intermingle, are *impressionistic devices* (another term borrowed from painting). Here the emphasis is upon realistic psychological processes as opposed to simulated, brutal physical processes. The writer gives us a series of interrelated impressions to create a sense of an experience, as in art, Monet, Cézanne, Renoir, Degas; in music, Debussy's *La Mer;* and in the novel, Virginia Woolf *To the Lighthouse* and very differently, Jack Kerouac's *The Subterraneans*.

So some random light directing them with its pale footfall upon stair and mat, from some uncovered star, or wandering ship, or th Lighthouse even, the little airs mounted the staircase and nosed round bedroom doors. But here surely, they must cease. Whateve else may perish and disappear, what lies here is steadfast. Here one might say to those sliding lights, those fumbling airs that breathe and bend over the bed itself, here you can neither touch nor destroy. Upon which, wearily, ghostily, as if they had feather-light fingers and the light persistency of feathers, they would look once, on the shut eyes, and the loosely clasping fingers, and fold their garments wearily and disappear. And so, nosing, rubbing, they went to the window on the staircase, to the servants' bedrooms, to the boxes in the attics; descending, blanched the apples on the dining-room table, fumbled the petals of roses, tried the picture on the easel, brushed the mat and blew a little sand along the floor. At length, desisting, all ceased together, gathered together, all sighed together; all together gave off an aimless gust of lamentation to which some door in the kitchen replied; swung wide; admitted nothing; and slammed to.

(To the Lighthouse)

... the cold winter rainy nights when Charles would be crossing the campus saying something witty, the great epics almost here sounding phantom like and uninteresting if at all believable but the true position and bigburn importance of not only Charles but a good dozen others in the light rack of my brain, so Mardou seen in this light, is a little brown body in a gray sheet bed in the slums of Telegraph Hill, huge future in the history of the night yes but only one among many, the asexuality of the WORK—also the sudden gut joy of beer when the visions of great words in rhythmic order all in one giant archangel book go roaring thru my brain, so I lie in the dark also seeing also hearing the jargon the future worlds— damaje-eleout-ekeke-dhdkdk-dldoud, ——d, ekeoeu- hdhdkehgyt—better not a more than which strangely he doth mdodudltkdip—baseeaatra—for example because of mechanical needs of gyping, of the flow of river sounds, words, hark, leading to the future and attesting to the madness, hollowness, ring and roar of my mind which blessed or unblessed is where trees sing— in a funny wind—well-being believes he'll go to heaven—

(The Subterraneans)

A special effect can be created when two elements are set side by side, or juxtaposed. Some *juxtapositions* are accidental, others are deliberate. Sometimes a writer may juxtapose two images that have no special impact separately but that spark an idea or an emotion when set side by side. The two words, images, or events may be so deliberately and carefully chosen that they spark a third element that exists only in the reader's mind.

In *Portrait of the Artist as a Young Man*, Joyce allows Stephen to hold forth eloquently on the subject of beauty in art.

—This hypothesis, Stephen began.
A long dray laden with old iron came round the corner of Sir

Patrick Dun's hospital covering the end of Stephen's speech with the harsh roar of jangled and rattling metal. . . .

—This hypothesis, Stephen repeated, is . . . that, though the same object may not seem beautiful to all people, all people who admire a beautiful object find in it certain relations which satisfy and coincide with the stages themselves of all aesthetic apprehension.

By juxtaposing to Stephen's philosophical flights a description of a "dray laden with old iron," Joyce does not himself directly say, rather, he implies, that the ordinary realities of this world clash with aesthetic theorizing; but he also implies in the very use and effect of the technique of juxtaposition that in a novel *(Portrait)* all such contraries are reconciled, for both elements are part of the reader's aesthetic experience of that passage and of his apprehension of how it contributes to the unity of the novel.

In the movies this technique is called "*montage.*" Eisenstein, the Russian director, describes montage in this way: "Two pieces of film of any kind, placed together, inevitably combine into a new concept, a new quality, arising out of that juxtaposition." Juxtaposition or montage is a technique that involves the reader as a collaborator in the creative process so that he sees and feels much more.

Montage is used in novels, sometimes for expressionistic, sometimes impressionistic or psychological effects. When two or more different images (often radically separate in time and space) are juxtaposed, the effect is an image, insight, intuitive experience greater than the sum of the parts. The move *Hiroshima, Mon Amour* is full of such images: as the French woman gazes at her sleeping Japanese lover, memory images of her dead German lover flash rapidly, breaking up the living image before her. *Impingement* is another term in fiction for this device. Impingement is also a stylistic technique—one word or phrase impinges kinetically upon another, giving style an immediacy, an active, dynamic quality.

The term *flashback* is appropriated from the movies, also. Until recently a flashback was signalled by the screen's going blurry, but today many movies shift back and forth from present to past (sometimes forward to the future, and the movie catches up eventually) with very little warning And this kinetic way of experiencing the flux of time is part of the whole experience. In fiction, the same thing has happened, especially in *The Cannibal* by John Hawkes.

The ghosts raised their heads in unison by the canal and sniffed the night air.

I, Zizendorf, my gun drawn, crouching on my knees with my

comrades who were tensed like springers or swimmers, heard above gusts of wind the approaching light machine. The uprising must be successful, inspired, ruthless.

The Duke carefully reached out his hand and the boy fairy did not move, while the marquee banged to and fro, the projector steamed, and the invisible lost audience stamped booted feet and rummaged in box lunches.

Unconscious, drowned cold in acid, the Census-taker lay on the third floor, dressed, uncovered, where Jutta had dropped him.

The Mayor, at this hour, groaned, awoke, and found himself pained by a small black-pebble cluster of hemorrhoids, felt it blister upwards over his spine.

The ghosts returned to their cupped hands and sipped the green water, while soft faecal corbans rolled below their faces through the cluttered waves in tribute to Leevey.

Compared with the smooth use in movies, flashbacks are handled obviously and crudely even in some good fiction; but Conrad in *Lord Jim* and Faulkner in *Sanctuary* have used this device in complex and profound ways, so that one experiences, in the technique itself, the vision of the work.

Flashbacks and montage, the more subtly they are used, cause deliberate discontinuity in the plot sequence to achieve effects that would not be possible with continuity; this technique is based on sound psychological insights into the way the mind, emotions, perceptions, work. Discontinuity in technique is often an expression of the same quality in the lives of the characters, or it may be a more direct expression of the author's vision of life, which may differ from that of his characters.

A major characteristic of the language of poetry is *compression* or *condensation;* the same technique is often used effectively in the structure of a novel, as in, for instance, the panoramic passages described earlier. To some extent, of course, all works of fiction are compressions of the endless ramifications of real life, but a conscious use of this technique as a principle of structure has special results.

Focus and *emphasis* control the reader's responses so that his experience will be more concentrated, intense. To achieve emphasis, as distinguished from focus, a writer may select only those details that isolate a specific moment.

Most structures are logically put together, but the structure of some recent novels, especially French, are alogical; they follow a logic that is peculiar to themselves and ostensibly can't be repeated for other novels. The sense they make, the structure that results, may not be visible there in the work; it may occur only in the mind of the perceiver, the reader, and the main character may be engaged in the same task, as in Robbe-Grillet's *The Voyeur;* Nathalie Sarraute's *Tropisms;* and Claude Mauriac's *The Marquise Went Out at Five.* No novel is ever totally plotless, for we read on to the end to be able to look back on some kind of wholeness.

Action need not be narrative, or physical. Even style can in itself be action if what it describes is a developing attitude or state of mind. Psychological movement is the mind constantly reacting, so there is a feeling of mental movement forward toward a solution or realization. Words and phrases and perceptions interact, impinge upon each other, juxtapose violently, as in the novels of James, Virginia Woolf, Fitzgerald, Faulkner, Hemingway, and Wright Morris. Overt action is often too superficial and can be just as boring as inert description presented for its own sake. The proportion of action is sometimes an index to a novel's achievement. The balance of action with other major elements is another positive factor.

The depiction of action requires a great deal of special skill; some writers seem incapable, artistically or temperamentally, of presenting action credibly; some don't intend to (Henry James, for instance). Action is *too* active an ingredient in popular fiction; one thinks of westerns, crime stories, adventure tales of sea and air. But even a war story could be relatively actionless and still grip a reader. (See Edwin Muir, *The Structure of a Novel.*)

STYLE

As the novel matured, approached art, its medium—language—became more self-conscious, controlled, *made.* Style, narrowly speaking, is the author's use of language. Style is choice of words (diction) and syntax (arrangement of words in a sentence) and the handling of sentence and paragraph units by varying patterns to achieve a specific effect. "The sentence is a single cry," said Herbert Read. "It is a unit of expression, and its various qualities—length, rhythm, and structure—are determined by a right sense of this unity." About paragraphs, Read said: "As the thought takes shape in the mind, it takes *a* shape. ... There is about good writing a visual actuality. It exactly reproduces what we should metaphorically call the contour of our thought. ... The paragraph is the perception of this contour or shape" (*English Prose Style*). Katherine Mansfield says, "In 'Miss Brill' I chose not only the length of every sentence, but even the sound of every sentence. I chose the rise and fall of every paragraph to fit her, and to fit her on that day, at that very moment."

Despite its importance, style is one of the least discussed aspects of technique because desciptions of its effect are difficult. The term style should not be confused with the more general term technique, which is *all* the methods the writer uses to produce the whole literary creation. The term may be used as a general synonym of excellence—some have it, some don't. Or as a term of classification: a satirical, a lyrical, a witty, an objective style. When an analysis of a writer's style is carried far enough, it ends in the man himself—Hemingway, for instance.

The total of the qualities that characterize an individual writer's style (some of which may be too subtle ever to be detected) constitutes his literary personality and reflects his personal or psychological one. Style is, then, the man. If the man beguiles himself with his style, he ends up with a mannered style, as Hemingway did. Many of the secrets of style are matters of tone, of the perfect recognition of the writer's relation to the reader in view of what he wants to say and the congruence of his feelings with the reader's.

Style is texture of writing: verbal detail, imagery, connotations and sounds of words, their order in sentences, the lengths of sentences and of paragraphs. Together, style and point of view are the major technical considerations in analyzing fiction. Variations on the author's basic style are somewhat determined by the point of view an author decides to employ. One aspect of style is the use of rhetorical devices (proven ways of stimulating the desired emotion, attitude, or idea in the reader) and figurative language (the use of metaphors and similes, for instance). "Metaphorical language," says Mark Schorer in "The Analogical Matrix," "gives any style its special quality," "expresses, defines, evaluates theme," can be "the basis of structure," as "overthought" or "underthought," "reveals to us the character of any imaginative work." Our responses to a story are controlled by language artfully arranged to achieve carefully prepared effects.

To detect ways in which the writer tries to affect his reader, analyze his style. The words a writer chooses to express feelings, thoughts, and action will tell you a great deal about his relationship with his raw material and the way he wants his readers to respond to it. What are the dictates of style in a particular novel? Is the style appropriate to the subject matter and to the point of view the author uses?

Few writers really arrive at a distinctive style of their own; it is easier to recognize most writers by their handling of other techniques. The essential differences between great writers remain mysterious and cannot be discussed, but one may be more receptive to that essence if one learns to recognize distinguishing characteristics. It is distinctive style wedded to technique or craft that distinguishes most great novelists from each other. "... There is no branch of criticism in which learning as well as good sense," said Henry Fielding, "is more required than to the forming an accurate judgment of style. . . ." And Flaubert (whose *Madame Bovary* has taught many modern novelists to write) said: "One never tires of anything that is well written. Style is life! Indeed it is the life-blood of thought! . . . I shall try to show why aesthetic criticism has remained so far behind historical and scientific criticism: it *had no foundation*. The knowledge everyone lacked was *analysis of style*, the understanding of how a phrase is constructed and articulated." "I would sooner die like a dog than hurry my sentence by so much as a second before it is ripe. . . . A phrase is an adventure." He strove for the *"mot juste"* (the right word). Zola said, "A well-made phrase is a good action," giving good style an almost moral quality.

Generally, we may speak of simple, complex, and mid-styles.

Economy, objectivity, and indirection or underwriting characterize the *simple style*. It is concrete, clear, exact, vivid, brief, in combinations that are fresh. War-weary Frederick Henry in Hemingway's *A Farewell to Arms* offers a credo for underwriting: "There were many words you could not stand to hear and finally only the names of places had dignity. . . . Abstract words such as glory, honor, courage, or hallow were obscene beside the concrete names of villages, the numbers of roads, the names of rivers . . . and the dates." A fine example of underwriting is the fishing scene at Burgette in the middle of *The Sun Also Rises* (see essay in Part III). Gertrude Stein's simple style influenced Sherwood Anderson's. The dog "did not die with a real sickness. She just got older and more blind and coughed and then more quiet, and then slowly one bright summer's day, she died" *(The Good Anna)*. Stein's simplicity was consciously and deliberately artificial and literary, and finally complex. With a kind of folk simplicity in story-telling and in narrative line itself, Anderson made a breakthrough in style: "Wing Biddlebaum talked with his hands. . . . The story of Wing Biddlebaum is a story of hands." Anderson once said: "Any clearness I have in my own life is due to my feeling for words." Both Stein and Anderson influenced Hemingway's style. *A Farewell to Arms* opens with a muted portentous lyricism:

> In the late summer of that year we lived in a house in a village that looked across the river and the plain to the mountains. In the bed of the river there were pebbles and boulders, dry and white in the sun, and the water was clear and swiftly moving and blue in the channels. Troops went by the house and down the road and the dust they raised powdered the leaves of the trees. The trunks of the trees too were dusty and the leaves fell early that year and we saw the troops marching along the road and the dust rising and leaves, stirred by the breeze, falling and the soldiers marching and afterward the road bare and white except for the leaves.

John O'Hara exerts sophisticated control over the simple style in *An Appointment in Samarra*. James T. Farrell in the *Studs Lonigan Trilogy*, uses

a tough, functional, simple style to serve his ideas about life in city slums.
Graham Greene in *Brighton Rock* fuses purpose, technique, and style.

The complex style is elaborate, rhapsodic, lyrical, subjective, sometimes
overwritten, especially in the misuse of hyperbole (exaggeration, or rhetoric
in excess of the occasion). Henry James in *The Wings of the Dove* shows
himself a master of the baroquely complex style:

> The two ladies who, in advance of the Swiss season, had been
> warned that their design was unconsidered, that the passes would
> not be clear, nor the air mild, nor the inns open—the two ladies
> who, characteristically had braved a good deal of possibly in-
> terested remonstrance were finding themselves, as their adventure
> turned out, wonderfully sustained.

The complex style is at work in the arch, sophisticated, snobbish tone of
Mary McCarthy's *The Groves of Academe*. Frederick Buechner's modification of the Jamesian style in *A Long Day's Dying* is intricate and sensitive.
Personal anguish in the struggle between response to the subject and inability to capture or express one's feelings about the actual thing in words
produces the desperately reaching-out style of James Agee in *A Death in
the Family*. There is an expressionistic complexity in the style of Faulkner's
Absalom, Absalom!; a rhapsodic excess in Thomas Wolfe's *Look Homeward,
Angel;* an exploitation of the bizarre in Djuna Barnes' intricate, baroque,
highly metaphorical *Nightwood;* symbolic expressionism in the style of D.
H. Lawrence's *The Rainbow;* a tangle of puns and comic repetition gives
complexity to Joseph Heller's style in *Catch-22;* Herbert Read's style in *The
Green Child* alternates between the philosophical and the weirdly lyrical.

The *mid-style* consists of combinations of the simple and the complex;
it is conservative, traditional, characterized by wit and satire, and allows
more objectivity—the freedom but also the occasional dullness of neutrality.
Jane Austen's traditional style is at dead center in *Emma*.

> Happily it was not necessary to speak. There was only Harriet,
> who seemed not in spirits herself, fagged, and very willing to be si-
> lent; and Emma felt the tears running down her cheeks almost all
> the way home without being at any trouble to check them, ex-
> traordinary as they were.

The southern writer Carson McCullers is lyrical in her use of the mid-style
in *The Heart Is a Lonely Hunter*, speaking of Singer the mute:

> And then sometimes when he was alone and his thoughts were
> with his friend his hands would begin to shape the words before he
> knew about it. Then when he realized he was like a man caught

talking aloud to himself. It was almost as though he had done some moral wrong. The shame and sorrow mixed together and he doubled his hands and put them behind him. But they would not let him rest.

There is a midwestern laconic quality in Wright Morris' lyrical, impressionistic, nostalgic opening of *The Works of Love*.

In the dry places, men begin to dream. Where the rivers run sand, there is something in man that begins to flow. West of the 98th Meridian—where it sometimes rains and it sometimes doesn't—towns, like weeds, spring up when it rains, dry up when it stops. But in a dry climate, the husk of the plant remains. The stranger might find, as if preserved in amber, something of the green life that was once lived there, and the ghosts of men who have gone on to a better place. The withered towns are empty, but not uninhabited. Faces sometimes peer out the broken windows, or whisper from the sagging balconies, as if this place—now that it is dead—had come to life. As if empty, it is forever occupied. One of these towns, so the story would have it was Indian Bow.

There is a more controlled tone of nostalgia in the opening of Morris' *Ceremony in Lone Tree:* "Come to the window. The one at the rear of the Lone Tree hotel. The view is to the west." Even in setting a scene Morris' style moves. Other mid-stylists are: Flaubert *(Madame Bovary)*; Dreiser *(An American Tragedy*, with its many instances of pseudo-literary syntax); Sinclair Lewis *(Babbitt)*; James Gould Cozzens *(The Just and the Unjust)*; Willa Cather *(Song of the Lark)*; Steinbeck *(The Grapes of Wrath).*

Some novels employ a combination of styles. Melville's *Moby Dick* is a strange mixture of styles and techniques within the first person point of view. In *Bleak House*, Dickens employs the effective strategy of alternating chapters of narration by a *good* woman with his own omniscient, present tense roving-eye-view. modulating the style from chapter to chapter, as he shifts point of view. In *Howard's End*, E. M. Forster speaks often in his own voice, but modulates objective narration ironically with the thoughts of his characters. In *Portrait of the Artist as a Young Man*, Joyce's style is lyrical but controlled, becoming more and more complex as Stephen matures. Joyce's *Ulysses* uses many literary styles, conventional and experimental, serving a complex form and a profound theme.

The style of most fiction is a careful amalgam of words that denote and words that connotate. Some writers use denotative (explicit) words more than others: James T. Farrell, James M. Cain, and Erskine Caldwell.

Lov opened the sack, selected a large turnip, wiping it clean with his hands, and took three big bites one after the other. The Lester women stood in the yard and on the porch looking at Lov eat. Ellie May came from behind the chinaberry tree and sat down not far from Lov on a pine stump. Ada and the old grandmother were on the porch watching the turnip in Lov's hand become smaller and smaller with each bite. (Erskine Caldwell, *Tobacco Road*).

Some writers use connotative (suggestive) words, and thus move closer to poetry. Virginia Woolf, Jean Cocteau, J. P. Donleavy, Malcolm Lowry, Gabriel Miro, Vladimir Nabokov.

Their visits to that islet remained engraved in the memory of that summer with entwinements that no longer could be untangled. They saw themselves standing there, embraced, clothed only in mobile leafy shadows, and watching the red rowboat with its mobile inlay of reflected ripples carry them off, waving, waving their handkerchiefs; and that mystery of mixed sequences was enhanced by such things as the boat's floating back to them while it still receded, the oars crippled by refractions, the sunflecks now rippling the other way like the strobe effect of spokes counter-wheeling as the pageant rolls by.

(Vladimir Nabokov, *Ada*)

In fiction, language more often connotes than it denotes. The writer tries to evoke something that is not literally denoted in the lines on the page. We experience then what the words evoke. Sometimes the specific limitations of the point of view the author has chosen prevents him from literally stating, forces him to evoke explanations, for instance, and the reader then perceives them. "I want to use a minimum of words for a maximum effect," says Wright Morris. "Underwriting seems to be a species of underwater swimming. Is the pool empty? That is how it often looks." Hemingway said: "If a writer of prose knows enough about what he is writing about he may omit things that he knows and the reader, if the writer is writing truly enough, will have a feeling of those things as strongly as though the writer had stated them. The dignity of movement of an iceberg is due to only one-eighth of it being above water."

Zola felt style could be abused if wedded to excess emotion: "We are in fact rotten with lyricism; we believe, quite wrongly, that the grand style is the product of some sublime terror always on the verge of pitching over into frenzy; the grand style is achieved through logic and clarity." When a writer goes too far in his descriptive passages, becoming too lyrical, he ends up with a *"purple patch"* that calls attention to itself. "Under the pavements

trembling like a pulse, under the buildings trembling like a cry, under th
waste of time, under the hoof of the beast above the broken bones of citie
there will be something growing like a flower, something bursting from th
earth again, forever deathless, faithful, coming into life again like April"
(Thomas Wolfe, *You Can't Go Home Again*). Over-written prose is often
devoted to descriptions of the sky, of settings, or of the hero waking up ir
the morning or walking down the street. The realist despises "fine writing
which writers such as Walter Pater, J.-K. Huysmans, Ronald Firbank, and
Oscar Wilde strive for. The following is from J.-K. Huysmans' *Against Na
ture*.

> With a withdrawn, solemn, almost august expression on her
> face, she begins the lascivious dance which is to rouse the aged
> Herod's dormant senses; her breasts rise and fall, the nipples ha
> dening at the touch of her whirling necklaces; the strings of
> diamonds glitter against her moist flesh; her bracelets, her belts,
> her rings all spit out fiery sparks; and across her triumphal robe,
> sewn with pearls, patterned with silver, spangled with gold, the
> jewelled cuirass, of which every chain is a precious stone, seems
> be ablaze with little snakes of fire, swarming over the mat flesh,
> over the tea-rose skin, like gorgeous insects with dazzling shards
> mottled with carmine, spotted with pale yellow, speckled with
> steel blue, striped with peacock green.

The High style often ends up being affected. Overuse of exotic phrases, a
chaic words, or juiced up mannerisms can overornament a style. Some
writers strive, unfortunately, for a literary tone.

Another threat is *abstract language*. The first 80 pages of *Salt* by He
bert Gold (he is often a good writer) consist almost solely of two kinds of
general, abstract statements: "He ate, he slept, he worked, he juggled, ar
the identical days filed by." "'You love me?' He guessed that he did. He
pitied her, cherished her, admired her, and was bored by her. He did no
want to be bothered." Very little is immediate, dramatized in those 80
pages; the style is often scintillating, but almost always the experience is
abstract. In the first 150 pages of this 400-page novel, Gold much too ofte
uses such general, passive statements as, "He would take a shower and he
would call Janet." Too little happens in the immediate present. Too many
passive verbs render one's style sluggish or inert. Judiciously used, abstra
style has its function, but often a writer dupes himself into thinking a high
sounding abstraction contains more emotion and power than it possibly ca
Ezra Pound said to the Imagist poets, "Go in fear of abstractions."

By becoming too chummy with the reader, the writer may commit th
cute-tone fallacy, characteristic at one end of the literary spectrum of mar

women's magazine stories and at the other of "little" or underground
magazine pieces.

"That man has no soul," said Oscar Wilde, "who can read of the death
of Little Nell without laughing." Wilde was revolted by the *fallacy of sentimentality:* "The suspension of the activities of the intelligence, of the powers of ethical and intellectual judgment... emotion unimpeded by thought."
(Beckson, *A Reader's Guide to Literary Terms*). Sentimentality is sentiment
in excess of the occasion. Today, the use of the *pathetic fallacy* is associated
with sentimentality. Ruskin defined it as "the attribution of human characteristics to inanimate objects" (a device akin to personification). "Trees
looked down scornfully upon Jeb." Trying too hard for pathos, or sublimity,
the writer stumbles into bathos. A similar overreaching is displayed in the
unintentional hyperbole fallacy, which can be described as rhetoric in excess
of the subject or occasion: this fallacy often stands in for imagination when
the writer must describe extreme emotions, such as mental anguish, or extreme action, such as physical violence.

Certain qualities contribute to the power of either the complex or the
simple style. Deliberate *repetition* enhances the effect of a particular phrase
and contributes to a sense of unity. Joseph Heller's *Catch-22* is a good
example of effect by repetition.

> "Cut," said a doctor.
> "You cut," said another.
> "No cuts," said Yossarian with a thick, unwieldy tongue.
> "Now look who's butting in," complained one of the doctors.
> "Another country heard from. Are we going to operate or aren't
> we?"
> "He doesn't need an operation," complained the other. "It's a
> small wound. All we have to do is stop the bleeding, clean it out
> and put a few stitches in."
> "But I've never had a chance to operate before. Which one is
> the scalpel? Is this one the scalpel?"
> "No the other one is the scalpel. Well, go ahead and cut al-
> ready if you're going to. Make the incision."
> "Like this?"
> "Not there, you dope!"
> "No incisions," Yossarian said, perceiving through the lifting
> fog of insensibility that two strangers were ready to begin cutting
> him.

The reader settles down in his response to *texture* in structure and language; reading Hemingway, he feels a tight, though not complex texture;
reading James, he feels a woven texture (See passages quoted earlier). The

writer's style gives his work a surface texture and his voice a resonance. This texture acts upon the mind of the reader almost sensually. He feels the loose texture of Carson McCullers in *The Heart Is a Lonely Hunter;* the rough of Norman Mailer in *The Naked and the Dead* and James Jones in *From Here to Eternity;* the smooth of E. M. Forster in *Passage to India;* and the ragged of Dreiser in *An American Tragedy.* Texture affects a reader's attitude toward what he is reading, disposes him well or ill toward the writer, according to the reader's own temperament.

The reader also responds to prose-rhythm, even melody, which differs generally with the two styles, and specifically with every writer. The cadence of good prose differs from ordinary prose when the writer has a feeling for the rhythms of language beyond the sense.

Fictionists have less latitude for inventiveness in language than poets; since words are the medium for describing characters and telling stories, the illusion is broken if words call attention to themselves. Still, a few writers manage to create a highly volatile style and still sustain the illusion of a heightened reality. One way of giving a new power to language is in the creation of *portmanteau words;* used earlier by Lewis Carroll and Charles Dickens, portmanteau words were a vogue in the Twenties, beginning with the surrealists and perfected by Joyce. James Joyce created a new dream-language for *Finnegans Wake,* made up mainly of puns and portmanteau words, and mongrel words from many languages. "And look at here! This cara weeseed. Pretty mites, my sweetthings, was they poor-loves abandoned by wholawidey world? Neighboulotts for newtown. The Eblanamagn you behazyheld loomening up out of the dumblynass. But the still sama sitta. I've lapped so long." He suggested that the language is indeed protean, governed only by appropriateness, the terms of which are implicit in the choices the writer makes about raw material and techniques. In such words themselves we see the principle of juxtaposition or montage at work The writer's inventive use of words is encouraging a linguistic study of literature. Faulkner, Joyce, and other writers even make up new words; sometimes new words are coined after a character: Snopes, Babbitt, Scrooge.

A *cliché* is an expression that once had the force of originality and freshness but has become trite and stale through overuse. Some writers (and some readers) do not object as strongly as others to clichés, but a writer tries to be as original as he can without calling too much attention to his style. Some writers deliberately use clichés to give an aura of everyday reality to the world they are creating. Other writers prepare a special context for a cliché that resurrects its original vitality with a new meaning or emotional power. Clichés are sometimes used deliberately; Wright Morris resurrects and transforms the buried cliché frequently in his 19 novels. In *Man and Boy,* Warren Ormsby, an ordinary man, muses upon the fate of son, missing in action and remembers a Christmas they never shared: "How did one grasp something like that? ... Oh, it was one thing to be dead, but what was the word for describing what it was to have been not quite alive? Well, he knew. The words for that were *nipped in the bud*. During a war one heard them everywhere."

Colloquial language in the author's own narrating voice, along with ungrammatical elements, dialect, slang, profanity, even archaisms can achieve special effects: "Folks this here is the story of the Loop Garoo Kid. ... Men called him brother only to cop his coin" (Ishmael Reed, *Yellow Back Radio Broke-Down*).

A writer's style not only reflects the way *his* mind works, on conscious and unconscious levels, but the way the mind as an organ works. The mind is naturally involved in processes of condensation, concision, concentration of the miscellaneous data taken in by the senses. There are contrary forces at work in every part of the psyche (ego, superego, id, libido); the writer deliberately stimulates these forces, pits one against the other as he creates; as this conflict is dramatized implicitly and overtly in the narrative, the style of language in which it is expressed will convey to the reader a sense of the tensions between meaning and expression. Style is a dynamic process that imitates the psyche's own processes. The best style exploits this relationship to the full. Although the writer often speaks directly, he is seldom euphemistic (substitution of an inoffensive expression for one considered too explicit, or offensive)—less today than ever. An early novel by John Lyly, *Euphues, the Anatomy of Wit* (1579), introduced that stylistic concept, but it has almost disappeared from realistic fiction.

For writers such as Flaubert, James, and Joyce, style becomes a kind of absolute. Zola said, " . . . For the writer, genius is not to be found only in the feeling, in the *a priori* idea, but is also in the form and style." Stendhal also testifies: "Often I ponder a quarter of an hour whether to place an adjective before or after its noun." Maupassant is even more exact: "Whatever you want to say, there is only one word to express it, one verb to set it in motion and only one adjective to describe it." Conrad carries this attitude to a higher altitude. "A work that aspires, however humbly, to the condition of art should carry its justification in every line." And Pound gives it an absolute tone: "Literature is language charged with meaning. Great literature is simply language charged with meaning to the utmost degree."

Dialog is a major element in fiction. Stylistically, it is more a problem of imitation, relatively, than the straight prose passages. It differs in that it is always in the present, and thus dramatic, while most narration is in the past tense. "I can only reach my dramatic effect," said Flaubert, "by the interplay of dialogue and contrast of character." The novelist may learn from

the playwright, the movie scriptwriter, and the dramatic monolog in poetry
(Robert Browning). Striving for the illusion of immediacy, many writers
today overuse dialog. "Only the significant passages of their talk should be
recorded," said Edith Wharton, "in high relief against the narrative." Some
writers, such as Ivy Compton-Burnett in *A God and His Gifts* and Henry
Green in *Loving* are well-known for their deliberate, effective overuse of
dialog. If they are to seem real and alive, characters must speak, but a skillful writer can make passages of description also express character.

A skillful writer employs various techniques to make his lifelike dialog
serve more than one function: convey basic information; reiterate motifs;
keep the narrative going; suggest descriptions of other characters who are
present or absent from the scene. While most writers do not use sub-
standard English in the straight narrative passages, it can be used effectivel
in dialog and thus provide some relief and contrast to the general style.
"'Yes, Pip, dear boy, I've made a gentleman on you! It's me wot has done
it!' ... The abhorrence in which I held the man, the dread I had of him,
the repugnance with which I shrank from him, could not have been ex-
ceeded, if he had been some terrible beast" (Dickens, *Great Expectations*).
What may seem obvious or obtrusive elsewhere may seem quite natural
coming from the mouth of a character. When he attributes an idea or an
observation to a character in dialog, the author is not held responsible.
Ernest Hemingway is a master in the many uses of dialog, as in *The Sun
Also Rises*:

> We climbed down. It was clouding over again. In the park it
> was dark under the trees.
> "Do you still love me, Jake?"
> "Yes," I said.
> "Because I'm a goner," Brett said.
> "How?"
> "I'm a goner. I'm mad about the Romero boy. I'm in love w
> him, I think."
> "I wouldn't be if I were you."
> "I can't help it. I'm a goner. It's tearing me all up inside."
> "Don't do it."
> "I can't help it. I've never been able to help anything."
> "You ought to stop it."
> "How can I stop it? I can't stop things. Feel that?" Her han
> was trembling.
> "I'm like that all through."
> "You oughtn't to do it."
> "I can't help it. I'm a goner, now, anyway. Don't you see t
> difference?"
> "No."

"I've got to do something. I've got to do something I really
want to do. I've lost my self-respect."

"You don't have to do that."

"Oh, darling, don't be difficult. What do you think it's meant
to have that damned Jew about, and Mike the way he's acted?"

"Sure."

"I can't just stay tight all the time."

"No."

"Oh, darling, please stay by me. Please stay by me and see
me through this."

"Sure."

"I don't say it's right. It is right though for me. God knows,
I've never felt such a bitch."

"What do you want me to do?"

"Come on," Brett said, "Let's go and find him."

In dialog the writer attempts to be true to the way people *really* talk; he
may be much more careful, more unique, in narrative descriptive passages,
although too great a contrast may jar.

Although some writers today still rely heavily on *description* (C. P.
Snow, James Gould Cozzens, Harriette Arnow, Herbert Gold, John
Fowles), descriptive passages are not in themselves as important in today's
fiction as in the works of Hardy, Dickens, Tolstoy, Wolfe. Modern writers
have tried to make description active and expressive of character, especially
in the central intelligence and first person points of view, as does Wright
Morris' poetically conceived and stylistically compressed *In Orbit*.

This boy comes riding with his arms high and wide, his head dipped
low, his ass light in the saddle, as if about to be shot into orbit
from a forked sling.

.   .   .

That's the picture: there are those who can take it in at a glance.
. . . But perhaps the important detail escapes you. He is in
motion. Now you see him, now you don't. If you pin him down in
time he is lost in space. Somewhere between where he is from and
where he is going he wheels in an unpredictable orbit. He is as
free, and as captive, as the wind in his face. In the crown of his
helmet are the shoes of a dancer with one heel missing, one strap
broken. Such things come naturally to knaves, dancers, lovers and
twists of the wind. This cool spring morning the rain-scoured light
gleams on his helmet, like a saucer in orbit, where the supernatural is just naturally a part of his life.

Descriptions of nature, said Chekhov, and other background features, should be very brief.

Writers differ a great deal in their use of *detail;* the principle of selectivity is employed by most of the best writers; however, some good ones use the additive method (James Farrell, Joyce Carol Oates). But, generally, excessive details and character and background description are detrimental in today's fiction. "However detailed... description is," said Ivy Compton-Burnett, "I am sure that everyone forms his own conceptions, that are different from everyone else's, including the author's."

Description is always determined by the point of view. The third person omniscient author describes objectively, directly, for the reader's benefit. Classic novelists tended to offer chunks of description, inert blocks, that were passive: "The room is surrounded by sticky buffets holding carafes which are dirty and chipped, round mats with a metallic sheen, piles of plates of thick blue-bordered porcelain, manufactured at Tournai" (Balzac, *Pére Goriot*). An active style can make a passive passage of description move. (See the selection from *The Great Gatsby* quoted below; notice how quickly events are thrust forward in that passage.) The writer need not delay the reader while he passively describes a setting or character or events. One thing can be made, through style, to happen right after another, rapidly.

The third person/central intelligence point of view shows us only what the main character sees and how he responds, reveals the world filtered through his subjectivity, thus reveals his character and personality: "Scobie looked at the next stretcher load and looked away again. A small girl—she couldn't have been more than six—lay on it. She was deeply and unhealthily asleep; her fair hair was tangled and wet with sweat; her open mouth was dry and cracked, and she shuddered regularly and spasmodically. 'It's terrible,' Scobie said" (Graham Greene, *The Heart of the Matter*).

The first person narrator combines the subjective act of self-discovery with the desire to show the reader objectively what he has seen; he is both omniscient story-teller and subject of his story:

> A breeze blew through the room, blew curtains in at one end and out the other like pale flags, twisting them up toward the frosted wedding-cake of the ceiling, and then rippled over the wine-colored rug, making a shadow on it as wind does on the sea. The only completely stationary object in the room was an enormous couch on which two young women were buoyed up as though upon an anchored balloon.
>
> (Nick speaking, in Fitzgerald's *The Great Gatsb*

The style is active and the characters move within the setting Fitzgerald describes.

Description is colored by the mood and tone of the narrator of whatever type: melancholy, elegiac, ironic, tragic, sardonic, rhapsodic, lyrical. It is also affected by the physical point of view: time of day, season, range or scope (close or far away: size), and the senses that are affected. Any description must be consistent with the context of a specific scene and, beyond that, the entire story thus far.

Descriptions convey sensory impressions through imagery. Abstract descriptions, using general words ("beautiful," "terrific," "small") don't describe but merely offer information or exposition dully. If it's effective, description doesn't report, it recreates. Conventional descriptions of characters, scenes (landscapes, clouds, settings) are often abstract and inert. Figurative descriptions employ figures of speech: similes ("The red sun was pasted in the sky like a wafer," Stephen Crane, *The Red Badge of Courage*); metaphors ("The sun was a lordly lamp," Thomas Wolfe, *Look Homeward, Angel*). Concrete descriptions do not stop the action to describe a still-life. They create an active sense of movement; they appeal to the senses. They have a freshness of diction, avoiding overuse of adjectives.

The realistic writer (Zola) chooses his details to create the illusion of actuality; other writers (Flaubert) try to evoke a sense of life (verisimilitude) rather than render it fully and literally. The impressionistic writer evokes a sense of a complete and actual world through careful *selection* of details, with some use of symbolism, as does James Agee in *A Death in the Family*.

> On the rough wet grass of the back yard my father and mother have spead quilts. ... All my people are larger bodies than mine, quiet, with voices gentle and meaningless like the voices of sleeping birds. One is an artist, he is living at home. One is a musician, she is living at home. One is my mother who is good to me. One is my father who is good to me. By some chance, here they are, all on this earth; and who shall ever tell the sorrow of being on this earth, lying, on quilts, on the grass, in a summer evening, among the sounds of the night. ... After a little I am taken in and put to bed. Sleep, soft, smiling, draws me unto her: and those receive me, who quietly treat me, as one familiar and well-beloved in that home: but will not, oh, will not, not now, not ever: but will not ever tell me who I am.

Just as the technique of selection enables the writer to suggest a sense of fullness, the stylistic technique of *suggestion* enables him to evoke something more than the words in a sentence or paragraph literally state: "In her eyes she seemed to be afraid of him. Her face was full of little lines he had never seen before; they were as small as the lines in her mended best teacup" (James Agee, *A Death in the Family*). Some writers such as Henry James sometimes rely too much on suggestion; some writers are often not suggestive enough (James T. Farrell, John Steinbeck, Erskine Caldwell).

Some of the methods of suggesting or evoking qualities are the use of color or sense imagery: "I tried to fascinate his attention with roadside treasures (. . . an old soggy firecracker whose faded colored stripes were run together, half a ping pong ball containing rainwater) but he took no notice of anything. . ." (Stephen Millhauser, *Edwin Mullhouse*). "Colors, scents and sounds correspond," said Baudelaire.

In *The Great Gatsby*, Fitzgerald selects details carefully, rather than piling one on top of another. Omitting unnecessary details, he strives for emphasis. He strikes a dominant note, creates a dominant impression, subordinates minor details. Rather than cluster descriptions of a character (Daisy) or place (The Valley of Ashes), he breaks them up, presenting single details a bit at a time, placing them strategically. He creates a pattern of description throughout the novel (interiors and exteriors). He works indirectly, letting one character, for instance, describe another in dialog, thus raising the reader's expectations, as no direct description could: "Her voice is full of money," Gatsby says of Daisy. Fitzgerald orders and arranges, co-ordinates a succession of details along a narrative thread. Description and narrative are at best inseparable. The distinction is that description emphasizes the image and narrative the action: they are two different kinds of beads on a string.

Other features of point of view and of style are wit, irony, and paradox (important elements of modern poetry as well), seen at work most effectively in the works of Ford Madox Ford, E. M. Forster and G. K. Chesterton. These rhetorical devices lend intellectual vitality and meaning to a novel, but must be justified by the general context. The meaning of *wit* has changed through literary history; today, it is revealed in clever, mocking observations: in Richard Farina's *Been Down So Long It Looks Like Up to Me*, Stanley Elkin's *The Dick Gibson Show*, Kurt Vonnegut's *Breakfast of Champions*. "It's all very well to say smoking in the lobby only, but have you seen the lobby lately?" (Wilfred Sheed, *Max Jamison*). Some writers are especially well-known for their wit: Ronald Firbank, James Branch Cabell, John Updike, Mary McCarthy, Vladimir Nabokov, Kingsley Amis, Muriel Spark, Honor Tracy, Evelyn Waugh. Sarcasm is almost never used by the author himself, although he may betray a sardonic tone: "Nately's death almost killed the Chaplain" (Joseph Heller, *Catch-22*).

Irony exists when there is a discrepancy between the appearance and the reality of a situation or when the reverse or opposite of what a reader expects happens. Verbal irony occurs when a writer deliberately says the opposite of what he means. Often, a reader sees the irony in a situation while the characters do not. Verbal irony is the use of statements by the author that are contradicted by actual events: "At first he had not understood the four people at all. They talked and they talked—and as the months went on they talked more and more. He became so used to their lips that he undersood each word they said" (Carson McCullers, *The Heart Is a Lonely Hunter*). The irony is that Mr. Singer doesn't really understand any of the four people, and they are all convinced that he above all does. The novel is based on a paradoxical theme (the need for privacy and the fear of it) expressed in a series of ironic relationships. Irony is one of the chief sources of pleasure for readers of complex stories. Using subtle stylistic techniques, Ford Madox Ford gives readers one of the great first person ironic narrators in *The Good Soldier*.

Paradox and irony characterize the view of life presented in much of modern fiction. These attitudes sometimes promote objectivity, as against the sentimental indulgence of William Saroyan in *The Human Comedy*. A *paradox* is a seemingly contradictory statement with an underlying truth factor that reconciles the contradiction. For G. K. Chesterton, paradox is a mark of style, as in *The Man Who Was Thursday:* "Chaos is dull"; "It is always the humble man who talks too much." And for Wright Morris: "What is it that strikes you about a vacant house?. . . It's forever occupied" *(The Home Place)*. Today, in a time when most serious fiction is packed with irony, irony-hunting, like symbol-hunting, is a literary sport. The ironic experience is rather serious and limiting; while the paradoxical impulse encourages the imagination to play.

The term "symbolism" is often used for elements that aren't really symbolic or which might, for fiction, better be designated by other terms such as *motif,* counterpoint, parallel, analogues, correspondences, associations. "Comparisons consume me like flies," said Flaubert. And those comparisons must come together in patterns. In a famous essay, Mark Schorer discusses the "matrix of analogy" in *Persuasion, Wuthering Heights,* and *Middlemarch;* he traces the "dominant metaphorical" qualities of these novels—which other critics might call symbolic patterns. Motifs should not be confused with symbols. In *The Great Gatsby* noses (Jordan's, the butler's, etc.) are not used symbolically; they are motifs. Eyes, on the other hand, are used symbolically, so often in so many variations that they also become motifs, patterned throughout.

A *motif* is an element that is repeated, usually with variation, throughout a story. A motif may be a recurring subject, idea, or theme. The use of motif controls character, story, and theme in Aldous Huxley's *Point Counter Point*. Parallels are a type of motif. Motifs should not be confused with symbols, although symbols may be part of a pattern of motifs. Motifs and leitmotifs (terms from music) are aids to emphasis and focus. For example, all through *Gatsby* runs the motif of cars, to emphasize and focus the death car near the end. ("Motive" is sometimes used in this sense.) Some writers employ motif very consciously and consider it one of the major techniques of the art (Joyce, Faulkner, D. H. Lawrence, Proust), while other writers seem to leave such enhancements entirely up to chance (James M. Cain, John O'Hara, Nelson Algren). Motifs aid the process of anticipation. The knife-scissors motif in *To the Lighthouse* leads us to anticipate an event or insight related to or caused by some sharp object.

A *parallel* is an element that moves alongside another element; the two mutually enhance each other's effect, sometimes through contrast or comparison. A parallel is something like a motif in a pattern; it is sometimes mistaken for a symbol. In both Ernest Hemingway's *The Sun Also Rises* and Wright Morris' *The Field of Vision* aspects of the bullfight are related to aspects of character relationships. Some of those aspects are symbolic, some are motifs, but some are merely parallels that give unity to the novel. *Repetition* is a device that intensifies the reader's response by enabling him to remember imporant elements as the story moves ahead. An element is introduced, then repeated, with variations in a pattern, throughout the story. Repetition is a major unifying device.

A final word on style. In "The Analogical Matrix," Mark Schorer says, "Style is conception. It is style, and style primarily that first conceives, then expresses, and finally tests subject matter and theme." The forging of a style is a difficult and life-long task. Words cannot easily be forced into flesh.

It must be reiterated that the effects of techniques being described here operate at best unconsciously upon the reader, though the more receptive (because perhaps better trained) reader will be aware of some of these effects as he reads. Not all good novels strive for, or create, these effects, but they are at work to some degree in all fiction.

SYMBOLISM

Symbolism is the technique of representing one thing by means of another through resemblance or association. An object, image, event, or character may symbolize an idea or theme in a novel. The use of symbolism enables the writer to show relationships among people, nature, society, the intellect, and the spirit. Symbols may be incidental or a story may be unified by a symbolic design. Symbols, like charged images, help to focus ideas and feelings so that the story's impact is stronger and deeper. The term "symbolism" is often used for elements that aren't really symbolic or that might better be called by other names: "counterpoint," "parallel," "motif," "analogues," "correspondences," "associations."

The influence of the French Symbolists is still at work in world literature. Most symbolist poets were interested in the way words could signify
or evoke subtle sensory experiences. They tried to achieve for poetry the
condition of music. Because most novels must create an illusion of reality,
the writer's use of symbolist techniques must be very subtle. The purely
symbolic imagination is rather rare in fiction, but some writers are much
more symbolic than others, Jean Cocteau, Thomas Mann, and William
Faulkner more than John Dos Passos, James T. Farrell, and John Steinbeck.

One major kind of unity is achieved by symbolic design. In *The Rainbow* D. H. Lawrence develops a pattern consisting of the rainbow and the
cathedral, sexuality and the rhythms of rural life.

> The arc bended and strengthened itself till it arched indomitable,
> making great architecture of light and colour and the space of
> heaven, its pedestals luminous in the corruption of new houses on
> the low hill, its arch the top of heaven.
> And the rainbow stood on the earth. She knew that the sordid
> people who crept hard-scaled and separate on the face of the
> world's corruption were living still, that the rainbow was arched in
> their blood and would quiver to life in their spirit, that they would
> cast off their horny covering of disintegration, that new, clean,
> naked bodies would issue to a new generation, to a new growth,
> rising to the light and the wind and the clean rain of heaven. She
> saw in the rainbow the earth's new architecture, the old, brittle
> corruption of houses and factories swept away, the world built up
> in a living fabric of Truth, fitting to the over-arching heaven.
>
> .   .   .
>
> They worked together, coming and going, in a rhythm, which car-
> ried their feet and their bodies in tune. ... There was only the
> moving to and fro in the moonlight, engrossed, the swinging in the
> silence, that was marked only by the splash of sheaves, and si-
> lence, and a splash of sheaves. And ever the splash of his sheaves
> broke swifter, beating up to hers, and ever the splash of his
> sheaves beat nearer.
> Till at last, they met at the shock, facing each other, sheaves
> in hand. And he was silvery with moonlight, with a moonlit,
> shadowy face that frightened her. She waited for him.

In Michel Tournier's *The Ogre*, Tiffauges, the ogre, lives in a "universe of
signs and symbols," of symbolic and mythic patterns, and the reader shares
his perceptions of them. "For his vocation was not only to decipher essences
but also to exhalt them, to bring their qualities to the point of incandes-
cence. He was going to give this country a Tiffaugian interpretation, and at

the same time raise it to a higher power, never yet attained." Tiffauges perceives both benign and malign inversions of conventional signs and symbols. A symbolic design relates a blind elk, a blue horse, a bicycle to his own function as a person who carries other persons, experiencing euphoria. "Yes, it was a sort of euphoria that enfolded me from head to foot when I took Jeannot's inanimate body in my arms. . . . a total joy of all my being." Conrad rendered many of his stories against a symbolic landscape or seascape (*Victory*). The landscape in *The Magic Mountain* by Mann is obviously symbolic. A very obvious symbol is the letter A in Hawthorne's *The Scarlet Letter*. For Proust, in *Remembrance of Things Past*, the magic lantern is a symbol of memory and imagination.

> My bedroom became the fixed point on which my melancholy and anxious thoughts were centered. Some one had had the happy idea of giving me, to distract me on evenings when I seemed abnormally wretched, a magic lantern, which used to be set on top of my lamp while we waited for dinner-time to come: in the manner of the master-builders and glass-painters of gothic days it substituted for the opaqueness of my walls an impalpable irridescence, supernatural phenomena of many colours, in which legends were depicted, as on a shifting and transitory window.

Ezra Pound advised poets that the natural object is the most effective symbol (a wound is a "red badge of courage" in Stephen Crane's novel) as opposed to the rhetorical, the contrived, or the literary symbol that overpopulates Thomas Mann's *The Magic Mountain*, for instance. The habit of symbol-hunting in modern classrooms and in criticism, encouraged, of course, by the over-infatuation among writers with symbols (which seem to add a sense of importance to their work) has led to the impression that symbolism has harmed the novel. As James M. Cain (who made a shark stand for the terror in all beauty) has said, "Who can't make up symbols?" And most readers might ask, "And who wants to hunt them down once writers *do* make them up?" This attitude detracts from the vital importance of a subtle use of symbols and symbolic patterns in works produced by genuine symbolic imaginations: John Barth's *The Floating Opera*, Joyce's *Ulysses*, Camus' *The Plague*, William Styron's *Lie Down in Darkness*, and Kobo Abe's The *Woman in the Dunes*. In Fitzgerald's *The Great Gatsby*, the Valley of Ashes and the eyes of T. J. Eckleburg symbolize decay of the American vision of a garden of Eden, and Daisy and the green light at the end of her dock symbolize the idealistic American's vision of the American dream.

> This is the valley of ashes—a fantastic farm where ashes grow like wheat into ridges and hills and grotesque gardens. . . . Above the gray land and the spasms of bleak dust which drift endlessly over

it, you perceive, after a moment, the eyes of Doctor T. J.
Eckleburg... their retinas one yard high. They look out of no face,
but, instead, from a pair of enormous yellow spectacles. ... his
eyes, dimmed a little by many paintless days under sun and rain,
brood on over the solemn dumping ground.

.   .   .

And as I sat there brooding on the old, unknown world, I
thought of Gatsby's wonder when he first picked out the green
light at the end of Daisy's dock. He had come a long way to this
blue lawn, and his dream must have seemed so close that he could
hardly fail to grasp it. He did not know that it was already behind
him, somewhere back in that vast obscurity beyond the city, where
the dark fields of the republic rolled on under the night.

Gatsby believed in the green light, the orgiastic future that
year by year recedes before us. It eluded us then, but that's no
matter—tomorrow we will run faster, stretch out our arms
farther. ... And one fine morning—

So we beat on, boats against the current, borne back
ceaselessly into the past.

IMAGERY

In the beginning was the word, and the word was the author, and the
word was with the author, if one may, respectfully, paraphrase St. John.
The philosopher Ernst Cassirer says that all thinking, all knowledge began
with language itself, and language started as poetry, the compressing of the
many into the one (all the aspects of a tiger into the word tiger). "Word
magic is everywhere accompanied by picture magic," he said. "Wisdom
speaks first in images," said Yeats. Figurative language is language expanded
beyond its usual literal meaning to achieve intensity and vividness. A figurative expression usually contains a stated or implied comparison to express a
relationship between things essentially unlike. *Metaphors* and *similes* are
two common types of figures of speech. The metaphor "John is a lion" is an
implied comparison which is more immediate and dramatic than "John has
some of the characteristics of a lion." "John is *like* a lion" is a simile, a
stated comparison. The word "like" specifies that a similarity exists between
John and a lion. "As if" and "as though" are other signals that a simile is
being introduced in a sentence.

Writers of fiction use similes more often than metaphors because
metaphors tend to try a reader's patience. "John is a lion" may make some
readers reply, "No, he isn't." A reader is more likely to accept the simile

"John is like a lion." Metaphors and similes may be implied rather than overtly stated. They are most effective when the reader feels that they are appropriate to the context of the story, that they seem to be part of a pattern, rather than created for a passing occasion.

Imagery is the collection of descriptive details in a literary work that appeal to the senses. An author uses an image to arouse emotion in the reader and to help create the predominant mood of the story. The writer attempts to embody in vivid images all abstractions and generalizations about character and meaning; to stimulate the reader's senses; to arouse his emotions; to stimulate his imagination.

"An image," said Pound, is "that which presents an intellectual and emotional complex in an instant of time." Yasunari Kawabata is known for his startling images; in *Snow Country* the hero on the train sees a girl's face reflected in the window as the mountain landscape flows by outside: "Shimamura had the illusion that the evening landscape was actually passing over the face, and the flow did not stop. . . . It was a distant cold light. As it sent its small ray through the pupil of the girl's eye, as the eye and the light were superimposed one on the other, the eye became a weirdly beautiful bit of phosphorescence on the sea of evening mountains." Novels are made up of many other kinds of images: auditory, sensory, intellectual.

When Ezra Pound defines literature as "language charged with meaning," the word "meaning" may be taken as a fusion of emotion and idea in the imagination. The controlling or dominant image, the image-nucleus in a work that is organically unified has the potency of a poetic image, discharging its power gradually, as the story moves from part to part. After the reader has fully experienced the story, fully perceived it in a picture, that focal image continues to discharge its power. The symbolic image of the green light at the end of Daisy's dock in *The Great Gatsby* becomes a condensation and abstraction of many other images in the novel. The developing elements in a novel become integrated finally, Croce tells us, in an image, and "what is known as an image is always a tissue of images." Yeats said, "I seek not a book but an image."

The concept of the charged image is a way of talking about coherence and synthesis in a work of art. The important elements of a story are condensed and compressed into this charged image; it can evoke all the other elements—theme, character, setting, conflict, style, and so on. The image is highly charged with emotion and meaning. Some examples are: Don Quixote and Sancho Panza on the road approaching the windmills; Huckleberry Finn and Jim on the raft on the Mississippi River between adventures; the green light passage from *Gatsby* quoted earlier; Mick Kelly, Jake Blount, Doctor Copeland, Biff Brannon sitting around Mr. Singer in his kitchen in Carson McCullers' *The Heart Is a Lonely Hunter*. In Yves Berger's *The*

Garden, the charged image is the symbolic polarity of the garden of the imagination surrounded by the world of actuality.

> On Virginia's shoulders I stroke the wheels of the wagons, the runaway mules, the fur of the guzzling bears. I listen to an earthquake which quiets down, subsides. ". . . Words, nothing but words and when you have said them, when you have wallowed in them, on them, when you have made yourself drunk with words, then you open your eyes, they fall on me who am waiting, waiting for you, a real Virginia, of flesh and blood—"

This charged image from early and late (a separation of 500 years) in Virginia Woolf's fantasy *Orlando* captures the concept of timelessness and of the simultaneity of all time.

> Flinging himself from his horse, he made, in his rage, as if he would breast the flood. Standing knee deep in water he hurled at the faithless woman all the insults that have ever been the lot of her sex. Faithless, mutable, fickle, he called her; devil, adulteress, deceiver; and the whirling waters took his words, and tossed at his feet a broken pot and a little straw.
>
> .   .   .
>
> But descending in the lift again—so insidious is the repetition of any scene—she was again sunk far beneath the present moment; and thought when the lift bumped on the ground, that she heard a pot broken against a river bank.

The charged image in Camus' *The Stranger* comes at the exact center of the novel.

> Then everything began to reel before my eyes, a fiery gust came from the sea, while the sky cracked in two, from end to end, and a great sheet of flame poured down through the rift. Every nerve in my body was a steel spring, and my grip closed on the revolver. The trigger gave, and the smooth underbelly of the butt jogged my palm. And so, with that crisp, whipcrack sound, it all began. I shook off my sweat and the clinging veil of light. I knew I'd shattered the balance of the day, the spacious calm of this beach on which I had been happy. But I fired four shots more into the inert body, on which they left no visible trace. And each successive shot was another loud, fateful rap on the door of my undoing.

The novelist, no less than the poet, is the maker of images; in a novel, the images are less concentrated, and are dispersed among discursive pas-

sages. Conrad said, "My task which I am trying to achieve is, by the pow
of the written word to make you hear, to make you feel—it is, before all,
make you see. That—and no more, and it is everything."

The *epiphany* is a special kind of image that creates a moment of illumination more for the character perhaps than the reader. James Joyce
fected the epiphany: "A sudden spiritual manifestation, whether in the v
garity of speech or of gesture or in a memorable phase of the mind itself.
the most delicate and evanescent of moments." We experience this perfe
moment in many novels, including Joyce's *Portrait of the Artist as a You
Man.*

> A girl stood before him in midstream, alone and still, gazing ou
> sea. She seemed like one whom magic had changed into the lik
> ness of a strange and beautiful seabird. Her long slender bare l
> were delicate as a crane's and pure save where an emerald trail
> seaweed has fashioned itself as a sign upon the flesh. . . .
>
> She was alone and still, gazing out to sea; and when she fe
> his presence and the worship of his eyes her eyes turned to him
> quiet sufferance of his gaze without shame or wantonness. . . .
> Her image has passed into his soul for ever and no word ha
> broken the holy silence of his ecstasy. Her eyes had called him
> his soul had leaped at the call. To live, to err, to fall, to triump
> to recreate life out of life! A wild angel had appeared to him, th
> angel of mortal youth and beauty, an envoy from the fair courts
> life, to throw open before him in an instant of ecstasy the gates
> all the ways of error and glory. On and on and on and on!
>
>   .   .   .
>
> He felt above him the vast indifferent dome and the calm
> cesses of the heavenly bodies; and the earth beneath him, the
> earth that had borne him, had taken him to her breast.

There are very similar epiphanies involving the idealized woman in *The
Great Gatsby, Look Homeward, Angel, Raintree County, The Rainbow,*
Bloom experiences an anti-epiphany in Joyce's *Ulysses* when he gazes at
Gertie.

Motifs, symbols, parallels, images, epiphanies culminate, into a patt
or contrasting sets of patterns that contribute to organic unity, as in Ford
Madox Ford's *The Good Soldier,* Albert Camus' *The Stranger,* Ralph El
son's *Invisible Man.*

Patterns emphasize the relationships among all the characters and elements in a novel. In the best novels, we don't want merely to find out what happens; we enjoy accumulatively apprehending some order over the content, and through that order an emotion and some insight into its meaning. We respond to design, to incremental, converging patterns, whether they are narrative or mainly expressive of character.

Pattern or *design* is the repetition through complications of the central incident or idea. As we sense the pattern or design of the story we feel that it is moving forward at the same time that the main line of interest is being sustained. Pattern has to do with the organized relationships between the various elements or aspects of the story. Through a careful concern with these elements, form evolves and we have a sense of unity when we have finished the story. Each part functions in its relationship to the whole. The story's form enables us to keep before us as the story moves a comprehension of the whole. The effectiveness of a pattern is in the way the reader follows it to its completion.

Some may argue that such patterns are mere embroidery, and may be described modestly as amplification with various gradations and modulations, employing contrast as a device. Perhaps in its simplest form this process may be thus mechanically described; but in most of the finest novels, handling of designs and patterns unifies the work and thus transmits its power. A major principle at work in achieving this end is the technique of *selectivity*.

"Life being all inclusion and confusion, and art being all discrimination and selection. . . . life persistently blunders and deviates. . . life . . . is capable . . . of nothing but splendid waste," said Henry James. Robert Louis Stevenson said, more succinctly, that the writer must "suppress much and omit more." A good example of a work that would have benefited from selection is Alexander Solzhenitzyn's *The Gulag Archipelago*. A novel in which selection is intelligently employed is Turgenev's *Fathers and Sons*.

The technique of selectivity enables the writer to choose scenes that reveal something, rather than just scenes that would occur in life; artistry, not life, is the final criterion for what the writer leaves in his story. Out of all the possibilities in a situation, he attempts to choose, select, those details that tell the most, that suggest the whole scene, and perhaps give "clues to character, situation, and theme." Since a writer cannot tell all, he must select what will be most effective; and sometimes he does not *tell* at all—he merely suggests, and the reader proceeds from there. The importance of selectivity applies not only to scenes and dialog but to the writer's choice of details as well. He strives to create, imagine details that reveal. Such repeated details not only give a sense of unity to the story but evoke aspects of character and mood.

An irritating type of misplaced emphasis is the tedious reproduction of *trivia,* or the *lighting a cigarette fallacy.* The hero's most trivial action is described as though stars were altered in their courses. The reader regards that kind of cause and effect as purely literary. The writer must also take care not to commit the *claims fallacy.* "McPheeters was the funniest man in the world." The reader expects the writer to demonstrate proof of that claim.

The repetition of motifs, situations, character relationships contributes to the effect of *unity.* The reader is pleased to sense that some kind of harmony of the elements of a novel is slowly being achieved; to make the reader aware of this harmony, the writer may use devices of dissonance, as in music, by contrast; the four parts of Faulkner's *The Sound and the Fury* with their very different narrative voices rasp against each other.

In all novels, some principle of integration is at work, striving for structural, thematic, symbolic, spatial, temporal unity, the effect of which is an intense, and, most important for many novelists, lasting experience for the reader. They cause, sometimes, a metamorphosis or transformation. Every novel is an act of metamorphosis or transformation; but the deliberate effect of some novels is to make the reader experience more intensely the process of transformation.

In a process novel, or a psychological novel, coherence may not show until near the end; meanwhile one experiences a "suspended coherence" (see Humphrey).

UNITY

The total effect of the devices that contribute to unity is to create a sense at the end of *simultaneity* and *inevitability.* When all the elements in a story are coordinated and controlled by techniques, the effect is a sense of simultaneity, a feeling at any given moment that all the elements interact in our minds and emotions; the reader holds all the elements in the consciousness at once, as in a *gestalt.* If the reader has this sense of simultaneity throughout the story, he feels at the end a sense of inevitability: everything has happened as it has because it has to. When we feel that what happens in a story, especially in the end, *must* happen because of the way the elements have been set in motion, we feel a sense of inevitability. "Before everything," said Ford Madox Ford, "a story must convey a sense of inevitability."

Form and unity work against chaos in the reader's responses; the reader doesn't like to feel that the elements of a novel are there gratuitously or accidentally.

Many recent novels strive for something different from unity. We may experience in some so-called plotless novels the on-going stages of a process that flows and shifts, with moments of lifelikeness and a general feeling of anti-form, anti-structure; process is a more apt term for these novels than plot (the novels of Nathalie Sarraute, Claude Simon, Alain Robbe-Grillet, is defined by a carefully created context. Context may suggest a rather mechanical building up; ambience is created by a more impressionistic technique (Virginia Woolf's *To the Lighthouse*).

Structure as used today is not quite the same thing as form; the one is relatively mechanical, the other organic; the one is apt more for aesthetic works, the other for traditional novels. Form follows function, said Susanne K. Langer. If the function of the novel is to tell a story, the structure will be sequential, architectural, and when the roof goes on, and smoke goes out the chimney, the reader has had a very different kind of experience from one involving form. If the novel's function is to stimulate in the reader the same perceptions the character experiences, with a sense of wholeness at the end that is denied the character, then the form will seem to follow the gestalt-making mental process, the convolutions of emotions rather than the mechanics of episodes, while simultaneously growing, through various techniques, toward an organic whole; the reader apprehends this process of growth and beholds it at the end, recognizes that it has been prefigured every moment along the way. Stephen Dedalus in James Joyce's *Portrait of the Artist as a Young Man* says "Three things are needed for beauty, wholeness, harmony, and radiance." Form and structure generate energy, life, emotion, and they shape meaning. But form is a mysterious phenomenon when it is achieved by a master, structure less so; still, talk about form alerts the reader to its manifestations; one must develop a facility for responding to the evolution of form; it does not come easily for many of those readers who find the structural approach more readily apprehendable. "Form alone *takes*, and holds and preserves substance," said Henry James.

The fundamental opposition between the Apollonian and the Dionysian mentality takes another shape in the formalist-mimetic conflict. In criticism and in fictional practice there is a dualism of word and idea, expression and thought, manner and matter, form and content or substance, treatment and subject, language or style and content, theme and form. Paralleling questions about form is a less trenchant question: are some subjects more suitable to fiction than others?

There are various general notions of form that spring from subject matter itself: imitative or mimetic form (the writer imitates things, people, events just as they are found in reality); expressive form (intense feeling produces its own natural form); and a metaphorical use of space as a basis for form (spatial form). The most artistic novels of the twentieth century (Faulkner's *The Sound and the Fury*, for instance) exhibit "organic form" (Samuel Coleridge's term) which is "innate" in content, as in nature: the idea and the form of a snake are one. "Cut a good story anywhere," said Chekhov, "and it will bleed." The organic analogy asserts that art follows processes similar to those in nature. "A novel is a living thing," said Jame "all one and continuous, like every other organism." The organic concept requires the detachment of an architect or a musician. "The less one feels thing," said Flaubert, "the more likely one is to express it as it really is." kind of dynamism arises from the deliberate cultivation of the tensions be tween content and form. The conflict here with the notion of expressive form is obvious.

The organic formalists are inclined to use musical analogies (fugue, symphonic) when discussing form; and James used the metaphor "architec tonics" when discussing structure. The formalist approach harks back to classical principles of symmetry and proportion, and to strict concepts of genre, such as Joyce's Stephen sets forth in "lyric, epic, and dramatic." B a principle that applies to all these approaches is dynamics, for any approa to form will work in its own way if it has its own special means of present its elements dynamically.

The novel is a protean form—it can take any shape, even, as James o served, "great fluid puddings." The traditional concept of the aesthetic ex perience is that, though it shimmers with many vibrations, it should come to an end, it should close. Recent novelists have rejected conventional structure, but have also reacted against the notion of aesthetic harmony. The aesthetic experience is a series of explosions that go on and on, they suggest. The novel can be a launching pad for endless reiterations of the novel's basic elements, as we see in Julio Cortazar's *Hopscotch*. Thomas Pynchon's *Gravity's Rainbow* is another such "open-ended" work.

Whether the writer works best with structure or in creating closed o open forms, he acts out his will to *make*, his compulsion to create order c of fragmentation and chaos. Some novels are much more ordered than life itself, and some seem to be much less. The nature of the elements of the novel defeat any nihilistic attempt to copy disorder; the imitative fallacy o erates here: an imitation of boredom can be very fascinating; and thus it ceases to be boredom and becomes fiction. Chaos on paper is order impe sonating chaos.

One also ought to ask whether the novel can ever tell the truth as sc ence seems to. The novel must necessarily distort in order to clarify. Its paradoxes of form and function are the source of its triumphs and its failures; some readers mistake the obvious triumphs for the only possibilities and some writers mistake the failures for the only route to possibilities. For instance, words are the medium, but most of the best writers make you forget that and create an illusion of reality as the reader on his part willingly suspends disbelief in the transaction; however, some superb writers, recognizing that words are the medium, devote all their energies to pursuing all the ramifications of language—lesser writers go the same way to failure.

A novel's structure may be described in many ways. For instance, there is the Marxian triad concept: thesis, anti-thesis, and synthesis results in form. In an Epic novel, the term "amalgam" (of various components) or "epic synthesis" is used. More critics than novelists cling consciously to one or another structural approach. What is needed among critics, and also among novelists and their readers, is a pluralistic overview or eclectic approach to matters of technique. Few will disagree that the novel's subject matter is the entire province of human experience, but controversy about technique continues. Few writers work out of multiple possibilities.

RELATIONSHIPS BETWEEN THE READER AND THE WRITER

Is the novel a criticism of life? Most serious novels give a grim, skeptical or cynical view of life, full of doubt; some offer no conclusions or solutions. It might be argued that such novels lie, for they give only half of reality. Is an optimistic view unreal? Is only a grim view real? Keats spoke of "negative capability" and Fitzgerald said that "the test of a first rate intelligence is the ability to hold two opposed ideas in the mind at the time and retain the ability to function." Few writers or readers pass that test.

The novelist as activist must take one point of view or another. The novelist as moralist sees only what his morals allow him to see. Many of the problems of the relationship between the writer and his audience has been attributed to the decline of a consensus of moral vision, making it difficult for either the writer or the reader to form moral judgments about characters and events depicted in novels; relativism has caused a distaste for terms such as "good" and "bad"; but the fact remains that current fiction is highly moral and hence somewhat hypocritical. The radical novelist who would destroy conventions often fails to realize how conservative he is, for he is usually criticizing the imperfect manifestations of those conventions. The new morality of revolutionary victors is the same old morality with a new, sometimes monstrously fervent, resolve to abide by it.

Moral concerns have been replaced by something called "relevance." To some a novel is relevant if it can be used as a kind of guide or handbook

or how-to-cope manual in the solving of life's "real" problems; this approach
moves away from the novel. Another concept of relevance moves more deeply into the novel than some think it necessary to plunge; this approach
argues that literature becomes relevant when equal attention is given to the
reader's experience as is now generally given to the "text." Relevance occurs when the reader, avoiding an over-emphasis on analysis, makes a total
emotional and intellectual response to the work.

Another approach is to see the novelist's role as a special one: to attempt to show the world simply as it is, without distorting it to favor one
approach or another. Human feeling could go into creation for its own sake,
rather than to promote one morality over another. The phrase "art for art's
sake" distorts a reality that has never really had a chance to flourish. "Art
for humanity's sake" is more accurate. Let the novel deal with everything
under the sun, but let its transcendent quality be its achievement as an
aesthetic object to be enjoyed finally for its own sake, as is the sun itself.

Indirectly, the study of the novel is a study of the relationship between
author and reader, a measuring of the distance between them, and an
analysis of the way that distance is handled. But this relationship has not
been studied nearly enough directly (see Booth, *Rhetoric of Fiction*). The
relationship begins with the writer in his compulsion to tell a story, but it
has become increasingly complex. James said that the author makes "his
reader much as he makes his characters." Recently, Wright Morris has said
much the same thing *(About Fiction)*. Thus, related to the question of distance is the question of the artist's relationship to his readers within the
present human condition. Is his writing a direct result of his participation in
the great social issues of his time—is he a man of his time primarily; or is
he the aesthetic writer who is primarily trying to create a work of art that is
timeless, even though his theme may be relevant to the problems of his
time? Such attitudes affect every aspect of the novel. "Gentle Reader," the
conventional way of addressing the reader in the early history of the novel,
has become a sardonic salutation. The reader was once approached as an
equal, to instruct and delight him; now he is often considered an inferior,
who is to be shocked into recognizing his inferiority. The techniques for
managing these two contrasting relationships are very different; rather, the
techniques may remain basically the same, but the handling, the use of
them has changed.

From the inception of printing, there have been many reading publics
or "fiction publics." Between the writer and the reader, there has always
been what Booth calls a secret contract, collaboration, collusion, communio
which determines the degree of literary involvement or engagement that is
achieved. The writer must understand his audience if he is to induce it to
use its imagination; some writers have always respected the demands of an

made concessions to the audience; some have catered to its prejudices and assumptions.

Nevertheless, each writer has, consciously or not, an ideal reader, sometimes a reflection of himself. In the past, he was the general public, made up of different types; the author often made direct appeals to his ideal reader's prejudices and predilections. It is on such relationships that fame is based; authors and certain works become popular, and audiences crave the popular. Some writers appeal to the general fiction public because of their urbanity (John P. Marquand), others because of their pseudo-primitiveness (James Jones in *From Here to Eternity*, for instance). A smaller group delights in being part of an elite; the more powerfully inbred this group becomes, the more inclined they are toward decadence, as in the symbolist movement.

The most mysterious area in this reader-author relationship is *taste*. Education in the forms and techniques of literature is one thing; the tenacity of taste is another. Taste is a personal preference or liking for something, often influenced by mysterious emotional factors. Tastes and critical judgments may clash. For instance, a reader may have a taste for a certain type of fiction that his critical faculties tell him is inferior. Of all the forces outside the story that affect the reader's responses, taste is the most powerful. It is likely that as a reader reaches a better understanding of the nature of taste and of fiction, his own tastes will change.

Many kinds of environmental and educational forces converge with personal make-up to create an individual's tastes in literature. We speak of good and bad, cultivated and unformed, fine and gross, healthy and depraved or perverted (by good and bad literature), true and false, just taste (which coincides with a consensus as to pure morality), catholic and narrow tastes. Some groups promote the supremacy of their own tastes and attempt to arbitrate for others. When author and reader's prejudices coincide good taste is claimed. But taste, combined with other qualities, is all we have; each man must be his own final arbiter. Poe said that in the evaluation of literature taste was the arbiter between Pure Intellect and Moral Sense. Judging by the preconceived tastes of the individual critic is called the "good taste" fallacy. We should rise above our own individual feelings, our predispositions and prejudices to an objective self. The taste that is not aware of its own nature may promote a static interest in more of the same. But Henry James has said, "I am quite at a loss to imagine anything that people ought to like or dislike." He also said, "We must grant the writer his donnée" (the basic elements he has chosen to work with); and many readers have no taste for James' own donnée.

Critics have stayed out of the murky realms of taste but a deeper understanding of the process whereby it is shaped will illuminate a great deal about the creative process itself. In any given era, the so-called general reader develops a taste for particular kinds of novels—trends, fashions evolve. We ought to remember that often the touchstones of the present *are* the tombstones of the future. If tastes are indeed formed, new tastes can be learned. But how may they be taught? More important, how may the horizons of the individual's tastes be broadened? Taste often prevents a person from entering new realms of the novel—a form in which everything is possible.

Because he has strong tastes of his own, each writer makes certain *assumptions* about his reader's tastes and morality. Unconsciously, though sometimes very deliberately, a writer writes out of certain assumptions about the kinds of readers he imagines will read his story; working out of these assumptions, he appeals, more consciously than unconsciously, to certain *attitudes* he thinks his readers have about love, violence, religion, morality, politics, education (and other institutions), sex, masculinity (heroes and villains), femininity (heroines), in a style which his readers will find acceptable. Usually, the writer shares these attitudes and assumptions with his readers and himself reads the kinds of stories that appeal to those attitudes and assumptions. In some stories the writer has assumed too much, in others too little about his readers.

A study of the novel should include a study of the way these assumptions operate; are they implicit or explicit, and with what results, technical and otherwise? A simple way to begin is to examine very different kinds of magazines, to study their ads. These ads make certain assumptions about the readers of magazines; similar assumptions are at work in a novel. The reader will be sympathetic or hostile to the novel depending on the degree to which he senses and agrees with these assumptions. The popular writer is known to manipulate stock responses which he can assume his readers will make to stereotyped characters, situations, and themes, as in Jack Schaefer's *Shane*, James M. Cain's *Serenade*, Frank Yerby's *The Foxes of Harrow*. But in subtler ways, the more serious writers work the same way: Walter Van Tilburg Clark's *The Ox-Bow Incident*, Wright Morris' *Love Among the Cannibals*, and Robert Penn Warren's *Band of Angels*.

An area even less studied than the author-reader relationship is the reader-author transaction. The reader comes to a novel with certain expectations and when the writer's assumptions and the reader's expectations coincide, the reader has a pleasurable experience. The reader moves from anticipation to expectation to gratification. Sometimes the equilibrium is the same with a Lloyd C. Douglas religious novel as with a novel by Kurt Vonnegut. Another kind of experience is a head-on collision between the reader's expectations and the author's assumptions, resulting either in "injury" to the reader or in an opportunity to make the acquaintance of a writer very different from those he has known before.

The difference between the act of creation and that act of reading must be taken into account when we set about studying the novel in greater depth. How do these contrasts end up complementing each other, and what might result if some of the conflicts could be resolved? There needs to be, in other words, a psychology of reading, understood by both reader and writer, student and teacher.

To involve his reader, the writer appeals to and often manipulates the reader's response to aspects of the nature of fiction. The reader comes to the form with certain conventional expectations; if the writer is to surprise the reader, or to jolt his perspective by violating these conventions, the conventions themselves must be employed; so the writer who hopes to do away with conventions entirely undercuts his relationship with the reader to that extent. Each work, of course, sets up its own peculiar expectations and anticipations, and the reader enjoys either having them realized or re-versed. A major source of energy in the fictive experience is the reader's curiosity, which the writer arouses and satisfies. The reader's natural re-sponses carry him through much of a novel, but he enjoys situations in which the writer causes him to reverse his natural response. Most writers set out to draw the reader into an emotional involvement; although the writer may strive for a certain distance, he wants to play upon and evoke in-tense emotions and persuade the reader to become emotionally attached to one of the characters, at least.

How does fiction affect the reader? It affects him ethically, aestheti-cally, psychologically, politically, perhaps religiously. Judging literature by how it affects us often leads us away from the work into subjective and im-pressionistic responses only (the *affective fallacy*). Effects are relative; thus, it is extremely difficult to judge a work by whether it has the effects the writer seems to intend. But certainly the writer wishes to move his reader, and if he fails, the work fails. He may persuade the reader in-tellectually; he may move him to laughter or to tears—which some critics and writers consider inauthentic responses; he may charm him; he may en-courage sensory, instinctive responses; he may deliberately make the reader uncomfortable; he may offer him a "voyeuristic" experience. There is an in-finite range of individual differences among readers in this realm of possible emotional and intellectual and purely literary responses. What counts is the reader's experience on personal (subjective, taste, fashionable) and public (objective, conventional, traditional) levels; a synthesis of these levels in-tensifies the reader's experience.

The concept of "the interesting" as a vital reader experience is seldom discussed, except by David Daiches and Booth. A reader is often heard to say, "I didn't finish that novel because it wasn't very interesting." "Interest ingness," said Daiches, "is a criterion no serious critic has dared to apply to art, but I can see no reason why it should not be applied." There are simple, obvious, categorical areas of interest for the reader: tragic and comic pleasure in experiencing suffering or in observing the suffering of others; commiserating with the pitiable; being in awe of the marvelous. One of the writer's main objectives is to astonish, to cause the reader to wonder.

All these experiences are vicarious, induced by illusion, with the use o abstract symbols called words, which are merely black marks on a page. Both literature and society depend heavily upon man's need to go beyond himself into the selves of others. In some forms, some types of literature, that experience is more intense than in others. If the reader fails to identify with at least one person in a novel, the experience is unsatisfying. There are many kinds of sympathy, involving degrees of intimacy; there is a difference between commiserating with a character and having compassion for him; be tween having sympathy and feeling empathy. In the romantic novel, we might admire the hero for his actions, his intellect, his morals. In today's fiction, we often sympathize with a person who commits evil. But because we identify in some way with the characters, we vicariously feel fear, horror, pity, terror, even hatred. When empathy rises to a certain level we might even speak of the writer's successful communication with the reader as being an act of communion in the brotherhood of man. But in some novels, the emotion reader and writer share may be scorn.

The writer has many responsibilities to the reader, but some writers in sist that such responsibilities require a two-way relationship. "We ought to have readers who do as much goddamn work," said Mark Harris, "as we who write." Many readers do themselves and the writer an injustice when they say that a novel is good if it's easy to read. "Easy writing makes difficult reading," said S. J. Perelman. Other readers perhaps go too far in say ing that those books are best which are most difficult. In such works, obscurity poses as profundity. The writer himself is often a victim of this de lusion. A certain degree of bewilderment in the reader is necessary if an illusion is to be sustained; bewilderment in the writer himself is a limited asset.

There needs to be training in the art of reading, not simply in the limited pleasures of deciphering codes, puzzles, and hunting symbols and motifs. "A good novel needs all the attention the reader can give it," said Ford Madox Ford. "And then some more." Appreciation, taste, and enthusiasm, says Welleck and Warren, are the province of the reader, as distinguished from the scholar or critic. The act of reading in its various aspects parallels in many ways the act of creating. It was a poet, after all, who coined the phrase "the willing suspension of disbelief" to describe the initial act of the reader that makes all else possible. And the reader's total response makes it possible for a mere character to become a "phantasm," something that leads a life of its own once the reader-writer transaction is over. "The novelist does not as a rule rely sufficiently," says Gide's protagonist in *The Counterfeiters,* "on the reader's imagination."

While objectivity in reading and studying literature can be carried too far, more readers are turned away from literature by objectivity in required study than by objectivity in their own patient reading. Submersion in self makes other selves unavailable. Objectivity is enforced by second readings of a novel. Repeated readings enable a reader not only to enjoy new facets and to experience already-felt elements more deeply but to cultivate their responses, to observe and evaluate their own reading mechanisms, and thus make their responses to another work richer, more sensitive and complete. "And when the process is over," says E. M. Forster, describing the reader's experience also, "the artist, looking back on it, will wonder how on earth he did it. And indeed he did not do it on earth." Conrad said, " . . . the demand of the individual to the artist is, in effect, the cry 'Take me out of myself' meaning really, out of my perishable activity into the light of imperishable consciousness."

A study of a writer's techniques through an examination of the various versions of a work (from notes through conception and revision to final product) develops the student's receptivity to the effects of those techniques (what they *do* to the reader and *how* they do it) and enables the student to understand the nature and appreciate the effects of the various forms: not only fiction, but poetry, plays, films, imaginative nonfiction. What the student learns from studying *revisions* of a particular work enables him to apply what he has learned to any other work in the genre. The emphasis is not on studying the specific work for its own sake (although that occurs) but on studying the form in which the work is written.

Here is what some writers have said about the importance of rewriting:

"The art of writing is re-writing" (Seán O'Faoláin).

"The best reason for putting something down on paper is that one may then change it" (Bernard de Voto).

"Rewrite—the effort always brings some profit, whatever this may be. Those who do not succeed fail because they are lazy" (Albert Camus).

"It is in order to shine sooner that authors refuse to rewrite. Dispicable. Begin again" (Camus).

"It is not everyday that the world arranges itself into a poem" (Wallace Stevens, poet).

Joseph Conrad's wife locked him into his study, as she did every morning. When she released him for lunch, she asked, "Joseph, what did you do this morning?" "I put in a comma," he replied. After lunch, she locked him in again. When she released him for dinner, she asked, "And what did you accomplish this afternoon, Joseph?" And he replied, "I took the comma out." A very serious illustration of the importance of style, and of revision, in the creative process.

Writers rewrite for many reasons and make many kinds of revisions. One kind of stylistic revision is the attempt to move from *telling* the reader how a character feels to *implying*. Suppose that in telling a reader how a character feels, the writer has given the reader three statements in logical order. "John gazed out the window. Because he felt disgusted with the whole world. He pulled the shade." The task in revision is to cut out one of those three statements and to reword the remaining two so that they imply how the character feels. "Restless, John went to the window and gazed out at the city. Smog hazed his vision. He pulled the shade." The experience of "disgust" is not described on the page, it is evoked in the reader through a phantom circuit of the imagination. The best style is one that requires the reader's active, imaginative, intellectual, emotional collaboration.

Compare two versions of a key scene in Wright Morris' *Man and Boy*, expanded from a short story "The Ram in the Thicket." Most of Morris' revisions are omissions; he removes (or slightly rewrites) phrases or lines that too obviously *tell* the reader. His aim is to evoke, to suggest, to reveal. A major stylistic technique is his deliberate use of clichés (discussed earlier in the section on clichés under "style").

A Key passage in Wright Morris' "The Ram in the Thicket," as revised for the novel, *Man and Boy* (revised version underlined)

1 The basement toilet had been put in to accommodate the help,
   The basement toilet had been put in to accommodate the help,

2 who had to use something, and Mother wouldn't have them on her
   who had to use something, and Mother would not have them on her

3 Oriental rug. But until the day he dropped some money on the
   oriental rug. Until the day he dropped some money out of his

4 floor, and had to stike a match, inside, to look for it, Mr. Ormsby
   pants, and had to strike a match   to look for it, he

5 hadn't noticed just what kind of a stool it was. Mother had picked it
  had never noticed what kind of a stool it was. Mother had picked it

6 up, as she had told him, second-hand. There was no use, as she had
  up secondhand—she had never told him where—because she couldn't

7 pointed out, why she should buy anything new or fancy for a place
  see buying something   new   for a place

8 that was meant to be in the dark. He hadn't pushed the matter and
  always in the dark.

9 she hadn't offered more than that. What he saw was very old.
                                        It was very old,

10 with a chain pull, and operated on a principle that was very
  with a chain pull, and operated on a principle that

11 effective, but invariably produced quite a splash. The boy had
                invariably produced quite a splash.

12 named it the Ormsby Falls. That described it pretty well, it was

13 constructed on that principle, and in spite of the splash they both
                      But in spite of that, he

14 preferred it to the
  preferred it to the one at the store and very much more than the

15 one upstairs. This was a hard thing to explain, as the seat was
  one upstairs. This was rather hard to explain since the seat was

16 pretty cold over the winter:
  pretty cold in the winter and the water sometimes nearly froze.

17 but it was private, like no other room in the house.
  But it was private like no other room in the house.

18 Considering that the house was as good as empty, that was a strange

19 thing to say, but it was the only way to say how he felt. If he

20 went for a walk like the boy, Mother would miss him, somebody

21 would see him, and he wouldn't feel right about it anyhow. All

22 he wanted was a dark quiet place and the feeling that for five

23 minutes, just five minutes, nobody would be looking for him.

24 Who would ever believe five minutes like that were so hard to

25 come by? The closest he had ever been to the boy—after he had

26 The first time the boy had turned up missing, he had been there.
given him the gun—was the morning he had found him here on the
stool.

27 It was that time when the boy had said—when his father nearly
It was then that the boy had said,

28 stepped on him—"Et tu, Brutus," and sat there blowing through his
et tu, Brutus, and they had both laughed so hard

29 nose. Laughing so hard Mr. Ormsby thought he might be sick.
they had to hold their sides. The boy had put his head in a basket

30   Like everything the boy said
of wash so Mother wouldn't hear. Like everything the boy said

31 there had been two or three ways to take it, and there in the dark
there were two or three ways to take it, and in the dark Mr. Ormsby

32 Mr. Ormsby couldn't see his face. He had just stood there, not
could not see his face.

33 knowing what to say. Then the boy stopped laughing and said:
When he stopped laughing the boy said,

34 "You think we ought to make one flush do, Pop?" and Mr. Ormsby
Well, Pop, I suppose one flush ought to do, but Mr. Ormsby

35 had had to brace himself on the door. To be called Pop had made him
had not been able to say anything. (To be called Pop made him so weak

36 so weak he couldn't speak, his legs felt hollow, and when he
so weak that he had to sit right down on the stool, just like he was

37 got himself back to the stairs he had to sit down.
and support his head in his hands.)

8 Just as he had never had a name for the boy, the boy had never
  Just as he had never had a name for the boy, the boy had never

9 had a name for him—one, that is, that Mother would permit him to use.
  had a name for him—none, that is, that Mother would permit him to use.

0 And of all the names she couldn't stand, Pop was the worst.
  Of all the names Mother couldn't stand, Pop was the worst,

1 Mr. Ormsby didn't like it either, he thought it just a vulgar
  and he agreed with her, it was

2 common name, a comic name used by smart alecks to flatter old men.
  common, and used by strangers to intimidate old men.

3 He agreed with her, completely—until he heard the word in the
  He agreed with her, completely—until he heard the word in the

4 boy's mouth.
  boy's mouth. It was only natural that the boy would use it if

5   It was hard to believe a common word
  he ever had the chance—but he never dreamed that any word,

6   like that could mean what it did.
  especially *that* word, could mean what it did. It made him weak,

7 he had to sit down and pretend he was going about his business,

8 and what a blessing it was that the place was dark.

9 Nothing more had been said, ever, but it remained their most
  Nothing more   was said, ever, but it remained their most

0 important conversation—so important that they were both afraid
  important conversation—so important that they were both afraid

1 to   improve on it (*Man and Boy* 26–29).
  to try and improve on it (*Wright Morris: A Reader*, 594–595).

Here are a few suggestions for the study of revisions: Compare the two
published versions of F. Scott Fitzgerald's *Tender Is the Night*. Compare *A
Happy Death* by Camus with the related novel *The Stranger* (also consult
his notebooks). Compare *Stephen Hero* with the later *A Portrait of the Artist as a Young Man* by James Joyce. Compare William Faulkner's *Flags in
the Dust* with the shorter, revised *Sartoris*. Compare the two published

versions of John Fowles' *The Magus*. Read John Steinbeck's *Journal of a Novel: The East of Eden Letters*. Read the notebooks, diaries, letters of Fitzgerald, Conrad, James, Mansfield, Woolf, Thomas Wolfe, Maugham, Anaïs Nin, James Joyce, Gide, Dostoyevsky, D. H. Lawrence, Flaubert.

Some understanding of the ways the *imagination* works in the revisi process may illuminate the nature of fiction. The role of the imagination today seriously, perhaps perilously neglected when the creative process i discussed. "Write about what you know" is the most misused piece of ad vice ever pontificated upon young writers. "What you know" can be a ric world created out of one's imagination—rather than simply what it's like grow up in a middle-class suburb. "By refusing to write about anything which is not thoroughly familiar," says Saul Bellow, author of the imagin tive novel *Henderson the Rain King*, "the American writer confesses the powerlessness of the imagination and accepts its relegation to an inferior place." Imagination is perhaps more important than experience and inspi tion. Many writers do not want to give a faithful report on real life inci dents; they want to transform them in their imaginations so that the stor self becomes an event—not just a report referring to something else. A child prefers to be told a story that is made up than to listen to one bein read. He wants to experience *the process itself* as the imagination invent

It is while looking closely, imaginatively at every word (every comm in the revision process that the imagination may suddenly soar, and see larger possibilities. As the writer first imagines characters and their story the source of creative energy is usually inspiration. In the imagination, i the revision stage (the re-seeing stage) of the creative process, characters and their story are reshaped many times, in many possible ways. When *reshaping imagination* is at work, the source of creative energy is almost ways the techniques of writing themselves. We do not often discuss the third way the imagination works. It is of absolute importance. One may it the technical imagination. Often, the writer is inspired to see the char ters and their stories in the imagination, but cannot see *how* the story ca be told. He must wait for a *technical inspiration*. Or he must willfully in ine a technique for telling that story. Some writers get just as great a thr discovering the right technique to solve problems in a story's first draft a they do from the initial inspiration. Inspiration dies very quickly, but tec nique opens up many possibilities. Unconsciously in the first draft and c sciously in the revision stage, the *stylistic imagination* is at work. Imagin tion does not work simply on the larger elements of plot and characters, in the realm of technique; it works line by line in style.

(See John Kuehl, *Creative Writing and Rewriting;* Thomas McCorm *Afterwords: Novelists on Their Novels;* William E. Buckler, *Novels in the Making;* John Braine, *Writing a Novel;* Wallace Hildick, *Word for Word* and *Writing With Care*.)

INNOVATIVE TECHNIQUES

To some degree every fiction, even the simplest, defies definite interpretation, and that is especially true of innovative fictions. They are so far outside recognizable contexts that they cannot be judged good or poor—they simply *are*. Avant-garde stories seem immune to literary analysis. No literary criteria can be applied to the question, "Are the writers in control of their materials?" Some critics labor to explain and describe what innovative fiction strives to achieve; but there is an inherent contradiction in trying to explain a story that was originally conceived to defy analysis. All we can expect to do here, then, is suggest a *few* ways of approaching and perhaps getting into stories (or "fictions") by avant-garde, experimental, or innovative writers ("fictionists" is the name most prefer).

Generally, the novel has been the most conservative of art forms. It lends itself to greater variety in subject matter, but fewer possibilities in form. "'The novel, of all literary genres, is the freest, the most lawless,' held forth Edouard.'... Is it for that very reason, for fear of that very liberty (the artists who are always sighing after liberty are often the most bewildered when they get it), that the novel has always clung to reality with such timidity?'" (Gide, *The Counterfeiters*). Gide's novel itself was a narrative innovation, but within this genre few distinct innovations have made a lasting and pervasive impression.

The most influential avant-garde movements in the novel were affected by the French Symbolist poets who reacted against the rationalism of the Victorian Age and the old-fashioned romanticism of earlier eras. They turned art to the complex operation of the senses. They explored the unconscious and the dream world as a major area of human experience not adequately depicted in art. Because conventional concepts of human experience and beauty were related mainly to bourgeois ethics and religion, these poets explored experiences not previously touched upon. They were drawn to the world of the poor, the criminal, the forbidden, to the abnormal. These poets described states of being that verged on the illegal, that posed a threat to conventional society. They used irrational means to explore the irrational and the subconscious. Relativism reigned. Words and their associations were examined in numerous combinations, in what might be called the poetic license explosion (in such a combustion, mistakes, faults, inferior qualities are easily concealed). Self-expression became, as never before, an end in itself. They introduced symbolism to the literary world, although, of course, it had been used less consciously in such works as Melville's *Moby Dick* (see the chapter on the Whiteness of the Whale). Proust, Joyce, Woolf, and James were directly affected by the symbolists.

The surrealists decided the symbolists had not gone far enough. They focused upon the life of the subconscious and dreams as manifestations of

mankind's true nature. André Breton's *Nadja* was the first, perhaps best, of
the surreal romances.

> When the dessert is served, Nadja begins looking around her. She
> is certain that an underground tunnel passes under our feet, start-
> ing at the Palais de Justice (she shows me which part of the build-
> ing, slightly to the right of the white flight of steps) and circling
> the Hotel Henry IV. She is disturbed by the thought of what has
> already occurred in this square and will occur here in the future.
> Where only two or three couples are at this moment fading into
> the darkness, she seems to see a crowd. "And the dead, the dead!"
> The drunkard lugubriously continues cracking jokes. Nadja's eyes
> now sweep over the surrounding houses. "Do you see that window
> up there? It's black, like all the rest. Look hard. In a minute it will
> light up. It will be red." The minute passes. The window lights
> up. There are, as a matter of fact, red curtains. ... I confess that
> this place frightens me, as it is beginning to frighten Nadja too.
> "How terrible! Can you see what's going on in the trees? The blue
> and the wind, the blue wind. I've seen that blue wind pass
> through these same trees only once before. It was there, from a
> window in the Hotel Henry IV, and my friend, the second man I
> told you about, was about to leave. And there was a voice saying:
> 'You're going to die, you're going to die.' I didn't want to die, but
> I felt so dizzy. ..."

Anaïs Nin, in such novels as *House of Incest*, is one of the few writers who
remained committed to the surrealistic vision. (Compare style and technique with Barnes' *Nightwood*.)

> Men recognized her always: the same effulgent face, the same rus
> voice. And she and I, we recognized each other; I her face and sh
> my legend.
> Around my pulse she put a flat steel bracelet and my pulse
> beat as she willed, losing its human cadence, thumping like a sav
> age in orgiastic frenzy. The lamentations of flutes, the double cha
> of wind through our slender bones, the cracking of our bones dis
> tantly remembered when on beds of down the worship we inspir
> turned to lust.
> As we walked along, rockets burst from the street lamps; we
> swallowed the asphalt road with a jungle roar and the houses wit
> their closed eyes and geranium eyelashes; swallowed the telegra
> poles trembling with messages; swallowed stray cats, trees, hills,
> hedges, Sabina's labyrinthian smile on the keyhole. The door
> moaning, opening. Her smile closed. A nightingale disleafing me
> liferous honey-suckle. Honey-suckled. Fluted fingers. The house

opened its green gate mouth and swallowed us. The bed was floating.

The poems and novels of the surrealists were ways of exploding the
barriers between the conscious and the unconscious life. There was a great
emphasis on spontaneity: automatic writing, championed by Gertrude Stein.
Free-association writing was prevalent in the movement (Joyce's *Ulysses*,
passages in Virginia Woolf's novels). In free-association, these writers discovered relationships among objects and events that rational means cannot
uncover. The process stimulated remembrance of things forgotten, and
there was an associational progression in their works. Images that stylized
reality filled their novels. Some writers employ surrealistic passages, without producing a sustained surreal vision: Nathanael West in *The Dream Life
of Balso Snell;* John Hawkes in *The Cannibal;* Djuna Barnes in *Nightwood;*
Susan Sontag in *The Benefactor;* Kenneth Patchen in *The Journal of Albion
Moonlight;* Henry Miller in *Tropic of Capricorn;* William Burroughs in
Naked Lunch.

> white flash... mangled insect screams...
> I woke up with the taste of metal in my mouth back from the dead
> trailing the colorless death smell
> afterbirth of a withered grey monkey
> phantom twinges of amputation...
> "Taxi boys waiting for a pickup," Eduardo said and died of an
> overdose in Madrid...
> Powder trains burn back through pink convolutions of tumes-
> cent flesh... set off flash bulbs of orgasm. ... pin-point photos of
> arrested motion... smooth brown side twisted to light a ciga-
> rette. ...
> He stood there in a 1920 straw hat somebody gave him...
> soft medicant words falling like dead birds in the dark street....
> "No... No more... No mas...."

Surrealists banded together—painters, playwrights, poets, movie makers, novelists—and published their own works in their own magazines, issu-
ing manifestoes: "The writer expresses. He does not communicate," declared Eugene Jolas in *transition* magazine in 1929.

If most of the symbolists were too disciplined for the surrealists, for the
dadaists the surrealists weren't revolutionary enough. While the symbolists
were eminently unpolitical, although they were sometimes moralists and social critics (especially Baudelaire), many of the surrealists and dadaists became communists or socialists, working for a new order (which ironically,
would certainly reject their art). The dadaists were anti-aesthetic as well as
anti-rational, but they were at the same time anarchists and revolutionaries,

deliberately causing confusions in every aspect of their activities. They set out to destroy all art forms and show through their own methods the madness of all human existence. Nothing was sacred; nothing was absolute; no patterns in life, society, or art were valid. They juxtaposed images that had no logical relation whatsoever. Louis Aragon's *Anicet* is the best of the few novels the dadaist movement spawned.

The surrealists and the dadaists together were truly avant-garde in seeking the frontiers of human (and perhaps animal) sensual experience and in testing conventional aesthetic notions. The result, once the shock wore off, was that their techniques and attitudes were absorbed by less militant writers, and with great self-control and artistic discipline, those writers were able to make use of the discoveries and new emphases of the surrealists and the dadaists. The movements themselves did not produce a single poem, novel, or play of lasting value; while some of the paintings are fascinating, especially those of surrealists Dali, Max Ernst, Chirico, Paul Klee, Miro, Magritte, Chagall, Yves Tanguy, and a few others, most of the work looks old-fashioned, outmoded. The French Symbolist poets have fared far better the works of Mallarmé, Corbière, Valéry, Nerval, Baudelaire, Verlaine, Rimbaud are, of course, still vital, exciting, and relevant as art, and their effect continue to be felt. These lines from "Golden Verses" by Nerval anticipate the anti-novelists, especially Robbe-Grillet:

> ... life bursts from all things
> "Everything's sentient!" and works on you.

> Beware! from the blind wall one watches you:
> even matter has a logos all its own. . . .
> Pure spirit grows beneath the surface of stones.

The experimental novel uses new forms and techniques (symbolism, impressionism, expressionism, surrealism, dadaism, automatic writing) to express new insights and attitudes. Many of the works of the avant-garde are as ephemeral as thesis-ridden or subject-dominated novels because the claim to the reader's attention is that they are new and unique and depart from or revolt against the conventional novel. But when experimental or avant-garde techniques have become accepted and are used frequently, sometimes even in so-called popular fiction, the particular innovative work ceases to be exciting and becomes a curiosity in the history of literature. Most surrealistic novels are almost as unreadable as most popular novels of the twenties and proletarian novels of the thirties. Their achievements have been skillfully absorbed into the mainstream of literature. That is as it should be, for the very nature of an experiment is that it prepares for something more important and lasting than itself.

Most writers experiment constantly, but in private; the so-called experimental writer offers his experiments to a limited public that finds the mere act of experimenting intrinsically important and meaningful. But often, the meaning is exterior to the work; it is valued as an act of rebellion against an established literature that has withered or ceased to interest the experimental writer and his audience.

The experimental writer knows and writes for his audience—unconsciously perhaps—as obviously as the best-seller writer. In fact, avant-garde art of every kind has always had a great deal in common with folk and popular art; it came into being *with* the mass media. Innovative writing often derives as much from pop as from high-culture models. The avant-garde writer often uses popular fiction elements as his material and distorts them to his purposes, to explode conventional forms and to outrage the bourgeoise. (Camus patterned *The Stranger* on Cain's *The Postman Always Rings Twice*). Both popular and experimental writers emphasize pure experience over meanings.

The audience for experimental writing is limited, perhaps because it is difficult to see the value of form divorced from logical meaning. There is a predisposition to be confused—why make a part of an experience the whole? With the increasing sophistication of the mass media and its audience, avant-garde may be in danger of becoming totally absorbed, for few techniques are shocking in a culture that has few norms to which the majority conforms.

The major innovations of the deliberately avant-garde or experimental writer are: stream of consciousness (Dujardin and Joyce); collage (William Burroughs' *Nova Express*); surrealism (Breton, Cocteau); dadaism (Louis Aragon, *Anicet*); black humor (Bruce Jay Friedman, Donald Barthelme, Kurt Vonnegut, Jr.) montage (Lautréamont, Patchen); new uses of language (Gertrude Stein, Joyce).

Avant-garde and experimental novelists try new things with form and language, seldom with theme and content (Joyce, Stein, Cortazar); this observation suggests that the basic effect of the novel, like most art forms, is aesthetic. But too often experimentalists simply take a device or technique used by many novelists, as one among many techniques, and exaggerate it; for instance there is Joseph Heller's stylistic technique in *Catch-22* of repeating phrases in comic rhythms.

> One afternoon when she came a second time to the soldier in white, she read the thermometer and discovered he was dead.
> "Murderer," Dunbar said quietly.
> The Texan looked up at him with an uncertain grin.

"Killer," Yossarian said.

"What are you fellas talkin about?" The Texan asked nervously.

"You murdered him," said Yossarian.

The Texan shrank back. "You fellas are crazy. I didn't even touch him.

"You murdered him," said Dunbar.

"You fellas are crazy," the Texan said, "I didn't even touch him."

"You killed him," said Yossarian. "I heard you kill him."

"You killed him because he was a nigger," Dunbar said.

"You fellas are crazy," the Texan cried. "They don't allow niggers in here. They got a special place for niggers."

"The sergeant smuggled him in," Dunbar said.

"The Communist sergeant," Yossarian said.

"And you knew it."

This technique is used also by Gertrude Stein in *Three Lives;* Günter Grass in *The Tin Drum;* Curzio Malaparte in *The Skin;* but also by Dickens, somewhat less comically, in *Bleak House.*

One delayed consequence of the dadaist movement, joined with existentialism and the concept of the absurd, is the black humor movement, which is also political in nature, as was the dadaist movement. The black humorists of today are not as philosophically grounded in the absurd and in existentialism as were the writers who inspired black humor. Black humor often deliberately employs lowcomedy kinds of humor to express the senselessness and futility of life in the electronic age; a style composed of disjointed syntax and barren clichés expresses man's inability to communicate Life is an absurd, black, terrifying farce. The black or absurd humorist attempts to exorcize every vestige of sentimental allegiance to decayed institutions and paralyzing attitudes and values. Here are a few examples: J. P. Donleavy, *The Ginger Man;* Terry Southern, *The Magic Christian;* Kurt Vonnegut, *Mother Night;* James Purdy, *Cabot Wright Begins;* John Barth, *The Sot-Weed Factor;* Joseph Heller, *Catch-22;* and Bruce Jay Friedman, *Mother's Kisses.*

He wanted badly for her to leave, yet there were times he fe that maybe she was right. That he would not be able to get along on his own. He would go hungry and not know what to say to people and wind up just standing in one place somewhere, finally have to be put in a large box with air holes and sent home to he He came around finally to the idea that he would let her stay on semester and that was all. After that she would have to leave or would go home and not go to college again, just staying indoors and listening to radio shows until he died at thirty-four. Once, at night, when she was standing near the hotel room window in her nightgown, he wondered what would happen if he shoved her out, whether she would flip end over end or drop, pancake style, to the pavement. He wondered what would happen legally if a son did that to his mother.

Black humor is a source of power to writer and reader, appealing strongly to somewhat impotent people who feel incapable of coping with the forces that victimize man in our computerized age. The cruel laughter is directed mainly at those who create the horrible conditions in our world, but includes the passive victims as well. The hero is liberated by his black vision to little more than endless gallows humor. The idea of a solution is painfully laughable. Like most destructive visions, this one thrives on an inverted sentimentality. Some readers' hatred of literature makes them warm to a literature of hatred.

The anti-novel uses techniques devised to frustrate the reader's expectations about fiction, derived from reading traditional novels. The responsive reader is then open to new kinds of fictive experience. By violating traditional concepts of the novel, the author attempts to set it free, to delineate new states of consciousness. Today, the terms "anti-novel," "anovel," "aliterature," "noveau roman" (the new novel), "*ante*-novel" or "thingism," "realistic formalism," "objectivism," or "phenomenalism" describe the work mainly of the French: Robbe-Grillet (*Jealousy*); Natalie Sarraute; Samuel Beckett (an Irishman who writes in French); Michel Butor (*The Modification*); Claude Mauriac (*The Marquise Went Out at Five*). Bernard Pingaud has said of the "*anti*novel": "what the new novelists describe or relate is what takes place before the novel in the classic sense has begun, previous to any characters or story." Calling for a new realism, Robbe-Grillet asserts that "the discovery of reality will continue only if we abandon outworn forms." The novel "does not express... it explores itself" (*For a New Novel*). Mainly, these writers want to throw out conventional notions of story and characterization and focus upon the phenomenal world of objects and natural events (Natalie Sarruate, *Tropismes*) and through them evoke the inner life of anti-heroes.

Just as naturalism depicted the hero as victim, the psychological experimental novel usually presents a character whose distinguishing characteristic is self-pity. The self-pitying or self-contemptuous hero in-search-of-himself often results in a book in-search-of-its-form as in Julio Cortazar's *Hopscotch*. Some of the experimental novels exhibit an alogical structure (a logic peculiar to the specific work) employing a plastic language, multiple vision, an image in process of taking shape, kaleidoscopic progression. (See Richard Ellmann, *The Modern Tradition*.) With Samuel Beckett, the focus is mainly on language; it, and what it describes, is reduced to the bare essentials, style without substance, as in the *Unnamable*, in which the narrator clings to life by the frail strands of rhetoric.

> Where now? Who now? When now? Unquestioning. I, say I. Unbelieving. Questions, hypotheses, call them that. Keep going, going on, call that going, call that on. Can it be that one day, off it goes on, that one day I simply stayed in, in where, instead of going out, in the old way, out to spend day and night as far away as possible, it wasn't far. Perhaps that is how it began. You think you are simply resting, the better to act when the time comes, or for no reason, and you soon find yourself powerless ever to do anything again. No matter how it happened. It, say it, now knowing what. Perhaps I simply assented at least to an old thing. But I did nothing. I seem to speak, it is not I, about me, it is not about me. These few general remarks to begin with. What am I to do, what shall I do, what should I do, in my situation, how proceed? By aporia pure and simple? Or by affirmations and negations invalidated as uttered, or sooner or later? Generally speaking. . . .

Some of these writers (Robbe-Grillet, Susan Sontag, Marguerite Duras) have turned to film as a way of capturing *the thing itself*, evoking sterility, déjà vu, ennui, and the nostalgia of despair.

Here are some arguments defending avant-garde fiction's effects. Experimental writers reject traditional techniques because those techniques fail to depict facets of our contemporary experience. Glibly, sympathetic commentators continue to cite conditions that by now have become clichés: Bureaucracy and technology have dehumanized civilized man; overwhelming social dislocations have fragmented individual identity; even group identity has proven inadequate; scientific and psychological models for living have failed; life since the end of World War II has become boring, insipid, banal, dull, conformist.

Racial, social, and economic inequality, the threat of the bomb, insane wars, ecological breakdown, and political treachery inspire in many innovative fictionists a pessimistic view of man as a degraded creature. They argue that as mankind experiences rapid social and psychological changes, fiction should simultaneously reflect and contribute to the process of change. But traditional fiction has failed to do that, they charge, because the possibilities of its forms have been exhausted. Experimental writers often point out that while other art media reflect a changing world, fiction remains the most "conservative art of midcentury," the "most self-imitative," the most predictable and formulaic. Fictionists are inspired by innovations in other media more than by those in their own: abstract expressionist painting, free-form sculpture, method acting, modern dance, the improvisations of jazz, the music of chance.

In the opening paragraphs of *The Death of the Novel* (a novella), Ronald Sukenick expresses the view of many fictionists.

> Fiction constitutes a way of looking at the world. Therefore I will begin by considering how the world looks in what I think we may now begin to call the contemporary post-realistic novel. Realistic fiction presupposed chronological time as the medium of a plotted narrative, an irreducible individual psyche as the subject of its characterization, and, above all, the ultimate, concrete reality of things as the object and rationale of its description. In the world of post-realism, however, all of these absolutes have become absolutely problematic.
>
> The contemporary writer—the writer who is acutely in touch with the life of which he is part—is forced to start from scratch: Reality doesn't exist, time doesn't exist, personality doesn't exist. God was the omniscient author, but he died; now no one knows the plot, and since our reality lacks the sanction of a creator, there's no guarantee as to the authenticity of the received version. Time is reduced to presence, the content of a series of discontinuous moments. Time is no longer purposive, and so there is no destiny, only chance. Reality is, simply, our experience, and objectivity is, of course, an illusion. Personality, after passing through a phase of awkward self-consciousness has become, quite minimally a mere locus for our experience. In view of these annihilations, it should be no surprise that literature, also, does not exist—how could it? There is only reading and writing, which are things we do, like eating and making love, to pass the time, ways of maintaining a considered boredom in face of the abyss. Not to mention a series of overwhelming social dislocations.

Sukenick, therefore, writes in this way (ending his novel *Out*):

this way this way this way this way this way this way this

way out this

way out

0

In "Title," a short story, John Barth's writer-narrator recognizes the fictionist's special problem: "I believe literature's not likely ever to manage abstractions successfully, like sculpture for example. . . . Well, because wood and iron have a native appeal and first-order reality, whereas words are artificial to begin with, invented specifically to represent" something else. In the short story "The Birds," Ronald Sukenick's writer-narrator, like Barth's wants to do what sculpture, theater, even music are doing, what prose fiction hasn't done, isn't doing, won't, perhaps can't do: "Destroy this as you read it. It is printed in a soluble ink which you can lick off the page sentence by sentence. The ink has various flavors depending on the parts of speech to make this easier to understand and swallow." The conditions of his medium allow him only to pretend to offer the reader such an experience.

Innovative writers are trying to add their own contributions to those of other art media in the effort to break out of traditional forms. In several introductions to collections of avant-garde writing, commentators offer the following characteristics of the new fiction: It makes use of aspects of past innovations; of the symbolist, dada, surrealist, impressionistic, expressionistic, imagist movements in various media. It reflects elements of bohemian, beatnik, hippie, and other subcultures. Its techniques are those of the con man and the magician. It has an aggressively comic spirit that revels in nonsense as an end in itself, that employs elements of satire, parody, burlesque, lampoon, invective, and black humor. Not afraid to take uncalculated risks, this new fiction strives to be vital, exuberant, and audacious.

Innovative writers attempt, their defenders tell us, to experience phenomena purely, innocently: The naked "I" sees with a naked eye. They use techniques that "fracture" the "purely personal flow of perception," producing a "non-narrative succession of fragmented impressions" and "revelatory moments." The focus is "on the experiencing mind" of the author (and/or character) and the reader. It is no wonder that much avant-garde writing has an air of being under the influence of mysterious, mythic forces. It is incantatory, visionary, and prophetic. To achieve those effects, each experimental writer reaches for a unique style, using techniques that "shatter syntax" to recycle, revive, or resurrect what such writers consider to be a used-up or dead language; they labor to forge a pure language, free of empty rhetoric.

Innovative writers attempt, we are told, a "calculated demolition of the conventions" of fiction to break down "the applicability of traditional categories both of judgment and description," categories such as "perceptiveness, good taste, intelligence, the ability to create credible characters, the satisfactory resolution of themes." They are against chronological structure and plot (against the elements of conflict, exposition, complication, revelation, resolution). Refusing to create illusions of real life, they are attracted to bizarre subject matter and depict "implausible people doing incredible things." They are against such messages and themes as "the discovery of love, the loss of innocence, reconciliation to the fact of death, the renunciation of self-interest, the recognition of evil."

Anti-Story (1971) is an anthology of fiction that reveals what is happening in the experimental realm. Philip Stevick, the editor, provides us with some very suggestive titles and subtitles of sections: The new fiction is "against mimesis" (imitation of life); it is fiction about fiction, he says. It is against "reality," preferring to explore the uses of fantasy. It is against depicting "events," asserting instead the primacy of the author's creative voice. Against "subject," it is "fiction in search of something to be about." It is against "the middle range of experience," reaching for "new forms of extremity." It is against intellectual "analysis," trying to make us experience "the phenomenal world" directly. It is against "meaning," exploring instead "forms of the absurd." It is against "scale," insisting that a novel can be as short as one paragraph.

Commentators on innovative fiction argue that willful obscurity may enable the imagination to explore possibilities and to push into far-out realms where transformations may occur. In the innovative approach, they point out, there is an infinite range of structural possibilities. Many innovative works reach beyond the limitations of the normal printed page. Each page becomes a visual unit; the reader encounters the fiction first through the naked eye, words are mixed with photos and other page-exploding graphics, causing impingement of words upon images. Each fiction extends the possibilities of life and art.

Innovative fiction breaks up the surface appearances of everyday life and remains unresolved on levels of action, theme, and character. Refusing to impose order upon disorder, innovators force their readers to ride the wild horses of chaos. To force us to experience the relativity of all things, they distort chronology, thwart continuity. They offer us experiences in disintegration, for their fictions do not progressively cohere; they self-destruct, line by line. Unlike traditional stories, the commentators warn, innovative fictions offer not patterns to live by, but freedom from patterns. Everything in the fiction is pure invention; and what we experience is the imagination at play. The fiction does not reflect the real world; it is its own world, and we must accept it as an alternative world. Each fiction is atypical, idiosyncratic, an act of pure creation; the world the author creates exists nowhere beyond the page, it exists only in a language continuum. It does not report on already made and finished things and events; it is in itself a new thing, a new event. Each fiction is *about* the process of its own creation. A world created by imagination and intuition, it is an aesthetic object, a "self-contained, artificial universe."

André Gide's personal credo may stand for the innovative fictionist: "My function is to disturb." Innovative writers and critics assume or claim that the new fiction, using "techniques that perpetually astonish," has certain effects on the reader (even those that sound negative are, in these writers' frame of reference, positive). Innovative fiction does violence to the reader; it startles, provokes, disorients, disturbs, frightens, alienates him—blows his mind. Its impact is almost physical; it rapes the reader's senses and sensibility. It violates his preconceptions and expectations about life and art; it shatter ethical and spiritual certainties. Inviting the reader's subjective responses, it "foments radically unusual states of mind." It can inspire the reader's own experimentations in perception and behavior that may change his life. Ronald Sukenick has said in an interview that innovative "fiction is one of the ways we have of creating ourselves." For the reader, experimental fictions offer "experiences to respond to, not problems to figure out." We should "improvise our art as we improvise our lives. No hysterical impositions of meaning."

And here are some arguments attacking avant-garde fiction's effects. Readers who resist innovative writing cite many of the characteristics described so far as reasons for their rejection of it. The majority's most powerful resistance to these experiements is neglect or indifference. But some readers react with overt hostility, charging that innovative writers are arrogantly subjective, willfully perverse, self-indulgent, self-conscious and, in their leftist views, self-righteous. They produce claustrophobic, irrational, deranged, and paranoid works that reek of futility. They write out of destructive, anti-social impulses. Dark, decadent, amoral, subversive, anarchistic, offensively violent, often pornographic, and blasphemous, their abstract, abstruse, arbitrary, ambiguous, bizarre, obscure works lack form, unity, coherence, and control. Because these writers assume too much of the reader, their fictions are to some readers too complex, difficult, exasperating, depressing; to others they are simply too cute, shallow, and boring; and they are often in bad taste. The anti-heroes of these unrealistic concoctions fail to achieve insights, to learn from their experiences. Innovative works, these readers insist, are of only passing interest or relevance; and some are fraudulent put-ons.

These unsympathetic readers further argue that a major limitation of avant-garde writing lies in its very nature: Because the innovative writer can choose only to be free, his freedom is a self-contradiction. On the other hand, the eclectic writer is much freer to choose, he can skillfully use both traditional and innovative techniques. The innovative writer often simply exaggerates a single device or technique that most writers use as one among many in the creative process. The anti-story's basic problem, the unsympathetic reader insists, lies in its negative impulse: It thrives by virtue of being what something else is not, and thus narrows rather than expands possibilities. And the world of the novel—of all types—has been an expansive one.

Samuel Beckett has not gone far beyond *Watt*; Joseph Heller has written two novels, *Catch-22* and *Something Happened*, in fifteen years; John Barth's *Giles Goat-Boy* contains little new and anticipates all consequent Barth; Jean Genet's *Our Lady of the Flowers* contains all Genet's possibilities. The so-called freedom of the avant-garde is a contradiction.

Since their visions differ radically from the majority view, innovative writers often feel they are outlaws in society; as outsiders, they pride themselves on the labels their critics paste on them; they turn every hostile objection into a possible description of their experimental intent; thus when a critic shows how an innovative work violates the rules of traditional fiction, he succeeds only in describing the work's achievement.

Hostile critics charge that innovative writers make pretentious, sometimes hysterical claims to originality in vision and technique, seemingly ignorant of a fact of literary history: that innovation always runs parallel to tradition, that the one never does or should replace the other. In the stream of literature, turbulence comes and goes; the sediment remains. Scholars are fond of citing one of the very earliest novels—*The Life and Opinions of Tristram Shandy, Gent.* (1760)—which contains numerous innovative devices, techniques, and ways of rendering human perception. "The machinery of my work is a species by itself," says the author, Laurence Sterne, through Shandy. "Two contrary motions are introduced into it, and reconciled, which were thought to be at variance with each other. In a word, my work is digressive, and it is progressive, too, and at the same time." Many graphic devices, such as blank or black pages, and drawings or signs and symbols, were introduced in *Tristram Shandy*. A recent young French novelist offered a novel in a box; readers were invited to reassemble the loose pages any way they wished; few readers did. Steve Katz in *The Exaggerations of Peter Prince* (1968), an odd-sized book, employs photographs, rejected or revised pages of the novel, different sizes and styles of print, drawings, blank spaces, marginalia, as though Sterne had never lived. You can blow up the same monument only once, these scholars observe and Sterne lit the first fuse.

Experimental writing may prove less difficult if one keeps the foregoing pro and con observations in mind, and if one realizes that every novel offers the reader hints about the ways it should be read. The reader of a story always goes through a creative process that parallels the writer's; that, too, is especially clear in experimental fictions. All art is in a primary sense about *itself;* every story is about the process of storytelling, *about* the relationship between the writer and the reader. That is more obvious in experimental than in traditional novels. The reader should let each fiction happen to him the first time he reads it. Many innovators remind us that "in the beginning was the word . . . and the word was made flesh." They try to expose us to the pure, bracing potency of the word. The best way to get into innovative fiction's sometimes murky waters, then, is to plunge from the highest diving board.

Several of the following sources provided concepts and a few succinct phrases (in quotes) for this section: (1) Joe David Bellamy (ed.), *The New Fiction, Interviews with Innovative American Writers* (Barthelme, Barth, Sukenick, Oates). (2) Madeline Gins, "Brief Autobiography of a Non-existent," in David Madden (ed.), *Creative Choices.* (3) Beverly Gross and Richard Giannone (eds.), *The Shapes of Fiction.* (4) Rust Hills (ed.), *Writer's Choice.* (5) Frederick Karl and Leo Hamalian (eds.), *The Naked i.* (6) Jerome Klinkowitz (ed.), *Innovative Fiction.* (7) Richard Kostelanetz (ed.), *Twelve from the Sixties* and *Breakthrough Fictions.* (8) Terry Southern (ed.), *Writers in Revolt.* (9) Philip Stevick (ed.), *Anti-Story.* (10) Ronald Sukenick, *The Death of the Novel;* "The New Tradition," *Partisan Review* XXXIX (1972), 580–588; interview in *The Falcon* Numbers 2/3 (Spring 1971), 5–25.

THE FUTURE OF THE NOVEL

The effect of the mass media (journalism, magazines) and of electronics (radio, movies, television) on the novel has been both stimulating and threatening. There has long been a debate as to whether the novel's competition has caused a decline in its vitality, whether it is, in fact, dead, or at least dying. The novel provided the early movies with narrative content and a few techniques; and as early as the 1920's the novel was borrowing techniques from the movies. As narrative modes, the movies and novels are closer to each other than they are to plays, for both employ controlled point-of-view techniques: in the case of the movies, the camera-eye is intimately controlled by the director. Since the movies have some of the best qualities of plays and novels, they may supplant those media. For the consumer, movies are easier, more immediate, more accesible, cheaper than novels.

In the early 1960's numerous articles appeared, proclaiming the approaching death of the novel, among them: a piece by the English novelist John Wain, "The Conflict of Forms," "The Novel Again" by Steven Marcus "The Fact in Fiction" by Mary McCarthy, "The Article as Art" by Norman

Podhoretz, and, a defense, "The Curious Death of the Novel: or, What to Do About Tired Literary Critics" by Louis Rubin.

John Wain sees the novel's great period of fertility and change as between 1850 and 1925; after that, with its divorce from life and its allegiance to art, it lost its prestige as a means of conveying information, as a vehicle for destroying pretense, and as a way to truth; the novel is no longer the major popular entertainment form (except, one might add, such novels as *Airport, Hotel,* and various police novels, which do inform their readers about certain special areas of life).

Marcus despairs because of two characteristics of the current novel: it fails to deal with ideas relevant to man living in a society that may lack a future and it is written, read, and studied as if it were a poem; these characteristics suggest serious ill-health. Criticism itself competes in potency with the novels it scrutinizes.

Mary McCarthy wonders whether it is still possible to write novels today. "The staple ingredient" of all novels has been "fact." The novel is "disappearing from view" because the world we live in—a world of Buchenwald, Hiroshima, the Kennedy and King assassinations, Watergate, global pollution, and moon-landings—is unreal, unimaginable. The everyday world of common sense seems insignificant. "The novel seems to be dissolving into its component parts: the essay, the travel book, reporting... the 'pure' fiction of the tale. ... We know that the real world exists but we can no longer imagine it." Mary McCarthy, who has written several novels since, one of them a best-seller, *The Group,* concludes with faint optimism: "Someone may be able to believe again in the reality, the factuality, of the world."

Podhoretz's thesis is not so much that the novel is dying but that it has been preempted by non-fiction. "The discursive writing of people who think of themselves as novelists turns out to be more interesting, more lively, more penetrating, more intelligent, more forceful, more original—in short, *better,* than their fiction." He continues: "And what the novel has abdicated has been taken over by discursive writers. Imagination has not died (how could it?) but it has gone into other channels," into magazine articles that reveal a "remarkable fusion of feeling and intelligence." Some excellent recent non-fiction, written in a few instances by novelists, has indeed used some of the devices of fiction: Truman Capote's *In Cold Blood;* Norman Mailer's *The Armies of the Night;* Jean Stafford's *A Mother in History;* Frank Conroy's *Stop-Time;* Willie Morris' *North Toward Home;* Anne Dillard's *Pilgrim at Tinker Creek;* Robert M. Pusig's *Zen and the Art of Motorcycle Maintenance.*

The trouble with these arguments, says Rubin, is "that they are no more true now than during those past times when the novel was supposedly at it heyday." The only thing that can destroy the novel is bad novels. This is a time of transition; but when the next major phase in the novel's evolution comes we probably won't be able to recognize it. We should stop listening to those critics who hate fiction in the first place and "spend more time reading living novels."

PART III: CLOSE ANALYSES

Note: While the best procedure is to read the novel, then the essay, one may get a sense of the use of techniques by reading the essays even if one has not read the novels.

STYLE

The Dynamics of Style in a Key Passage
of Hemingway's *The Sun Also Rises*

The fishing trip in Hemingway's *The Sun Also Rises* is an important episode, which invites comparison with the bullfight—from the solitary confrontation of Jake and fish, to Jake as spectator among thousands, to the confrontation of man and bull; the fishing passage appears on page 119, and Romero kills the bull about 110 pages later. I point out this relationship, which I do not intend to elaborate upon, to emphasize the importance of the fishing passage.

The actual fishing doesn't take long in prose time or bulk.

> He was a good trout, and I banged his head against the timber so that he quivered out straight and then slipped him into my bag.
>
> While I had him on, several trout had jumped at the falls. As soon as I baited up and dropped in again I hooked another and brought him out the same way. In a little while I had six. They were all about the same size. I laid them out, side by side, all their heads pointing the same way, and looked at them. They were beautifully colored and firm and hard from the cold water. It was hot day, so I split them all and shucked out the insides, gills and all, and tossed them over across the river. I took the trout ashore washed them in the cold, smoothly heavy water above the dam, and then picked some ferns and packed them all in the bag, three trout on a layer of ferns, then another layer of ferns, then three more trout, and then covered them with ferns. They looked nice the ferns, and now the bag was bulky, and I put it in the shade o the tree.

With the passage quoted above and several other lines, that's it; Hemingway's few words render the experience as fully as it demands. At first reading the treatment may seem perfunctory. In a way it is, because most of the experience has already occurred and what is left of it doesn't have to be explicitly presented—first, the desire came, then the prolonge anticipation progressed to the actual moment, which came and was over quickly, followed by the viewing of the catch and satisfaction in the shade of the tree. Hemingway does not have to tell how Jake feels either during or after catching the fish—he had better not if the effect of his underwriting is to work. But Jake's choice words, his syntax, the ordering of his data suggest how he feels. The dead-pan reportage—this happened, and then this and then this—creates a sense of ritual, an essential aspect of the novel.

In the 17 lines, Jake refers to himself 9 times and to the trout about 20. Given the man and the trout, we don't need, and we don't get, more than 2 or 3 references to the water and the vegetation ashore. The usual Hemingway conjunctions and connecting adverbs (15 "ands" and 4 "thens") create a steady rhythm like the heavy flow of the river, and lay out the *prose units* as Jake lays out the fish—neatly.

The active verbs, fish-hook sharp, neatly snag their objects, and whip them into the stream of the prose, bag them firmly into the impression Hemingway wants to convey. In order, not greatly simplified, the verbs go like this: I banged, he quivered, brought, then laid them all out and looked; then I split, shucked, tossed, took, washed, picked, packed, covered, and put.

The adjectives and the adverbs function even more austerely. The first trout is "good," a word that covers everything about a trout in a way that it couldn't cover everything about a fisherman, who being human, demands qualifiers. Packed together in ferns, in order, in the bag, the trout look "nice." "Beautifully colored and firm and hard from the cold water," the trout are vividly pictured. Learning that the water is cold, we sense that the fish are, too, and we feel cool. But in the next sentence, we are told that the day is hot, and because it is hot, Jake immediately splits and disembowels the fish, thereby keeping the fish as close to the freshness of the cold water as possible. Later, he washes them in the "cold, smoothly heavy water," and with the green ferns and the tree shade, the heat (potential source of decay and debility) is kept out of an invigoratingly cold experience. Of course the general heat of the day, by contrast, makes the freshness of the experience. We are not told that the fish are heavy, but we are made to feel that they are, first, suggestively, by the description of the water—"smoothly heavy"—and then by the line "now the bag was bulky." The progression of the relation of the fish to the bag is this: "slipped him into my bag," "packed them all in the bag," and "now the bag was heavy." But an implied progression is this: each fish comes out of the water and is slipped into the bag, then, because he can't wait until he is ashore for the washing to look at them, Jake takes each one out, lines them all up as though in military formation, and then he puts them in the bag again, takes them ashore and out of the bag, washes them, packs them in the bag.

How Jake feels is in the feel of the style. His appraisal of the first tro
may seem unrelated to the action of banging its head, but by not breakin
up the sentence into two Hemingway suggests that Jake's banging express
his gladness at the fish's being a good one, and that he feels a satisfaction
seeing the quivering fish go straight is expressed in the smooth line "and
slipped him into my bag"—"bang!" becomes "slip." We can imagine how
Jake felt seeing "several trout" jump at the falls while he had one on the
line. He brings the second fish in in "the same way," and probably he fee
even better. Presently, he has six, and the whole run seems sudden—six
beautiful moments, "all about the same size." The whole passage is full of
symmetrical elements. Symmetry, too, satisfies Jake. For he lays the fish
out, and the "side by side" phrase is so quiet that we sense his delight an
then his thrill in looking at them all, "their heads pointing the same way."
The single most revealing sentence in the passage is the one in which we
are told that he tossed the innards and the gills "over across the river," n
into it—he doesn't want to foul it with death. The rest of the fish will become life again in Jake. This is part of the romantic attitude of twentieth
century "natural" man. Jake's description of the water—"smoothly
heavy"—suggests how he feels during the washing ritual, for "smoothly
heavy water" is a fine thing to have one's hands active in. First he tells us
that he packed the fish in ferns, but information alone is not enough. He
has to detail the operation, because the ordering of the fish is so satisfying
that it is good to tell of it in an ordered way. That the fish look nice, that
the bag which was empty is now bulky (and therefore heavy like the wate
that he can sit in the shade at the end of the experience with the fish besi
him makes him feel good. If we are not told explicitly how Jake feels fishing, Hemingway's style connotes how he feels. Hemingway puts the read
through the experience himself, and he feels as any man would—even as
would, and I can't stand to touch fish or see them caught.

THEME:

Meaning and Form in
Albert Camus' *The Stranger**

In modern literature there are characters *like* Meursault but none of them affect us quite the way *he* does nor mean as much to us, provided we understand him completely enough to see in him a reflection of ourselves. Since Meursault has no history the novel, ultimately, insists that we remove that lack with the particulars of our own history. But in a more vital sense, neither he nor we have any history until we realize it in a moment of rebellion, and remember it in the realization of imminent death. But in this novel, as it is a work of art, we experience the whole process, from part to part, vicariously.

Like Christ, Meursault is a pure symbol, presented to us only in those moments which most lucidly reveal his essential significance for us. Meursault's story begins at that point when his destiny enters its denouement, and the working out consumes only about a week—the rest is one long day during the night of which he achieves recognition. The most exemplary tragic hero has, really, no personality or history except for that fatal moment in which all is consummated; about him we need to know only what relates to the one pure flame that consumes him in the same instant that it illuminates him. But the illumination occurs in life, the final consuming in death; the moment which results in the illumination for Meursault occurs when he kills the Arab. Modern literature seems obsessed with the Christ figure and what it can make of it. Meursault, in the end, wonders, "How had I failed to recognize that nothing was more important than an execution; that, viewed from one angle, it's the only thing that can genuinely interest a man?" In death by execution man's absurd predicament is epitomized; those who cannot endure the absurd surrender themselves to the promises of the resurrection of Christ; much depends upon the angle from which one views execution. Meursault does not seem much of a tragic hero, but as Camus

---

*Reprinted by permission from David Madden, "Camus' *The Stranger:* An Achievement in Simultaneity," *Renascence*, Vol. XX, No. 4, (Summer 1968) pp. 186–97. Copyright © 1968 by the Catholic Renascence Society, Inc.

says, "He's the only Christ we deserve;" and, as a mortal Christ, he is the only one who can ultimately have any meaning for us.

Meursault is Everyman—as he is, shorn of sham and pretense—and *The Stranger* is, from one perspective, a morality tale. That's why his story is *not* extraordinary; he seems unordinary only because a naked man is spectacular and attracts undue attention. Not only does he have no past by virtue of his forgetting, not until the end does he remember the past and anticipate the future—albeit a future cut short as the result of an indifferent past but cherished all the more for its brevity; past and future really matter only in the realization of how fully the present is imperiled, so that, though briefly, the condemned man lives keenly. As an innocent man, he lived only passively, to gratify his senses. A stranger to himself, to society, which insists upon false simplifications of identity that Meursault cannot satisfy, an outsider in an indifferent world, he is *de trop*, because nothing he can ever do will amount to anything. Like Jean-Baptiste in *The Fall*, he is absent at the moment when he takes up the most space—in his own life when he kills the Arab and in public when his life is on trial. The refrain of Jean-Baptiste's life is *I,I,I*, but for Meursault the I is muted, although it exercises and satisfies its demands. Like Caesonia of *Caligula*, he might say of himself, "The only god I ever had is my body," and like Jean-Baptiste, he would disown his mother for ten minutes of sensual love (as, in society's eyes, he does the day after her funeral) even if he knew he'd regret it later (he wouldn't). He seems not only to have few or no illusions but no wishes either, or aspirations, except to continue as he is; his employer's offer of a better job, a change of life, in Paris leaves him cold because he is quite satisfied with his life, and in Paris the people have washed-out faces; and marriage? he would if Marie, or any other girl, wanted. It's not that he is disengaged—he was never *en*gaged; not that he isn't committed to life—he *is*—to his own life, but only as a cat is committed to its life.

He is never able to consider life seriously; if it is either a game or tiresome for Jean-Baptiste, it is, for Meursault, mostly tiresome. He sleeps more than any hero in modern literature, except Raskolnikov. In *The Rebel* Camus declares, "To breathe is to judge," and on this minimal level Meursault lives. Seldom in the novel does he make a particularly decent move, or make a moral choice or morally assert himself. Passively, he is nice to Salamano but only until he becomes sleepy. On the beach, he does admonish Raymond not to shoot in cold blood—but more of that later. Only when he is living in anticipation of the execution, does he begin to reflect, to react, to evaluate, to make the "human inquiry." Until then he is indifferent, passive to events. In a sense, he moves through society and neither touches the other until the events of the novel occur, and even then, superficially, he *seems* to move as through a vacuum. As for society's dictates, somehow they just never got across to him. Or was it that unconsciously,

passively, he *felt* an assumption about life that negated social certainties,
such as those of the Priest, and numbed every thing in his conscious experience except an awareness of appetites? But perhaps he has always sensed,
with an animal instinct and revulsion, the ambiguities of the organization of
society, sensed that it is organized like the tiny Brazilian killer fish that, if a
bleeding man fall into the water, will make of him a gleaming skeleton in
seconds. The best defense is indifference; indifferent to the plague, unconsciously, he pushes his rock up the mountain.

Meursault's behavior merely indicates that the absurd is something *a
priori* in his nature; he behaves as man would if he did not refuse to be
what he is. But not until the end does he *discover* the absurd, experience
those Sisyphian moments of exaltation between the prolonged periods of
futile travail, and become consciously the hero and achieve tragic recognition of a kind peculiar to modern man. If he experiences dread, anguish,
anxiety, and despair, those emotions felt by the existentialist who is aware
of his sickness unto death, the experience is unconscious, and becomes man-
ifest only after the murder of the Arab.

Virtually a perfect book, *The Stranger* is cleanly written. But the
simplicity of the novel is misleading because its largest meanings emerge
from what *isn't* said. If the reader is moved to make an inquiry of the book's
silence, he will begin by perceiving that the novel's formal symmetry, like
that of *The Fall*, is balanced by the occurrence of its major pivotal event in
the exact center of the book, an indication of the careful calculation that in-
forms its entire design; the book proves not to be as casual as it may at first
seem. The very design of the book seems a conspiracy against Meursault at
the same time that it explains him. The first part moves with a tremendous
deliberation toward its climax. We feel an awesome sense of the inexorable.
Nothing in the book refers to or depends upon anything outside it. Most of
the symbolism and the purpose of the repetitions are clear even as they retain remarkable subtleties and complex implications. Nothing is gratuitous;
every detail functions. The language is mostly denotative, seldom overtly
connotative. Adjectives are scarce and seem to cluster only around the sun,
the dominant image. Meursault is like Grand, the writer in *The Plague* who
has spent years writing the opening line of a book and who after the plague
tells Rieux, "My writing is coming along. I've deleted all the adjectives."
The purity of presentation of events and ideas reminds one of a line in *The
Fall:* "For the statue to stand bare, the fine speeches must take flight like
pigeons." A character like Meursault frightens the pigeons. We behold him
bare.

Occasionally, there is a shift from past to present tense: "Mother died
today," "Today I refused again to see the Chaplain." This use of tense not
only gives a sense of immediacy but emphasizes Meursault's fixity in the

present; one may consider either that the confession (testimony) is all past tense or that it is being told as it happens, day by day. But it's all one. If time seems not to exist in the prison prior to the sentencing, it is fitting that time should be ambiguous during the events that culminate in Meursault's doom; for in a sense, all the events are aspects of the one moment that is consummated in his recognition of their meaning.

For a novel in which nothing seems to happen, in which the viewpoint character doesn't seem to react except with a growl of his empty stomach, a blinking of his sleepy eyes, a quiet upsurge of sexual alcohol to his brain, a great many fine tensions exist here. The major tension is between the reader and the narrator. One cannot react lightly to Meursault's indifference no matter how fully one must ultimately sympathize with him. At first there is mostly revulsion, a morbid fascination, and Meursault remains for a long time a stranger to us. But insidiously, there are early identifications. I had been suspicious of him all along until he was asked for the fourth time what his mother's age was and I realized with a shiver that I didn't know my own mother's age. From then on I was on my guard, with Camus' offensive pawing at it from every page. Meursault is as you desire him—provided you understand your fundamental kinship to him. In writing a novel about alien-ation, Camus begins by alienating the reader, but in the end, as we join Meursault in the little-ease, the guilty and the "innocent" are reconciled, a moral amelioration occurs.

Meursault speaks to us in a very quietly sardonic tone, a tone that does not seem to assume any definite response. He relates his story with an air of indifference that is belied by the fact that he *does* tell it. Some kind of plea, it seems, is being made. Or is it that we are overhearing an "encounter be-tween human inquiry, and the silence of the universe," that once the sen-tence is pronounced, becomes increasingly more subjective and meaningful? With all Meursault's headaches and wine-food-cigarette-sex-and sun-induced sleep or drowsiness, one might like to conclude that it is all an absurd dream. Indeed, for Meursault, in a sense, his whole life has been a dream and he is painfully asleep when he pulls the trigger, but when he awakes in the little-ease, he doesn't have to be told that he isn't dreaming, nor do we. At the risk of triteness, I suggest that he has come back to the womb—not for rebirth or for death alone but for brief moments of both, for to breathe is also to be reborn and to die.

With the first line of the novel we know that Meursault is living in the present; the past, being inconsequential until it is consummated, is uncer-tain. But at least, he has the basis for something. Camus says in *The Rebel*, "Real generosity toward the future lies in giving all to the present"; but "all" includes, ultimately, an assessment of the past. Meursault's nemesis is that he doesn't give enough until it is too late. Meanwhile, the telegram reads like a newspaper headline and gets about as much reaction from Meursault as would: GOD ANNOUNCES WORLD WILL END TOMORROW AT FOUR A.M. He had rather she hadn't died, that the world not end, but there it is in black and white. Just *when* she died is doubtful but then it doesn't matter—she's dead, and he will keep the *usual* vigil (and so forth); the adjective "usual" is characteristic of his reactions throughout most of the novel. But she doesn't seem dead. "The funeral will bring it home to me, put an official seal on it, so to speak. . . . " The funeral will bring, finally, *everything* home to him and the judicial system will put the official seal on it, so to speak. Nothing—the funeral, the killing, the sentence, the loss of Marie's body—has any reality until they are consummated by recognition and finally death in the midst of remembrance. He says to his employer, regarding his mother, as he says to the jury regarding the murder, "Sorry, sir, but it's not my fault, you know." No, they *don't* know. And we wonder, after five instances of this kind of apology or denial: is this why he is so cold, indifferent, passively amoral—to elude judgment, which changes everything?

There are three major events in the novel: the funeral, the killing, and the recognition; as for the sentence with which the trial ends, that has been there all the time—the event brings it home to him, puts the official seal on it. In the funeral section, all the events of the future are prefigured: the funeral casts its shadow upon the future. In merely going through the motions, he expresses the fundamental dead-end of death. In the death cell, he realizes that if Marie were dead he wouldn't be able to feel anything for her. At the funeral, he seems to be vividly aware of everything but the presence of his mother's dead body and he declines to have the coffin opened. Why? "Well, I really couldn't say." It is because he knows he would not be looking at his mother but at a corpse? Every detail of Meursault's behavior is later used as evidence against him; but the sun, that witnesses everything, alone sees him kill the Arab. In *The Fall*, Jean-Baptiste analyzes the motives behind funeral attendance: It is ourselves we love in the recently dead. But Meursault doesn't love himself. Maybe unconsciously, he *sees* himself in her death, and that is fitting since through her he came into life; from the death of the Arab he will learn more, and in the imminence of his own death it will all become clear. A funeral is a cheap source of tragedy for the spectator, says John-Baptiste. "Something must happen—and that explains most human commitments . . . Hurray then for funerals!" That something *must* happen perhaps does explain Meursault's commitment to the killing of the Arab; but as for funerals, he doesn't feel up to saying "hurray"; he only feels sleepy.

His lack of desire for a last look at his mother, his failure to recall her age (if he ever knew it), his drinking, smoking, sleeping, and his interest in the difference between burials in Paris and in Morocco are natural manifestations of his true attitude. Here and in the other sections, when he candidly expresses his seeming lack of conventional feeling about love, jealousy, about being a "pal," Salamano's dog, job prestige, the murder (no regret), God, and so on, we see all the most precious objects of society's illusions and pretense devastated by Meursault's indifference; but it is not a question of *lack*, for as the Prosecutor says, "We cannot blame a man for lacking what is was never in his power to acquire." So that *he* isn't on trial, but an abstract concept that he fails to measure up to and by which he is judged; the talking in the courtroom is like, then, the drone of hornets in the vigil room and flies in the magistrate's examining room. What matters, then? To eat, sleep, work, fornicate, swim, enjoy life, and keep out of the hot sun.

The warden makes unwittingly tactless comments, speaking impersonally of her death as the warden of a prison would. The Home (or earth), simply called, *is* a prison inhabited by men and women condemned to death by old age and forsakenness. His mother and Perez confront the absurdity of death with the hope of true friendship. The novel begins in this symbolic prison and ends in a real prison that is symbolic of man's predicament—from the mother to the son (except that the nonreligious mother does fall back upon the church). The padre comes a bit ahead of time for her, just as the Priest does for Meursault. The padre calls him "My son" and leads the way to the mortuary; later, the Priest angers him by calling him "My son" and would lead him to the guillotine.

Once Meursault enters the vigil room, he never really leaves it; in it he contemplates death and his awareness slowly increases; from it, he observes life. The room where she lies is as bare as his own room or as a cell or like the magistrate's room in which most of the questions asked him pertain to his behavior in the vigil room. The doorman lives under the illusion that he isn't an inmate—*they are*—thus keeping his distance from the absurd; just as the magistrate refuses to admit his own guilt, to see his true nature in Meursault but insists upon being outraged at Meursault's lack of conventional feeling. The scene with the doorman begins on page 7 and is followed by sleep and then by the entrance of the old people; on the seventh page of Part Two is the very similar scene with the magistrate, followed by sleep in the cell and then confrontation of the judge and jury.

He is awakened by the rustle of the old people coming in, come to mourn his mother's death—to perform the ritual, that is. "For a moment I had the absurd impression that they had come to sit in judgment on me." Even so, "It was hard to believe that they really existed." But later, the jury, similarly seated, seem like people on a trolley, "who look for something in a man that will amuse them." Since he is really tried for burying his mother rather than for killing a mere Arab, the judgment began in the room where he failed to show grief, failed to fake innocence, and when the trial comes it all seems harmless. It *seemed* as though the night had created an intimacy between himself and the old mourners; during the trial he has "an absurd impression of being one of the family," sees as Rieux does in *The Plague* a family resemblance in the faces of those who face the absurdity of the plague together. Rightly, he assumes that he is an ordinary man like everyone else.

During the wake, one old man is staring at Meursault when he awakes from a doze; at the trial, a young journalist constantly stares at him, giving him the odd impression of being scrutinized by himself: after the sentence, he does just that. The young man and the robot woman are rather like himself and his mother, watching the trial with fascination; when he meets the robot woman at Celeste's, she seems indifferent to him but he is interested enough to follow her, perhaps because she reminds him of his mother: also, she exemplifies those empty people who *need* to watch the Brazilian fish at work. This mother-son motif is reiterated in the scene in which Marie visits Meursault in prison. On either side of Marie are two women; one, a mother, gazes endearingly, silently across the thirty-foot no-man's land into the eyes of her son; the other one, a wife, loudly advises, gossips to her silent husband. The man and wife are what Meursault and Marie might have become, the son and mother are what Meursault was and, in a sense, still is.

In the vigil room, he can see only death, but from his own room and his cell and the police van, he observes life; his apartment, incidentally, is like his own mind—he lives in only one bare room of it. He spends that first Sunday in his room, a non-involved but fascinated stranger, observing those who go to stadiums and theatres (Jean-Baptiste claims he always felt most innocent in those places). Having gotten through another Sunday, he can conclude that "Really, nothing in my life had changed"; but in a sense, *everything* has. The daylong observing has hurt his neck; the guillotine will end that. In the cell, he believes that he could get used even to living in a hole in a tree with only the sky to look at, and in the death cell that is what he does; his mother was right: in time one can get used to anything; as with cigarettes, once you lose the craving, the punishment ends. From the courtroom and from the police van, he hears, sees, smells the beauty of nature, which he will remember and for which he will long. Riding in the van, he "learned that familiar paths traced in the dusk of summer evenings may lead as well to prisons as to innocent, untroubled sleep."

The various disguises of love presented in the book are prefigured in his attitude toward his mother at the funeral. Her coffin only makes him think of the pen-trays in the office where his real life goes on. A woman friend of his mother does cry, but she has reason to—both women being old, they were friends. As Salamano, having lost his dog, says, "In a Home one makes friends." Though he had mistreated his dog, who had replaced his wife whom he'd never loved, he had also taken care of it and now life without it will be a problem. For the first time, he puts out his hand to Meursault, who, he hopes, may replace the dog. The dog's moan was "like a flower, growing out of the silence and the darkness." Marie and Meursault love each other physically. But she wants to introduce mental love into it, the seed that would corrupt his solitude. "That sort of question had no meaning really." He senses, when his blood runs cold on hearing the screams of Raymond's deceitful mistress, what the real meaning of the question is; and formerly Raymond, who condemns Salamano's "cruelty," beat her only "affectionately." Perhaps, Meursault's mother was his dog, or he hers, but now he has no such needs as those of Salamano, Raymond and Marie; he does not intentionally thrive on the sorrows of others, but to a point, he will allow himself to be used. Like Rieux in the absurdity of the plague, Meursault becomes reconciled with his mother.

The morning promises a nice day for the funeral, but the tangy breeze is consumed in the hellish noon blaze of the sun on the road just as Meursault himself shatters the balance of the day on the beach. The black hearse reappears on the beach in the form of the black rock under which the Arab lies; the Arab is playing on the three-noted reed a kind of threnody, although the reed has another significance. Perez collapses like a rag doll in the sun; later, before he kills, Meursault feels limp as a rag. His mother's nurse's voice is musical, tremulous when she warns him of heatstroke. "But if you go too fast, you perspire, and the cold air of the church gives you a chill." Either way, one is in for it; just as Salamano's dog is whipped both when it halts to pee and when it runs ahead. And in the cell, Meursault reflects: the nurse was right, there's no way out, "and no one can imagine what the evenings are like in prison." We see then that in many ways the funeral and the rest of the book are welded together as aspects of the same moment.

The Sunday morning of the killing, Meursault feels burnt out, and Marie tells him that he looks like a mourner at a funeral. A week ago, he met Marie at a swimming pool; now they go *in* a bus (hearse) to the sea (maternal source of birth and death). To him, the sun is deadening, to her enlivening. But in the womb-warmth of the water and lying on the beach, he and Marie experience a sensual harmony; he feels sleepy, then hungry, the contentment of an innocent child. Drowsy with wine, cigarettes, food, and struck by the sun as by a clenched fist, he goes with Mason and Raymond to the beach. The sand is hot as fire, glowing red—the center of hell. When Raymond goes back and wants to shoot the Arab, Meursault voices his first moral reaction. "It would be a low-down trick to shoot him like that, in cold blood." He means it; his own act is not deliberate. But isn't it also that, like Christ, who once said, "My time is not yet come," he is protecting the object of his own fate? But he does evaluate—to fire or not to fire, to move or not to move: all comes to the same, because it *will* happen some day. All his life, he has felt that breeze blowing toward him, that breeze that liberates him from the fiery insistence of the sun, at the instant he fires the revolver, and enslaves him to man's judgment, which commits him to the little-ease of his own mind. He *has* to go back to the beach, just as Oedipus has to know. It is his fate—not predestined by God, but inevitable by virtue of his life as a mortal.

The sun glints on Raymond's revolver as he hands it to Meursault. Later, he confronts the Arab alone and the shaft of light on the thin blade seems to transfix his forehead. What is it but the guillotine itself, already raised to chop off his head? At that moment, he recognizes, the sun insists upon his fate. He notes that the heat is the same as at his mother's funeral and he has the same disagreeable sensations. And, of course, he wants to "retrieve that pool of shadow by the rock and its cool silence." The Arab is after all only "a blurred dark form, wobbling in the heat haze," that stands between him and the shade.

The sun is the source and symbol of life, of death, and rebirth. Throughout the novel, from nearly every page, the sun insists upon two things: one, that it, not God, is the source and sustainer of life, and Meursault must realize the full implications of that fact; two, that, being also that which decomposes life, it must be the source of Meursault's death, also. He kills, he says, because of the sun. That is not false. In the same moment, he revolts against and he submits to the sun's insistence, the flame of life that consumes as it vitalizes and illuminates. He says, "This has gone far enough." He, in a sense, shoots the sun as he shoots the Arab. This first act of rebellion precedes the "human inquiry" that enables him to live with his freedom and his captivity. The sun as pagan god is further emphasized by the Arab's playing of the reed, suggestive of Pan.

We may list many possible *reasons* that would explain Meursault's senseless act, but even if they were all true, the most important fact is that he killed the man, and that he did is absurd. He does not reason about his crime or defend himself; in recent years he has lost the habit of noting his feelings; and though he comes to believe that he is guilty and feels like weeping when he senses that others loathe him, he can't feel regret because he had never been able to regret anything in his life, and regret comes only when one knows one has fouled one's chances for Heaven or broken one's own rules; so how can he regret what he never intended? As Caligula says, "Who can condemn me in this world where there is no judge, where nobody is innocent?" Regret is the luxury of judges. Meursault can never reconcile himself to the idea that he is a criminal; other men may behead him for it but acknowledgement of sin and remorse are his alone. Actually, he is only vexed. Realistically, his act is consummately symbolic of modern man's ignorance of himself.

But a more profound symbolism seems to be operating here. There are two Christs in the novel: the Arab and Meursault. That the Arab is a Christ is suggested by the five shots: the first is the gratuitous spear thrust, followed, to reverse the sequence, by the four nails which crucify him on the sand. The Arab is the true Christ because Meursault, sensing in the Arab's death the absurdity of life that can end so meaninglessly, makes of the death a resurrection for himself; the Arab is his *personal* Christ. And just as we are supposed to be the cause of Jesus's death, in order to gain redemption by believing the significance of it, so Meursault must kill the Arab and is thus redeemed. Now this is only a symbolic action. Camus isn't saying that every man needs to kill in order to become aware of life, to make such a desperate commitment, but only that *Meursault* must kill for all. Although it seems unreal, he realizes himself in that one extreme moment; but the effect is delayed until after the official seal is affixed to what he learns and an official of the church comes and outrages him by trying to rob him of his moment; in that ecstasy of rage he is fully aware.

What does Meursault learn? That no matter how we die, we all die as absurdly as the Arab did. The court, failing to see the meaning, or refusing to by misplacing the attention upon Meursault's callousness, makes an anonymous man of the Arab; he *and* Meursault are *de trop* at the trial: Meursault is alone with his Christ. Meursault himself is a Christ only in that he is crucified, by the guillotine, twentieth century man's appropriate cross. From his execution only a false value would redound to society: the satisfaction of having proved the efficacy of its illusions and pretenses (by which the absurd is obscured) by destroying a man who threatens those false values. His crucifying of the Arab resulted in the only positive value his own crucifixion could have; as though Jesus died only to prove certain things to himself.

At the trial, there seems to be a conspiracy to exclude Meursault. Actually, it is not *Meursault* but a symbol, a victim, they want. He feels like a gatecrasher because those at the trial seem to be a club gathered for a small-town social; they all know each other very well in terms of those false appearances they all share—they are, that is, in the most extreme sense, strangers. Because he is a symbol, they can easily accuse him of the parenticide as well. Both lawyers have read his soul; that one found a blank, the other read it like a book, only means that society, insisting for its own protection upon a cross-eyed blindness, sees only what it wants to. He has a great urge to speak but realizes he has nothing to say. Life has him by the throat; he wants to vomit, to sleep. Seeing Marie, his heart turns to stone. After Meursault is sentenced, he is treated kindly, respectfully, like the sacrificial goat he is. The young man knew what the outcome would be and for the first time averted his eyes (just as Rieux did when Cottard, raving mad, was dragged away). There, but for my dissembling, go I.

Now he and society have touched each other and he is no longer innocent. The judicial machinations reflect what life is about and only officially inform us of the sentence under which we all live. Here in the trial, that of which he had been subconsciously aware, and in which he had tried to avoid involvement, is manifested. The touch that kills also liberates. "Execution relieves and liberates," says Caligula; relieves the populace, liberates the victim. "It's a universal tonic." But he never reasons about his crime, and the punishment inspires in him only fear, which is noble Caligula says, because it is straight from the guts. It's what caused the gut-up-roar of Meursault's father's stomach when he witnessed an execution; now his son is consummating the truth the father perceived. Meursault wants the howls of execration when he goes to the cross because it is the Christ's consolation: knowledge of the guilt of others, the ecstasy of the chosen one who is aware of his function. He transcends them all in the knowledge of his own guilt perceived in the most extreme moment of confrontation with the absurdity of virtue, of life itself.

Now that he is condemned to death, yesterday and tomorrow have meaning. By expecting the worst regarding his appeal, he has the *right* to hope; acknowledgement of the absurd gives him the *right* to hope. For when the book ends, it is not certain that he will be executed; but an appeal can result only in a reprieve because die he will someday, maybe even the senseless way the Arab died, although any way is, essentially, just as senseless. Who is *lucky?* He will not waste his last hours on God. They will come for him at dawn. When? He doesn't know. But each dawn he agrees with his mother that no matter how miserable, one always has something to be thankful for.

The magistrate had *brandished* a crucifix in front of him. "Know who this is?" he asked. ("It's *me*," he might have answered.) The magistrate has to believe that Meursault believes in God or his own certainty would be threatened. The Priest has the same trouble. Immersed in the moment of his reconciliation with life, Meursault hates the Priest for bringing the reek of death and renunciation into his cell. He is rebelling against death by saying yes to life, by daring to hope even in the recognition of his absurd predicament.

"There is nothing when I die," he tells the Priest, who is certain the appeal will succeed. He had thought of the afterlife only as one who might wish to be rich, or as a place wherein he might "remember his life on earth. That's all I want." On that wall, "drenched in human suffering," he has tried to see Marie's face take form, but he has failed; anyway, a single strand of a woman's hair is worth more to him than all the Priest's certain ties. He had passed his life in a certain way, and he might have passed it a different way, if he'd felt like it. But he is convinced he was right, beca all his life he had been waiting for the moment of death that would justify him. He rejects the Priest's request to kiss him, although he would have kissed his friend, Celeste. But when the Priest insists that he will pray fo him, Meursault reacts with rage, experiences an enlivening joy in his vio lence and invective:

> ... when I awoke, the stars were shining down on my face. Sounds of the countryside came faintly in, and the cool night air veined with smells of earth and salt, fanned my cheeks. The mar velous peace of the sleepbound summer night flooded through m like a tide. Then, just on the edge of daybreak, I heard a steame siren. People were starting on a voyage to a world that had ceas to concern me forever. Almost for the first time in many months thought of my mother. And now, it seemed to me, I understood why at her life's end she had taken on a "fiancé"; why she'd play at making a fresh start. There, too, in that Home where lives we flickering out, the dusk came as a mournful solace. With death s near, Mother must have felt like someone on the brink of freedo ready to start life all over again. No one, no one in the world ha any right to weep for her. And I, too, felt ready to start life all over again. It was as if that great rush of anger had washed me clean, emptied me of hope, and, gazing up at the dark sky spangled with its signs and stars, for the first, the first time, I la my heart open to the benign indifference of the universe.

With one of the most eloquent and remarkable passages in modern litera- ture, the novel draws to a close. While his trial, the "proceedings," belon to the public, his fate belongs to him. "His rock is his thing," as Camus s of Sisyphus. Meursault refuses "to be a god in order to be a man." He be gins an inquiry into the silence of the universe. He knows the absurd and knowing *that* means "a living warmth and a picture of death." But Meur- sault does have a kind of hope. "And indeed it could be said," as Rieux says, "that once the faintest stirring of hope became possible the dominio of the plague was ended." One must imagine Meursault happy.

STRUCTURE:

Chapter 17 of Emily Brontë's *Wuthering Heights**

One of the most crucial chapters in Emily Brontë's *Wuthering Heights* is seventeen. Its particular function, situated midpoint in this book, is to effect a transition from the first half of the novel, which ends with Catherine's death, and to act as pivot for the second thrust of action. Incidentally, it provides references to previous and anticipations of forthcoming actions, images, and *leitmotifs;* with these, in a close reading of the chapter, I shall be most concerned. (References are to the Riverside Edition.)

When the chapter opens, Catherine has been buried and little Cathy is only a few days old. Heathcliff and Edgar, in characteristically contrasting moods, in their dissimilar abodes (Wuthering Heights and Thrushcross Grange), mourn Catherine's death. The old rancor between Heathcliff and Hindley finally seethes to its final volcanic overflow, and, only six months after Catherine, Earnshaw dies, somewhat mysteriously, leaving Heathcliff master over the property and Hareton. Heathcliff's brutal behavior towards Isabella finally forces her to flee. In London, she gives birth to Linton, a contemptible imitation of Edgar, and dies twelve years later. A death and a birth in the previous chapter are here followed by two deaths and a birth. Major events occur then, and begin to move, in this chapter.

Pulsating with contrasts and insidious shiftings, reversals, repetitions of relationships and symbolic exchanges of identity among the characters, this chapter erupts with more blood and violence than any other. On page 183, where no actual violence is depicted, we encounter a great verbal violence. Weather and nature images are relevant and abundant here. The tenebrous mood of childhood is sustained in some of the behavior. The obtrusive but pertinent window device is further developed. Feelings of suspense, of momentary suspensions and tensions prevail. Vital information, necessary for immediate purposes or as illumination of the past and "plants" for the future, is provided. A closer scrutiny, page by page, may offer a deeper

*Reprinted by permission from *The English Record*, Vol. XVII, No. 3, (Feb. 1967) pp. 2–8. Copyright © 1967 by the New York State English Council.

penetration into the meaning of the novel and may simulate the sense of un-
folding which the chapter effects.

[180] After Catherine's burial, the weather becomes dreary, chill, dismal.
The long autumn and winter of Heathcliff's sorrow follows the summer day
of her death, but 18 years later, he dies in April, with the spring rain on his
face. Now that they are both dead, their love undergoes a renascence; only
in some spiritual realm can their kind of love thrive.

We are made aware of the window; uncurtained, it is banked with
snow. In Isabella's story, the window at Wuthering Heights is very important.

[181] An intruder has come into the house, laughing. Brontë does not have
Nellie reveal her to be Isabella until after a page of narrative. Brontë often
utilizes this suspense-generating device, subtly creating an unsettled atmosphere; and, in a house of mourning, Isabella's nervous laughter of relief in-
tensifies this effect. Isabella is "dripping with snow and water" (when she
tells of Heathcliff breaking through the window, she describes him as being
"white with snow"). Nellie talks to this married woman, who wears "a gir-
lish dress," as though she were a child. A good anticipation of the bloody
story Isabella will tell is the "deep cut under one ear," the cause of which
we can suspect, but the reader is prepared to expect the occasion of it when
Nellie says she will "stir nowhere, hear nothing" until Mrs. Heathcliff has
changed her wet clothes. Isabella's running through the moors, propelled by
terror, contrasts with all the voluntary walking and running there of
Catherine and Heathcliff, usually in stormy weather.

[182] Isabella's smashing her wedding ring with a poker, "striking it with
childish spite," is more of the childhood motif fostered by Nellie's point of
view. This feeble act is her only way of attacking Heathcliff in physical
terms. (In Freudian terms, she denies him her sex, symbolized by the ring.
She derives sadistic pleasure from inflicting mental torture upon him, via
references to Catherine, a process she calls "pulling nerves with red hot
pinchers."

In this and other chapters, fire is a recurrent image, both metaphorically and literally; for instance, Joseph feels Hindley is saved "so as by fire."

"Do you think he could bear to see me grow fat, and merry; and could
bear to think that we were tranquil, and not resolve on poisoning our comfort?" Isabella asks Nellie. This question anticipates what Heathcliff, later,
almost systematically does. [183] Heathcliff's facial expressions of his loathing
for Isabella (as described by her) become a familiar reflex whenever Heathcliff is afflicted with the presence of any one he detests.

If she once desired that he should kill her (indicating her rather masochistic-sadistic personality). Isabella now would rather "he'd kill himself!" For the reader, aware of the real effect upon Heathcliff of Catherine's death, that is a possibility—realized in the end.

Isabella's line ("I . . . can dimly imagine that I could still be loving him, if—no, no!") not only testifies to Heathcliff's effect upon women, particularly Isabella, but also betrays her masochistic impulses; earlier, Heathcliff himself spoke of this trait in her.

Isabella speaks of Catherine's perverted taste in loving so dearly such a monster, knowing him as well as Catherine did. But Catherine did not *know* Heathcliff as Isabella does, in the Biblical sense; their love was of a different kind, into which Isabella unwittingly offers the reader an insight when (on page 192) she says, "But then if poor Catherine had trusted you, and assumed the ridiculous, contemptible, degrading title of Mrs. Heathcliff, she would soon have presented a similar picture! She wouldn't have borne your abominable behavior quietly; her detestation and disgust must have found voice." Knowing what we know of their relationship, it *is* almost ridiculous to imagine Heathcliff and Catherine as man and wife; in such a condition they might have detested each other.

Isabella declares to Nellie that she wouldn't "feel" for Heathcliff though he should weep "tears of blood for Catherine!" Metaphorically, that is, the reader feels, just what Heathcliff has done and shall continue to do. Nellie insists that she be more charitable, that Heathcliff is a human being and that "there are worse men than he is yet!" This is more pertinent as advice to the reader, who will, later in the book, often recoil from Heathcliff's violence and cruelty. Once might also continue to bear in mind what Isabella says to Hindley (p. 191): "he's only half a man. . . . " *Her* meaning aside, he *is* half a man, because he has lost Catherine, his soul, and when he is about to die, about to be reunited with her, he is happy and relatively kind to others; this has been a persistent motif, declared both by Heathcliff and Catherine throughout the book.

[184] Isabella's description of Heathcliff's wandering on to the moors, his fasting, his locking himself in at dawn (throughout the book, people are forcibly or voluntarily locked in or out of rooms or houses), anticipates his behavior years later during the days preceding his self-conditioned death.

Isabella mentions "Joseph's eternal lectures," which Catherine in her diary, as read by Lockwood early in the book, lists as among the unbearable conditions of living in Hindley's house, compelling Heathcliff and her to seek refuge together in the moors. Their natural element. "That odious old man" is Hareton's "staunch supporter." After Heathcliff's death, he "returns thanks that the lawful master and the ancient stock were restored to their rights" (p. 356).

[185] Isabella sets the scene for the major event of her story. She is reading some old books, "till late on towards twelve," just as Lockwood was doing before his dream of Catherine's ghostly attempt to enter through the locked window. Heathcliff, mourning Catherine's recent death, has been wandering on the moors in a storm when he comes to the locked window and tries to get in. Violent resistance awaits him, too, but by Hindley with Isabella's complicity. The snow is blowing outside, as it was the night of Lockwood's stay, and her thoughts revert to Catherine's new-made grave. Heathcliff has been tormented by apparitions of Cathy. Like Lockwood, Isabella feels the oppressive atmosphere of melancholy, "all joy vanished from the world, never to be restored." With this line, Brontë achieves a fine effect: Isabella, who hates Heathcliff, is actually expressing for the reader what Heathcliff now feels and continues to feel.

[186] Isabella's reply to Hindley's assassination plot further reveals her character: "I'd be glad of a retaliation that wouldn't recoil on myself, but treachery, and violence, are spears pointed at both ends—" She rejects Hindley's invocation of Old Testament law: "Treachery and violence are a just return from treachery and violence!" But later (p. 191) she advocates it herself. In final desperation, Hindley cries, "It's time to make an end!" Finally, years later, Heathcliff himself must have come to such a conclusion.

[187] Isabella warns Heathcliff (as Lockwood warned Catherine) not to attempt entry through the window. But unlike Catherine, Heathcliff, the male force, triumphs. He crashes through the window. Isabella remarks his "sharp cannibal teeth," one of numerous bestial images in this chapter and in the book; years later, Nellie observes that the dead Heathcliff's teeth are "sharp, white," sneering.

[188] With a Lockwoodian flippancy, Isabella tells Heathcliff to stretch himself over Catherine's grave and "die like a faithful dog." One recalls her casually relating the incident in which Heathcliff, as they were eloping, hanged Isabella's faithful dog, the one which bit Catherine. Nearly every scene at Wuthering Heights contains dogs, metaphorically or actually; as Isabella leaves the house to flee to Thrushcross Grange, she sees Hareton hanging some puppies from a chair, and this incident she unfeelingly relate to Nellie.

"I can't imagine how you think of surviving her loss." Again, Isabella suggests one of the most overwhelming feelings the reader has and shall continue to have about Heathcliff. Through such *doubles entendres* Brontë provides the reader with an understanding of much of Heathcliff's behavio

When Heathcliff causes Hindley to inflict a knife wound upon his own wrist, the reader is reminded of the wound Isabella bore when she arrived at Thrushcross Grange. In this manner, future action in the scene is subtly set in motion and anticipated, and this is one of Brontë's recurrent devices. Actually, the wound is not inflicted until the following morning. That Heathcliff is not a cannibal, but is a passionate man capable of control and pity, is evidenced by the immediacy with which he tends Hindley's wound.

[189] The dialogue between Heathcliff and Joseph, and the latter's behavior, introduces a slight touch of humor amidst the blood letting. In this scene, Heathcliff almost realizes a childhood wish, expressed in one of the most vivid images in the book: "the privilege... of painting the housefront with Hindley's blood."

[190] We have more of Isabella's hypocrisy and gloating satisfaction when she says that the next morning "I... felt the comfort of a quiet conscience within me." Nellie, characteristically, admonishes her for reveling in such satisfaction. When Heathcliff is nearing death, Nellie exhorts him to read the Bible, but he replies, "I've done no injustice, and I repent of nothing—I'm too happy, and yet I'm not happy enough. My soul's bliss kills my body, but does not satisfy itself"—one of the most significant insights into his behavior and his relationship with Catherine to come out of his own mouth.

[191] Isabella speaks of wanting to "reduce Heathcliff to my level"; we remember Hindley's desire to put him on his proper level; and later, when Heathcliff is dead, and the shepherd boy tells Nellie of seeing the ghosts, she tells the boy to take a lower road. These comments tend to emphasize Heathcliff's actual stature, not only in the character's but the reader's eyes as well.

"It's well people don't *really* rise from their graves," Isabella tells Heathcliff, implying that Catherine would be horrified by the havoc he has wreaked. This sets a kind of distance between other people and Heathcliff's experience with the risen Catherine. Isabella cannot forgive Heathcliff for being beyond the reach of revenge.

[192–93] Isabella accuses Heathcliff of having contributed to the death of Catherine. "After all, it is preferable to be hated than loved by him." Knowing what we now and will later know about his capacity for hatred, this line is an indication of the passionate, almost destructive intensity of Heathcliff's love for Catherine.

Again, Isabella's faulty perspective provides an emphasis on Heathcliff's spiritual kinship with Catherine: "Now that she's dead, I see her in Hindley." With Hindley, Catherine never had anything in common.

Isabella provokes Heathcliff into throwing a knife at her; it strikes her under the ear. She runs away, leaving Heathcliff and Hindley "locked together on the hearth."

[193] When Heathcliff inquires about Isabella and the child, hinting that he might force them to return, we are prepared for the coming of Linton and are somewhat informed as to his character. Linton is described as being, from the first, an ailing, peevish creature.

[194] On hearing his son's name, Heathcliff "smiled grimly, and observed: 'They wish me to hate it too, do they?'" It is as though hatred for another creature is being forced upon him by the sentimentality of those he already loathes. That we shall indeed witness his active hatred of his son, Linton, is foreshadowed by Nellie's observation, "Fortunately, its mother died before the time arrived. . . . "

The profound difference between Heathcliff and Edgar is significantly demonstrated in their contrasting manner of mourning. According to Nellie, Edgar, too, took walks on the moor alone when no one else would be about visited his wife's grave, and abandoned his duties. "But he was too good to be thoroughly unhappy long. *He* didn't pray for Catherine's ghost to haunt him: Time brought resignation, and a melancholy sweeter than common joy." Of course, we see both these men through the questionable vision of Nellie.

Not until this point in the chapter is Edgar's child named and given some sort of personality. His coldness toward her "melted as fast as snow in April"; it is April, incidentally, when Heathcliff, just before his death, softens toward the young Cathy.

[195] Now Nellie contrasts Hindley with Edgar in the light of her moral attitude, and curiously makes this judgment: "One hoped, and the other despaired; they chose their own lots, and were righteously doomed to endure them." This again, seems an oblique comment upon Heathcliff as compared with Linton. Nellie breaks her narrative here to align her own moral standards with Lockwood's.

Humor once more momentarily disperses the gloom in Mr. Kenneth's manner of reporting the death of Hindley, but not until after Brontë, tastefully, gives us the direct information. This humor acts not only as balance beside the grimness, but tends to rob the event of any undue importance. Of the many deaths in the book, only Catherine's and Heathcliff's are given any careful attention; the others are given short shrift.

(Hindley seems much older than 27; perhaps Brontë has too masterful permeated her novel with a sense of time.)

[196] One of the most interesting double-meaning remarks supplied by imperceptive characters in this chapter is Mr. Kenneth's: "He's rapidly regaining flesh since he lost his better half." Isabella is meant here, but on a more meaningful level it is true that Heathcliff's flesh is dominant now that his spirit, the better half of it, is lost.

[197] Mr. Kenneth suggests to Nellie that the only way for Hareton to benefit at all from his father's money would be to ingratiate himself with Heathcliff. The reader is going to be looking for some manifestations of this advice: one remembers that the orphan Heathcliff became Mr. Earnshaw's favorite. Later, we learn that little Hareton does like Heathcliff.

Hindley is described as being "both dead, and cold, and stark." This iamge will tend to intensify the similar image of Heathcliff as "dead and stark!"

It is ironic that Heathcliff reminds Nellie that the expense for Hindley's funeral will come out of his pocket; actually, it comes from the pockets of the dead man. Later, Heathcliff says, about his legacy, "I wish I could annihilate it from the face of the earth" (p. 353). Property as such never really meant anything to him; and he wants to leave no trace of his physical self behind.

[198] Nellie observes that Heathcliff's attitude during the funeral ". . . expressed a flinty gratification at a piece of difficult work, successfully executed." A sinister mystification is cast over the manner of Hindley's death. When he says of Hareton, "And we'll see if one tree won't grow as crooked as another, with the same wind to twist it!" we suspect that Heathcliff shall be that wind, that Hareton and others may become the object of more "difficult work," and certainly, his later treatment of young Linton is a complex example of that kind of intention. The treewind image is of course a reference to Lockwood's observation on p. 2: "One may guess the power of the North wind . . . by the excessive slant of a few stunted firs at the end of the house." And near the end (p. 346), Catherine and Hareton, the new generation, sit under these very fir trees and discuss the strange behavior of Heathcliff.

Heathcliff says he will not give up Hareton except in exchange for little Cathy. Ultimately, according to the plan we expect him to execute, he is in command of Linton, Hareton, and Cathy. In more ways than one, Nellie is right: "The guest was now the master of Wuthering Heights." But, in a sense, in respect to the force he has all along exerted, he has always been master of events and director of lives.

IMAGERY:

Wright Morris's *In Orbit,*
An Unbroken Series of Poetic Gestures*

Once focused in his field of vision, an element in a Wright Morris
novel becomes reusable raw material. For every element in the latest nov
In Orbit, some prototype exists in his other books. The method is familia
to readers of Morris' work: many key characters, concepts, images, even
phrases from previous novels are reassembled in new conbinations in this
one. More poetically compressed, the major themes of his other novels a
made new in this brief book: the relationship between the hero and his w
nesses; the conflict of the phony and the real; the conflict of the habitual
and the natural; improvisation; the acting out of the American Nightmare
the context of the American Dream; audacity; the transformation of the
cliché; the cross-fertilization of fact and fiction; the impersonality of love;
life of objects; the transforming effects of travel. Yet Morris never repeats
himself, and the familiar never looked so new and strange as in this novel

In Orbit shows the interaction of sexual, psychological, intellectual,
mechanical, and natural forces. Their paths crisscross by chance and finall
converge in a tornado. The controlling energy is Morris' conceptual powe
which compresses chaos into a pattern and gives these forces life as well a
symbolic value. Morris opens and closes the novel with this catalytic poet
image: "This boy comes riding with his arms high and wide, his head dippe
low, his ass light in the saddle, as if about to be shot into orbit from a
forked sling. . . . All this can be taken in at a glance, but the important de
might escape you. He is in motion. Now you see him, now you don't. If
pin him down in time, he is lost in space. Between where he is from and
where he is going he wheels in an unpredictable orbit. To that extent he
free." To achieve transcendence beyond the "ordinary" lives he is about t
shake up, the boy risks chance encounters: "At any moment it might cost
him his life." He is doing what comes naturally, and that takes talent. "T
he has. The supernatural is his natural way of life." The boy, Jubal, is rur

*Reprinted by permission from David Madden, *The Poetic Image in Six
Genres* (Carbondale, Ill., Southern Illinois University Press, 1969) p. 141-
162. Copyright 1969 by Southern Illinois University Press.

ning for his life away from one of his own kind, LeRoy Cluett, whose motorcycle he has stolen. Morris rehearsed Jubal in the characters of Calvin, Lee Roy Momeyer and Munger in *Ceremony in Lone Tree,* and he has traits that recall the Oswald of *One Day.* Jubal responds to the immediate moment spontaneously with speed, and the spectacle of his response affects the "ordinary" people who encounter him.

The image of the motorcyclist expresses the nature of the contemporary American character and scene; most of our experiences are moments in motion, seeming to have no relevant past. Is part of our nature a desire to go against nature, and is the machine an extension of that desire? Haffner, the foreigner, observes that "as the Huns were once believed to be part of their horses, these riders look... like part of their machines. Gas percolates in their veins. Batteries light up their eyes.... When this new breed of creature was perfected the one stop at the diner would be a short one. The model would feature interchangeable parts. A bulb taken from the headlamp would screw into the eyes. A glance at the dials would report what was on its mind." As Jubal approaches Haffner's Volkswagen after he has supposedly raped Holly Stohrmeyer, Pickett's feeble-minded old beauty, Haffner asks, "Out of gas?" A profoundly serious question for a young man like Jubal, for whom to be out of gas is to be nothing—a force wandering from its natural modus vivendi. Charlotte, a young beauty living in Pickett, sees Jubal in animal-sexual-natural, rather than mechanical, terms: "the overall impression of the boy on the bike... is that of two cats, piggyback: hard at it." The novel is full of machines, various kinds of cars and airplanes— human imitations of forces in nature. Hodler, editor of the *Pickett Courier,* "doesn't know if the sound he hears if thunder or a passing jet. He doesn't know, that is, if it is the will of God or man." Holly, impressed by Jubal's crash helmet, inspires Hodler to visualize the headline: "*VISITING SPACE-MAN ASSAULTS HOLLY STOHRMEYER.*" Similarly, a tornado will assault the town.

The natural and the antinatural are the opposing forces Morris depicts. If some things "come natural to knaves, dancers, lovers and twists of the wind," some people are "too clean-cut to bleed." The women incline toward the spontaneous, the natural: "When Hodler thinks of people in their natural state—when he thinks of it as being a good one—he thinks of Pauline Bergdahl," who runs the One-Stop Diner on the outskirts of Pickett. In his novels, Morris often stresses the irony of the American's persistent suppression of the natural desire to expose oneself to risk. When Pickett's historic elm falls in the wind, "small fry stand in a circle anxious to be hit by falling branches." The elm greeted the first settlers, "hardy, stubborn men who worked like slaves to deprive their children of all simple pleasures, and most reasons to live." After decades of suppression the natural pioneer recklessness comes out perversely in the President's accused assassin in Morris' *One Day;* if he could not act creatively, he could protest in an act of impotence.

Early in the novel the motorcycle and the twister as complementary forces are juxtaposed: "Pauline had merely called to say that in her opinion it was twister weather, and while hosing down her cinders she had seen, just in passing, this boy on the swiped motorbike." At the beginning and at the end, Morris says: "Perhaps the most important detail escapes you. Now you see him, now you don't." Jubal is "as free, and as captive, as the wind in his face." Like the wind captive in a twister, Jubal does what comes naturally: he runs. "He is never doing more than what comes naturally, but it is amazing how many things seem to." Just after his third run-in with a Pickett resident, "the wind thrusts at his back" as he runs. At the end of the second third of the novel, Hodler "listens to the ominous weather forecast [natural and human]: the barometer is falling. More rain is expected with rising winds. More trouble is expected from the spaceman, still on the loose." Symbolically, the weather is an expansion of the boy and his effect on others: "The windshields of the cars reflected a low, turbulent sky. Would this curtail or expand the goings-on of the man at large?" To Hodler's eyes, Jubal, seen in his fantastic garb just before the twister strikes, appears to be one of the puzzling effects produced by electrical storms.

The motorcyclist and the twister are supernatural and natural forces which happen on Pickett "as luck would have it." The psychological weathers of those among whom the rider moves disturbes his "weather," just as a twister is wind that just happens to undergo the proper atmospheric conditions produced by chance which violently disturb and concentrate it in a core of energy that must move. "Now you see it, now you don't." In *One Day,* Morris sets the scene in fog. "That we are such stuff as fog is made of is hardly a fresh impression, but events have a way of making it new." Are the weathers for our era alternately fog and twister weather? "Is it weather," Haffner asks, "if you can forecast it?" Are people alive and interesting to each other if they're predictable? Weather can be interesting because no matter how accurately we try to predict it, it often enough prove unpredictable. It is this phenomenon in people that intrigues Morris. Aberrant behavior, like aberrant weather, often seems the most natural, and, though violent, the loveliest. "The will of God," Pauline says, "you have to see it." The shambles after a twister is lovely? asks the passive Hodler. "The shambles ain't but it's the will to do it," says Pauline. Even Hodler "is saddened by the thought of the cloud-seeders who will one day take the twist out of the twisters, the fear out of the storm." In this novel we se ways in which the human climate builds up along lines of tension similar to the climate that produces the twister. Hodler sees that twisters are like those people who can't stand being crowded in cities or in strained situations. In the time-span of Morris' works, the twister is a constant factor, a force that always exists in the present alone. And Jubal, child of the present, on his motorbike recalls Lee Roy in his hotrod in *Ceremony;* both are somewhat deranged hangovers of the Lone Eagle in his *Spirit of St. Louis.*

American culture is always Morris' subject. Editor Hodler has written a book about the Swiss who shaped American culture. "But little consolation it gives him. What, if any, *shape* has it?" Just as weather becomes most visible when it condenses, shapes up into a twister, so we see ourselves, our town, our national character most sharply when a violent catalyst gives shape to various impulses and makes them visible a moment before they disperse again. Three major images are compressed in Hodler's metaphoric summing up of American culture. On his "troubled mind's eye it seems a mindless force, like the dipping, dancing funnel of the twister, the top spread wide to spew into space all that it has sucked up. It is like nothing so much as the dreams of men on the launching pad. Or those boys who come riding, nameless as elemental forces, their arms spread wide and with coiled springs in their asses, ticking off the countdown they hope will blast them out of this world."

More than any other Morris novel *In Orbit* illustrates Croce's concept of a novel as a tissue of images, over which lingers finally a single image. Few American novels come quite as close to poetic immediacy as *In Orbit.* Facets of the opening image interpret moments to come; nuances in the same passage when it is repeated at the very end of the novel poetically summarize and interpret the moments that have passed. Most of the images comment thematically; all others at least seem to say more than they are saying. In his selection and controlled condensation and juxtaposition of images, Morris achieves the dynamisms of the dance. Susanne K. Langer's description of what happens in the dance offers one perspective on Morris' magic: "In a world perceived as a realm of mystic Powers, the first created image is the dynamic image; the first objectification of human nature, the first true art, is Dance," which makes the "world of powers" visible by an unbroken fabric of gestures charged with feeling. In this novel, the images are struck on the anvil of the present tense because everything happens in that immediate present in which twisters and motorcycles rampage. "That's the picture: there are those who can take it in at a glance." Poetic simultaneity enables the active reader to do just that.

Morris employs his recurring method: he sets the scene and introduces most of the characters in Chapter 1, alluding to the major public event which will transform, if only momentarily, their private worlds. Familiar Morris characters (often in danger of becoming caricatures) undergo yet another metamorphosis. The long scrutiny in Chapter 2 of Haffner and Charlotte in the car en route to the vet is an example of the sort of static character analysis in Morris which sometimes seems a mere cataloging of quirks.

In Orbit, like most of Morris' novels, examines the human nature of time. This is such an important element in Morris' novels, perhaps the most important, that we ought to trace its evolution. In his early novels (My Uncle Dudley, The Man Who Was There, The World in the Attic, The Works of Love) and photo-text experiments (The Inhabitants, The Home Place) Morris nostalgically sifted the dust in the grave of our rural past, looked at (photographed) things at rest, static situations, attempted to convey a sense of worn artifacts that are metaphysically inhabited and holy (in his most recent book, God's Country and My People, Morris returns to this photo-epiphany technique). The author, like the recurring character who is his central intelligence, was captive in the past, observing Nebraskan home folk immolated in clichés. Unconsciously, then consciously, these books were attempts to bury those bearded giants in their self-dug graves. Several transitional novels dealing with the contemporary scene, each reaching more desperately for firmer ground in the shifting sands of the present, were gestures of freedom from enthrallment: Man and Boy, The Deep Sleep, The Huge Season. Then, in The Field of Vision he showed how the mind superimposes the home place and the past upon a foreign landscape (Mexico) in the present. Love Among the Cannibals, his first major break with the past, dealt solely with contemporary characters in the immediate present on timeless beaches in Hollywood and Mexico. He returned to the Nebraska landscape in Ceremony in Lone Tree to make a deliberate break with the past in the midst of its own habitat; that this is the second part of a trilogy whose third part is yet to come suggests that the break is not complete.

A look at the author's last four novels reveals Morris' impressive success in making his characters active in the immediate present. The depiction of neither Horter, the commercial songwriter in Cannibals, nor Soby, the professor in What a Way to Go (1962), is encumbered by a past; by responding spontaneously to the wisdom of the body, the Greek and Cynthia teach Horter and Soby that sex is one means of living contentedly in the immediate present. On ancient ground (Venice and Greece) wisecracking Cynthia is the nerve center of the lively present; as she helps him get to the simplicity of the Greeks, Soby brings the dead mythic past alive again in his imaginative field of vision. At its best, travel, new scenes, arouse the impulse to "make it new!" The past is set in stone until one's present emotion give it flesh. In the midst of oldworld clichés, Soby observes life imitating art, fact and fiction merging ambiguously. He learns to transform imaginatively his environment and his relationships with the people he meets by chance.

If Soby re-experiences Western culture's past, Warren Howe, middle-aged television script-writer in Cause for Wonder (1963) deliberately re-experiences his own past. This book, the realization finally of a novel Morris had tried to write when he was very young and had embellished with zany drawings, demonstrates the simultaneity of past and present in skull time-and-space; past and present in both America and Europe are the ambience of self-discovery. Even forgotten moments of the past sometimes overwhelm the immediacy of the present. Time-past and place-distant are preserved in the creative memory that reconstructs as it resurrects. Howe contemplates as he experiences it the human nature of time-and-space, which are coexistent dimensions of each other. "If you live in the present," he discovers, "you can't help but be ahead of your time." The usable past is "the here and now." Morris shows how the moment of individual creative vision synthesizes memory and immediate perception, time and space.

In *One Day* (1965) Morris makes public and private events impinge significantly upon each other in the immediate present on the American scene; he parallels the trivial events of every day with a single, enormous, historical event (the assassination of President Kennedy) of a single day. Each character is so stimulated by a frightening present to immerse, if not immolate himself, in memories of a haunting, distant past, that the events of the day, even the assassination, pale. Veterinarian Cowie, the Morris voice, wonders: "Who could say when this day had begun, or would ever end?" Morris suggests an answer in the way he restructures time and space in his characters' various fields of vision.

In his latest collection of essays, *A Bill of Rites, A Bill of Wrongs, A Bill of Goods,* Morris writes about fads, fashions, foibles, and follies in our civilization that may make us die laughing. Why is it that when one gets "lost in thought" about the future, one often ends up stupefied by the immediate present? Why does nostalgia for the past so often turn into a timeless nausea? Morris suggests an answer: "What's new makes its debut, and receives our blessings, in the theatre of advertising. The newest thing in our lives of importance is prime time. . . . Who makes it prime? You and me. *Prime* is what is made in our image." Morris arrives on target more by intuitive punning, by image and epigram than by sustained logic. These image fragments pose the question: What ever happened to the American Dream? In the suburbs of Eden, it came true—revealing itself as a nightmare. From the Nebraska Plains (the navel of the world) to the Golden Gate, in sixteen novels, Morris has contemplated American landscapes, inscapes, escapes, and outscapes in Space. Written in California, where the past went that-a-way, this is Morris' intellectual autobiography, his Summing Up; it is in the artifacts and pseudofacts of just a moment ago that his past is mirrored.

In Orbit is set in Indiana, similar to the Nebraska scene; here Morris contemplates volatile images of the present as they presage the future. Instead of describing artifacts that are imbued metaphysically with the past, Morris sets in orbit objects that exist only for the present. As in most of his novels, the time span is one day, but here Morris intermingles everyday events with a natural and a public human event that affects only one representative American small-town cosmos. The task of imaginative synthesis is mainly the reader's.

The structure of *In Orbit* visibly expresses the theme. Each chapter, except the last, opens with a brief scene in which Jubal encounters one of the other characters; the novel closes, effectively, with the image that opened it, repeated almost verbatim, with a few key variations. The point of view in most of the Jubal sections is shared with Jubal's so-called victims: Holly, Haffner, Charlotte, and Kashperl, the proprietor of an Army and Navy Surplus store. Sometimes the links between one event or consciousness and another seem merely rhetorical: "Like William Holden he is on his own now, and out of gas." A break, then: "In matters of gas Charlotte Hatfield knows that her husband, Alan, runs out of it." But generally the multiple-point-of-view technique operates more subtly here than in most of his novels. The montage of points of view is meaningful, as when Jubal's and Holly's combined vision is followed by Hodler's. Morris shuttles back and forth, interpretively, from one vision to another: having just knifed Kashperl, Jubal is about to encounter Charlotte when we go back to Haffner, whose run-in with Jubal was similar to Kashperl's. Jubal's tornado-like encounters with the townspeople are complemented by the way one character's psychological weather impinges upon another's.

We experience this method in the first chapter: the action of the boy passing on the motorcycle affects Pauline, the passive observer, who stimulates Hodler to contemplate elaborately what she reports; then Sanford Avery, the farmer who keeps an eye on Holly, calls Hodler to report the effect of what Pauline saw: the apparent rape of Holly. Holly is sitting on her porch, her hair drying, wearing nothing over her breasts, peeling apples in a swarm of bees, and when Jubal approaches her to ask for gas, she thrusts her thumb, which she has cut, toward Jubal, as though he is expected to suck it for her, and that is what he does. She falls and they roll on the porch, entangled. When Jubal leaves Holly, he comes upon Haffner, who laughs at him insanely; then he encounters Kashperl who appears to make a pass at him. Holly, Haffner, Kashperl provoke him, and Charlotte arouses him—all four encounters, after we've looked at the first two from many angles, impinge within three pages in the middle of the novel. Appropriately, Morris filters the day's swift events most often through the pattern-perceiving mind of a newspaper editor, Hodler.

In Orbit is vision-structured in time. What Morris sees raises the rhetorical question, often repeated in his novels, "How explain it?" He demands the reader's active involvement in the answering process. "That's the picture. You might want to add a few details of your own." This is the reader's field of vision, in which time is fragmented. With immediate poetic force, we experience a single instant from various points of view and achieve a sense of simultaneity. The time scramble may seem arbitrary, but the fragmentary approach enables one to look at separate moments from different time and character perspectives, and thus we see more, and more deeply, each time. Conventional "time," says Haffner, "is for people who live on the installment plan."

Morris evokes the pathos of the isolation from each other of similar minds by showing how separate lives plug into a common current of feeling and perception unaware. Separate visions come up with the same or similar similes, as when Jubal (then Hodler) sees Holly's farmhouse porch, then later Charlotte's terrace, as a stage. Both Hodler and Alan come up with the same paradoxical question about the mystery of human perception: "Does it charm him to the extent that it escapes him?" When Holly says her assailant was a spaceman, Hodler looks up as if he might see him in the sky. This "as if he might see" motif appears in most Morris novels, a constant rhetorical reference to the importance of creative vision. Like a phantom, the boy moves in and out of the literal fields of vision of the townspeople, but he is very vivid in the private movie theaters of the character's minds. Jubal knows none of the people he encounters, nor does he perceive the pattern of relationships among them as they meet him; each thinks his encounter with Jubal is singular.

The reader takes it all in with a glance. "Is that so funny?" asks Haffner, laughing at Pauline hosing down the cinders. "So much depends on your point of view." Tableaux and events are even funnier from the reader's complex point of view, for he sees her spray Jubal, also; and the plane that sprays the orchards gradually sprays most of the characters. The comedy in Morris is, at times, pretty broad, as when Haffner, then Jubal, chases his runaway car, calling it as though it were an unleashed pet. But in every image, Morris' is a black comic vision that sometimes sees things with a cross-eyed folksiness. Morris wants the reader to end with the "disturbingly impersonal" and timeless vision of a Holly or a Charlotte, of a child (like little Brian in Cause for Wonder).

The vision-structure of the novel enhances the profundity of the character relationships. The hero-witness relationships pattern that has made this vision-structure in most of Morris' novels meaningful reached the end of one line of development in Ceremony; a new line had already been established in Cannibals, with a female hero, the Greek, affecting change in Horter. A similar sexual relationship was further developed in What a Way to Go between Cynthia and Soby. In Cause for Wonder, the hero was once more a man, but a very old man. Madman Dulac's witnesses, especially Howe, are willing accomplices to the hero's acts of lunacy. And under the influence of

Dulac and his castle, the natural impulsiveness of most of the characters comes out. Unlike Dulac, Jubal only appears to go berserk; it is his witnesses who, misinterpreting his actions, surrender to impulse. In *One Day,* Morris shows how suppressed emotions in the American character exploded in a perverse hero, the President's accused assassin, as a "meaningful accident." Several such accidents occur in *In Orbit.* Most of the characters in *One Day* identify with—or Morris relates them in some way to—the assassin. Unable to understand himself, he seemed to behave as though others would. In *In Orbit* both Jubal, who rather closely resembles today's typical American boy, and the twister are heroic forces affecting their witnesses: "Is it more than a tree that falls? It falls to give this day its meaning." The communal and personal pasts of the town are marked off from the future by the events of the day, "which were already being assembled according to the needs of the survivors." "On the radar screen" of the mind "a spaceman and a twister left the same track. Both were in orbit, or out of it." Their effect on the townspeople is impersonal, like the effect on Kashperl of a man who happened to read a few chance lines aloud in a bookstore, then "creaked off ignorant of what he had done to Kashperl."

Thus, Jubal is unaware that he has "raped" Holly *for* Hodler and Avery, both of whom wanted to make love to her. In this new variation of the hero-witness relationship, the weird behavior of witnesses, whose gestures Jubal misinterprets, sets off impulses in him. We see here more clearly than in earlier novels the ways in which suppressed but wild people affect the hero. The magnetism of their need draws out, energizes, encourages the hero's own wild streak, authorizes his acts, then authenticates them by the witnesses' responses to them. These responses then transform the witnesses "Hodler sees it all through the rapist's eyes," and he observes that "part of the pleasure Avery feels in this rehearsal is to see it on the face of Hodler." Each of Jubal's "victims" smiles as though enchanted. Confronted with such events, Hodler can't remember Haffner's name: "His mind is a blank. Has he lost it?" Morris shows the beneficial effects of losing one's mind now and then.

It is the mind that is most important. Even with a twister, attempted rape and seduction, and assault with a bag of wild cherries and a knife, Morris is determined to subordinate, as is his custom, the action of events to psychological epiphanies. When Hodler and Avery think a spaceman raped Miss Holly, the psychological effect on them is more violent than Holly's actual encounter with Jubal. When Jubal sticks Kashperl with a knife, "no holes of blood are visible." Morris depicts the infliction of unhealable, invisible wounds which are good for the victim because partly self inflicted. Normally, people are too normal to be natural. Kashperl sees the "his friends have labels, they play roles, and they think they have been discovered. The shock—and it is a shock—is of familiarity. To see in a face n more, and no less, than what one knows. While Kashperl shows Jubal a knife, unaware that he is Miss Holly's assailant, the mailman's cryptic message—"Ought to leave him at large as a public service"—becomes gospel to the reader.

Each person in Morris' representative sampling of small-town people nurtures a wild streak similar to the berserk, marauding stranger's; his, however, is mostly their invention. "Bit of the mad dog in us all, eh, Hodler?" says the young intern. Morris reconceives the current idea that there's a little of Eichmann and Oswald in us all. "The mad dog in Hodler is not on the surface, but McCain knows it is there, and he finds it reassuring, almost comforting." This passage suggests the source of the witnesses' inner disposition to produce, then respond to the hero. "Did they all dream of being a man on the loose?" Hodler wonders. "Envied by inhibited red-blooded men, pursued by comical galoots like the Sheriff. He went that-a-way. With the thoughts, fantasies, and envious good wishes of them all." Morris scales this appalling thesis down to manageable, and thus more frightening, size. People emerge from certain seemingly trivial moments with something of their old selves missing. "A dozen or more people are known to be missing. Are Hodler, Charlotte, and Alan three of them?"

It is Alan, the witness, who puts his wife Charlotte into orbit when he puts Kid Ory's horn on the hi-fi. "Somebody not in orbit has to lower the needle carefully into the groove." So-called normal, or successfully suppressed, people need supposedly abnormal people: Alan needs Charlotte, Hodler needs Holly, Charlotte herself needs Haffner, who seems odd to her, and on this day of the twister they all need and use Jubal. Psychologically, man daily subsists, it seems on the tiny deviations from or reversals of the generally accepted. People are adept at making a thing something of their own, something opposite from the thing's intended purpose. People also need, now and then, a violent disruption of their normal mode of life. Wild as Holly's behavior is, her life has its habitual ceremonies. "Sanford?" she always asks, hearing a man approach her from behind. One day it is not Sanford Avery, but a person who reluctantly enacts Sanford's own erotic daydreams. Hodler's response to the day's violent disruption is typical: "it scares the shit out of him, but he likes it. He would gladly take the twist out of that boy who seemed to strike in the same, irresponsible manner, but a twister had obligations that he felt this boy did not. There were these opposing forces, high and low pressures, moist and dry air in unpredictable mixtures, great heat and cold, fantastic combinations that built up like nuclear fission, and most important of all there was the element of chance that dissolved it in vapor, or brought it to perfection, a tube that dipped from the sky and rearranged most of the matter it touched." He "feels a pleasurable apprehension in the knowledge of this potential killer." Like most witnesses, Hodler discovers that "destructive elements are not merely on the

loose, but some of them are rubbing off" on him. Hodler and Kashperl, fe
ing the impact of the hero and the imminence of the twister is the vacuum
at the center causing objects that are sealed up tight to explode." "Know
what nature abhors, Hodler?—a vacuum. Know what a man on the loose
heads for? A vacuum!" This twister-fugitive metaphor powerfully expresse
the condition of the American character at this moment in the nightmare
history.

Holly is the first of Jubal's "victims." She resembles Miss Caddy in *T
World in the Attic*, and Avery is like Mr. Purdy (also like Mr. Parsons in
The Deep Sleep). Holly belongs to the Morris breed of lovable simpletons
sometimes they are young, sometimes old, and animals prefer them to the
more rational adults. But by now their unpredictability has become a little
banal, and only the Morris genius for embellishing the simple type keeps
from atrophying into caricature. The impersonality of such human and
natural events as motorcyclists and twisters passing through is reflected in
Holly's childlike, "serene unblinking gaze." To Hodler, Holly looks like "a
woman patiently awaiting further visitations," because impersonal human
encounters sometimes satisfy a deeper need than personal ones.

As Jubal steps up to the car window, Haffner thrusts his bag of wild
cherries at him. (Jubal's crowning Haffner with the bag recalls Scanlon's
dumping a cigar pot on his own head in *The World in the Attic* and
Ormsby's pushing the helmet down over Lipido's head in *Man and Boy*.)
"'Poy on the loose!' Haffner repeats, and the idea delights him." Haffner
(who resembles Herr Perkheimer in *What a Way to Go*) is to Charlotte
what Hodler and Avery are to Holly. Unable to take care of himself, Haff
ner takes care of Charlotte. Like most Morris characters, he "showed spe
promise as a clown." He prefers "the flawed performance," and likes the
idea of a sonata for one needle in, one *out* of the record groove. Happily
stunned by the boy—the figurative twister—Haffner sleeps through the li
eral twister.

Propelled by his wild encounters with Holly and then with Haffner,
Jubal runs into Kashperl. The cut Holly gave herself somehow inspires th
cut Jubal impulsively gives Kashperl with the knife Kashperl is trying to s
him. Kashperl (who is like Sol Spiegel of *Cause for Wonder*) collects book
with "a preference for the fading title, or the missing author, or better ye
the rare volume that proved to lack both." He prefers disorder. "The play
chance" gives him room in which to influence human events. Even in his
quieter moments, Jubal affects his witnesses, as when Kashperl watches h
padlock his duffle bag and guitar to a parking meter with time left on the
dial. "With a gesture the meter is now a grave marker. Does it tick off th
time before the dead will arise? In Kashperl's book this is style, and he is
impressed. With a gesture, no more, this boy makes old things new." Jok

ingly responding to the boy as though he were the rapist at large, Kashperl asks him about it: "He wanted what Jubal had had without all the trouble." Jubal's comment reveals one aspect of the hero-witness relationship: "She wasn't so old she didn't enjoy it, fat man. I'd say she got more out of it than I did," for in love-making, the woman "gets most of the fun, and all the poor guy gets is the credit!" Jubal is like a natural force that people foolishly stand in the way of, and his knifing Kashperl is another "meaningful accident." "I asked for it," says Kashperl," "and I got it"—naturally, just by being himself.

"Anything at all might interest Alan. It had to be alive to interest his wife Charlotte." "After one year in Pickett she prefers creatures who don't think"—cats, and people who resemble cats, as Haffner does. "Charlotte herself is alive in a way electricity is, and it makes her unruly. On certain days, like this one, she seems charged with it." Alan "would rather live with it than do without it." Hodler makes a similar observation about Jubal, and in many other descriptive passages the parallels between Charlotte's and Jubal's natures are stressed. Like Jubal, Charlotte just seems to be with it naturally. "She does not like the thought, or the poem that submits to typing. She does not like the music until it becomes the dance." After his run-in with Kashperl, Jubal encounters Charlotte whose grocery cart, like Haffner's car, drifts away from her down a ramp (the runaway car motif is carried over from *One Day*). Just as he sucked Holly's cut, he rescues Charlotte, whose heels are caught in the doormat. Charlotte is a more self-aware version of Holly, but both experience events purely. "What next?" thinks Jubal, echoing Horter in *Cannibals*. "At the thought of it, he laughs. All this time he has been on the run from something; what he feels now is the pull of something." A woman—natural, pure force, acts on him. While nature herself works up a dance, Charlotte, having felt Jubal's charge, whirls "in a manner of a person possessed." But just as male and female sexual forces are about to converge in Jubal and Charlotte, Morris delays this most intensely immediate moment in the novel with the longest excursion into the past—Jubal's.

At the climax of the novel, Morris moves the center of consciousness from the journalist's mind, Hodler's, to the poet's; this is the only section from Alan's point of view. In a novel poetically performed, this sensible, overly cerebral writer and teacher of poetry is the least poetic character, though he achieves the finest epiphany. If Avery arrived too late to watch the Holly-Jubal encounter, Alan witnesses the Charlotte-Jubal scene. Jubal and the twister converge simultaneously on the conceptual thinker and his wife, the solo dancer. Twister, male energy, poetic compression, the dynamics of the dance—all these forces merge for an instant, while the passive observer, Hodler, is caught in a rain drain.

While the novel's allusions are predominantly cultural, Alan offers an important literary one: Yeats's "How can we know the dancer from the dance?" concept, which Eliot developed further. Alan watches "this mute figure [Jubal] watch the dance. He wonders how it must look through the stranger's eyes." Simultaneously, he observes that a baby's legs on a porch nearby seem to move in time to Charlotte's dance music—the natural "dance that preceded the music. The beat preceding the dance." "No rhythm to it, no meaning to it, just a pointless, mindless movement." Affected by witnessing these other spontaneous creatures—the baby, the boy, the dancer—Alan experiences pure being, impersonal vision: "He hardly knows, or cares, if the flash he sees is in the air or in his head." "Is it possible to say he no longer sees the dancer, only the dance?" Such an eternal moment of pure duration is holy to Morris, and he goes beyond Browning in poetic rendering of *the moment*. But having survived the literal twister, Alan reverts to his Herzogian stupor of thought: contemplating the aftermath of the twister, he muses, "One's first thought is 'What is it like? What does it remind me of?'" Charlotte declares: "I'm not reminded of *anything*."

Hodler is the novel's Morris-mind, but like Soby, Horter, and Cowie, he is more removed from Morris autobiographically than are Clyde Muncy, Foley, Boyd, and Howe. It is what escapes his conceptualizing that Hodler likes most about what he witnesses: "The meaning that escapes exceeds whatever he has grasped." Hodler arrives at the "scene of the crime," but he sees that the real crimes are all in his and Avery's heads; no crime, it is later discovered, has really been committed here, for "penetration" of Holly did not occur. Morris often echoes Blake: "It occurs to Hodler that the evil men do is less depressing than their vagrant, idle thoughts." Hodler is relieved to see no cuts on Avery, who "suffers from a crime he failed to commit." Hodler himself feels defensive when Avery calls Jubal a pervert. "Hodler wears no space helmet, but one might think that he had just been shot into orbit." Though he is usually the witness of the aftermath, Hodler feels as though he is Jubal's accomplice. As a man who controls his impulses, he does help create the psychological climate of restraint that finally turns boy like Jubal loose. But his collusion differs from Avery's leering delight. "Hodler is a sober man, but for this boy on the loose, free to indulge in his whims, he feels a twinge of envy. There is something to be said for impulsive behavior, although Hodler is perhaps not the man to say it. Visiting spacemen are free to act in a way he is not." Actually, we know that Jubal doesn't indulge his whims; he is driven by others, beginning with one of his own sort, LeRoy. Like the reader, Hodler is a bystander, but near the end he becomes an active observer who will give his own "eyewitness report." Having traced the signs of a human twister, he finally witnesses him in action just when the actual twister steals the show. As the boy rides on out the other end of town, following the twister, Hodler sleeps. "Something in his nature, as well as in nature, seems to find release."

Compared with all his witnesses, Jubal, Morris suggests, is stable. Ironically, Jubal is fleeing his bully buddy's violence against him when he arrives by chance in Pickett; and it is to protect himself from its citizens that he reacts violently in his encounters with them; he assaults the men because their impulsive behavior startles him; he merely attempts to control them. The Sheriff himself, having interviewed the smiling "victims," declares that it is he and the kid who need protection. In the midst of the rain that precedes the twister, Jubal exhibits the conservatism that streaks through most apparently wild men: "he waits, a remarkable example of a responsible, law-abiding citizen, until the green flashes on, giving him the all-clear up ahead."

If his own appearance is bizarre, many things in acceptable society, especially businesses, also look weird: propeller-type banners that twirl between the gas pumps of the One-Stop Diner; his exotic costume could have been provided by Kashperl's store: "Everything is familiar, in stock, and selling—except the face," smeared with soot. Hodler wonders, looking at the numerous low "camp" pictures on the wall of Holly's room: "Was a spaceman so unusual?" Like rider and motorcycle, Holly and house are equally haywire; house and inhabitant cohabit on similar planes of aberration.

Jubal decides that the movie view of life and of war is crazy; then the view of "real" life and peace that he glimpses while on the run seems even crazier. "The crazy ways of the world silence Jubal." Looking for a gun in Kashperl's store with which to protect himself, he says, "You run into some awful nutty people," and Kashperl himself proves to be one of them. People either act nutty like Holly and Haffner, or think only evil like Kashperl. "If the army is no place for a growing boy," Morris concludes, "neither is the world." Juxtaposing Jubal with the "normal" people who think Jubal is a madman, Morris shows that it is the peculiar that is normal.

Though Morris never takes his eyes off the berserk elements in the American character, the style he uses to describe disorder, chance, and contingency is the most perfectly controlled style in contemporary American literature. Everything style has been trained over the centuries to do, Morris makes it do in his novels. In this one, he restricts himself to a comparatively few images, but his mind savors them so persistently that we always feel the weather of his mind; as in old-fashioned novels—Fielding's, for instance—we are always aware of an ambient sensibility as part of the fictive experience. All descriptions are double-edged; of course, this stylistic excellence, sustained line by line, can be wearing. But though we are constantly aware that he is actively using style, the way he uses it is unpredictable.

Sometimes the author is too transparently clever, as in dialog that echoes his own key phrases. His rhetoric sometimes so exceeds the occasion that one is too conscious of Morris' predilection for the non-event. His wit is sometimes too dependent upon rhetorical reversals, bizarre parallels, Blakean or Chestertonian paradoxes. Hodler thinks, "Cold tips often prove to be hot ones"—Morris worries this phrase, for instance, over a whole page. In revitalizing the cliché, Morris often depicts the triumph of the commonplace over the spectacular, as when Hodler perceives that the date makes more sense out of the news than he can make of it. Still, a proliferation of such reversals—Haffner carries a pipe tool but does not smoke a pipe, loses all his pocketknives, but never the sharpening stone, and is "delighted to see the healthy dogs with their ailing owners on leashes" enter the vet's—evokes chuckles that verge on exasperation. Some of his conceits are worked over in a muddy context, as when Haffner sees Jubal coming: "A white man emerging from a black man, or the two in one?" Jubal's face, blackened by his buddy with a cigar stub dipped in stovelid soot, evokes too many such speculations from the author and the characters. Some of his puns respond negatively to analysis. But the wordplay throughout the novel on such controlling terms as "in orbit" and "spaceman" has become quite vital by the end—the word has become flesh.

Morris' rhetorical interrogation of his raw material is a stylistic trademark. In this novel rhetorical questions elicit actual events. "And how is Miss Holly?" Hodler asks Avery, as a routine rhetorical question, to which Avery always answers, "Who the hell would know that?" But today, "Somebody finally knew. It is a torment to Hodler that this essential knowledge is what he once desired for himself." When the mailman reports that a spaceman raped Miss Holly, Kashperl asks Jubal a typical, kidding question: "Now why'd a boy like you do that?" Today, just by chance, he asks the right person. If "Hodler admits to the frailty of language," Morris forces that frailty to perform amazing feats of style and signficance.

Briefer than Man and Boy, In Orbit is Morris' shortest novel. After sixteen novels, the best of which are brief, one is tempted to conclude that the long, large-canvas, many-faceted novel which so many readers have looked for may not come, that the short novel is after all Morris' forte. But mindful of what he can accomplish in the margin of unpredictability allowed by his continuing development of familiar raw material, we ought to resist that temptation.

Though he continues to be an observer of current trends in American character, Morris is less than ever a critic; his is an impersonal vision which selects details that fascinate him. Cerebral though he is often accused of being, so much so that even in this age of criticism, of Herzogian readers, he alienates many who must still admire him, Morris strives first of all to put his reader through a pure experience. In a work of art "the transitory, illusive facts," he said in *The Territory Ahead*, "are shaped into a fiction of permanence." *In Orbit* is a work of art that, to use Conrad's phrase, carries "its justification in every line." And Morris' first task, like Conrad's, is to "make you *see*." He shows us the American landscape and makes us see into the American character. In "The Lunatic, the Lover, and the Poet" (*Kenyon Review*, Autumn, 1965), Morris could have been speaking of his own inclination: "Grown accustomed to monsters, real or imaginary, perhaps we know this new world better than Shakespeare, whose instinct was to speak his mind through the mouths of clowns and fools." Though the implications of his novels are terrifying, Morris (to use Conrad's words once more) "speaks to our capacity for delight and wonder, to the sense of mystery surrounding our lives."

TIME:

Time as Theme, Structure, Character and Symbol in Faulkner's *The Sound and the Fury*

William Faulkner's *The Sound and the Fury* depends for the integrity of its form upon a uniquely organic structure of which Time is the generative principle. In most of Faulkner, Time is out of joint, and in this novel it operates in no single mode but in several simultaneously. Flowing, irregular, often seemingly static, Time provides primary perspective upon narrative (the sequence of which is obscure until the complex operation of Time is explicated), theme (of which Time is the focal consideration), character (enigmatic without an awareness of the active function of Time) and symbol (for which Time is the pivotal referent).

TIME AS THEME

This is Faulkner's most universal book. Although it is set in the Southern culture, the glories and virtues of the Southern tradition and details of Mississippi culture are less specified in this than in any other Faulkner novel. There is little mention of General and of Governor Compson and frequent reference to "your own flesh and blood," hovering out of the past or decaying in the present. Mainly, the cultural and consanguineous past is present only in the manner of the statue of the Confederate soldier in the square, gazing "with empty eyes beneath his marble hand into wind and weather."

Quentin's father's speech, in the opening paragraph of Quentin's section, is essentially an echo of Macbeth's famous speech.

> It [the watch] was Grandfather's and when Father gave it to me he said, Quentin, I give you the mausoleum of all hope and desire; it's rather excrutiatingly apt that you will use it to gain the reducto absurdum of all human experience which can fit your individual needs no better than it fitted his or his fathers. I give it to you not that you may remember time, but that you might forget it now and then for a moment and not spend all your breath trying t

conquer it. Because no battle is ever won, he said. They are not even fought. The field only reveals to man his own folly and despair, and victory is an illusion of philosophers and fools. (*The Sound and the Fury*, p. 95, Modern Library Edition.)

.   .   .

> Tomorrow and tomorrow, and tomorrow,
> Creeps in this petty pace from day to day,
> To the last syllable of recorded time;
> And all our yesterdays have lighted fools
> The way to dusty death. Out, out, brief candle!
> Life's but a walking shadow, a poor player
> That struts and frets his hour upon the stage
> And then is heard no more: it is a tale
> Told by an idiot, full of sound and fury,
> Signifying nothing.

These two speeches indicate how Time operates thematically, reflecting Faulkner's vision of time in life. While these speeches primarily reveal the characters who utter them, they also provide insight into theme as well, since theme is manifested in characters in action.

During sleep, not only tomorrow, yesterday, too, "creeps in this petty pace," and although nothing ceases, perhaps anguish is, in the absence of dream, lulled. "And then I was in time again, hearing the watch," Quentin says on awaking. But for Benjy, the pure, animal imperturbable ego, sleep is not an escape. "I have been asleep," ends his day in the novel, and describes his mode of life: whining, wailing, bellowing (animalistically, not mentally, perturbed), "all time and injustice and sorrow become vocal for an instant" in a timeless dream. In this world, such innocence and immunity from the anguish of conceptual thought is possible only in a state of serene idiocy. "All our yesterdays have lighted fools / The way to dusty death" is man's epitaph, to the extent that his vision, viewing the field, fails to reveal to him his own folly and despair. The illusion is greatest when men wish defeat into victory. Man then foolishly struts and frets his hour, each tomorrow, upon the stage of yesterday, idiotically telling a tale of no substance, "full of sound and fury."

All Quentin's ancestral yesterdays have day by day impinged upon his own present, lighting him the way to a watery escape from temporal time and its freight of shadows, into an eternity of expiation by fire. Living, he can't forget or conquer Time. His father and Rosa Coldfield (See Faulkner's *Absalom, Absalom!*) told him a tale of yesterday which should have taught him to reject that part of it which cast a blinding light; but the story too painfully paralleled his ancestor's and his own past, which, in this book is obliquely told by an idiot, Benjy. Told through the dead Quentin and the idiot Benjy, the ancestral and the personal story (organically integrated) seem *more* sound and fury, although there is significance for the reader, as witness, overhearing these stories.

The ascribed values of the past live malignantly in Quentin because he lives in a time that breeds and nourishes only Jasons in the old, barren ground. The mother, inflicting a petty pace of decay upon herself, nags her family with clichés from a past she knows only too despairingly is dead; she emasculates her males, renders virginity in her females as irritable as a hangnail to them. The father, who philosophically views everything as absurd, drifts in a dipsomaniacal euphoria. In Quentin, the guilt of the ancestral, and of his own past (particularly the incest parallel between Judith and Henry Sutpen and himself and Caddy), the incestuous inversion, reaches that point where the only way is down. The past exists in the Snopes-like Jason only at that stage where it signifies nothing (that stage beginning with his birth); its sound and fury is gone with Quentin and Caddy and only the niggardliness of the emasculated present prevails. Caddy, unlike Dilsey, refuses to enact even nominally (as her mother does) the traditional burden-bearing role of the female; she is the fecund female life force that knows no bond to the past, for whom each tomorrow is another time for random expenditure of that for which she refuses responsibility—her reproductive capacity and maternal role. Benjy, the all-inclusive manifestation of sound and fury, the last, unprogenitive son (in him the Compson-Bascomb line ends, Time stops), with his pure ego, knows no malignant concept of Time or loss, and the bright shapes of fire continue to provide hypnotic tranquillity, never teaching him its burning quality; for Quentin fire is infernal punishment and cleansing for sins only conceived yet worse than real: "the clean flame the two of us dead amid the pointing and the horror beyond the clean flame." If Benjy tells of Time in decay, though in him it is pure, through Dilsey, Time is manifested more purely in the quality of her endurance; though her children do not turn out perfectly, she is free of all trappings except an elementary religiosity and daily travail in such a way as to enable her sanely to endure.

We cannot discuss Time as theme without involving character manifestations of it, another indication of the organic interdependency of the parts of this novel.

TIME AS STRUCTURE

Although ingenious, organic functioning of point of view (that is, each section is composed of elements intricately related to and dependent upon those of other sections) contributes to the structure of *The Sound and the Fury*, character is so dependent upon the Time principle that Time performs the major structural function. The sequence of Point-of-view shift, both within a given character (within a sort of free associational, involuted continuum) and from one to another, suggests a kind of time succession.

In Benjy's tale, told April 7, 1928, his birthday, the day before Easter (he was born in 1895), the novel's major narrative events and most of its symbolism is presented or implied. In this section, time past and present seem frozen or static. The sound and the fury of the Compsons is rendered in a light most natural to it: the sensorially excited memory of a Compson idiot. Although we do not fully understand the implications of Benjy's *apparently* incoherent memories, the entire novel is telescoped in them. Quentin's story (June 2, 1910; he was born in 1891) develops the major theme, and provides elaborations, clarifications, and further complexities of Benjy's section. Quentin's section is dominated by time past. Jason's story (April 6, 1928; he was born in 1895)—in which most of the symbolic patterns, the leitmotifs, refrains, are recapitulated—develops secondary themes. His section is dominated by time present. The fourth section, related in Faulkner's third person omniscient point of view, with emphasis upon Dilsey's point of view, is concerned with time past, present, and future.

Since, because of the novel's theme, Benjy's tale has to begin the novel, and since he could not have known the major (to Jason) events of April 6, the peculiar arrangement of the three days is necessitated. The overall action transpired from the turn of the century, the new era, to Easter, 1928, a year before the great crash. April 8, Easter Day, logically (in terms of theme) ends the novel in order to turn the seasonal frame of the story (one of its many frames) to ironic effect: much is finally buried, ended, although the past rises and walks abroad. (Benjy is 33, Christ's age when he died, Easter Day ends the novel, Christmas is a recurrently emphasized time during which major events occur, and Quentin makes many religious references, but I won't attempt to describe the Christ or Christian allegory.) The novel is composed somewhat like a musical composition (further testimony to the Time principle), with the three days at Easter suggesting a threnody.

A kind of time movement may be detected in another aspect of point of view as structure. Benjy's ego, asserting itself with innocent selfishness, remembers in the manner of an animal or of an arrested three year old, memories being evoked by sensory stimuli that have their analogues in the past; but he exists in the present, unaware that it is constituted by disordered references to the past and is not motivated by expectations of the future. The world exists in his mind in a state of almost pure immutability. To that world, Quentin and Jason, impelled by the demands of their individual personalities, bring to bear a rational, ordering scrutiny.

However, a kind of logical pattern of order pervades Benjy's memories. A modified stream-of-consciousness method is employed in the three sections; often, though there is a seemingly more discernible line, Quentin's thoughts are just as chaotic as Benjy's. Benjy remembers out of pure need for love and kindness; Quentin is compelled by guilt, grounded in a commitment to the past based on illusion, that has brought him to the verge of self-destruction; and Jason, purely, basely selfish, remembers only what is of immediate, usually utilitarian value, only what helps to explain or comments upon his immediate situation and his selfish future prospects, and in this sense, but for different reasons, he is closer to Benjy than to Quentin. In the fourth section, Faulkner depicts in the present a mesh of selfish activity (Jason, Quentin, Caddy, Mrs. Compson, Luster) around which Dilsey moves in an orbit of selfless servitude and endurance. Her life provides a temporal cycle: "Never you mind me ... I seed de beginnin, en now I sees de endin." Like Benjy, she is immutable; unlike him, she is racially alien but humanely committed.

Only in the concluding section does a conventionally fictional sense of event operate: that what is *told* has happened; but even here, Faulkner's facility for creating the impression of immediate representation is at work. In Jason's section, this sense of immediacy is now and then clearly indicated: "*this* store." In Quentin's section there are different time effects. He, too, speaks in the past tense but with no clear indications of time present, although a feeling of it is generated, despite his long reveries into the past. More important for the novel, he is dead (since we leave him not long before his death, to whom could he have told the story?) but speaking as though he were alive: to him the past spoke through Rosa Coldfield and various other agencies but *his* story only the reader knows, and it can concern or affect only the reader.

That Time via point of view, as operating structurally in the organism of the novel, is even more complex than has been suggested may be implied in a close, but by no means exhaustive, scrutiny of Benjy's section in which we may note how time operates in other ways too.

Benjy's narrative, to use the term freely, presents unique problems in fictional craft. Obviously, the reader is not expected to believe that he is in the mind of an idiot who is recalling events in the first person. How may a sense of idiocy, the feeling of chaos and irrationality, emotional disparateness be conveyed, while still achieving the fictional purpose of depicting event, establishing symbolic and other devices, and delineating character? Benjy is given, gratuitously, the faculty and the vocabulary of intelligible recall, but only apparently. Though they fail to cohere sequentially, relate, and become concepts, he would receive all the impressions of sight, hearing, smell, touch and taste. One must settle, then, within this framework, upon a semblance of idiotic perception and memory; animal response is dominant, mental evaluation is minimal. The diction is simple throughout: "I could see them hitting." Once in the past, he is made to experience as though he were in the present.

If Benjy's and Luster's wandering in the present is the organizing event, a schematization of the directional line of events reveals that: event five recurs 13 times; six, 5; fourteen, 9; fifteen, 5; the present, 27, distributed widely, interspersed with other events, all related by similar images, sounds, smells, tastes, touches; that there are approximately 16 separate incidents, 80 sections and 55 transitions in 72 pages. This suggests that a complex, almost mathematical formula governs the arrangment of the incidents: behind the semblence of idiotic chaos, resides order, calculated to produce appropriate effects, to be enhanced by recapitulations in Jason's and Quentin's sections.

Faulkner uses musical, poetic, and mathematical (time) techniques to give organicity to this and the other sections. The monotonous repetition of "He said, She said" creates a unifying effect in Benjy, and in parts of the other, sections: like the ticking of a clock or a metronome. The various refrains and repetitions create a sense of time present, of the past embodied, active, insistent in the present. There is, however, very little deliberate or obvious anticipation of future events; a causal line is sacrificed in order to create a feeling of past and present as being immobile. The past lies heavily dead upon the present, impeding progression into the future.

An obvious time refrain in Benjy's and Quentin's sections is the representation of all the seasons and of several holidays, funerals, and weddings. Quentin's watch and the Harvard clock and bells, and the transformations of his shadow pervade his section. A sense of day passing, with mealtimes, bells, regular (though delayed) stock market reports, and the impending show time, prevails in Jason's section. In the final section there is the ominous doomsday motif, heightened in the sermon.

Among the multitudinous and various refrains and repetitions which become, essentially, time factors, some of the more obvious are: fire, people as beasts, birds, religious references, the succession of baby sitters for Ben (Versh, T. P., Luster), Benjy's bellowing and whining throughout, clocks, Benjy's and, especially, Quentin's preoccupation with their shadows, Caddy's and her daughter's smelling of trees, the various incestuous overtones, someone always "telling on" someone, carriage and automobile trips, and meals. These refrains undergo numerous variations.

Faulkner's transitions are remarkably effective and here enhance the functions of Time. One of the subtlest is on page 57 in Benjy's section. A parallel has been patterned between Caddy's wedding, viewed by T. P. and Benjy, and Damuddy's lying in state, viewed by Caddy, Benjy and others. T. P. said, "Git on the box and see is they started." Without using italics, Faulkner immediately reverts to Caddy as a child, "They haven't started because the band hasn't come yet," Caddy said. Thus, the present and two events of the past become compounded. Transitions in Quentin's section, too, are subtle and effective. Jason often establishes the entrance of a character or a change of scene by a sudden direct reference, as though the character or the scene were already introduced. Faulkner's facile transitional techniques are another aspect of his meticulous exemplification of Time as structure.

TIME AS CHARACTER AND AS SYMBOL

It follows from the complexity of *The Sound and the Fury* that a discussion of Time as organic principle operative in theme and structure would necessarily, by implication at least, provide insight into Time as character and as symbol. True of most good novels, it is an even greater consideration here. For instance, Time in the mode of symbolic action affects theme, structure and character; though they may be examined separately, they function in unison, organically. Benjy is first a character in a compelling story, but he is no less vitally a source of symbolic action, a pivotal thematic image, and an effective structural device; of Quentin, Jason, Dilsey and, in a different way, Caddy, the same may be said. Time is such a pervasive force in the novel that it takes on qualities of character.

Upon the stage, where the romantic tragedy of the past is re-enacted among decaying props in the present, the lines either obviously memorized, distorted, imperfectly learned or forgotten, the action absurdly florid, stilted or reluctant, and impotent, Benjy's timeless ego is as uncomprehending as a mirror. Being an idiot, he has no character if it is not composed of the collective images that flit, flutter, and falter, now vaguely, now only too calamitously clearly, across the mirror he is. Individually configured in the characters, the common despair and disorder enacts before the mirror of Benjy's mind intricate postures of deformity. Benjy's function as mirror is suggested in the scene in the bedroom (beginning on p. 80): "but we could see Caddy fighting in the mirror and Father put me down and went into the mirror and fought too. He lifted Caddy up. She fought. Jason lay on the floor, crying. He had the scissors in his hand. Father held Caddy (p. 83). He rolled into the corner out of the mirror" (p. 84). Benjy's own need focuses in the mirror upon the reflection of the warm, bright fire, for he *exists* in pure sensory immediacy; and he is aware of his shadow as a companion.

Quentin is attracted to hellfire as a source of eternal torment. "Niggers say a drowned man's shadow was watching for him in the water all the time," thinks Quentin (p. 109). All his life, he has followed his shadow, conspiring with him in his progress toward doom, to this eternal, all-embracing sea; his shadow, embodying that aspect of the past which wreaks his personal nemesis, and Benjy's, embodying the collective idiocy of times frozen out of joint, merge in this final reflection, to be shattered by suicide, the "reducto absurdum of all human experience." The major climaxes of Quentin's guilt-ridden life occur in or by the creek in the pasture, which is Benjy's favorite domain—from the narrow creek of Quentin's life to the everlasting sea. He is compelled to "out" the brief candle of life (for which the embracing symbol is Benjy's fire) to immerse himself in eternal fire. Only there may he and Caddy be together, cleansing themselves of incest, existing purely.

The will of the past decays symbolically in Benjy, the vessel of arrested time; in his mother it decays day by day with a morbid willfullness; Caddy's heedless, furious plunge into sex is an escape from guilt (she, like Electra, leave expiation to Quentin) and time; burdened with and paralyzed by the decaying past, Quentin adds iron weights and sinks to hell and cleansing; Jason constructs the petty edifice of his life upon the ruins, consciously disowning the past; among the ruins, Dilsey endures because for her time is "in the book, honey, Dilsey said. Writ out. . . . They'll read it for me. All I got to do is say Ise here." Roskus, the doomsayer, contrasts with Dilsey: "I seen the sign an you is too—" but Dilsey is too busy living to be intimidated by it, although she would agree with him that "Dying ain't all," and thus condemn Quentin's suicide as a "sinful waste."

This involuted plotting, by the Time principle, of intricate relationships, could continue endlessly, by the nature of organic structure. Let a few more observations regarding Quentin suffice.

For Quentin, the year at Harvard is a time of internal examination. The long story of the Sutpens, heard during the summer (in *Absalom, Absalom!*), provides external impetus to the unavoidable investigation of his own moral disintegration the following summer; his own damnation is too intimate for him to be able to relate it to Shreve.

On the morning of his suicide he renounces recorded time (or thinks he does) by unhanding the ancestral watch, although it continues to tick and the clocks of the indifferent world (at Harvard) toll the hour to remind him that he is not yet free to suffer the purer, eternal hell. In a symbolic sense, Benjy (the collective past), smells Quentin's impending death now; the vulture (the bird of time) has finished undressing the dog Nancy (or the dog

Benjy), the nakedness is revealed, the final decay is setting in. Quentin, like Christ, is not crucified—no such lofty thing; he has been, rather, "worn away by the minute clicking of little wheels (his own conscience)." For him, now, like Benjy, moments of the past are arrested in the present moment: "One minute she was standing in the door." In that moment, Caddy is revealed in her true nature, but when she tells him that "When they touched me I died," he recognizes his tragic predicament, that only by willing himself as her partner in sin, lowering it to nadir, incest, can he free her from dishonor among the lowly (Ames, and others); though it would mean the lowest dishonor among kin, they can atone together.

That the past is still immediate, even, or especially, as he is about to will it to its final culmination, is symbolically established throughout his last day. "I have committed incest, Father," is symbolically addressed to God, in whom he despairingly can no longer believe (except as he will feel his wrath in hell). For Mrs. Compson religion is reduced to a Bible she is too lazy to retrieve from under her bed but must order Dilsey, who can barely climb stairs, to hand it to her. Mr. Compson's attitude toward female honor has degenerated into a philosophical sophistication that is a painfully inadequate response to Quentin's initial confession. God seems to offer hell as the solution.

Gerald is an aristocratic counterpart to Dalton Ames, with whose "They're all bitches" not only he but Jason, too, would agree; Jason, now Snopes-like in his awe of money, has no reverence for anything to which Quentin would ascribe value. When Quentin fights Gerald he is vividly reliving the indignity of his past failure of manhood with Dalton.

With the little Italian girl, whom he calls sister, Quentin relives his early sexual failures with Natalie and Caddy, and ironically, he is attacked by the girl's brother. It was by a stream, too, that he first realized his desire for his sister and began a suicide pact with her which he couldn't execute then but is completing alone now. Symbolically, two things happened that night years ago. The incest was mentally consummated (according to the Pauline doctrine that if one lusts for a woman one has already committed fornication); in a sense, the girl Quentin, who became another Caddy (smelling of trees) rather than another Quentin (reeking of the decay of the past) was conceived. And the losing of the knife, the intended instrument of suicide, was the losing, in Freudian terms, of Quentin's manhood; in the wishing of this all-destructive sexual act, incest, he emasculates himself.

Emasculation is a recurrent motif, representing the essence of the theme of impotency that appears in various forms. Ironically, Jason gelds Benjy, who, being sexless already, least of all needed to procreate or even fornicate, but he himself (Jason) spills his seed upon barren ground (whore for his mother has, in the sense that he could even consent to marriage, emasculated him, despite his hands-in-pockets effort as a child to guard his genitals (an act which later becomes the miserly protecting of his money). Jason senior is driven to a dipsomaniacal loss of sexual drive. Caddy and her daughter waste their female fecundity in extreme misanthropic philanthropy. Time as character and as symbol in this consideration results in the end of the ancestral line. These people having failed, ultimately, to endure, Time will cease to affect, work its influences, and wreak its ravages upon the Compsons in their folly and despair.

The total impact of *The Sound and the Fury* is negative and pessimistic to such a tremendous, intense, and final extreme (the obvious hope manifested in Dilsey notwithstanding) that only a contrasting significance is possible. In his Elijah-Ecclesiastes novel, Faulkner achieves that height of warning, ringing with the very ding-dong of doom, from which hope may be inferred, because when warnings cease, doom *is*.

[The first draft of this essay was written in 1957; it has been revised for this book and is published here for the first time.]

PSYCHOLOGICAL CRITICISM:

The Paradox of the Need for Privacy and the Need for Understanding in Carson McCullers' *The Heart Is a Lonely Hunter**

The theme of *The Heart Is a Lonely Hunter* could hardly be more vital and universal; the immemorial, individual dilemma of loneliness, the spiritual isolation of human beings. It is not a realistic novel about the modern South, nor is it, despite certain critics or whatever McCullers' original intention may have been, a political polemic against capitalism and racism. The memorable characters are all excruciatingly real, but they retain a poetic simplicity which raises them to the level of universal significance. I do not mean "spiritual" in either the religious or even the mystical sense. I, and I think McCullers, mean that inexplicable force in each man which makes him ask why, which compels him to go deeply beneath the surface complex of himself into a more intensive, extensive reality. The validity of McCullers' vision of the psychic realm of her characters, or of man, depends a great deal upon the accuracy and consistency with which she achieves a very acute psychological understanding of her characters and of the nature of loneliness which moves them so grotesquely.

The effect of environment upon the personalities of the five focal characters is not detailed. One feels the environment, past and present, as a hovering, insidious menace. But the evidence available in the novel persuades us that extreme poverty powerfully effected in Jake Blount certain anti-social, pro-martyr compulsions; that southern cruelty against Negroes and the Negro's own ignorance compelled Copeland to become a doctor and a Marxist; that Singer's childhood in an institution for deaf-mutes impeded his ability to move smoothly among the unafflicted; that his early love for and dependence upon his mother has caused Biff Brannon to fail sexually; and that poverty, living in a large family, and being born at an awkward time contributed much to directing Mick along certain channels of malad-

*Reprinted by permission from *Literature and Psychology*, Vol. XVII, No. 2–3, (1967) pp. 128–40. Copyright © 1967 by Leonard P. Manheim and Morton Kaplan.

justment. But the novel is not only *not* an indictment of environment (no social institutions are directly vilified, except by Copeland and Blount, who are not necessarily McCullers' spokesmen); it is not an indictment of anything. McCullers was only 21 when she wrote this book, but she was too mature to condemn abstractions either, although it is a rather abstract, paradoxical conflict that she is primarily concerned with: everyone hungers for human understanding while simultaneously desiring an inviolable privacy.

The need for privacy is no less crucial than the need for understanding, but in the context of society both needs are frustrated, or, in the desperate attempt to satiate one, the other is neglected or deprived. Society is becoming more and more suspicious of the desire for, or at least detrimental to the search for, privacy, to which even the family unit is a threat. But, despite the attempts of educationists to teach "communications" and "understanding skills" regarding various contemporary problems and phases of modern life, society has *not* evolved conditions wherein one person's understanding of another is significantly increased. "Group dynamics" and "life-adjustment techniques" invade privacy and discourage real understanding of what matters most, in spiritual terms, to the individual, especially such extreme isolates as this novel's five characters. Basically, neither the society nor the individual is to blame, and where there is blame, it must be shared. The irremediable paradox of anguish can be partially controlled, that is, Negroes can be completely freed, but the essential loneliness and despair of Doctor Copeland cannot be entirely assuaged.

That man first learned to speak, most probably, out of a practical need—"Which way did the dinosaur go?"—is one indication that his desire for privacy is greater than his need for understanding, else he would first have asked, "Who am I and why am I?" Or perhaps, intuitively aware of the tremendousness of the Inexplicable, each man needs to believe that he is individually important by virtue of a unique expression in his psyche of that Inexplicable, whereby his fear of it is sometimes eclipsed. Being by nature a solitary spirit, each man, perhaps in his nethermost subliminal regions of being, desires privacy *first*, and from the dichotomy effected by this paradoxical conflict arise anguish and despair and the continuance of loneliness in which he thrives. In solitude emerge those very private intuitions about self and others that compel one to share or seek sympathetic understanding, either because these intuitions are terrifyingly perplexing or sublimely beautiful. Yet one might assume that were Mick able to tell everything to everyone, she would be unhappy, or at least less happy than she is in telling Singer only. Blount's trouble is that he wants to tell *everyone* a public "truth" in order to satisfy a private craving for friendliness, respect, and an end to loneliness. His failure results in near-paranoid psychosis.

Only when he can talk to one man who only listens can he, when the talking is over, feel tranquil for a while.

This, then, is a novel based on a paradoxical theme stated in a series of ironic situations. The symbolism is mostly thematic; there is very little internal symbolism and metaphor. John Singer is obviously that recurrent device in modern literature, Jesus our Savior, but McCullers' theme and treatment justify its use. Many of the people in the town idealize him in the way that the four "apostles" do: "Each man described the mute as they wished him to be." Man makes God in his own image. Singer wanders alone in the town, his face sad because he longs for his friend Antonapoulos; people think they see compassion and wisdom in his "tragic" visage. But Biff, the practical, curious cogitator, although himself in awe of Singer, anticipates the irony: "And why did everyone persist in thinking the mute was exactly as they wanted him to be when most likely it was all a very queer mistake?"

Singer is a father substitute for, or extension of, Mick's father, as he is partially for the others, but he is also a father confessor, a sort of religious idol (none of the four is religious in an orthodox way). It is a combination of "lacks," the fulfillment of which they seek, which people find abundantly embodied in or which they readily project onto Singer. But he is none of these things. He is merely a pleasant, polite young gentleman, a latent homosexual grieving over the absence of his lover, who is an obese, obtuse, uncouth, psychotic Greek. Obsessed with his love for the Greek, his loneliness, Singer has an illusory concept of the Greek: "I am not meant to be alone and without you who understand." Insane Antonapoulos understands even less about Singer than Singer understands about his "visitors."

Singer is, in a word, "bewildered" by these people. "For something had happened in this year. He had been left in an alien land. Alone. He had opened his eyes and around him there was much he could not understand. He was bewildered." In his loneliness, Singer welcomes his visitors, caters to them, but they cannot understand (only Biff really wants to) or listen to *him*.

Perhaps subconsciously they know that Singer doesn't understand, but maybe this is a satisfying middle-way, a compromise—to have at least a sympathetic listener, a human adjunct to oneself, but one who does not fully understand; thus one's privacy is not violated in the relationship. He almost like a strange god, one who listens with his eyes; this indirect mean of communication, this sort of siphoning process, creates a distance at the same time that it achieves a comforting intimacy, like praying in the palpable presence of the god. Unlike one's own conscience, Singer cannot talk back, ask questions; this increases his politeness and sustains his "sympathetic" smile. In such a relationship, the "confessor" may fully idealize the nature, the characteristics of the listener. The deepest anguish is in the sub-liminal realization that even this is cold comfort. The old frustrations, an-xieties are merely momentarily assuaged, not destroyed or even really di-minished.

If Singer is Christ, Antonapoulos is his god, and the cruelty of his friend's uncomprehending insanity (though not really cruel since Singer's il-lusion is stubbornly firm) suggests an allegorical statement about illusion. Perhaps for Jesus there was no more a father in Heaven than for Singer there was understanding and love in Antonapoulos. Belief in Jesus or reli-gion is like having the illusion that Singer understands the inner torment of his visitors, that he is a wise man at peace with himself. Whether or not our prayers expire in an indifferent universe, one derives only a fleeting pallia-tion. Perhaps religion, reservoir of man's errors and hopes, is as much a myth as Singer, who finally kills himself when the object of his own illusion perishes. For those who survive, he is a sort of spiritual Richard Cory. But no doubt the people who "confessed" to this innocent impostor are some-how, for a while, the better for having known, talked to him. His listening helped them through critical phases in their lives. (The therapeutic effect of the clinical psychiatrist's function as a listener becomes more clearly under-stood when one closely examines the relationships between Singer and the four neurotics; it also may indicate that, in this regard, the listener need not himself be free of neurosis.)

To sharpen focus on what has already been said, to provide a frame for further remarks, and to prepare for concluding observations, I want to look more closely at the individual characters. I will try to select passages and in-formation which will not only delineate the personalities of respective characters but which will also indicate insights into their behavior, their di-lemma. A very fine design, enriched by leitmotifs, in which alternate sec-tions are devoted to the intimate viewpoints of the various characters, uni-fies the novel. The characters move in a similar psychic and material realm in which each is painfully lonely, isolated from society by its conditions and their own constitutions; and each is obsessed with one single idea, purpose, or personality trait.

John Singer: Singer, a silver engraver, tall and thin, dresses very so-berly; Antonapoulos, who works in his cousin's fruit store, is obese, glutton-ous, sensual, and dresses very sloppily. They are the two extremes of Shel-don's theory of constitutional types: endomorphic and ectomorphic. These two opposites, the one intelligent and the other almost feeble-minded, brought together by their mutual affliction and their latent homosexuality, live compatibly, contentedly together for ten years in the average-sized southern town. Partly due to Antonapoulos' irrational temperament and his impulsive behavior, which later becomes compulsive, they have no other friends, even among other mutes, and live a routine, introverted life.

After his friend's commitment to the asylum, Singer becomes nervous and depressed, wanders about the town, moves to another house (where Mick Kelly lives), and eats in the New York Café. (Biff is the proprietor; the café is the world, its name emphasizes the alienation of its patrons from the immediate environment.) But then, "In his face there came to be a brooding peace that is seen most often in the faces of the very sorrowful or the very wise. But still he wandered through the streets of the town, always silent and alone." Walking or sitting, he keeps his hands in his pockets, ashamed as one would be who always goes about with his mouth open. Sometimes, referring to his four visitors, "The faces crowded in on him out of the darkness so that he felt smothered." He is not only bewildered, but like Christ, feels the burden of the despair of others; unlike Christ, he doesn't invite it. He thinks always of the Greek, and when he visits him, "the bliss of their reunion almost stifled him." Both the loneliness and the bliss are excessive.

After he learns of his friend's death, Singer, usually so very reserved, rages when a hotel slot machine fails to operate, and as he checks out, even steals some articles (steals as Antonapoulos had, trying to feel a closeness thereby). In the strange town, he tries to commune with three mutes, but the coldness in him toward anyone but Antonapoulos (anyone with whom he can communicate, deaf-mutes) repulses them. Being a very fastidious person, he characteristically washes the ash tray he has been using before he shoots himself. McCullers renders his behavior after his friend's death with psychological consistency and accuracy.

Biff Brannon: Biff says to his wife, in defense of the drunken, raving Jake Blount, "I like freaks!" Alice: "You're one yourself!" Biff is kind, tender-hearted, cuts prices for all customers who are maimed, and even salvages house-trapped bees. His wife, who teaches Sunday school is callous; with her, Biff can achieve no rapport and feels that silence is best. (Perhaps it would have been better if they had been deaf-mutes like Singer and Antonapoulos.) Around Alice, Biff is not his real self: "It made him tough and small and common as she was." But the major difference is that she never "watches, thinks, tries to figure things out. . . . But you don't know what it is to store up a whole lot of details and then come upon something real."

Looking at the tomboy, Mick Kelly, Biff feels tender but uneasy and pretends to be gruff with her. He is a sensible man but he, too, is "by himself." When Alice suddenly dies, he is no more lonely than before. After arranging for her funeral, he goes home: "To put things in order—" He completely cleans (and later redecorates) the house and bathes himself all over

(He had seldom washed below the waist, probably to make himself physically repellent to Alice.) The cleaning process rids him, in part, of Alice's
lingering presence. "When he tried to remember her face there was a queer
blankness in him."

Biff is almost desperately observant. He likes Blount because he is unpredictable, fascinating. He notices that "in nearly every person there was
some special physical part kept always guarded." Biff guards his genitals
with his hands; touching them reminds him that they are safe. He also observes that "in some men it is in them to give up everything personal at
some time, before it ferments and poisons—throw it to some human being
or some human idea." Often Biff says more than he realizes, for here is a
good description of what the other three visitors do. "Throw" is the word,
not *share* or seek *understanding;* Singer is both a "human" and the "idea"
each man has of him. This is less a description of Biff than of the others.
When *he* goes to Singer, he usually asks questions and wonders about
Singer himself. Biff keeps most of his feelings private; although he often
asks profound questions, he is willing to share or seek surface knowledge.
Even when his wife dies, he asks the undertaker, "And what is the percent-
age of cremations in your business?" Unable to answer the huge *whys* that
torment him—the why of Singer's peculiar effect on people, the why of
loneliness, of Jake's, of Mick's behavior—he gluts himself with facts, as Antonapoulos gluts himself with food.

Biff, like Singer, is a latent homosexual. He wears his mother's wedding ring. Symbolically, he has always been wed to her and therefore sees
Alice as dirtier than she is. As a child he used to play with, to sew scraps of
cloth, until his mother had to take them from him. His only friend is a woman, Lucille, Alice's sister. When she says that he would make a "mighty
good mother," he considers that a compliment. He "sometimes almost
wished he was a mother and that Mick and Baby were his kids." He would
like to adopt some children and make clothes for them. He would prefer to
live in ancient Greece, wear a toga (a dress), and walk among children.
Ashamedly, he desires to fondle Mick, for children seem more submissive,
and his uneasy feeling about her ends when her adolescence does. Often he
puts some of Alice's perfume behind his ears; after she is dead, he washes
his hair in a lemon preparation as she had. That he adopts certain of her
whims and habits, suggests that perhaps he had always envied her for her
feminine role. He delights in decorating the apartment and the café window. His favorite place for privacy is a back room filled with old newspapers, from which he derives a sense of security in possessing at least the
facts of his, of the world's past; there, in a rocking chair, he sings and thinks
in a "womb-like" intimacy, except that the room (reality), unlike the womb
(illusion or regression), is cold. Then there came the time (after Alice and
whores) "When he could lie with a woman no longer."

The image of Biff in the cold room rocking, singing, thinking, is one of the most poetic expressions of loneliness in all literature:

> At last he put away his mandolin and rocked slowly in the darkness. Death. Sometimes he could almost feel it in the room with him. He rocked to and fro in the chair. What did he understand? Nothing. Where was he headed? Nowhere. What did he want? To know. What? A meaning. Why? A riddle.

Every other café in town is closed during the night, but Biff's is always open to receive the world and its riddles, to stifle his loneliness: "Night was the time. There were those he would never have seen otherwise." When the novel ends, he realizes that "He had known his loves and they were over. . . . There was no one." Alone in the café, too late to call Lucille, no customers expected, all he has is the riddle. "And the riddle was still in him, so that he could not be tranquil. There was something not natural about it all—something like an ugly joke. When he thought of it, he felt uneasy and in some unknown way afraid." But, ironically, at Singer's funeral there was a huge crowd, while Biff, alive, stands alone in his café, "suspended between radiance and darkness. Between bitter irony and faith." Terrified, he calls to the Negro waiter, Louis, desperate for companionship. But a practical concern—the raising of the awning—brings him back to mundane routine.

Mick Kelly: The least neurotic, Mick and Biff are the most fully drawn of the five major characters. With them, the reader can more easily identify. Not that they are ordinary. Mick is a unique, individual adolescent and will be a neurotic, bitter woman; Biff is already neurotic. Copeland, obsessed with the one true purpose, and Blount, obsessed with the gospel of social reform, are both subject to monomania, and it is in this light that we see them.

The portrait of Mick is complete. We see her in various situations, reacting variously, exhibiting in her own eccentric way all the characteristics of an adolescent girl trying to achieve womanhood, but fearing to succeed. Unable to identify with her unsympathetic, older sisters, who ignore her, Mick used to follow, take her cues from her older brother Bill. But when the novel opens, she realizes, "Sometimes she hated Bill more than anyone else in the world. He was different entirely from what he used to be." In growing up, he has failed her. The mother is too busy to answer questions, and one assumes that Portia, the Negro cook, is the only adult female from whom Mick can learn what a girl must do.

Portia accurately diagnoses what *seems* to be Mick's problem;

> But you haven't never loved God nor even nair person. You
> hard and tough as cowhide. But just the same I knows you. This
> afternoon you going to roam all over the place without ever being
> satisfied. You going to traipse all around like you haves to find
> something lost. You going to work yourself up with excitement.
> Your heart going to beat hard enough to kill you because you don't
> love and don't have peace. And then some day you going to bust
> loose and be ruined. Won't nothing help you then.

But Mick knows "that always there had been one person after
another. . . . But she had always kept it to herself and no person had ever
known." There had been male and female schoolmates and female teachers
whom she had secretly loved. Now all she has is Bubber, her little brother,
Mr. Singer, and her father. There is a fine scene between Mick and her
father in which their mutual longing for familial love and sympathy very
nearly achieves satisfaction. "Yet for some reason she couldn't tell him about
the things in her mind—about the hot, dark nights."

More than any of the other characters, Mick needs solitude, privacy.
"Some things you just naturally want to keep private. Not because they are
bad, but because you just want them secret." But when they are about to
"poison" her, she "throws" them at her "idea" of Singer; she responds to his
impersonal air as she could not respond to her father's intense personal
need. Having no physical room of her own, she imagines one as existing in
her own mind. The only person allowed in that room is Mister Singer. It is
filled with dreams of the future, with music she has heard or imagined herself.

Mick not only writes music and spends her lunch money for private
piano lessons, but she also paints very imaginatively. She is trying to make a
violin, which, along with other fragments of things, she keeps in a special
box. (When she is famous, she will print M. K. on all her possessions.) She
takes long walks at night, where ordinary girls would be afraid to go, and
one time she sits under a window, thrills to a Beethoven symphony, coming
over the radio. "Wonderful music like this was the worst hurt there could
be." To divert herself from it, she subjects herself to physical pain by scrap-
ing rocks against her thigh until her hand is bloody.

Always now she is aware of a feeling of change. "All the time she was
excited. In the morning, she couldn't wait to get out of bed and start going
for the day. And at night she hated like hell to have to sleep again." She
daydreams of herself as a heroine, saving Mr. Singer from disaster, conduct-
ing an orchestra with all her heroes and friends in the audience. Refusing to
wear her sister's cast-off clothes, she also refuses to take the same courses in

school; she takes mechanical shop. She has in her mind plans (as strong as those for music) for belonging to one of the "bunches" of kids in school. She decides that a party will help. She is surprised when the seemingly grown-up kids respond gaily to the party-crashing antics of the younger kids in the neighborhood, but relieved, too. "And about the bunch she wanted to be with everyday. She would feel different in the halls now, knowing that they were not something special but like any other kids. It was O.K. about the ruined party. But it was all over. It was the end." Realizing this night that she has changed, she dismisses the party and dresses for the last time in her tomboy clothes.

"Mick, I come to believe we all gonna drown," says Bubber, watching the relentless rain. What he says is very true, certainly; this is what is happening to all Mick's plans. First, she loses Bubber's companionship when, with childlike cruelty but more out of her extravagant imagination, she frightens him with the prospect of the electric chair in Sing Sing for having shot Baby Wilson. That night, Mick, sorry, kisses his little body desperately. But "After he shot Baby the kid was not ever like little Bubber again." Everyone began to call him by his right name, George. McCullers' insight into George's behavior, his change suddenly from a quiet, sweet child to an introverted, solitary premature adolescent, is frighteningly real. "But he was a different kid—George—going around by himself always like a person much older and with nobody, not even her, knowing what was really on his mind." She retreats further into the "inside room."

Mick's self-respect becomes insidiously impaired as the family grows poorer. "They were nearly as poor as factory workers. Only nobody could look down on them." She follows Mr. Singer, talks to him. "For some reason it was like they had a secret together. Or like they waited to tell each other things that had never been said before," except that *he* tells *her* nothing. She imitates his habits. Ironically, she believes that Brannon hates her because she and Bubber once stole some candy from the café. Actually, he is one of the few people with whom she might have freely, naturally talked. Harry, her Jewish neighbor, is her friend: they talk, play together and plot to kill Hitler. Harry has a crush on Jake Blount, whose raging against society gives Harry, who is hypersensitive about his Jewishness, new ideas.

McCullers subtly builds up the process of sexual awakening. Sitting on the steps talking to Harry, Mick notices that "There was a warm boy smell about him." Confused, she reverts to their early childhood horse-play, but in the midst of it they become aware of each other's bodies.

> She felt his ribs against her knees and his hard breathing as she sat on him. They got up together. They did not laugh any more and the alley was very quiet. As they walked across the dark

back yard for some reason she felt funny. There was nothing to feel queer about, but suddenly it had just happened. She gave him a little push and he pushed her back. Then she laughed again and felt all right.

When they go swimming in the country, Mick suggests that they swim naked. Facing each other's nudity, they are suddenly very bashful. But lying on the grass, they naturally succumb to the urges within them. Afterwards, Harry thinks they have sinned, so he runs away to work in Birmingham. "She felt very old, and it was like something was heavy inside her. She was a grown person now, whether she wanted to be or not."

Later, although her family kindly forbids it, she is obliged to work in the ten-cent store. Once, in need of Mr. Singer, she goes to look for him but is frightened by the darkness that as a child she had loved. After Singer's suicide, she feels trapped into womanhood and servitude.

> Next to music, beer was best... But now no music was in her mind... It was like she was shut out from the inside room... It was like she was too tense. Or maybe because it was like the store took all her energy and time.
> It was like she was mad all the time. Not how a kid gets mad quick so that soon it is all over—but in another way. Only there was nothing to be mad at ... the store hadn't asked her to take the job... It was like she was cheated... Only nobody had cheated her. So there was nobody to take it out on. However, just the same she had that feeling. Cheated.
> But maybe it would be true about the piano and turn out O.K. Else what the hell good had it all been... It had to be some good if anything made sense. And it was too and it was too and it was too and it was too. It was some good.
> All right!
> O.K.!
> Some good.

Doctor Copeland: Educated in the North, Doctor Copeland returned to the South to lead his people out of sickness and servitude. He has read the great writers on spiritual and economic freedom and named his children after them. To them, "He would talk and talk, but none of them wanted to understand." He was almost Calvinistic in the way of life he wanted to prescribe for his family: "He knew how the house should be. There could be no fanciness—no gaudy calendars or lace pillows or knick-knacks—but everything in the house must be plain and dark and indicative of work and the real true purpose." But his wife, Daisy, taught them meekness, submission, superstition. Years later, Portia says,

> "Us talk like our own Mama and her peoples and their peoples be
> fore them. You think out everything in your brain. While us rathe
> talk from something in our hearts that has been there for a long
> time. That's one of them [our] differences."
>
> "You all the time using that word—Negro," said Portia. "And
> that word haves a way of hurting peoples' feelings . . . "

When *her* talk hurts *his* feelings, he refuses her gentleness: "No. It is
foolish and primitive to keep repeating this about hurt feelings." His stern
dedication to his "true purpose" has alienated all his children but Portia; ye
between them no understanding and mutual sympathy is possible.

Meeting his son for the first time in a long time, he can not submit to
his desire for common emotional expression, can only reproach him for not
becoming the ideal leader of his people Copeland had tried to teach him to
be. All his life Copeland has carried within him the hurt and humiliation o
the white man's domination. To protect himself from the excessive emotional responses he naturally feels compelled to make, he has adopted a
stoic attitude. The fervor of his dedication to ideas, "to the one strong true
purpose," his obsession with his mission, his really valiant devotion to his
duty as a doctor, divert his thoughts and energies and become media for
sublimation of violence and forces of repression upon the real violence, the
genuine Negro feelings smouldering inside him, that cause him such frustra
tion and anxiety. Dying of T.B., he realizes that he has failed, but actually
he has probably saved himself from the gallows. When he was young,

> The feeling that would come on him was a black, terrible,
> Negro feeling. He would try to sit in his office and read and medi
> tate until he could be calm and start again. . . . But sometimes th
> calmness would not come. He was young and the terrible feeling
> would not go away with study.

When he is old, the Negro blues of his people, that wonderful emotional cathartic, tries to come out of him: "it happened that he began sway-
ing slowly from side to side and from his throat there came a sound like a
kind of singing moan." But even the singing he suppresses, does not surrender to. One time, years ago, he struck down his wife with a poker. The
"He wrestled in his spirit and fought down the evil blackness" with very
hard work and a lofty, impossible ideal. When, with the dignity of a white
man, he goes to the court house to object to the atrocity perpetrated upon
his son, Willie, in prison, he is beaten as though he were a lowly "nigger."

> He waited for the terrible anger and felt it arise in him . . . he
> broke loose sudenly from their grasp. In a corner he was sur-
> rounded. They struck him on the head and shoulders with their

clubs. A glorious strength was in him and he heard himself laughing aloud as he fought. ... He kicked wildly with his feet... even struck at them with his head... Someone behind kicked him in the groin and he fell to his knees on the floor.

The old, suppressed violence finally came out and was suppressed again by other forces.

Copeland and Blount are afflicted with the same problem. They try to sublimate their personal frustrations into public causes and their manner of fighting for these causes further intensifies their neuroses by alienating the very people they wish to convince; this increases their own loneliness, and the poison of narcissism festers in their spirits. Copeland is happiest when he is being listened to even though he knows it will do no good; his joy comes from the feeling of being respected, of being unlike other Negroes, of having a part of himself become absorbed into the minds of his listeners. "In the room there was a murmur. Hysteria mounted. Doctor Copeland choked and clinched his fists. He felt as though he had swelled up to the size of a giant. The love in him made his chest a dynamo, and he wanted to shout so that his voice could be heard throughout the town."

That he might have found a friend in Blount is indicated in the scene in which they talk all night, but finally end in disagreement. Although the torment in their souls is similar, their ideas and their race ultimately conflict. More than the success of their reform programs, they need friendship, an end to loneliness. "Yet now he [Copeland] could not clearly recall those issues which were the cause of their dispute." Copeland was more at peace when he could talk to the uncomprehending deaf-mute, Singer. Even when men have the opportunity to admit into their solitude a kindred spirit, the habit and nature of introversion prevent it. Copeland goes, a sick, broken failure, to his wife's father's farm where he will die alone in a house full of his own people. Hope, a feeble hope that the future will be better is all any of them have. "I will return soon," Doctor Copeland says. The reader is less optimistic.

Jake Blount: Blount is even less fortunate than Dr. Copeland, who at least leads a routine, useful life as nominal compensation for spiritual stagnation. Intellectually, geographically, Blount is a drifter. He, like Copeland, must be obsessed with a purpose if his neurosis is not to become psychosis. Doctor Copeland early observes, "Then with a sudden clinical interest he observed the white man's face, for in his eyes he saw a strange, fixed, and withdrawn look of madness." When he was younger, Blount drove a nail into his own hand. This self initiation into martyrdom was a neurotic act of identification with the universal significance of Christ's suffering. To be like Christ, loudly, defiantly to preach anarchy for the benefit of men even as those men laugh and scorn, gives Blount a feeling of importance, usefulness and a cold kind of fraternal feeling that pathetically has little effect upon his loneliness. He speaks of "we" who understand, thus creating a mythical brotherhood to which he belongs, an "in-the-know" minority, whose uniqueness reflects a superiority upon and generates a feeling of lofty "to-getherness" in him. "We have opened our eyes and have seen. We're like people from way off yonder somewhere."

His emotional release is in talking, ranting, raving drunkenly about the brotherhood of man and in fighting those who laugh at him. Singer is a will-ing, attentive, supposedly comprehending listening-post. Afterwards, he is immensely relieved as though talking achieved a recalcitrant orgasm. He lives in mangy rooms. "The loneliness in him was so keen that he was filled with terror." One night, he yells into the street a bitter denunciation of those who are sleeping nearby, but what he really wants is attention, to feel that in that nightmare hour he is not entirely alone. *His* privacy is *too* in-tense.

He likes working at the side-show because "It eased him to push through the crowds of people. The noise, the rank stinks, the shouldering contact of human flesh soothed his jangled nerves." Writing slogans on buildings with chalk, exchanging comments in this way with a fanatical evangelist, also gives him an evanescent feeling of importance and fellow-ship. When he fails to achieve unanimity with Copeland, "Jake looked at him once before, sobbing with violence, he rushed headlong from the room." Also, he is a little paranoid: "Always he felt someone was laughing a him."

A riot develops at the side-show. Jake runs from it. "In his confusion h had run all the way across the town to reach the room of his friend. And Singer was dead. He began to cry." And he thinks of Copeland and goes to find him.

> ... Copeland had said to him, "Do not attempt to stand alone." There were times when that was best.... Still the terrible anger that they had felt that night had later been hard to under-stand. Copeland *knew* ... And what had they done? They had turned to quarrel with each other... they might be able to work together after all. If they didn't talk too much.

But Copeland is gone to the country to die among his own people, a stranger. Jake is very tired now. He has accomplished nothing except to meet a few friends and to lose them. Without even knowing it, he, like Mick, loses Biff, the one steady, sane man who really wants to be his frien but who is allowed to help him only in a material fashion. He leaves the town. "And in the dream there was a peculiar horror in wandering on and on through the crowd and not knowing where to lay down the burden he had carried in his arms so long." The burden is not really the great unknown truth but his own individual personality and loneliness. "But was this flight or was it onslaught? Anyway, he was going. All was to begin another time... He would not leave the South... There was hope in him, and soon perhaps the outline of his journey would take form."

McCullers very subtly designs a pattern of attraction and repulsion among the four characters. Biff is potentially a friend with whom any of them might talk. Like Singer, he would listen, but unlike Singer, he would ask questions, be too overtly interested. Mick likes Blount and is very tender toward Copeland; Copeland and Blound are drawn together only to finally repel each other. (Probably the happiest people in the book are the other Negroes, especially Portia, Highboy and Willie, who have a warm bond.) Aside from their loneliness, they have their regard for Singer in common. But when, one day, they all appear at his room at once, the atmosphere is irremediably strained. Singer reflects upon this, in a letter to the feeble-minded Antonapoulos,

> Then you would think when they are together they would be like those of the Society [of the deaf and dumb] who meet at the convention in Macon this week. But that is not so. They all came to my room at the same time today. They sat like they were from different cities. They were even rude, and you know how I have always said that to be rude and not attend to the feelings of others is wrong... I write it to you because I think you will understand.

One explanation may be that they were all very conscious that they had mutually shared their lives (worse than sharing their lovers) with Singer and each felt naked in the presence of the others. This further supports the idea that people do not really desire a wide understanding, that one confidant is all they can afford their spirits. The real dilemma is that even the telling to one person does not destroy the loneliness, the sense of isolation. Each man is doomed to be an island unto himself in the midst of a swarming continent of outside pressures, demands and responsibilities.

NATURALISM:

Joyce Carol Oates's
*With Shuddering Fall**

The young writer who has a vision is rare; rarer still is one who succeeds in a first novel in projecting a haunting sense of that vision. At
twenty-six, Joyce Carol Oates in *With Shuddering Fall* is focusing a vision,
glimpses of which she offered in her collection of short stories, *By the North
Gate*, published last year to unusual critical celebration. While *With Shuddering Fall* can hardly be the novel many predicted, it is much too early to
expect genius from one who has so recently shown signs of it.

Miss Oates sees life as a race track where men take chances, chance
being in the very nature of things. Because she depicts everything at the
point of extremity, she has been compared with Faulkner. But violence is
not just a literary reality; it is a fact we live with. And the author succeeds,
finally, in persuading us that the compulsion to violence is a universal so
familiar she need not always trace motives. Melodrama is the risk she runs.

Karen, the central character, a sixteen-year-old small-town girl, is obsessed with a guilt that defines her long before she commits traceable acts of
her own. Amid catastrophe and death, Karen's family and neighbors find
sustenance in the conventions, rituals, ceremonies of the Catholic Church
and their rural way of life. But Karen has always been a stranger among
them. Another stranger, but one who has no sense of guilt, is Shar Rule, a
thirty-year-old auto racer who returns to his dying father's bedside only to
set him and the house afire.

When Shar attempts to seduce her, Karen's sense of guilt and shame
compel her to jerk the car off the road. Shar tells Karen that it will be her
fault if he is forced to kill her father. During a fight between Shar and
Herz, Karen feels first a rapport with, then an estrangement from her
father. "For the moment her shame and guilt might be transformed into

---

pain, concentrated into physical pain; that way she could bear it." Seeking pain as atonement for guilt, she has wrecked the car; later, she allows Shar to rape her; she endures his manifold cruelties and, finally, lets him beat her until he destroys their child. But she is also fulfilling her father's commandment to kill Shar and not to return until she does. Leaving her father beaten almost to death by Shar, she sets out into the world with him, blessed with a temporary damnation. "How right he was to judge her; to find her guilty! She understood his judgment and accepted it." She must leave the father who has understood her and return to him defiled, and thus become one with the community of murderers.

Violence is both willed and accidental in this novel. If some of it seems gratuitous, it is a constant reminder that no one is safe. But man even helps these accidents along. Shar's life is a series of accidents; he is the target of some, the agent of others. His will and blind contingency conspire. The riot at Cherry River began, in a sense, with his "accidental" birth—perhaps before. Numerous incidents in the novel do not relate directly to the main action; but accidents express a submerged community will. "And, as if in answer to the crowd's secret desire, the car spun suddenly out of control." A continually shifting circular design emerges. Out of the violent encounter between Herz and Shar, Karen, the lamb of innocence, is born as a creature of experience.

The novel depicts the dynamic thrust of a complex dialectic. There are those who act and those who repress; those who race, those who don't: sometimes one is a participant, sometimes a witness, sometimes a mere spectator. The central metaphor, the controlling poetic image for the interaction of these opposing relationships, is the circular automobile race track. Lives collide as they race in a cirle; both reckless spectators and daring drivers move closest to death along the rail, on the curves. Karen, a witness, and Shar, a participant, collide at that outer circle. Shar "had always been on the periphery of" Karen's family, and she draws him closer to the rim, where he finally crashes. In the race itself, Shar and Herz collide; the paradox and irony lie in the fact that Karen's nature as witness causes Shar to be drawn to her and thus her father to encounter Shar. So Karen's very passive innocence sets in motion a series of human encounters which end in the massive explosion of the Fourth of July race riots at Cherry River.

The race is "a mock communion" in which spectators are cheated because, though they become the driver, the violence cannot touch them. Shar strives for "speed poised on the invisible point at which control turned into chaos," and the race is a ritual in which the center seems to hold for a moment as the threat of death that terrifies us all is brought careening to the brink, then "mere anarchy is loosed upon the world" once more. Shar wins, kills, dies for us all. Our rejoicing over the victory of the winner is mingled with regret that he has not put an end to anxiety, consummated the inevitable, for his triumph reminds us that other races lie ahead. Ultimately the mock Christ pays the extreme price for his walks on the water. It is this spectacle—of spectators and racers in mock communion—that makes witnesses like Karen suffer. The chaotic landscape, with its little circle of controlled violence, is an outward manifestation of Karen's shattered inscape.

Miss Oates conducts us through the labyrinth of blood kinship and of accidental spiritual and psychological kinships; around dark corners we glimpse our ghostly kin as they elude us, collide with us, but seldom accompany us. Though each character may only vaguely sense his community with certain other characters, the reader knows he is kin to others he knows not of, for the author constantly implies various kinds of kinship. And the race track image helps to control, to enhance, elucidate the significance of this web of relationship. Most of the minor characters exemplify various facets of the major figures and are variations or extensions of the three basic types: witness, spectator, racer.

Next to Karen and Shar, Max is the most significant character. Max is Shar's manager—"a bloated, insatiable spectator, a product of a refined civilization," who can love only those who ritualistically risk death, so that only death makes love possible. "Just as Karen realized she had no existence without the greater presence of someone to acknowledge her (her father; God), so did Max realize that his existence depended upon the life of others." And he loves Karen because she makes all Shar's qualities more vivid with her fears. Max is "the center of their lives! He drew them in to him, sucked them in, his appetite was insatiable."

Shar sums up his own function in life: "I drive a car." For the other drivers "it's money and for me, waiting to die." He has been "so many times around a circle" that he is "sick to death of it; how do you get out of circle but carried out in parts?" He conceives of a good way to die—to feel his body and his car as one soul, then to plow into the spectators. "When I'm out there, there's no bastard that owns me." He forces "cars or people or myself, all the way out, to the limit." His affinity is with machines, but none is as "finely geared and meshed as he," who knows his car better than his own body. Happy only when in control of things, as when he drives, "he came from nowhere and went nowhere. He seemed also to notice nothing. Max says of him, "There was only Shar's will, the deadly whimsical range of his desire," and "the whole world is shrunk down to fit him—he carries it around in his head." Neither good nor evil, sinless, he is a child. Max sees both Shar and Karen as targets and instruments of accidents. But while Sh operates from the stomach and can respond to love only with rage, Karen operates from the heart.

This novel attends, with sometimes too tenacious a scrutiny, to the development of one of the strangest love stories in recent fiction. To carry out her father's command, Karen must plunge into an entanglement with Shar, but since she is incapable of physical violence, she commits the slow psychological violence that the victim uses to destroy the tormentor. She makes sex a means of slowly stripping away Shar's various defenses. Rage is one of them, but it only defines her purpose, helps her to hate him more lucidly, reminding her of what he did to her father. Karen becomes accustomed to "a life that began nowhere and headed nowhere, geographically or morally." Though she screams, "Shar is filled with death!" she discovers soon after that he has filled her with life, with a child; he kills, and he regenerates, both accidentally. But Shar becomes a father-brother-lover image, and Karen achieves both Shar's birth as a loving human being and the death she has willed for him as murderer.

A few times Shar works Karen up to a sexual pitch; and several times he just misses communion with her. But slowly, through his relationship with her, especially the effects of it during their separation, Shar becomes aware of realities outside himself. When Karen finds him at Cherry River, his longing turns instantly to violence upon her, for he wishes to destroy the girl who makes him feel, suffer, and who destroys his control. He does not know that she wants him dead, nor has she told him she is pregnant. "Anger at himself expressed itself in anger at Karen," and he unwittingly aborts the child. Though she now wants the child, she lets him kill it to give him further cause to kill himself. And though her discovery that Shar has learned to love her moves her to love him, she uses his love as a final weapon. "She saw him with wonder. Her heart went out to him, she felt shame for her emotion. I can't help it if I have fallen in love, she thought defensively." But what she says to him is, "You make me sick," and this time it is he who turns the car off the track.

"A hell of a world," Shar said suddenly and self-consciously, "but at least it's my own fault." Thus he is still in control. Full of love for Karen, Shar extends affection to others. "Wish me luck," he says to Mitch, and hugs him. "Had he wasted his life? All life before he had fallen in love was empty, a mockery, a half-world; he could not really remember it as his own." As he races, he thinks of taking the young Negro driver with him, but love excludes the old spite, and Shar, who has always felt that he would never live to be thirty, crashes into the wall. Full of love for Karen, he is convinced, ironically, she can never love him, murderer of her child and (so he thinks) of her father. Max now sees that Karen has set an elaborate, in-

sane trap for Shar; he points at her body as though it were a weapon and
accuses her of murder.

This private psychological and physical violence is enacted on a publi
scale in Cherry River, an hour after Shar's death, which the spectators
blame on the Negro driver. Ironically, the Negro Mitch, the pure-hearted
sacrificial scapegoat and Shar's good friend, becomes the mob's target.

Karen moves barefoot among the rioters, blood from her miscarriage
streaming down her legs. As she begs God to forgive her for killing Shar,
she turns on some rioters and includes them in the communion of guilt, t
community of sinners. One of them, in an anguish of pity, guilt, and
helplessness, kicks her. The riot, sparked by Shar's death, is also her faul
The fact that she is not directly guilty has no psychological relevance for
her; all are guilty of being human, of becoming murderers, and the sentence is life. But after long suffering, grace, of sorts, is possible.

There is in this novel an undeclared but overpowering sense of sin, s
vation, and religion. Karen had almost fainted with happiness after her fir
communion. Through experience she comes to see the soul's struggle as a
reconciliation of paradoxes: "It was as if God were struggling to appear to
her, not in sunlight but in darkness." To rise with Christ, one must first l
down with the devil. The fires of Miss Oates' vision are fueled with the
paradoxes of Blake and Kierkegaard.

By virtue of such power as we have seen at work upon Shar, Karen
emerges cured after a stay in an asylum. Having fulfilled her father's com
mand so well, she returns. But home seems unreal. "Was it a betrayal? N
ground is holy, no land divine, but that we make it so by an exhausting,
deadly straining of our hearts." Bereft of Shar, she is afraid her father wil
disown her, even though he, like Shar, is a killer; like the mob at Cherry
River, he once killed a Negro. Witnessing Shar's and Herz's violence, Ka
had realized that she "could absorb their wrath, drown shuddering in the
fury." She has emerged contaminated. During mass in the hometown
church she realizes that everybody has "initiated me into the communion
killers." She knows she can blame her father for what she did, and still d
her guilt, but she takes full responsibility, for to be the agent of psycholo
cal incitements of violence is to be just as guilty as the person who acts. S
senses also that her neighbors love her for suffering, to "prove to them th
justice of their universe . . . the vague beliefs they mouthed and heard
mouthed to them in the ceremony of the mass." Thus, their relation to h
parallels the spectators' relation to Shar.

Karen and her father forgive and vow love for each other. But brief a
most begrudged declarations are purchased at an exorbitant price; Shar e

periences an hour of human love before his death. Karen, no longer innocent, but no longer a stranger, still has a lifetime before her.

It may be neither possible nor desirable to separate Joyce Carol Oates'
faults from the ultimate excellence of her effects. Could a better crafted
novel have worked its spell as strikingly? Perhaps she belongs with Dos-
toevski and D. H. Lawrence, among those prophetic novelists who achieve
expressive form; without art, they shatter us with vision. If art becalms, vision both damns and saves.

The faults, however, ought to be cited. Too many false moves in technique and structure and false notes in style provide the reader with countless opportunities for directing his gaze elsewhere. Miss Oates seems to
have no ear for the cadences of good prose; brilliant passages have the
charm of accidents. She indulges in an exceeding amount of generalization;
page follows page of description of psychological states over vague periods of
time through an undefined series of episodic situations.

We need to believe every moment that the world really is as bleak,
mean, foul, joyless, and violent as the author, with her total lack of humor,
insists. When we see the world as Karen sees it and encounter men like her
demon lover through her responses, we are convinced. But there appears to
be no method in the author's point-of-view technique. While most of the
novel is appropriately told through the third-person central intelligence of
either Karen or Shar, the author rather arbitrarily shifts to minor characters
without justification. The resulting diffusion of focus is a serious flaw.

With Shuddering Fall could have been a profoundly terrifying novel,
and for brief moments it is. Miss Oates has it in her power to frighten us
much more profoundly than certain recent books that arrogantly insist upon
shock. Had she succeeded in achieving complete credibility in every aspect
of her fable, the result may have been artistically fine, but perhaps humanly
unbearable. We are witnessing the struggles of a major talent who may possibly rise to the level of Eudora Welty, Carson McCullers, Katherine Anne
Porter, and Flannery O'Connor. One can only hope that she will find the
time to devote greater attention to style, technique, and structure without
dilluting the intensity of her vision or scaling down the magnificent terror of
her themes.

EXPERIMENTATION:

Juxtaposition in John Hawkes' *The Cannibal**

In *The Cannibal,* one of the most accomplished American "experimental" novels of the 1940's, John Hawkes makes Spitzen-on-the-Dein representative of Germany during the early stages of the Allied occupation after World War II; it is also the scene of an extended flashback to World War I. With the collapse of normality in every phase of their daily lives during both wars, the people of the town move upon a nightmare landscape. Even in the midst of almost total ruin, aristocratic, majestic Madame Stella Snow, who runs a boardinghouse, feels a sense of community. Most of the major characters are tenants in Stella's house. Stella's sister Jutta, who was about the age of her little girl, Selvaggie, at the end of the first war, has always lived a life of rigid restraint, but now, neither man nor woman, she wallows in listless sexuality with Zizendorf, leader of the insurrection, while the drunken Census-Taker watches. The Duke, a brave tank commander during the war, is already in pursuit of Jutta's effeminate son when the novel begins. Resentful of Stella, Jutta fears her family's and the Duke's aristocratic heritage and has no sense of patriotism. The only person Selvaggia fears is Herr Stintz, the one-eyed school teacher, who plays a dirge on his tuba every night and who is perversely attracted to her. Balamir, escapee from the local asylum, lives in the basement; the real or imagined son of the Kaiser, he thinks of Stella as the Queen Mother.

Fragmented images of the landscape, past and present, are repeated as haunting motifs throughout the novel. The scenic props of the glorious German past rot in the present: flags, brass band instruments. The architecture is expressive of the Germanic concept of the race's soul: the focus in 1914 is the *Sportswelt Brauhaus* and Stella's ancestral house; in 1945, it is the asylum and Stella's rooming house. The novel begins, repeatedly refers to, and ends with the asylum, situated just outside town. Animals make their lairs in rooms vacated by patients. Balamir and his brother inmates do not realize they are out; they merely move on a landscape that is an objec-

*Reprinted from *Masterplots,* edited by Frank N. Magill, copyright 1949, 1952, 1953, 1954, 1960, 1968, 1976, by Frank N. Magill. By permission of the publisher, Salem Press, Inc.

tification of their own private lunacies. The novel is rife with images expressive of the Nordi-Teutonic-Prussian heroic stance and nationalistic tradition; of the relationship between father and son, an exalted notion of family, seen in terms of generations perpetuating ancestral pride; of blustering notions of masculinity and of the enduring long-suffering of females. The degeneration of the race is manifested in dry, sterile, impotent copulation—promiscuity, prostitution, perversion; infected men and women with shaven heads dance a waltz like zombies in a storehouse on the asylum grounds; Allied parachutists rape women whose vaginas are packed with poison; pregnant women expose themselves to death by freezing, while others suckle children as old as six; German soldiers carry suicidal cyanide capsules. These people struggle to survive in a town where there are no clocks, no postal service, no radios, no newspapers, no fluid for embalming corpses; where all the keys for the machines are welded together; where excrement burns in pits, gas explodes in sewers, typhoid breeds in wells, and flabby rubber rafts, corpses, and fog drift in the canal where the ghosts of British tank soldiers come to drink. Across this landscape creep maimed horses, dry cows, terrified birds, mangy chickens, wild dogs that snarl at train wheels, rabid monkeys, and rats. When ravaging animals are turned loose in a world of violent death, mutilation, and disease, and become assimilated into the human population, people begin to respond to one another in animal terms and resort, finally, to cannibalism. In 1914 and again in 1945, an incredible cold grips the landscape; then a damp air descends, the cold dissolves into a fog, and moonlight reveals things soft with rot and the final acts of horror.

Although he has been compared with Kafka, Hawkes resembles him not at all in technique. Kafka's seemingly unreal world is presented rationally. While Hawkes' images seize the reader and hold him in a tension created by forces of repulsion and abnormal attraction, he deliberately attempts to break the illusion of reality by employing literary elements and devices that act upon one another in such a way that the dream becomes reality, making questions of literary appropriateness irrelevant. Elements of parody, black humor, lyricism, mock sentimentality, farce, and the conscious, controlled use of clichés causes frequent, sudden, and absurd shifts in tone and perspective. Through an eclectic method that is more often expressionistic than impressionistic, Hawkes attempts to project a series of images that reflect the mental climate of an ignobly defeated people whose aspirations were pathologically nationalistic. Hawkes uses a point of view strategy which makes great demands of the reader; if the reader co-operates, he finds himself in the same relation to the author that exists between the novel's victims and victimizers. Obsessed by the past, Zizendorf, editor of the town's defunct newspaper, *The Crooked Zeitung,* is the surrounding narrator. As the present action begins, he is preparing to kill Leevey, the Jewish-American soldier who patrols one third of the nation on a rusty motorcycle as its sole overseer. Zizendorf's monomaniacal purpose is to free his people, rebuild the town, and resuscitate the old nationalistic pride. Thus it is appropriate that all the streams of consciousness, the nighttime reveries and nightmare of the other characters, converge and become assimilated in him. He is the voice, the mind, the collective subconscious of vanquished Germany.

With this device, so expressive of his theme, Hawkes shifts frequently from one character to another—illogically, in view of Zizendorf's limited access to the raw materials of his narrative; but there is a kind of Jungian truth in this technique. The shifts are made without preparation, as thoughts shift erratically in a deranged mind. The reader is into a scene; then, suddenly, he is briefly somewhere else; then he is thrust into yet another character's field of vision. Sometimes the shift is made within a sentence. Though there are few scenes of sustained length, Hawkes will present, after a relatively long scene, a series of brief images, bringing the separate action of each character forward a little, usually with ironic effect.

But there is almost none of the sustained stream of consciousness passages one finds in Virginia Woolf or Joyce. Hawkes' characters simply respond to the stimuli the author provides for all their senses. In Hawkes' surreal (but all too real) world, the reader's senses are assaulted by violent odors, ghastly sights, eerie sounds, foul tastes; and he feels the touch of so rot. The characters are defined in terms of extreme experiences to which they are always subordinate. A relative lack of individualization gives the effect of a single, many-faceted character. Thus, the all-embracive mind of Zizendorf, the Hitlerian temperament re-emergent, becomes the reader's own consciousness; to his horror, he discovers that it is a consciousness in which values of all kinds are suspended, just as in a dream we commit or witness atrocities upon which we make no judgments. What the reader experiences are extreme moments of bestiality, not as a social creature, but a a beast would experience them—purely.

Hawkes uses a technique that is more poetic and cinematic than novelistic. The shifts among points of view are made by a method of juxtaposition, or montage. The juxtaposition of poetic images, which are charged with vivid visual components expressive of theme, character, and event, has the effect one experiences when two shots in a movie are juxtaposed to create a third dimension of emotion or thematic significance. The rhythm of the movie camera is, at its best, the rhythm of poetry rather than that of prose. The montage is essentially the method of Eliot's *The Waste Land*, which, along with "The Hollow Men," is one poetic influence upon *The Cannibal*. Eliot's principle of the objective correlative is basic to this novel. Hawkes externalizes the internal neuroses of a people. The method of juxtaposition operates throughout the book, within each section, each scene, and often within each paragraph and sentence, creating a kind of continuity that proceeds according to a logic quite different from that of a

conventional novel. Here again the effect of pure vision—of things seen as
they are—is apparent. Hawkes' images come to the reader as though from
electronic impulses bounced off the moon rather than from an author; with
the distance of a movie director, he achieves control and restraint in the way
he handles images which assail us as though poured out chaotically by an
extremely undisciplined writer. The roving camera eye—going in and out of
focus, zooming in like a telephoto lens for a microscopic scrutiny of, for instance, the mouth of the dead merchant clotted with cobwebs—is being
very coldly guided. A vividly descriptive style which employs all the devices
of rhetoric enhances the impact of these images.

There is as little order in the sequence of images as there is in the
spread of shrapnel; as though a camera caught it in slow motion, that is
what we see—the explosion of a mine which the reader steps on in Hawkes'
field of view. Just as there are lines of force in an explosion that give it a
unity, which the victim cares little to imagine, so beneath the apparent chaos
of the novel's images and occasional scenes, a pattern of events may be dis-
cerned. The novel is in three parts; the present action in 1945 surrounds an
extended flashback to events in 1914. This structure emphasizes the oneness
of the two wars; and within each chapter the method of juxtaposition conveys
a sense of the simultaneity of all events.

If in Part I Hawkes tries to make the reader feel he is having hallucina-
tions, he deliberately eases him into a rather traditional narrative occurring
around 1914. Stella sings in the Sportswelt Brauhaus; Ernst, the son of
Herman Snow, the proprietor, falls in love with her. A coward, Ernst re-
sents his father, a virile lover, sportsman, and soldier, who urges him to
"join in the chase"; sullenly, bitterly observing the masculine way of the
frequenters of the Brauhaus, Ernst, too, wants to earn a place in Valhalla.
When Cromwell, a friend of Herman, takes Stella home in a carriage, Ernst
desperately runs after them. An English traitor, Cromwell admires the
German spirit of nationalism, tradition of heroism, and ideals of conquest;
he is eager to see it demonstrated in a prolonged war.

War begins the next day. Hawkes presents the members of Stella's family, including the children's nurse Gerta. The mother dislikes the world she
sees, but the ninety-year-old father, a general, who is dying, shouts "War!"
at breakfast and "Victory!" at noon, thinking the war is already over. Women
and children, Hawkes shows, are the innocent victims of such insane masculinity: a lone British plane falls in the marketplace and the mother is killed.
Stella nurses the old general, who dies with his plumed helmet on his chest.
Already prefigured in the death of Stella's parents, the decline of the German
nation is symbolized by the death of the old horse that moves between the
lower world of dogs and the upper world of the mountains where Stella and
Ernst go on their honeymoon. A parallel to this old horse is the legless,

headless statue of a horse in the square, a monument to the heroic past. When Cromwell arrives in the mountains, gleefully reciting the details of the war and praising the German troops, Ernst and Stella return to Stella's house; in her father's room, Ernst is dying of a fever.

A further suggestion of decline is Herman Snow's failure as a soldier and a lover; he encounters Gerta in the wreckage of the Brauhaus where she goes in the course of her promiscuous prowling among soldiers. Hawkes' montage method operates with great rapidity, shuttling back and forth over the ruined town (images of which are a mild foreshadowing of the devastation of World War II) between Gerta and Herman and Stella and Ernst; the strong women take care of the weak men. The role of coincidence in such a world is demonstrated when Gerta brings Herman to the very room where Stella is nursing Ernst. Herman, who had imagined, in his own delirium, of passing on to Ernst the spirit of love and war, accuses his son of "feigning."

At the conclusion of the 1914 section, Hawkes focuses on Jutta. A student of architecture when the war began, she has gone into a convent and is seriously ill with a fever; she is a victim of the stern love of the mother superior and is violated by the Ober-Leutnant who is staying overnight at the convent. It is her vision of life that Hawkes would have us see: not miraculous, yet clear; not right, though undeniable. The perspective on life which circumstances give these people is one divested of a moral dimension; it is simply clear (and by it we see clearly and are terrified) and undeniable (though under "normal" circumstances we daily deny it to maintain our precarious sanity).

By returning, at the opening of Part III, to Zizendorf where he left him on the embankment of the Autobahn, Hawkes makes his structure comment thematically upon his raw material: the present encloses and carries forward the past. The bizarre parallels of nightmares pervade the novel, merging past and present. While the Duke pursues Jutta's son, Jutta, who has been taking care of the drunken Census-Taker, sleeps; but her little girl, Selvaggia, watches for her brother at the window. Passing through the sleeping mother's room, Herr Stintz finally goes to Selvaggia. Though his single eye is the threatening moon in whose glare all horror occurs, Selvaggia goes with him, and thus, like most Hawkes victims, collaborates in her own violation. He wants the child, who has been protected from the slaughter of the Allied offensive, to witness her father's, Zizendorf's, murder of Leevey; then Stintz intends to inform. While this psychological rape is going on, the Duke corners Jutta's son in a wrecked movie theater, where Stella's son, who returned from the war with only one leg, lives with his wife; Stella's son is flattered by the Duke's visit. Before Zizendorf kills Leevey, Hawkes provides a long flashback to the day when the American Colonel and

Leevey first came to the town to execute Miller, the pastor who had
changed his views during the war. Stintz, out of a motiveless malice, and
the Mayor, from fear of the Colonel, had co-operated: Zizendorf had been
forced to join the firing squad and it was his bullet that killed the pastor.
Miller fell into the frozen canal, where his body thawed and bloated in the
fog. It is appropriate that Zizendorf should begin his insurrection by killing
a Jew. But Hawkes makes of Leevey merely a simple soldier who says, "Hi
ya, Mac," and wishes he were back in the delicatessen. When Jutta's husband was reported missing in Siberia, Zizendorf took over both Jutta and
the editorship; Hawkes connects Zizendorf with the husband by having
Jutta, seconds before Zizendorf kills Leevey, reread a letter in which her
husband tells of shooting a Russian leader from his horse. After Leevey
strikes the log in the road, Hawkes shifts back to the morning of his death
when, ironically, he had lain with a vicious German girl who infected him
with disease. With the insurrection under way, Hawkes has Stella, the
strong woman whom Zizendorf admires, recall the riot in the insane asylum,
a riot that began among the monkeys kept for experiments and spread to
the psychopaths. Under Stella's leadership, it was the women, bereft of
men, who put down the riot. The continuation of this ironic juxtaposition
climaxes the book: with the institution of a new government, the insane
people who have been at large return to the madhouse. Society's pathologi-
cal drives are pushed underground once more, while their manifestations
are worked out in various guises of normality until the nightmare of history
visits us again. Childhood fears, in Hawkes' prophetic vision, prove to refer
to the childhood of the race which civilization never entirely outgrows.

When the riot began, Stella was strangling a mangy chicken under the
gaze of Balamir, who had just escaped from the asylum. As the Duke hacks
up the body of Jutta's son with a rusty cane sword as though the child were
a fox, furious with himself for his lack of aristocratic finesse, Zizendorf tosses
Leevey's body among countless other dead soldiers in the swamp; handbills
inciting the people to rise up against the Allies are being printed in the
chicken house behind Stella's place; Stella is nursing Balamir, who, ironically, is thinking of himself as the one who will free his people and rebuild
the town; learning from Selvaggia of Stintz's betrayal, Zizendorf bludgeons
him with the old man's tuba, carts the body to the Mayor's house, sets fire
to it, while the Mayor sleeps fitfully, as he has throughout the novel,
afflicted with chronic nightmares of Miller. As Zizendorf goes to sleep with
Jutta, Selvaggia, seeing the fire, stays awake with her fears. Stella accepts
the Duke's invitation to dinner (she does not know that she will eat the
body of her nephew whom she has rejected as having no resemblence to
her aristocratic family); a few seconds later Zizendorf's handbill invites her to
kill Americans. Thus, she becomes one of the cannibals of her reverie in
1914. Ironically, the Duke is driven to the extreme act of cannibalism at
that very moment when Zizendorf has succeeded (or so he is convinced) in

restoring order and well-being; nor does the Duke know that Zizendorf has made him Chancellor; other "qualified" persons have been appointed to positions in the new government. Hawkes' irony asserts that Zizendorf's methods perpetuate and will ultimately reaffirm the kind of atrocity the Duke has committed, for the German (and in a sense all) national ego grows out of the carnage of its past wars. The piecemeal mutilation of Ernst in his bungling duels anticipates the butchering of Jutta's son; Ernst dies clutching one of the Christ figures carved by an old idiot in a shack near the mountain hotel. Men become Christs or cannibals.

The Cannibal is a short novel. It can be experienced in one sitting, just as one can suffer a nightmare in one sleeping. But just as the aura of some nightmares persists throughout the day, this is a nightmare from which the reader as cannibal is a long time waking.

THE POPULAR NOVEL:

James M. Cain's *The Postman Always Rings Twice**

Three related genres that developed in the novel form during the 1930's were the hard-boiled private detective (which departed from the genteel English novel of detection), the proletarian (which derived from European naturalism and American selective realism), and the tough guy (which derived from the former two). But perhaps for the best and most influential work of all three genres "the tough-guy novel" is a good term: Dashiell Hammett's *The Maltese Falcon,* published in 1929, and Raymond Chandler's *The Big Sleep,* published in 1939, in the private detective realm; B. Traven's *The Death Ship,* which appeared in an American edition in 1934, among proletarian novels; and Horace McCoy's *They Shoot Horses, Don't They?* published in 1935, among the pure tough-guy books are all minor classics in American literature. These and similar novels expressed the mood of American society during the depression, influenced action in motion pictures, affected the tone and attitude of more serious writers, and inspired certain European novelists during the 1940's. The quintessence of all these is James M. Cain's *The Postman Always Rings Twice.*

Although Frank Chambers, the twenty-four-year-old narrator of Cain's novel, belongs to that legion of unemployed who became tramps of the road, hoboes of the rails, and migrant workers, Cain is not deliberately interested in depicting the social ills of his time; if there is an attack on conditions that produced a man like Frank, it is only implicit. Frank is an easygoing fellow, remarkably free of bitterness, even when given cause; although he commits murder and pistol whips a blackmailer, he is not willfully vicious. A spontaneous creature of action whose psychological nature readily accommodates ambivalent attitudes, he can be fond of Nick Papadakis and weep at his funeral, yet seduce his young wife Cora, and twice attempt to kill him.

And although this novel is concerned, as many of Cain's are, with murder and other forms of violence, and although it satisfies momentarily the average American's inexhaustible craving for details of crime and punishment, it cannot be classified as a detective tale. Cain, like the readers he has in mind, is fascinated by the intricacies of the law and of insurance claims, but his primary interest is in presenting an inside view of the criminal act. However, Frank is no gangster and Cora is no moll; they are not far removed in status or aspiration from the average anticipated reader of Cain.

For Frank and Cora lie down in the great American dreambed of the 1920's only to wake up in a living nightmare in the 1930's. A lurid decade produced such a lurid relationship and such a lurid tale. When they meet at Nick's Twin Oaks Tavern on a highway outside Los Angeles, Frank has just been thrown off a truck, having sneaked into the back for a ride up from Tiajuana, and Cora is washing dishes in the restaurant. To demonstrate the animal impact of their encounter, Cain has them meet on page 5, make love on page 15, and decide to murder the obese, middle-aged Greek on page 23. Sharing the dream of getting drunk and making love without hiding, they go on what Cain calls "the Love-Rack." He regards the concept of "the wish that comes true" as a terrifying thing. This terror becomes palpable as soon as Frank and Cora believe that they have gotten away with murder and have acquired money, property, and freedom.

But in the background each has another dream which mocks the shared realization of the immediate wish. Cora came to Hollywood from a small town in Iowa bemused by the dream most girls of the Thirties cherished: to become a movie star. She failed, and Nick rescued her from a hash house. But basically her values are middle-class, and above all she wants respectability, even if murder is the prerequisite. An anachronism in the age of technology, though he has a certain skill as a garage mechanic, Frank desires to be always on the move, compelled by something of the spirit of the open road that Whitman celebrated. For a moment, but only for a moment, he shares this romantic, idyllic vision with Cora. After the failure of their first attempt to murder Nick, they set out together for a life of wandering. Thus, in the criminal affair of these lovers, these deliberate outsiders, two central dreams of the American experience—unrestrained mobility and respectable sedentariness—and two views of the American landscape—the open road and the mortgaged house—collide. As the dreams finally betray them, they begin, ironically, to turn on each other, for basically what Frank wants is Cora, the sexual dynamo, and what Cora wants is an instrument to be used to gain her ends—money and respectability. Though she may convince herself that the right man, instead of a fat foreigner, is a necessary part of her aspirations, this man would soon wake up in the wrong dream.

While the novel's larger thematic dimensions exist in the background, as a kind of fable of the American experience, giving it a lasting value in our literature, Cain is more immediately concerned with the lovers and with the action that results from their wish. This action keeps in motion certain elements that almost guarantee the reader's interest: illicit love; murder; the smell of tainted money; sexual violence that verges on the abnormal; and the strong characterizations of such men as Sackett, the district attorney; Katz, the eccentric lawyer; and Madge, the pick-up who takes Frank to South America to capture jaguars. Cain plays upon the universal wishes of the average American male.

What fascinates serious readers of literature is Cain's technique for manipulating reader response. Not only does he almost automatically achieve certain thematic ironies inherent in his raw material, but the ironies of action are stunningly executed. For instance, Frank cons Nick out of a free meal, but the con backfires in a way when Nick cons Frank into staying on to operate the service station; thus Frank becomes involved in a situation that will leave three people dead. After recovering from what he took to be an accident in the bathtub, Nick searches for Frank and persuades him to return to the roadside restaurant, thus helping to bring about his own death. Cleared of killing the Greek, Frank and Cora collect the insurance. Later, when she is waiting for a taxi to leave Frank, Cora sticks a note for him in the cash register; it refers to their having killed the Greek for his money. But Frank catches her and insists that he loves her; to test his love, Cora, who is now pregnant, swims so far out to sea that Frank will have to help her back; he does help her, but driving back from the beach, they have a wreck and she is killed. The police find the note in the cash register and conclude that Frank has engineered the wreck so that he can have all the money. Because he cannot be tried twice for killing the Greek, they will execute him for murdering Cora. A careful pattern of minor ironies contributes to the impact of the major ones.

Cain's structural techniques are impressive. The swift execution of the basic situation in the first twenty-three pages has been noted, and each development, each scene, is controlled with the same narrative skill; inherent in each episode is the inevitability of the next. Everything is kept strictly to the essentials; the characters, for instance, exist only for the immediate action; there is almost no exposition as such. Cain is the acknowledged master of pace. Violence and sexual passion are thrust forward at a rate that is itself part of the reader's vicarious experience. Contributing to this sense of pace is the swift rhythm of the dialogue, which also manages to keep certain undercurrents flowing. Frank's character justifies the economy of style, the nerve-end adherence to the spine of the action. Albert Camus modeled the style of *The Stranger* on Cain's novel, and Meursault is cut to the pattern of

Frank Chambers. But Cain has written what has been called a pure novel, for his deliberate intentions go no further than the immediate experience, brief as a movie is, as unified in its impression as a poem usually is. Though Frank writes his story on the eve of his execution, Cain does not even suggest the simplest moral: crime does not pay. An intense experience, which a man tells in such a way as to make it, briefly, our experience, it is its own reason for being. Camus' novel, however, operates on this premise only in the first half; in the second, he begins to develop a philosophical point of view that affects man in every phase of life.

For Cain, the postman, whose custom is always to ring twice, rang thrice. This first novel is one of America's all-time best sellers and has gone through a great many editions; Cain adapted it to the stage; and it was made into a famous motion picture. After thirty years it is still being read widely, both as popular entertainment and as a work of art of a very peculiar sort, respected, with severe qualifications, by students of literature.

VISION:

Conrad's Vision and the Hero-Witness Relationship in
Victory, Lord Jim, "Heart of Darkness," "Youth," and
"The Secret Sharer"

In *Victory*, Conrad is concerned with that tremendous theme which
commands his best works: civilized man's conflict with himself, with civilization and with the natural environment. Modern man's behavior is rooted in
the manners and morals of his society but the roots go deeper, into man's
actively primitive drives; not free from the elemental environment that
spawned him, the reek of primordial mud still clinging to him, civilized man
continues to be compelled by the tenebrous, inscrutable, irrepressible
forces that moved primitive men; in our mechanized, ultra-mental civilization, man still gropes in darkness by the light of an illusory vision of the
world made in the image of his aspirations.

The book is concerned primarily with Western civilization, in which the
male is not only the creator of technological marvels but is the romantic
quester, too, encouraged in his folly, in various ways, by the female. But it
is always the woman who remains sufficiently grounded in the elemental
drives to survive and, by sacrifice and dissembling, to protect the man to
whom she belongs. In *Victory*, Conrad creates a certain embracive vision of
life in which the basically primitive, animal, irrational nature of civilized
man is made to perform in an area of sea and island wilderness, an environment that is fundamentally wild and hostile, especially to men who think
they have, spiritually and materially, risen above it.

Before looking with detailed scrutiny at the book, to indicate what kind
of world, of men and women, the book depicts and to explicate what we
discover, a few technical considerations, which bear upon the novel's intention, should be noted.

The narrator, if he is not the author himself, is sufficiently close to
Conrad's basic view that his interpretive remarks may be taken as commentary meant to elucidate the theme, to make clear the author's point of view.
Out of a careful examination of the narrator's remarks, a character may
emerge, but he becomes so boldly inventive in those events which David-

son could not have related to him, about which no one person could have known, that one must accept him, not as a person whose intelligence of events is inconsistent with credibility but as one who *invents* with impunity; at a certain point he ceases to be a *witnessing character* and becomes a *creative witness*.

The narrator's diction is very florid but precise, both aspects enhancing the lushness, the hugeness of the theme, of the wild environment, the large actions and of the thoughts of the characters. A high key of tone is maintained; a complexity of texture is created. The rhetoric always renders with a heavy hand but the strange effect achieved is one of pervasive subtlety. Tension, suspense and character revelation are actually enhanced by a style that seems to leave very little unstated. Nature is made to reflect, in overwhelming imagery, the conflicts between men and between men and women who are recurrently described in characteristic images: Ricardo, for instance, is seldom mentioned without some variation on a feline image, which is emphasized when violence, insidious or overt, is imminent. In this way, little doubt is permitted as to what, how, where, why and by whom events occur. While in some writers this may be a fault, in Conrad it is a forceful virtue.

The book's most obvious device is that of repetition in many of its possible functions: symbolic images, colors, certain actions recur in variations; character description is constantly reiterated; certain relationships, events reappear in variation, for instance, Jones and his henchmen insidiously take over Schomberg's hotel just as they do Heyst's settlement, in each case forcing Pedro upon the "host" as a servant. These repetitions not only emphasize character traits and relationships, the state of the environment, but from them emerge many of the book's most meaningful statements; for instance, Lena says to both Heyst, whom she loves, and to Ricardo, whom she resolves to kill for Heyst, "I will be what you want," which not only makes a comment about all three characters but becomes a statement about woman's role as she feels it and as man, in a different way, imagines it.

The story is rich in symbols that are repeated with a frequency commensurate to their value. Secondarily, the characters are symbols, and certain environmental aspects operate symbolically, as do both human and natural acts. Every fictional element is thoroughly detailed and fully operative, nothing irrelevant is stated, and every statement functions to its full value.

Time functions in many aspects as a structural principle; for instance, out of the not always obvious shifts in time from present to past to future or from future to past (especially in the section dealing with Jones' siege of the island) much of the suspense and tension is created. In the first 54 pages (the first part), all the strands are set out and the novel is telescoped, end-

ing on a note of suspense which introduces Jones and his men. In the ensu-
ing sections, those events are recaptitulated in dramatically rendered detail,
which serves to engross the reader in that which, foreshadowed in the first
part, excited his curiosity. The viewpoint of the first section is primarily
that of the world, with Davidson as messenger, and following the intensive
middle section, in which events occur away from the world's scrutiny,
Davidson reappears to witness and to relate the tale's *denouement*. To
achieve the book's superb dramatic effects, the modified third person omniscient viewpoint is almost imperative.

. . .

One of the major principles operative in the book is that of opposition,
suggested immediately by the discussion of coal and diamonds: storm and
stress versus stasis; civilization and the primitive; East and West; national
rivalry; racial opposition—whites dominating yellow and black races; the sea
and the land; man and nature; survival and nonsurvival; thought and action;
force and passivity; submission and resistance; insidious and overt evil versus
the ways of good; idealism and romanticism versus practicality and reality;
dissembling and diplomacy versus overt behavior; piety and impiety;
civilized and primitive; good and evil; animalistic and rational; tame and ferocious, men and women characters. But the mere conflict of opposites is
not allowed to prevail. Opposites attract not only to conflict but to com-
mingle, to issue in meaningful combinations. The interdependence or attraction of like and unlike results in relationships which are either harmonious
or eventually erupt into further dissociations which provide the book's
meanings: Heyst, the imperfect, reflective, loveless, impious man is attracted to Lena, the near-perfect, unreflective, loving, pious woman, resulting in the harmony of lovers; Ricardo, the common man, the animal, "follows" Jones, the gentleman, the reflective villain, resulting in a complex operation of evil that finally disrupts into mutual destruction, having caused
Heyst and Lena to achieve mutual understanding and recognition: evil be-
gets good, good intentions beget evil nemesis.

Nature is a flux of opposite forces of destruction and creation, decay
and fructification, which affects human endeavor. Civilization is poised pre-
cariously on primitive imbalance. This may be seen most clearly in the
fringe areas where civilization (the Western world is meant here) and primitive conditions meet in relationships of "hazard and adventure." A kind of
geographical scheme may indicate the natural and social situation in which
the novel is set: in the East Indian islands, Western technology, the white
man (the Teutonic, the Anglo-Saxon, most of the Western ethnic groups are
represented in the novel) and his parasitic society overlays the abiding society of the black and yellow reluctant hosts. Here the comforts of civilization

palliate, for the white man, the rigors of the wilderness, the loneliness of exile; here sea and land are interwoven in the island network. A kind of magic circle (defined by the area of Heyst's wanderings) encloses the islands from both the Occidental and the Oriental mainlands, with which the various island inhabitants maintain a nominal contact. Slowly, the action of the novel narrows the circle until the crucial events occur only on Heyst's island where vestiges of Western civilization, represented by the characters who conflict there and by the defunct coal company, and the enduring primitive, Alfuro people lead their separate lives. Here all the interrelations of opposing forces are resolved in conflict and in amelioration, but the primitive triumphs; the jungle, as in "Heart of Darkness," shares Lena's victory, which was achieved by her primitive action.

Civilization remains remote and all references to it are negative: damp England kills Morrison, Alma suffered in poverty there, Heyst's father's rejection of it results in his own, Jones is driven out of it in failing to be recognized as one of its aristocracy, Ricardo is a renegade from it, and the sanest men, the story teller and Davidson, choose to live outside it by nominal allegiance to it in their occupation as merchant seamen. And civilization as personified in most of the characters is negative; the women, Lena and Mrs. Schomberg, are more primitive in that they pursue "respectable" or naturally worthy motives. The primitive, then, is the dominant *milieu* in which the various primitive drives become manifested in events.

> He (Heyst) marched into the long grass and vanished—all but the top of his white cork helmet, which seemed to swim in a green sea. Then that too disappeared, as if it had sunk into the living depths of the tropical vegetation, which is more jealous of men's conquests than the ocean, and which was about to close over the last vestiges of the liquidated Tropical Belt Coal Company—A. Heyst, manager in the East. (Anchor edition, p. 24)

Here is an early indication not only of the relationship between civilized man and primitive nature but an implication that nature will triumph, that man's ventures to control, to exploit it are ultimately doomed not only in the large, collective enterprises but in the specific personal one as well. Jones says: "The world is still one great, wild jungle without law." What the natural world is, men too are. Lena notices, in the midst of the crisis, the immobile patience of the forest. But when the conflict comes, the volcano acts up, a thunder storm rages, dies when man is finished with his violence. The "treacherous breeze" that chills Davidson when he comes to Schomberg's to meet Heyst, who has abducted Lena and precipitated the final stage of his nemesis, Lena and Heyst feel too, just before the final conflict. Schomberg's hotel is full of shade, solitude, gloomy silence just as the island is before Jones' arrival. For the white man, this is a very "feverish locality." To suggest the similarity of place and of action, Conrad has Ricardo and Jones set up a gambling room in Schomberg's hotel; the table is green, the room is lit by candles; in the corner is a pile of chairs, and Pedro hovers in the background. On the island, Jones decides to win Heyst's money in gambling; the green table becomes the jungle, strategic use is made of Heyst's candles, the pile of chairs becomes the pile of abandoned coal on the end of the dock, and Pedro hovers in the background.

Life is a gamble in which the basically tame are pitted against the basically wild men.

> It's my (Ricardo's) opinion that men will gamble so long as they have anything to put on a card. Gamble? That's nature. What's life itself? You never know what may turn up. The worst of it is that you never can tell exactly what cards you are holding yourself. What's trumps?—that is the question. See? Any man will gamble if only he's given a chance, for anything or everything. You too—(p. 121)

The gamble is a precarious one of which a man is not always aware. Speaking of the schooner captain who ignorantly escaped death by Ricardo's knife, Ricardo says: "Strange what a little thing a man's life hangs on sometimes—a single word." For Heyst, the word was Lena's "yes" to Ricardo; for Pedro, it was sheer chance that he wasn't knifed. The gamble is a serious matter for the intellectually tame, like Heyst (whose problem is partially that he is afraid to gamble with life): "I have been serious all my life," he tells Lena, and when this fails to suffice he is doomed, because for Jones, intellectually wild, it is a sport. "In fact, I am rather amused," Jones tells Ricardo; but when the game bores him, he is even more deadly. The unfeeling Ricardo tells Schomberg: "Artless, helpless humanity" is "a bloody lot of animated cucumbers." In appropriate contexts, Ricardo asks: "What do you think a man is, a wasp?" a mole, a baby, (to Lena) a reptile, an infant, a salamander, a graven image, a scarecrow? Throughout the book, men are characterized as one, a combination, or all of these.

Like gamblers, men, in moments of danger, think in flashes; thus Heyst's behavior is contrasted to Lena's emotionally profound deliberation. "To love, to slay—the greatest enterprises in life for a man," says Heyst, who has done neither of these. It is masculine to feel "the novelty, the flattered vanity of possessing a woman." Desperation is the lamentable substitute for courage.

The female merely watches the male gamble and when women interfere: "What will come of it?" Davidson asks, referring to Heyst and Lena. "Repentence, I should say," answers the narrator. There is nothing more odious to men in a card game than for a woman to make a noise. Even the nongambler Heyst is distracted by the women's musical noise-making to the extent that he is drawn to the music room.

Women seem to be outside men, closer to the primitive urges in lacking grandiose dreams. To the male, the female is inscrutable, a tempter, a dissembler; they encourage and inspire the dreams and ideals of men. Theirs is the final victory after the deadly, male folly of gambling. Lena and Mrs. Schomberg are passive among men, but when the chips are down, it is they who act. The female is both whore and spirit; Lena's real name is Magdalen Alma. Heyst, Schomberg, Jones, Ricardo are reduced to impotence by Lena, with the help of Mrs. Schomberg.

"You don't know what may be in the quietest of them," Davidson says of Mrs. Schomberg's surprising behavior; she who "seemed not to have enough pluck to lift her little finger." Heyst says of her, "She was protecting her position in life. A very respectable task"; one he fails later to meet, but which Lena doesn't. In a sense that transcends good or bad, women are selfish. Heyst: "Women can deceive men so completely," for which they have a special aptitude. "The petticoat's the trouble," says Ricardo of the dangers of robbing Heyst, but he also says, "There could be no half measures. A man has to trust a woman." Schomberg's cowardly behavior occasions the observation that the last thing women are willing to discover in their men is cowardice. Yet women have "an abstract horror of violence and murder." Lena had a rapturous, proud consciousness of her love for Heyst but she had an innate distrust of the masculine, that reductive strength allied to an absurd, delicate shrinking from recognition of the naked necessity of facts, which never frightened any woman worthy of the name. When Heyst and Lena are about to return to face Jones, "It was the man who broke the silence, but the woman who led the way."

Of mankind, Heyst, remembering his father, observed:

> . . . that the death of that bitter contemner did not trouble the flow of life's stream, where men and women go by thick as dust, revolving and jostling one another like figures cut out of cork and weighted with lead just sufficiently to keep them in their proudly upright posture. (p. 143)

This recalls Davidson's image of Heyst, walking proudly through the green sea of the jungle, his white cork helmet floating in the sunlight. "The use of reason is to justify obscure desires that move our conduct, impulses, passions, prejudices, follies, fears," Heyst's father thought. "For every man is fed on illusions, lest men should renounce life early and the human race come to an end." Heyst's father tried to save Heyst from illusions, causing

him to "renounce life early," but Lena's action does try to prevent the
human race from coming to an end. Action is the first impulse on earth, the
father realized, "the barbed hook, baited with illusions of progress, to bring
out of the lightless void, the shoals of unnumbered generations." But, trying
to avoid action, Heyst "had entered . . . the broad, human path of inconsistencies." Yet for man, there is nothing more painful than sharp contradictions; thus Heyst's desire for solitude, the source of his loneliness. Love is
Heyst's undoing *and* his salvation; in his final hour, when he is no longer
purely self-centered, he does live a few moments. In the ecstasy of sensual
lust, Ricardo is destroyed; Jones' horror of the female is his destruction.

Ricardo believes that a gentleman never loses his temper, is never
committed to ferocity; it is not good form. The world is made up, to him, of
the rich and the poor, of gentlemen and common men. There are money-
slaves who, treated like dogs, are neither grateful nor content, but Ricardo
follows a gentleman; he is in awe of the fact that a gentleman "never
shirks." Between renegade gentlemen and common men exists an attraction.
Of Jones, Ricardo says, "He seemed to touch me inside somewhere"; of
Ricardo, Jones says, "Ricardo is simple, faithful, wonderfully acute." Together they rise above the "buying and selling gang that bosses this rotten
show." To Ricardo, the snob, "foreign nobility (Heyst) ain't much." Jones
believes firmly in racial superiority; and to Heyst, one Chinaman is much
like another. Primitive man is frightened of the cunning, the complex
machinations of civilized evil; the natives seem to speak softly so as not to
break the magic spell that separates them from the invaders. Wang

> had some knowledge of the more superficial rites and ceremonies
> of white men's existence, otherwise so enigmatically remote to his
> mind, and containing unexpected possibilities of good and evil
> which had to be watched for with prudence and care. (p. 151)

Native life, for the whites, is a mere play of shadows among which the
white man "can walk . . . unaffected and disregarded in pursuit of incomprehensible aims and needs."

The negative Western culture is represented by many characters,
Schomberg, Ricardo, Jones, the music man and his wife, because it is complex. But the Oriental high culture is represented only by the Chinese merchant and by Wang, the impoverished rejecter of it. Because of its simplicity, only one representative is needed for the lower forms of Oriental culture: Pedro, the alligator hunter; although, suggestively, in a more positive
way, there are the Alfuro people, Wang's wife in particular.

In Conrad's view, generally, this is what the natural world, life, civilization, men and women, human nature is like.

[This first analysis, pages 295-99, has not been published previously. The following essay is reprinted as credited in the footnote.]

. . .

Joseph Conrad's three novellas "Youth," "The Secret Sharer," "Heart of Darkness," and his novel *Lord Jim* have in common the theme of romanticism and disillusionment, enhanced by the hero-witness relationship in which Charles Marlow is the central witness. Marlow is the narrator, or one of several narrators, of each of these stories. Though Conrad lived most of the adventures Marlow relates, Marlow is more the mind than the whole person of Conrad. The single most important event they share is the journey into "the heart of darkness": "Before the Congo," Conrad says, "I was just a mere animal." Conrad's body suffered for his soul's deliverance. In the Congo, he contracted a fever from which he never fully recovered: take a look at his thin frame, his gaunt, Quixote-like face in the photographs sometime. Conrad the sailor died in the fires of fever to rise like the phoenix from his ashes as Conrad the novelist. And Marlow, one of the first of his characters, serves as a bridge between Conrad the author and Conrad's ideal reader. Reflecting only *partially* the mind of Conrad, Marlow is no mere mouthpiece. He is a complete character in his own right.

One of Conrad's most significant characters, Marlow is also one of the most intriguing and representative characters in modern literature—certainly the most active of its reflective anti-heroes. Marlow grows from story to story, more as a thinking than as an acting character. A shadowy figure on the periphery of the action, he delves into the moral center of things. A former ship's captain, Marlow is quiet, mature, vital, friendly, cool, humane, and intelligent. He has firm opinions and prejudices, but he has a probing, ironic, generous mind, and an acute sensibility. Though he a disillusioned romantic, Marlow is a committed person. While to his fictional listeners he may seem to be an evasive middle-aged storyteller who slights the essential, it is *for* the essence that he reaches—in a kind of agony of reminiscence. Sometimes participant, sometimes mere observer, Marlow gets his narrative material from many sources. Chance, curiosity, and compassion compel him to become the secret sharer of several men. A Conrad's double, Marlow is haunted by *his* own doubles. Marlow's ordering, evaluating, selecting, mediating sensibility transforms the chaos of fac into a metaphor of the human quandary. It is as one who bears witness th Marlow embodies the theme of romanticism and disillusionment.

Reprinted by permission from *The Ohio University Review*, Vol. X, (1968 pp. 5–22. Copyright © by Ohio University.

Romanticism, like existentialism, is not so much a systematic philosophy as it is a way of life. With a childlike spontaneity, the romantic acts more on impulse than reason, though he may strive to integrate the two; he seeks variety rather than uniformity, thrives on the improbable rather than the mundane, aspires to the infinite rather than the finite, and hopes to achieve intuitive exaltation rather than objective certainty. Objective self-analysis and doubt are the death of romance and romantic idealism. As the romantic *aspires*, he prefers mystery over certainty. The quest, in its early stages, at least, is not for self-knowledge and mastery alone, but for a theater of self-theatricalization. The solitary romantic is drawn to dramatic and fantastic land- and seascapes that objectify the lush inscapes of his romantic ego; mountains, deserts, and jungles become stages for his gestures. In these dramas, the romantic protagonist, although he may challenge the social order as his enemy, is often his own antagonist. As hero, he is his own audience; the day of his triumph begins when others fulfill the function of witnessing audience. Sometimes the hero ceases to be a hero, as Marlow does, and becomes a witness to another hero.

It is in the hero-witness relationship that the common theme of these stories is worked out. What do I mean by the terms "hero" and "witness"? I don't mean "hero" in the public sense. None of the heroes—*young* Marlow, Leggatt, Kurtz, Lord Jim—perform a courageous, virtuous act in the usual meaning of the term. Nor do I use "hero" in the usual literary sense, because these men are not, except for Lord Jim, the main characters in the stories. Middle-aged Marlow, the witness, is the main character.

As I use the term here, the "hero" is a man whose way of life and whose acts have some profound effect on his witnesses. Obviously, Kurtz, in "Heart of Darkness," fits this description. He affects not only Marlow, but the young Russian adventurer Marlow finds at the inner station. In the young Russian, who resembles Marlow in his youth, the awe and admiration of Kurtz is personified. Marlow admires and envies the youth: "Glamour urged him on, glamour kept him unscathed.... If the absolutely pure, uncalculating, unpractical spirit of adventure had ever ruled a human being, it ruled this bepatched youth." The Russian accepts his illusory conception of Kurtz "with a sort of eager fatalism." There is between them the recurrent hero-witness relationship: "Kurtz wanted an audience," the youth wants a hero. The distant fiancée is another of Kurtz's witnesses, and in London several other witnesses come to see some of Kurtz's papers which Marlow possesses. Each of his witnesses saw a different greatness in Kurtz.

Although one might discuss the hero-witness theme in *Don Quixote, Moby Dick, Huckleberry Finn,* James' *The Ambassadors,* Faulkner's *Absalom, Absalom!,* Carson McCullers' *The Heart Is a Lonely Hunter,* Fitzgerald's *The Great Gatsby,* Warren's *All the King's Men,* John Knowles'

A *Separate Peace*, and several of the novels of Wright Morris (*The Huge Season, The Field of Vision*, and others), it is almost unique with Conrad, especially as it becomes the basis for the point-of-view technique. This relationship is simultaneously developed as a theme and as a device. Thus, as Conrad speaks in the guise of his character, Marlow himself is a literary, thematic and technical device. So Conrad's basic structural technique—indirection—works most brilliantly in one of his more direct characters: Charles Marlow. As a witness who testifies, Marlow functions as one of the most complex and profound point-of-view devices in modern literature.

In the character of Marlow, Conrad achieves a blend of the dramatic action of events and the reflective events of consciousness. In "Youth" and "Heart of Darkness"—the two most intimately connected of these four stories—Conrad recounts events so close to his own experience that he had to achieve some kind of distance to avoid the grave dangers of subjectivity. The reminiscing Marlow serves that function. Greek chorus to his own story ("Youth") as well as to Jim's and Kurtz's, Marlow analyzes motives like a "whispering demon." Through Marlow, the author is able to intrude by proxy; Marlow is Conrad's secret agent, spying on the characters. Marlow also serves various mechanical functions: he creates smooth transitions from one phase to another in a complex structure, the time sequence of which is often disjointed; he bridges otherwise awkward gaps in the narrative. His florid but precise rhetoric is appropriate for the lush, wild environments, the huge themes, the large actions and complex thoughts of the characters.

The original witness is, of course, the author himself, for it is the writer's business to witness the acts of others, more as a spectator than as a participant, and then to testify to mankind. Conrad goes a step further and creates a character who is primarily a witness who testifies to the other characters in the stories. In the hero-witness relationship in these stories, except "The Secret Sharer," Conrad sets up several levels of connection. In "Heart of Darkness" there are four: Marlow tells a story of a hero, Kurtz, whose acts he has witnessed, to a group of men; only one man seems to derive any lasting value from Marlow's testimony, and it is this man who tells the story to the reader. As the reader sits among the others in the group—a stranger to their common bond, the sea—he is placed at a superior distance from which he may witness and judge events. As Marlow talks, the reader understands even more than the man who retells Marlow's story to us. But it is the original witness, Conrad, the embracive speaker, who selects what is to be told, and who manipulates the judgment the reader will make. The hero-witness relationship provides the point-of-view framework for each of the stories and provides the reader with a dynamic means of evaluating the theme of romanticism and disillusionment.

What Marlow says to his listeners is true of all these stories: "You fellows know there are those voyages that seem ordered for the illustration of life, that might stand for a symbol of existence." But unlike the other three, "Youth" is almost pure romantic adventure drama (it was as such that most of Conrad's readers read all his stories when they first appeared). Except when he interrupts himself, Marlow tells his story straight in "Youth." His listeners are a director of companies, an accountant, a lawyer, and the anonymous person who retells Marlow's story. Although young Marlow doesn't change or experience recognition, Marlow as the narrator years later, and his listeners, experience keenly the loss of youth. Marlow of twenty is now dead, but Marlow at forty-five resurrects him by a feat of lyric recall, and at a distance of years, he casts over events a tone of nostalgic irony.

The hero-witness relationship is not as clear in "Youth" as it is in the other stories, but looking back, Marlow probably feels that the old ship, *Judea*, and the sea were heroic forces, and that he was a witness to their interaction; however, as a romantic young second mate, he sees himself as the heroic center of action and his subordinates his witnesses.

"Youth" is the simple story of Marlow's first assignment as second mate; but more exciting to him, it is his first trip to the East. An old, almost unseaworthy ship, the *Judea* is bound for Bangkok. "Bangkok! Magic name, blessed name." Despite tremendous misfortunes—six months of delays in inner harbors, a hole in the hull that requires pumping water during a storm, dissatisfaction among the crew, a fire in the cargo of coal—young Marlow reaches the East with his romantic illusions intact. But it is a middle-aged, worldly, disillusioned Marlow who tells the story.

After only a few pages, Marlow interrupts himself: "and youth, strength, genius, thoughts, achievements, simple hearts—all die. . . . No matter. . . . Pass the bottle." This refrain is reiterated throughout the story, counterpointing young Marlow's romantic effusions in the sweep of danger. For in the midst of the actual, young Marlow strives to transform reality into dream—to impose his fervid imagination upon events. As the crew desperately pumps water out of the leaking ship, middle-aged Marlow describes the real thing: "We pumped watch and watch, for dear life; and it seemed to last for months, for years, for all eternity, as though we had been dead and gone to a hell for sailors." But *young* Marlow is still in a heaven for romantics: "'By Jove! this is the deuce of an adventure—something you read about.'" Though he may die for ideals, the romantic does not insist simply on life's having meaning, but on its having a higher, nobler reality than everyday existence.

The romantic's first duty to himself is to reach exotic lands. After the ship burns and sinks, Marlow rows to the Java shore in the lifeboat—his first command. The beach gleams "faintly, like an illusion. . . . The mysterious East faced me, perfumed like a flower," but also "silent like death, dark like a grave." Thus Conrad fuses the vision of youth with that of middle-age. Now Marlow says: "I remember my youth and the feeling that will never come back any more—the feeling that I could last for ever, outlast the sea, the earth, and all men; the deceitful feeling that lures us on to joys, to perils, to love, to vain effort—to death." Marlow's listeners agree that when they were "young and had nothing, on the sea that gives nothing, except hard knocks" they were happiest. But perhaps that's just another illusion which makes declining years bearable. "I had been tried on that ship and had come out pretty well," Marlow concludes, but his voyage on the *Judea* is primarily a test of physical endurance. Having explored the outer regions of Erebus (that zone of darkness between earth and hell), Marlow is now ready for the "journey homeward," through the central zones of Erebus, during which he must undergo the more important initiation into full adulthood, and prove capable of a life of responsibility. For this part of the journey, he needs a secret sharer.

II

Although literally I have no evidence for placing "The Secret Sharer" among these stories, there is every artistic justification for its place in the design, and for seeing the unnamed Captain as Marlow. Internal evidence supports this move. (In *Conrad the Novelist*, Albert Guerard groups them together because of certain thematic similarities.)

In "The Secret Sharer," the point of view framework is much simpler, but no less significant, as the Captain (Marlow) speaks directly to the reader. This is not the report of a romantic journey, but Marlow, the novitiate, confesses to the reader, who becomes, in a sense, his secret sharer. It is in this story that the hero-witness relationship is most intimate and sustained, though still transitional in the general design that exists among the four stories. Conrad uses many techniques to weld together the identities of Marlow, the witness, and Leggatt, the hero. But as his other, darker, impulsive, anti-social self, Leggatt is so nearly Marlow, during the time of their conspiracy, that Marlow is, in a sense, witnessing himself; he is hero and witness compounded.

A greater test of his romantic self-concept comes when Marlow journeys to the inner station of the Congo, and experiences more decisive revelations in the heart of darkness. Marlow's witness relationship with the missionary-trader Kurtz is more valuable than the one with Leggatt. In

"Heart of Darkness," Conrad again uses the point-of-view frame of "Youth." Marlow tells his story to the same group as in "Youth," and, presumably, as in *Lord Jim*. Marlow's first words are: "And this also has been one of the dark places of the earth." He describes the colonization of once dark England by the Romans: "They were conquerers, and for that you want only brute force. ... What redeems it is the idea only... not a sentimental pretense but an idea; and an unselfish belief in the idea—something you can set up, and bow down before, and offer a sacrifice to. ...." What a person (*or* a nation), sets up and bows down before, is the romantic, idealistic, egocentric image he has of himself. Whatever threatens this image is sacrificed.

Although the romantic believes that civilization corrupts, Kurtz's inversion of this belief is romantic because of the intensity of his idealism. For romanticism can become a selfless subjugation to a general, exaggerated belief in the perfectibility of man. Kurtz martyrs himself in this cause. He goes from a racial, ethnic ego to a nightmarish perversion of his own subjective ego. The romantic attempts to remake the world in his own image, but *Kurtz* discovers that the primitive world that made him has claimed him once more. Marlow's early description of an imaginary young Roman applies to Kurtz in the jungle: "There's no initiation either into such mysteries. He has to live in the midst of the incomprehensible, which is also detestable. And it has a fascination, too, that goes to work upon him. The fascination of the abomination. ...." The romantic goes out into the world, and with his emotional imagination he transforms reality into dream. But in the clash between romantic idealism and the reality which it distorts, the outer world invades the romantic heart, and disillusionment occurs. The romantic longs to be in the midst of great things, but if he penetrates to the heart of great enterprises, as Kurtz does, he discovers the heart of darkness that beats in every man. When dark reality extinguishes the romantic beacon, one whispers, "The horror! the horror!" Journeying into the Congo, Marlow is returning, as Kurtz did, to what England was thousands of years ago. From the beginning Marlow observes nothing but contradictions of the evangelical ideal: absurd activity, callous expediency, greed, suicide, murder, and disease; he cannot escape the feeling that he also is a part "of the great cause of these high and just proceedings." Marlow's experience may be divided into two phases, each with an intention and a reversal: first, the journey to a new job, in which Kurtz turns out to be his destination; and second, the confrontation with the Congo and with Kurtz in which Marlow ends up confronting his inner self. In leaving the Congo and Kurtz behind, Marlow escapes conditions that might accentuate the dark side of his personality. The more Marlow experiences and gets to know the Congo river and the jungle, the more he already knows Kurtz before he even meets him. For nature is made to reflect, in overwhelming imagery, the dark conflicts within Kurtz, within Marlow himself, and between other men.

Marlow says to his listeners: "It seems to me I am trying to tell you a dream. ... that commingling of absurdity, surprise, and bewilderment. ..." The romantic spell of youth does become a primeval nightmare of bewitchment, and the spell is broken for Marlow when Kurtz cries: "The horror!" It is a dream, both in the sense that Marlow is journeying into the nightmare regions of man's nature, and in the sense that a dream—idealistic and romantic—wrought all this nightmarish ruin.

. . .

It is Marlow's mental experience in witnessing, then telling of Jim's adventures that interests Conrad. And as usual, the reader, and Marlow's one sympathetic listener, discovers that the experience is not inconclusive. In *Lord Jim,* Marlow, perhaps older now than when he told Kurtz's story, is a more prolonged witness and even less a hero himself than he was in the other stories. A wiser but disillusioned man now, Marlow is qualified to make of his observations on Jim a deeper spiritual assessment than his bitterness allowed him to make of the Kurtz experience. Though Marlow relates Jim's story from a mature distance, he is involved in the romance of Jim's wanderings; he lives vicariously the dream that Jim enacts. In a sense, Jim is Marlow's almost irretrievable secret self, and through Marlow, the reader intimately identifies with Jim. The novel is ironically subtitled "A Romance" because the more passionately the romantic quester seeks romance the more it eludes and finally deludes him. It is a quest doomed by its nature to failure, as one sees in the life of Jim.

In *Lord Jim,* the point-of-view frame is more complex than in other stories. The story is fragmented and the time sequence distorted. Marlow, the witness, gets the story partly at the inquiry, partly from Jim, the hero. It becomes a part of his life, and, haunted by it, he tells the story to friends, often. Told partly by Conrad, as omniscient author, partly in first person by Marlow, and partly through a letter written by Marlow, the story moves back and forth through time as Marlow pieces together the enigma of Jim's character which is solved only by the reader. Up to now, the reader has always understood a little more than Marlow himself; now Marlow and the reader are equals. As when they were anchored in the sea reach of the Thames, the group on the

In these hero-witness relationships Marlow is intiated in various trials by ordeal, he experiences ethical revelations, and at the end of his romantic quest achieves self-discovery, though immersed in disillusionment. He takes a long, delayed journey of initiation: In "Youth," Marlow is initiated into the immemorial peril of the human condition, best symbolized in the adventures of the sea voyage. (His earlier voyages were uneventful.) In "The Secret Sharer," he is initiated into the responsbilities of command. In "Heart of Darkness" he achieves insights into the deeper mysteries of human nature. And in *Lord Jim,* Marlow witnesses Jim's initiations into the same kinds of experiences he had himself in the previous stories. In "Youth," self-discovery comes only in the telling, when Marlow is middle-aged. In "The Secret Sharer," Marlow discovers his kinship with the fugitive personality (Leggatt). In "Heart of Darkness," he endures the most severe test of physical and moral fortitude, and discovers his kinship with primitive man and with Kurtz. And in *Lord Jim,* Marlow sees himself in a man who passes through Kurtz's despair to redemption.

So the witness is the person who stands to benefit in some intangible way from contact with the acts and way of life of the hero. In "Youth," Marlow witnesses his own romantic heroics and the heroic effect on him of the sea and the ship, *Judea.* In "The Secret Sharer," Marlow witnesses the heroic endurance of Leggatt, the fugitive. In "Heart of Darkness," Marlow witnesses the strange heroic endeavor and disintegration of Kurtz. In *Lord Jim,* he witnesses the heroic wanderings and final retribution of Jim. So it is always the witness, never the hero, who benefits from the relationship.

Marlow the witness responds to heroes who reveal himself to himself. Lord Jim is Marlow as he was in the story "Youth." Leggatt is Marlow as he could have been in the recent past, and as he might yet become in the near future. Kurtz is Marlow as the Congo might have remade him. The Marlow of *Lord Jim* has passed through the dream of youth and through the nightmare at the heart of darkness; he has crossed a shadowline into wisdom. He is now a witness who calls others to witness. Thus, in the four stories, Conrad's use of Marlow as a device, a point-of-view technique, is made profoundly meaningful also as a way of controlling and elucidating the significance of the theme. And if Marlow is the major fictional witness, we, as his listeners, end up being even more profoundly affected as witnesses.

Marlow's involvement in the lives of others results in enlightenment, and his missionary purpose is to enlighten others. As his Buddha-like posture in "Heart of Darkness" suggests, Marlow is a sort of priest who interprets the parables of human action. Men confide in him and confess to him: Lord Jim, Leggatt, Kurtz, and even villains like Jim's adversary, Gentleman Brown. What Conrad says of himself is true of his fictional counterpart, Marlow: "I would fain claim for myself the faculty of so much insight as can be expressed in a voice of sympathy and compassion." It is that voice that we hear in Marlow.

In this intricate point-of-view technique, one may sense Conrad's attitude toward his function as a writer: moved by compassion, endowed with imagination, he presents the heroic acts of his characters for the reader's own beneficial act of witnessing. "My task which I am trying to achieve," he

said, "is, by the power of the written word, to make you hear, to make yo
feel—it is, before all, to make you *see*. That—and no more, and it is ever
thing." Conrad believed that stories should be entertaining, by exercising
the reader's imagination, but the imagination should intensify and shape a
show forth the significance of its images. Thus, Marlow soon ceases to be a
witnessing person and becomes a creative witness, for Marlow seeks, as th
reader should, truth for its own sake; he makes of reminiscence a moral a
spiritual act, and ultimately becomes the witness as hero. In the mouths c
Conrad and Marlow, story telling becomes an ethical duty, listening creatively is an ethical obligation, and, ultimately, an act of existential piety.

CHRONOLOGICAL DEVELOPMENT OF THE NOVEL

If another general chronology of substantial length exists, the author has been unable to find it; thus, the usefulness of this one is clear.

All novelists and novels mentioned in the text are included here, with the exception of a few popular novels. Publication dates are, in most cases, those of original publication, *not* of first English translation. Birth and death dates for authors are given, except when exhaustive research failed to yield that information (some minor writers whose works are cited for purposes of illustration are not treated in reference volumes on writers and literature). Only the English titles of foreign novels are given here; foreign titles are often given in the text. With very few exceptions, the author's nationality is given; also, to aid students and teachers in designing courses in these areas, several ethnic and regional designations are provided: Afro-American, southern, etc. Many entries in the chronology are not mentioned in the text.

c850 B.C.	Homer (Greek) *The Odyssey*
6th cent B.C.	Aesop (Greek) *Aesop's Fables*
4th cent B.C.	Xenophon (Greek, c430–c354 B.C.) *Cyropaedia*
2nd cent A.D.	Heliodorus (Greek) *Aethiopica* Lucian (Syrian, c120–c200) *The True History*
c150	Apuleius, Lucius (Greek, 125?) *The Golden Ass*
3rd cent	Adigal, Ilangô (Indian) *The Ankle Bracelet* Longus (Greek) *Daphnis and Chloë*
300–500	Panchatantra (Indian) *Fables*
9th cent	Arihara No Narihira (Japanese, 825–880) *Tales of Ise*
1000	*Beowulf* (English)
1001–1015	Murasaki, Shikibu (Japanese, 978?–1015?) *The Tale of Genji*

11th cent   *The Finn Cycle* (Irish)

c1100   *The Mabinogion* (Welsh)
      The Song of Roland (French)

c1150   *Song of the Nibelungenlied* (German)

c1100–1250 *Grettir the Strong* (Norse)

c1235–1280 Lorris, Guillaume de (French) and Meung, Jean de
      (French) *Romance of the Rose*

12th cent   *Poem of the Cid* (Spanish)
      Reynard the Fox (Germanic)

Early 13th cent *Prose Edda* (Icelandic)

13th cent   *Burnt Nijal Saga* (Icelandic)
      Sturluson, Snorri (Norwegian, 1179–1241) *The
       Heimskringla*

14th cent   *Aucassin and Nicolette* (French)
      Lo Kuan-Chung (Chinese, c1320–1380) *Romance of the
       Three Kingdoms*
      Shih Nai-An (Chinese, fl. 14th century) *All Men Are
       Brothers*

1340–1345 Boccaccio, Giovanni (Italian, 1330–1375) *L'Amorosa
       Fiametta*

1350–1400 Pearl Poet (English) *Sir Gawain and the Green Knight*

1353   Boccaccio, Giovanni (Italian, 1313–1375) *Decameron*

1393–1400 Chaucer, Geoffrey (English, c1343?–1400) *The Canterbι
       Tales*

1400–1450 *Huon de Bordeaux* (French)

15th cent   *The Arabian Nights*
      La Sale, Antoine de (French, 1388–c1462)*The Fifteen
       Comforts of Matrimony*

1485   Malory, Sir Thomas (English, d. 1471) *Le Morte d'Arthι*

c1490   *Robin Hood's Adventures* (English)

1499   Rojas, Fernando de (Spanish, 1475?-1538?) *Celestina*

1508   Lobeira, Vasco de (Portuguese, c1360-c1403) *Amadís de Gaul*

1516   More, Thomas (English, 1478-1535) *Utopia*

1533-1567   Rabelais, François (French, 1490-1553) *The Lives, Heroic Deeds, and Sayings of Gargantua and Pantagruel*

16th cent   Wu, Ch'eng-ên (Chinese, 1505-c1580) *Monkey*

1554   *La Vida de Lazarillo de Tormes* (Spanish)

1559   Montemayor, Jorge de (Portuguese, 1520-1561) *La Diana*

1579   Lyly, John (English, c1554-1606) *Euphues, The Anatomy of Wit*

1588   Greene, Robert (English, d. 1592) *Pandosto*

1590   Sidney, Sir Philip (English, 1554-1586) *Arcadia*

1594   Nashe, Thomas (English, 1567-1601) *The Unfortunate Traveller*

Late 16th cent   Li Yü (Chinese) *The Golden Lotus*

1599-1604   Alemán, Mateo (Spanish, 1547-1613?) *Guzman de Alfarache*

Early 17th cent.   Fêng, Mêng-Lung (Chinese, 1574?-1645?) *Lieh Kuo Chih*

1605   Cervantes, Miguel de (Spanish, 1547-1616) *Don Quixote*

1621   Barclay, John (English, 1582-1621) *Argenis*

1627   Bacon, Francis (English, 1561-1626) *New Atlantis*

1646-1653   Scudéry, Madeleine de (French, 1607-1701) *Artamène*

Before 1657   Urfé, Honoré d' (French, 1576-1625) *Astrée* c1660   Quevedo (Spanish, 1580–1645) *Life of the Great Rascal*

1664   Petronius (Italian, ?–c66; translated 1664) *Satyricon*

1668–1694 La Fontaine, Jean de (French, 1621–1695) *Fables*

1669   Grimmelshausen, H. J. C. von (German, c1625–1676)
      Simplicissimus the Vagabond

1678   Bunyan, John (English, 1628–1688) *Pilgrim's Progress*
      La Fayette, Madame de (French, 1634–1693) *The Princess*
      of Clèves

c1685   Saikaku, Ihara (Japanese, c1642–1693) *Five Women Who*
      Loved Love

1688   Behn, Mrs. Aphra (English, 1640–1689) *Oroonoko*

1715–1735 Le Sage, Alain René (French, 1688–1747) *Gil Blas of San-*
      tillane

1719   Defoe, Daniel (English, c1659–1731) *Robinson Crusoe*

1722   Defoe, Daniel (English, c1659–1731) *The Journal of the*
      Plague Year; Moll Flanders

1726   Swift, Jonathan (English, 1667–1745) *Gulliver's Travels*

1731   Prévost, Abbé (French, 1697–1763) *Manon Lescaut*

1731–1741 Marivaux, Pierre Carlet de Chamblain de (French, 1688–
      1763) *Marianne*

1740   Richardson, Samuel (English, 1689–1761) *Pamela*

1741   Fielding, Henry (English, 1707–1754) *Shamela*
      Holberg, Ludwig (Norwegian, 1684–1754) *Journey of Nie*
      Klim to the World Underground

1747–1748 Richardson, Samuel (English, 1689–1761) *Clarissa*

1749   Cleland, John (English, c1710–1789) *Fanny Hill*
      Fielding, Henry (English, 1707–1754) *The History of To*
      Jones

1802-1814	Jippensha-Ikku (Japanese, 1765-1831) *Shank's Mare*
1804	Kyôden, Santô (Japanese, 1761-1816) *Fortune's Wheel* Sénancour, Etienne Pivert de (French, 1770-1846) *Obermann*
1806	Kyôden, Santô (Japanese, 1761-1816) *Inazuma-byôshi*
1808	Goethe, Johann Wolfgang (German, 1749-1832) *Elective Affinities* Kleist, Heinrich von (German, 1777-1811) *Michael Kohlhaas*
1811	La Motte-Fouqué, Friedrich de (German, 1777-1843) *Undine*
1812-1813	Wyss, Johann Rudolph (Swiss, 1781-1830) *The Swiss Family Robinson*
1813	Austen, Jane (English, 1775-1817) *Pride and Prejudice*
1814	Scott, Sir Walter (Scottish, 1771-1832) *Waverley*
1815	Austen, Jane (English, 1775-1817) *Emma*
1815-1816	Hoffman, Ernst Theodor Amadeus (German, 1776-1822) *The Devil's Elixir*
1816	Constant, Benjamin (French, 1767-1830) *Adolphe* Scott, Sir Walter (Scottish, 1771-1832) *The Antiquary*
1816-1830	Fernández de Lizardi, José Joaquín (Mexican, 1776-1827) *The Itching Parrot*
1817	Shelley, Mary (English, 1797-1851) *Frankenstein*
1818	Austen, Jane (English, 1775-1817) *Northanger Abbey; Persuasion* Peacock, Thomas Love (English, 1785-1866) *Nightmare Abbey* Scott, Sir Walter (Scottish, 1771-1832) *The Heart of Midlothian*
1820	Maturin, Charles (Irish, 1780-1824) *Melmoth the Wanderer*

1824   Moller, Poul (Danish, 1794–1838) *Adventures of a Danish Student*

1825–1826   Manzoni, Alessandro (Italian, 1785–1873) *The Betrothed*

1826   Cooper, James Fenimore (American, 1789–1851) *The Last of the Mohicans*
Disraeli, Benjamin (English, 1804–1881) *Vivian Grey*
Vigny, Alfred (French, 1797–1863) *Cinq Mars*

1828   Griffin, Gerald (English, 1803–1840) *The Collegians*

1830   Balzac, Honoré de (French, 1799–1850) *The Wild Ass's Skin*
Stendhal (French, 1783–1842) *The Red and the Black*

1831   Hugo, Victor (French, 1802–1885) *The Hunchback of Notre Dame*
Peacock, Thomas Love (English, 1785–1866) *Crotchet Castle*

1832   Mörike, Eduard (German, 1804–1875) *Maler Nolten*
Sainte-Beuve, Charles Augustin (French, 1804–1869) *Volupté*

1833   Balzac, Honoré de (French, 1799–1850) *Eugénie Grandet*

1834   Balzac, Honoré de (French, 1799–1850) *Père Goriot*
Bulwer-Lytton, Edward (English, 1803–1873) *The Last Days of Pompeii*

1835   Andersen, Hans Christian (Danish, 1805–1875) *The Improvisatore*
Simms, William Gilmore (American, 1806–1870) *The Yemassee*

1836   Marryat, Frederick (English, 1792–1848) *Mr. Midshipman Easy*
Pushkin, Alexander (Russian, 1799–1837) *The Captain's Daughter*

1837   Bird, Robert Montgomery (American, 1806–1854) *Nick of the Woods*

1837–1839   Dickens, Charles (English, 1812–1870) *Oliver Twist*

1838	Conscience, Hendrik (Flemish, 1812–1883) *The Lion of Flanders* Immerman, Karl Liberecht (German, 1796–1840) *Münchhausen* Poe, Edgar Allan (American, 1809–1849) *The Narrative of Arthur Gordon Pym*
1839	Lermontov, Mikhail Yurievich (Russian, 1814–1841) *A Hero of Our Time* Stendhal (French, 1783–1842) *Charterhouse of Parma* Thompson, Daniel Pierce (American, 1795–1868) *The Green Mountain Boys*
1841	Cooper, James Fenimore (American, 1789–1851) *The Deerslayer*
1842	Gogol, Nikolai Vasilyevich (Russian, 1808–1852) *Dead Souls* Sand, George (French, 1804–1876) *Consuelo*
1843	Surtees, Robert (English, 1803–1864) *Handley Cross*
1843–1844	Dickens, Charles (English, 1812–1870) *Martin Chuzzlewit*
1844	Disraeli, Benjamin (English, 1804–1881) *Coningsby* Dumas, Alexandre (French, 1802–1870) *The Count of Monte Cristo*
1844–1845	Sue, Eugène (French, 1804–1857) *The Wandering Jew*
1845	Mérimée, Prosper (French, 1803–1870) *Carmen*
1847	Brontë, Charlotte (English, 1816–1855) *Jane Eyre* Brontë, Emily (English, 1818–1848) *Wuthering Heights*
1847–1848	Thackeray, William Makepeace (English, 1811–1863) *Vanity Fair*
1847–1849	Murger, Henri (French, 1822–1861) *The Bohemians of the Latin Quarter*
1849	Melville, Herman (American, 1819–1891) *Mardi*
1849–1850	Dickens, Charles (English, 1812–1870) *David Copperfield*

1850   Hawthorne, Nathaniel (American, 1804–1864) *The Scarlet Letter*

1851   Borrow, George (English, 1803–1881) *Lavengro*
       Melville, Herman (American, 1819–1891) *Moby Dick*
       Ruskin, John (English, 1819–1900) *The King of the Golden River*

1852   Melville, Herman (American, 1819–1891) *Pierre, or The Ambiguities*
       Stowe, Harriet Beecher (American, 1811–1896) *Uncle Tom's Cabin*

1853   Gaskell, Elizabeth Cleghorn (English, 1810–1865) *Cranford*
       Nerval, Gérard de (Gérard Labrunie; French, 1808–1855) *Sylvie*

1854   Cooke, John Esten (American, 1830–1886) *The Virginia Comedians*

1854–1855 Keller, Gottfried (Swiss, 1819–1890) *The Green Henry*

1855   Freytag, Gustav (German, 1816–1895) *Debit and Credit*
       Kingsley, Charles (English, 1819–1875) *Westward Ho!*

1856   About, Edmond François (French, 1828–1885) *The King of the Mountains*

1857   Borrow, George (English, 1803–1881) *The Romany Rye*
       Flaubert, Gustave (French, 1821–1880) *Madame Bovary*
       Hughes, Thomas (English, 1822–1896) *Tom Brown's School Days*
       Trollope, Anthony (English, 1815–1882) *Barchester Towers*

1858   Björnson, Björnstjerne (Norwegian, 1832–1910) *Arne*
       Goncharov, Ivan Alexandrovich (Russian, 1812–1891) *Oblomov*

1859   Dickens, Charles (English, 1812–1870) *A Tale of Two Cities*
       Meredith, George (English, 1828–1909) *The Ordeal of Richard Feverel*
       Rydberg, Viktor (Swedish 1828–1895) *The Last Athenian*

1860 Eliot, George (English, 1819–1880) *The Mill on the Floss*
      Goncourt, Edmond (French, 1822–1897) and Jules de
          Goncourt (1830–1870) *Charles Damailly*
      Multatuli (Dutch, 1820–1887) *Max Havelaar*

1860–1861 Dickens, Charles (English, 1812–1870) *Great Expectations*

1861 Eliot, George (English, 1819–1880) *Silas Marner*
      Reade, Charles (English, 1814–1884) *The Cloister and the
          Hearth*
      Whyte-Melville, George J. (English, 1821–1878) *Market
          Harborough*

1862 Fromentin, Eugène (French, 1820–1876) *Dominique*
      Hugo, Victor (French, 1802–1885) *Les Misérables*
      Turgenev, Ivan (Russian, 1818–1883) *Fathers and Sons*

1863 Gautier, Théophile (French, 1811–1872) *Le Capitaine
          Fracasse*

1864 Goncourt, Edmond (French, 1822–1897) and Jules de
          Goncourt (1830–1870) *Renée Mauperin*

1865 Carroll, Lewis (English, 1832–1898) *Alice in Wonderland*
      Verne, Jules (French, 1828–1905) *A Trip to the Moon*

1865–1869 Tolstoy, Count Leo Nikolayevich (Russian, 1828–1910)
          War and Peace

1866 De Forest, John William (American, 1826–1906) *Miss
          Ravenel's Conversion from Secession to Loyalty*
      Dostoyevsky, Fydor Mikhailovich (Russian, 1821–1881)
          Crime and Punishment; The Idiot

1867 Coster, Charles de (Flemish, 1827–1879) *The Legend of
          Tyl Ulenspiegel*
      Dostoyevsky, Fydor Mikhailovich (Russian, 1821–1881)
          The Possessed
      Gaboriau, Emile (French, 1835–1873) *File No. 113*
      Goncourt, Edmond (French, 1822–1897) and Jules de
          Goncourt (1830–1870) *Manette Salomon*
      Nievo, Ippolito (Italian, 1831–1861) *The Castle of Fratta*
      Ouida (Ramée, Marie Louise de la; English, 1830–1908)
          Under Two Flags

1868   Björnson, Björnstjerne (Norwegian, 1832–1910) *The Fisher Maiden*
Collins, William Wilkie (English, 1824–1889) *The Moonstone*

1868–1869   Alcott, Louisa May (American, 1832–1888) *Little Women*
Lautréamont (French, 1846–1870) *Maldoror*

1869   Dostoyevsky, Fydor Mikhailovich (Russian, 1821–1881) *Notes from Underground*
Gaboriau, Émile (French, 1835–1873) *Monsieur Lecoq*
Trollope, Anthony (English, 1815–1882) *Phineas Finn*

1871   Carroll, Lewis (English, 1832–1898) *Alice in Wonderland; Through the Looking Glass*
Eggleston, Edward (American, 1873–1902) *The Hoosier Schoolmaster*

1872   Butler, Samuel (English, 1835–1902) *Erewhon*
Daudet, Alphonse (French, 1840–1897) *Tartarin of Tarascon*
Jókai, Maurius (Hungarian, 1825–1904) *A Modern Midas*

1873   Alger, Horatio (American, 1834–1899) *Bound to Rise or Up the Ladder*
Twain, Mark (American, 1835–1910) and Warner, Charles Dudley (American, 1829–1900) *The Gilded Age*

1873–1877   Tolstoy, Count Leo Nikolayevich (Russian, 1828–1910) *Anna Karenina*

1874   Alarcón, Pedro Antonio de (Spanish, 1833–1891) *The Three Cornered Hat*
Valera, Juan (Spanish, 1824–1905) *Pepita Jimenez*

1876   De Amicis, Edmondo (Italian, 1846–1908) *The Romance of a Schoolmaster*
Pérez Galdós, Benito (Spanish, 1843–1920) *Doña Perfecta*
Schchedrin, N. (Mikhail Saltykov; Russian, 1826–1889) *The Golovlevs*

1877   Zola, Émile (French, 1840–1903) *The Dram Shop*

1878   Chatterjee, Bankim-Chandra (Indian, 1838–1894) *Krishnakanta's Will*
Hardy, Thomas (English, 1840–1928) *Return of the Native*

1879   Daudet, Alphonse (French, 1840–1897) *Kings in Exile*
            Keller, Gottfried (Swiss, 1819–1890) *Der Grüne Heinrich*

1880   Cable, George Washington (American, 1844–1925) *The
                Grandissimes*
            Dostoyevsky, Fydor Mikhailovich (Russian, 1821–1881)
                The Brothers Karamazov
            Jacobsen, Jens Peter (Denmark, 1847–1885) *Niels Lyhne*
            Kielland, Alexander Lange (Norwegian, 1849–1906) *Gar-
                man and Worse*
            Machado de Assís, Joaquim Maria (Brazilian, 1839–1908)
                Epitaph of a Small Winner
            Wallace, Lew (American, 1827–1905) *Ben Hur: A Tale of
                the Christ*
            Zola, Émile (French, 1840–1902) *Nana*

1881   James, Henry (American, 1843–1916) *The Portrait of a
                Lady*
            Shorthouse, Joseph Henry (English, 1834–1903) *John Ing-
                lesant*
            Verga, Giovanni (Sicilian, 1840–1922) *House by the Med-
                lar Tree*

1882   Barbey d'Aurevilly, Jules Amédée (French, 1808–1889)
                The Story without a Name
            Halévy, Ludovic (French, 1834–1908) *The Abbé Constan-
                tin*

1883   Howe, Edgar W. (American, 1853–1937) *The Story of a
                Country Town*
            Lie, Jonas (Norwegian, 1833–1908) *The Family at Gilje*
            Maupassant, Guy de (French, 1850–1893) *A Woman's Life*
            Pereda, José María de (Spanish, 1833–1906) *Pedro Sán-
                chez*
            Schreiner, Olive (S. Africa, 1855–1920) *The Story of an
                African Farm*

1884   Daudet, Alphonse (French, 1840–1897) *Sappho*
            Huysmans, Joris-Karl (French, 1848–1907) *Against the
                Grain*
            Jackson, Helen Hunt (American, 1831–1885) *Ramona*
            Jewett, Sarah Orne (American, 1847–1909) *A Country
                Doctor*
            Pereda, José María de (Spanish, 1833–1906) *Sotileza*

1885   Howells, William Dean (American, 1837–1920) *The Rise of Silas Lapham*
Pater, Walter (French, 1839–1894) *Marius the Epicurean*
Twain, Mark (American, 1835–1910) *The Adventures of Huckleberry Finn*

1886   Haggard, H. Rider (English, 1856–1925) *King Solomon's Mines*
Lie, Jonas (Norwegian, 1833–1908) *The Commander's Daughter*
Loti, Pierre (French, 1850–1923) *An Iceland Fisherman*
Stevenson, Robert Louis (Scottish, 1850–1894) *Dr. Jekyll and Mr. Hyde*
Stevenson, Robert Louis (Scottish, 1850–1894) *Kidnapped*

1886–1887   Pérez Galdós, Benito (Spanish, 1843–1920) *Fortunata and Jacinta*

1887   Craddock, Charles Egbert (American, 1850–1922) *In the Clouds*
Dujardin, Édouard (French, 1861–1949) *We'll to the Woods No More*
Hardy, Thomas (English, 1840–1928) *The Woodlanders*
Strindberg, August (Swedish, 1849–1912) *The Natives of Hamsö*
Sudermann, Herman (German, 1857–1928) *Dame Care*

1888   Bellamy, Edward (American, 1850–1898) *Looking Backward*
Eça de Queiroz, José Maria de (Portuguese, 1845–1900) *Os Maias*

1889   Bourget, Paul (French, 1852–1935) *The Disciple*
Hearn, Lafcadio (American, 1850–1904) *Chita: A Memory of Last Island*
Verga, Giovanni (Sicilian, 1840–1922) *Mastro Don Gesnaldo*

1890   Hamsun, Knut (Norwegian, 1859–1952) *Hunger*
Howells, William Dean (American, 1837–1920) *A Hazard of New Fortunes*
Morris, William (English, 1834–1896) *News from Nowhere*

1890–1891   Pérez Galdós, Benito (Spanish, 1843–1920) *Angel Guerra*

1891 Diderot, Denis (French, 1713-1784) *Rameau's Nephew*
    (First authentic publication; composed 1761-1774)
    Freeman, Mary E. Wilkins (American, 1852-1930) *A New
     England Nun*
    Gissing, George Robert (English, 1857-1903) *The New
     Grub Street*
    Hardy, Thomas (English, 1840-1928) *Tess of the d'Urber-
     villes*
    Lagerlöf, Selma (Swedish, 1858-1940) *Gösta Berlings Saga*
    Wilde, Oscar (English, 1856-1900) *The Picture of Dorian
     Gray*

1892 Zangwill, Israel (English, 1864-1926) *Children of the
     Ghetto*

1893 Crane, Stephen (American, 1871-1900) *Maggie: A Girl of
     the Streets*
    Frederic, Harold (American, 1871-1898) *The Copperhead*
    Vazov, Ivan (Bulgarian, 1850-1921) *Under the Yoke*

1894 D'Annunzio, Gabriele (Italian, 1863-1938) *The Triumph of
     Death*
    Du Maurier, George (English, 1834-1896) *Trilby*
    Hardy, Thomas (English, 1840-1928) *Jude the Obscure*
    Hope, Anthony (English, 1863-1933) *The Prisoner of
     Zenda*
    Moore, George (Irish, 1852-1933) *Esther Waters*

1895 Crane, Stephen (American, 1871-1900) *The Red Badge of
     Courage*
    Fontane, Theodor (Prussian, 1819-1898) *Effi Briest*
    Kipling, Rudyard (English, 1865-1936) *The Jungle Book*
    Mikszáth, Kálmán (Hungarian, 1847-1910) *St. Peter's Um-
     brella*

1896 Crane, Stephen (American, 1871-1900) *George's Mother*
    Frederic, Harold (American, 1856-1898) *The Damnation
     of Theron Ware*
    Louÿs, Pierre (French, 1869-1925) *Aphrodite*
    Pontopiddan, Henrik (Danish, 1857-1943) *The Promised
     Land*

1897 Gide, André (French, 1869-1951) *Fruits of the Earth*
    James, Henry (American, 1869-1916) *The Spoils of Poyn-
     ton*

Kipling, Rudyard (English, 1865-1936) *Captains Coura-geous*

Mitchell, S. Weir (American, 1829-1914) *Hugh Wynne, Free Quaker*

Sheldon, Charles Monroe (American, 1857-1946) *In His Steps*

Stoker, Bram (Irish, 1847-1912) *Dracula*

1898   Crawford, F. Marion (American, 1854-1909) *Ave Roma Immortalis*

James, Henry (American, 1843-1916) *The Turn of the Screw*

Wells, H. G. (English, 1866-1946) *War of the Worlds*

Wescott, Edward Noyes (American, 1846-1898) *David Harum*

1899   Chesnutt, Charles Waddel (Afro-American, 1858-1932) *The Conjure Woman*

Chopin, Kate (American, 1851-1904) *The Awakening*

Tarkington, Booth (American, 1869-1946) *The Gentleman from Indiana*

Tolstoy, Count Leo Nikolayevich (Russian, 1828-1910) *The Resurrection*

1900   Conrad, Joseph (English, 1857-1924) *Lord Jim*

Dreiser, Theodore (American, 1871-1945) *Sister Carrie*

Johnston, Mary (American, 1870-1936) *To Have and to Hold*

Tarkington, Booth (American, 1869-1946) *Monsieur Beaucaire*

1900-1901   Jensen, Johannes V. (Danish, 1873-1950) *The Fall of the King*

1901   Altamirano, Ignacio (Mexican, 1834-1893) *The Bandit*

Churchill, Winston (American, 1871-1947) *The Crisis*

Kipling, Rudyard (English, 1865-1936) *Kim*

Mann, Thomas (German, 1875-1955) *Buddenbrooks*

Norris, Frank (American, 1870-1902) *The Octopus*

1901-1903   Couperus, Louis Marie Anne (Dutch, 1863-1923) *The Book of the Small Souls*

1902   Doyle, Sir Arthur Conan (English, 1859-1930) *The Hound of the Baskervilles*

Gide, André (French, 1869-1951) *The Immoralist*
Merejkowski, Dmitri (Russian, 1865-1941) *The Romance of Leonardo da Vinci*
Wister, Owen (American, 1860-1938) *The Virginian*

1902-1906   Leautaud, Paul (French, 1872-1955) *The Child of Montmartre*

1902-1909   James, Henry (American, 1843-1916) *The Wings of the Dove*
Reymont, Wladyslaw (Polish, 1868-1925) *The Peasants*

1903   Butler, Samuel (English, 1835-1902) *The Way of All Flesh*
Gissing, George Robert (English, 1857-1903) *The Private Papers of Henry Ryecroft*
James, Henry (American, 1843-1916) *The Ambassadors*
London, Jack (American, 1876-1916) *Call of the Wild*
Norris, Frank (American, 1870-1902) *The Pit*

1904   Conrad, Joseph (Polish, 1857-1924) *Nostromo*
Hudson, W. H. (English, 1841-1922) *Green Mansions*
London, Jack (American, 1876-1916) *The Sea Wolf*
Pirandello, Luigi (Italian, 1867-1936) *The Late Mattia Pascal*
Rolfe, Frederick William (Baron Corvo; English, 1860-1913) *Hadrian the Seventh*
Zeromski, Stefan (Polish, 1864-1925) *Ashes*

1904-1912   Rolland, Romain (French, 1866-1944) *Jean-Christophe*

1905   Fogazzaro, Antonio (Italian, 1842-1911) *The Saint*
Herrick, Robert (American, 1868-1938) *The Memoirs of an American Citizen*
Kuprin, Alexander (Russian, 1870-1938) *The Duel*
Mann, Heinrich (German, 1871-1950) *Professor Unrat*
Wells, H. G. (English, 1866-1946) *A Modern Utopia*

1905-1907   Heidenstam, Verner von (Swedish, 1859-1940) *The Tree of the Folkungs*
Sologub, Fëdor (Russian, 1863-1927) *The Petty Demon*

1906   Gourmont, Remy de (French, 1858-1915) *A Night in the Luxembourg*
Sinclair, Upton (American, 1878-1968) *The Jungle*

1906-1910   Nexø, Martin Anderson (Danish, 1869-1954) *Pelle, the
             Conqueror*

1906-1921   Galsworthy, John (English, 1867-1933) *The Forsyte Saga*

1907   Artsybashev, Mikhail (Russian, 1878-1927) *Sanin*
             Friedman, Isaac Kahn (American, 1870-1931) *The Radic*
             Gorki, Maxim (Russian, 1868-1936) *Mother*
             Harris, Joel Chandler (American, 1848-1908) *Brer Rabbi*
             London, Jack (American, 1876-1916) *The Iron Heel*
             Machen, Arthur (English, 1863-1947) *Hill of Dreams*

1908   Andreyev, Leonid (Russian, 1871-1919) *The Seven Who
                 Were Hanged*
             Bennett, Arnold (English, 1867-1931) *The Old Wives' Ta*
             Blasco-Ibáñez, V. (Spanish, 1867-1928) *Blood and Sand*
             Chesterton, G. K. (English, 1874-1936) *The Man Who
                 Was Thursday*
             Forster, E. M. (English, 1879-1970) *A Room with a Viev*
             Fox, John (American, Southern, 1862-1919) *Trail of the
                 Lonesome Pine*
             France, Anatole (French, 1844-1924) *Penguin Island*
             Grahame, Kenneth (English, 1859-1932) *The Wind in th*
                 Willows
             Rinehart, Mary Roberts (American, 1876-1958) *The Circ*
                 lar Staircase

1909   Stein, Gertrude (American, 1874-1946) *Three Lives*
             Wells, H. G. (English, 1866-1946) *Tono-Bungay*

1910   Bunin, Ivan (Russian, 1870-1950) *The Village*
             Forster, E. M. (English, 1879-1970) *Howard's End*
             Mulford, Clarence, E. (American, 1883-1956) *Hopalong
                 Cassidy*
             Rilke, Rainer Maria (German, 1875-1926) *The Notebook
                 Malte Laurids Brigge*

1911   Beerbohm, Max (English, 1871-1956) *Zuleika Dobson*
             Chesterton, G. K. (English, 1874-1936) *The Innocence o*
                 Father Brown
             Glaspell, Susan (American, 1882-1948) *The Visioning*
             Norris, Kathleen (American, 1880-1966) *Mother*
             Romains, Jules (French, 1885-1972) *Death of a Nobody*
             Wright, Harold Bell (American, 1872-1944) *The Winning
                 of Barbara Worth*

1912   Grey, Zane (American, 1872–1939) *Riders of the Purple
                Sage*
                Pérez de Ayala, Ramón (Spanish, 1880–1962) *The Fox's
                Paw*
                Saki (H. H. Munro; English, 1870–1915) *The Unbearable
                Bassington*

1912–1913   Sôseki, Natsume (Japanese, 1867–1916) *The Wayfarer*

1912–1914   Gunnarsson, Gunnar (Icelandic, 1889–1975) *Guest the
                One-Eyed*

1913   Alain-Fournier (French, 1886–1914) *The Wanderer*
                Bentley, E. C. (English, 1875–1958) *Trent's Last Case*
                Cather, Willa (American, 1873–1947) *O Pioneers*
                Singmaster, Elsie (American, 1879–1958) *A Boy at Gettysburg*

1913–1916   Biely, Andrei (Russian, 1880–1934) *Petersburg*

1913–1927   Proust, Marcel (French, 1871–1922) *Remembrance of
                Things Past*

1914   Burroughs, Edgar Rice (American, 1875–1950) *Tarzan of
                the Apes*
                Gide, André (French, 1839–1951) *Lafcadio's Adventures*
                Grey, Zane (American, 1875–1939) *Light of Western Stars*
                Russel, Mary Annette (Elizabeth; English, 1866–1941)
                The Pastor's Wife

1915   Azuela, Mariano (Mexican, 1873–1952) *The Underdogs*
                Conrad, Joseph (Polish, 1857–1924) *Victory*
                Ford, Ford Madox (English, 1873–1939) *The Good Soldier*
                Lawrence, D. H. (English, 1885–1930) *The Rainbow*
                Maugham, W. Somerset (English, 1874–1965) *Of Human
                Bondage*
                Poole, Ernest (American, 1880–1950) *The Harbor*
                Richardson, Dorothy M. (English, 1882–1957) *Pilgrimage*

1916   Barbusse, Henri (French, 1873–1935) *Under Fire*
                Blasco-Ibáñez, V. (Spanish, 1867–1928) *The Four Horse-
                men of the Apocalypse*
                Bojer, John (Norwegian, 1872–1959) *The Great Hunger*
                Hémon, Louis (Canadian, 1880–1913) *Maria Chapdelaine*

Joyce, James (Irish, 1882–1941) *Portrait of the Artist as a Young Man*
Lardner, Ring (American, 1885–1933) *You Know Me Al*
McFee, William (English, 1881–1966) *Casuals of the Sea*
Tarkington, Booth (American, 1869–1946) *Seventeen*

1917
Cabell, James Branch (American, 1879–1958) *Cream of the Jest*
Cahan, Abraham (American, 1860–1951) *The Rise of David Lavinsky*
Douglas, Norman (English, 1868–1952) *South Wind*
France, Anatole (French, 1844–1924) *The Gods Are Athirst*
Garland, Hamlin (American, 1860–1940) *A Son of the Middle Border*
Hamsun, Knut (Norwegian, 1859–1952) *Growth of the Soil*
Hergesheimer, Joseph (American, 1880–1954) *Three Black Pennies*
Phillips, David Graham (American, 1867–1911) *Susan Lenox, Her Rise and Fall*

1917–1929
Richardson, Henry Handel (Australian, 1880–1946) *The Fortunes of Richard Mahony*

1918
Cather, Willa (American, 1873–1947) *My Antonia*
Wast, Hugo (Gustavo Martínez Zuviría; Argentinian, 1883–1962) *Black Valley*

1918–1923
Duun, Olav (Norwegian, 1876–1939) *The People of Juvik*

1919
Anderson, Sherwood (American, 1876–1941) *Winesburg, Ohio*
Baroja y Nessi, Pío (Spanish, 1872–1956) *Caesar or Nothing*
Cabell, James Branch (American, 1879–1958) *Jurgen*
Gide, André (French, 1839–1951) *Pastorale Symphony*
Hergesheimer, Joseph (American, 1880–1954) *Java Head*
Maugham, W. Somerset (English, 1874–1965) *Moon and Sixpence*
Sillanpää, Frans Eemil (Finnish, 1888–1964) *Meek Heritage*
Wassermann, Jacob (German, 1873–1934) *The World's Illusion*

1919–1941
Tolstoy, Alexey (Russian, 1882–1945) *The Road to Calvar*

1920   Anderson, Sherwood, (American, 1876–1941) *Poor White*
Colette, Sidonie Gabrielle (French, 1873–1954) *Chéri*
Deledda, Grazia (Italian, 1872–1936) *The Mother*
Lawrence, D. H. (English, 1885–1930) *Women in Love*
Lewis, Sinclair (American, 1885–1951) *Main Street*
Masters, Edgar Lee (American, 1869–1950) *Mitch Miller*
Wharton, Edith (American, 1862–1937) *The Age of Innocence*

1920–1922   Undset, Sigrid (Danish, 1882–1949) *Kristin Lavransdatter*

1920–1931   Zamyatin, Yevgeny (Russian, 1884–1937) *We*

1920–1932   Duhamel, Georges (French, 1884–1966) *Salavin*

1921   Aragon, Louis (French, 1897) *Anicet*
Byrne, Donn (American, 1889–1928) *Messer Marco Polo*
De la Mare, Walter, (English, 1873–1956) *Memoirs of a Midget*
Hull, E. M. (English, n.d.) *The Sheik*
Macaulay, Rose (English, 1881–1958) *Dangerous Ages*
Maran, René (Martiniquian, 1887–1960) *Batouala*
Miro, Gabriel (Spanish, 1879–1930) *Our Father Daniel, Scenes of Clerical Life*
Sabatini, Rafael (Italian, 1875–1950) *Scaramouche*

1922   Barrios, Eduardo (Chilean, 1884–1963) *Brother Ass*
cummings, e. e. (American, 1894–1962) *The Enormous Room*
Garnett, David (English, 1892) *Lady into Fox*
Hesse, Hermann (German, 1877–1962) *Siddhartha*
Hough, Emerson (American, 1857–1923) *The Covered Wagon*
Ivanov, Vsevolod (Russian, 1895–1963) *Armoured Train 14-69)*
Joyce, James (Irish, 1882–1941) *Ulysses*
Lewis, Sinclair (American, 1885–1951) *Babbitt*
Pilnyak, Boris (Russian, 1894–1938) *The Naked Year*
Van Vechten, Carl (American, 1880–1966) *Peter Whiffle*

1922–1929   Martin Du Gard, Roger (French, 1881–1958) *The World of the Thibaults*

1923   Aldanov, Mark (Russian, 1886–1957) *The Ninth Thermidor*
Atherton, Gertrude (American, 1857–1948) *The Black Oxen*

Radiguet, Raymond (French, 1903–1923) *Devil in the Flesh*

Salten, Felix (Austrian, 1869–1945) *Bambi*

Svevo, Italo (Italian, 1860–1928) *Confessions of Zeno*

Stephens, James (Irish, 1882–1950) *Deidre*

Toomer, Jean (Afro-American, 1894–1967) *Cane*

1923–1924   Jensen, Johannes V. (Danish, 1873–1950) *The Long Journey*

1924   Ferber, Edna (American, 1887–1968) *So Big*

Forster, E. M. (American, 1879–1970) *Passage to India*

Mann, Thomas (German, 1875–1955) *The Magic Mountain*

Melville, Herman (American, 1819–1891) *Billy Budd* (first published, 1924)

Rivera, José Eustasio (Colombian, 1889–1928) *The Vortex*

Webb, Mary (English, 1883–1927) *Precious Bane*

1924–1926   Ford, Ford Madox (English, 1873–1939) *Parade's End*

1925   Ammers-Küller, Johanna van (Dutch, 1884) *The Rebel Generation*

Dos Passos, John (American, 1896–1970) *Manhattan Transfer*

Dreiser, Theodore (American, 1871–1945) *An American Tragedy*

Erskine, John (American, 1879–1951) *Private Life of Helen of Troy*

Feuchtwanger, Lion (German, 1884–1958) *Power*

Firbank, Ronald (English, 1886–1926) *Prancing Nigger*

Fitzgerald, F. Scott (American, 1896–1940) *The Great Gatsby*

Gide, André (French 1869–1951) *The Counterfeiters*

Glasgow, Ellen (American, Southern, 1874–1945) *Barren Ground*

Heyward, DuBose (American, Southern, 1885–1940) *Porgy*

Kafka, Franz (Czechoslovakian, 1883–1924) *The Trial*

Morley, Christopher (American, 1890–1957) *Thunder on the Left*

1926   Christie, Agatha (English, 1890–1976) *The Murder of Roger Ackroyd*

Glasgow, Ellen (American, Southern, 1874–1945) *The Romantic Comedians*

Güiraldes, Ricardo (Argentinian, 1882–1927) *Don Segundo Sombra*

Hasek, Jaroslav (Czechoslovakian, 1883–1923) *The Good Soldier Schweik*

Hemingway Ernest (American, 1899–1961) *The Sun Also Rises; The Torrents of Spring*

Kafka, Franz (Czechoslovakian, 1883–1924) *The Castle*

Lawrence, D. H. (English, 1885–1930) *The Plumed Serpent*

O'Flaherty, Liam (Irish, 1897) *The Informer*

Olyesha, Yuri Karlovich (Russian, 1899–1960) *Envy*

Roberts, Elizabeth Madox (American, Southern, 1886–1941) *The Time of Man*

Supervielle, Jules (French, 1884–1960) *The Colonel's Children*

Traven, B. (German-American 1882/1901–1969) *The Death Ship*

Wren, Percival Christopher (English, 1885–1941) *Beau Geste*

1927

Aiken, Conrad (American, 1889–1973) *Blue Voyage*

Cather, Willa (American, 1873–1947) *Death Comes for the Archbishop*

De La Roche, Mazo (Canadian, 1885–1961) *Jalna*

Hesse, Hermann (German, 1877–1962) *Steppenwolf*

Katayev, Valentine (Russian, 1897) *The Embezzlers*

Leonov, Leonid (Russian, 1899) *The Thief*

Lewis, Sinclair (American, 1885–1951) *Elmer Gantry*

Masters, Edgar Lee (American, 1869–1950) *Kit O'Brien*

Mauriac, François (French, 1885–1970) *Thérèse*

Powys, T. F. (English, 1875–1953) *Mr. Weston's Good Wine*

Queen, Ellery (Dannay, Frederick, American, 1905 and Lee, Manfred B.; American, 1905–1971) *The Roman Hat Mystery*

Rölvaag, O. E. (Norwegian, 1876–1931) *Giants in the Earth*

Traven, B. (German-American, 1882/1901–1969) *The Treasure of Sierra Madre*

Van Dine, S. S. (American, 1888–1939) *The Canary Murder Case*

Wescott, Glenway (American, 1901) *The Grandmothers*

Wilder, Thornton (American, 1897–1975) *The Bridge of San Luis Rey*

Woolf, Virginia (English, 1882–1941) *To the Lighthouse*

Zweig, Arnold (Prussian, 1887–1968) *The Case of Sergea* *Grischa*

1928   Breton, André (French, 1896–1966) *Nadja*
Delmar, Viña (American, 1905) *Bad Girl*
Grey, Zane (American, 1875–1939) *Nevada*
Guzmán, Martín Luis (Mexican, 1887–1959) *The Eagle and the Serpent*
Hall, Radclyffe (English, 188?–1943) *The Well of Loneliness*
Herbst, Josephine (American, 1897–1969) *Nothing Is Sacred*
Huxley, Aldous (English, 1894–1963) *Point Counter Point*
Il'f, Il'ia (Russian, 1897–1937) and Petrov, Eugene (Russian, 1903–1942) *Twelve Chairs*
Lawrence, D. H. (English, 1885–1930) *Lady Chatterley's Lover*
Remarque, Erich Maria (German, 1898–1970) *All Quiet o the Western Front*
Sholokhov, Mikhail (Russian, 1905) *And Quiet Flows the Don*
Waugh, Evelyn (English, 1903–1966) *Decline and Fall*
Woolf, Virginia (English, 1882–1941) *Orlando*

1928–1929   Tanizaki, Jun-ichiró (Japanese, 1886–1965) *Some Prefer Nettles*

1929   Burnett, W. R. (American, 1899) *Little Caesar*
Cocteau, Jean (French, 1889–1963) *The Holy Terrors*
Faulkner, William (American, Southern, 1897–1962) *The Sound and the Fury*
Gallegos, Rómulo (Venezuelan, 1884–1969) *Doña Barbar*
Green, Julien (American-French, 1900) *The Dark Journe*
Hemingway, Ernest (American, 1898–1961) *A Farewell t Arms*
Hughes, Richard (English, 1900–1976) *A High Wind in Jamaica (The Innocent Voyage)*
Priestley, J. B. (English, 1894) *The Good Companions*
Renn, Ludwig (German, 1889) *War*
Scott, Evelyn (American, Southern 1893–1963) *The Wav*
Tarkington, Booth (American, 1869–1946) *The Magnifice Ambersons*
Wolfe, Thomas (American, Southern, 1900–1938) *Look Homeward, Angel*

1930   Alvaro, Corrado (Italian, 1894–1956) *Revolt in Aspromonte*
Baroja y Nessi, Pío (Spanish, 1872–1956) *The Restlessness of Shanti Andia*
Baum, Vicki (Austrian, 1888/1896–1960) *Grand Hotel*
Brand, Max (American, 1892–1944) *Destry Rides Again*
Dahlberg, Edward (American, 1900–1977) *Bottom Dogs*
Faulkner, William (American, 1897–1962) *As I Lay Dying*
Fisher, Dorothy Canfield (American, 1879–1958) *The Deepening Stream*
Giraudoux, Jean (French, 1882–1944) *Living Woman*
Gold, Michael (American, 1894–1967) *Jews Without Money*
Hammett, Dashiell (American, 1894–1961) *The Maltese Falcon*
Lewis, Wyndham (English, 1886–1957) *The Apes of God*
Maugham, W. Somerset (English, 1874–1965) *Cakes and Ale*
Rhys, Jean (English, 1894) *After Leaving Mr. Mackenzie*
Seaver, Edwin (American, 1900) *The Company*
Vorse, Mary Heaton (American, ?–1966) *Strike!*

1930–1932 Broch, Hermann (German, 1886–1951) *The Sleepwalkers*

1930–1943 Musil, Robert (Austrian, 1880–1942) *The Man without Qualities*

1931   Buck, Pearl (American, 1892–1973) *The Good Earth*
Faulkner, William (American, Southern, 1897–1962) *Sanctuary*
Hurst, Fannie (American, 1889–1968) *Back Street*
Miller, Henry (American, 1891) *Tropic of Cancer*
Saint-Exupéry, Antoine de (French, 1900–1944) *Night Flight*
Strong, L. A. G. (English, 1896–1958) *The Garden*
Thayer, Tiffany (American, 1902) *Call Her Savage*
Uslar Pietri, Arturo (Venezuelan, 1905) *The Red Lances*
West, Nathanael (American, 1903–1940) *The Dream Life of Balso Snell*
Woolf, Virginia (English, 1882–1941) *The Waves*

1932   Bodenheim, Maxwell (American, 1893–1954) *Run, Sheep, Run*
Brody, Catherine (American, n.d.) *Nobody Starves*
Caldwell, Erskine (American, Southern, 1903) *Tobacco Road*

Céline, Louis Ferdinand (Louis Fuchs Destouches;
French, 1894–1961) *Journey to the End of the Night*
Faulkner, William (American, Southern 1897–1962) *Light
in August*
Gibbons, Stella (English, 1902) *Cold Comfort Farm*
Huxley, Aldous (English, 1894–1963) *Brave New World*
Lindsay, Norman (American, 1879–1969) *The Cautious
Amorist*
Lumpkin, Grace (American, Southern, n.d.) *To Make My
Bread*
Mauriac, François (French, 1885–1970) *Viper's Tangle*
Morgan, Charles (English, 1894–1958) *The Fountain*
Nordhoff, Charles (American, 1887–1947) and Hall, James
Norman (American, 1887–1951) *Mutiny on the Bounty*
Smith, Homer (American, 1895) *Kamongo*
Smith, Thorne (American, 1893–1934) *Topper Takes a
Trip*

1932–1935   Farrell, James T. (American, 1904) *Studs Lonigan*

1932–1946   Romains, Jules (French, 1885–1972) *Men of Good Will*

1933   Aiken, Conrad (American, 1889–1972) *Great Circle*
Allen, Hervey (American, 1889–1949) *Anthony Adverse*
Aymé, Marcel (French, 1902–1967) *The Green Mare*
Caldwell, Erskine (American, Southern, 1903) *God's Little
Acre*
Conroy, Jack (American, 1899) *The Disinherited*
Hilton, James (English, 1900–1954) *Lost Horizon*
Malraux, André (French, 1901–1976) *Man's Fate*
March, William (American, Southern, 1894–1954) *Com-
pany K*
Martin Du Gard, Roger (French, 1881–1958) *The Postman*
O'Faoláin, Séan (Irish, 1900) *A Nest of Simple Folk*
Silone, Ignazio (Italian, 1900) *Fontamara*
West, Nathanael (American, 1903–1940) *Miss Lonelyhearts*
Zoshchenko, Mikhail (Russian, 1895–1958) *Restored
Youth*

1934   Aragon, Louis (French, 1897) *The Bells of Basel*
Armstrong, Arnold B (American, n.d.) *Parched Earth*
Cain, James M. (American, 1892–1977) *The Postman Al-
ways Rings Twice*
Cantwell, Robert (American, 1908) *Land of Plenty*
Dinesen, Isak (Danish, 1885–1945) *Seven Gothic Tales*

Fitzgerald, F. Scott (American, 1896-1940) *Tender is the Night*

Giono, Jean (French, 1895-1970) *Song of the World*

Graves, Robert (English, 1895) *I, Claudius*

Halper, Albert (American, 1904) *The Foundry*

Icaza, Jorge (Ecuadorian, 1908) *Huasipungo*

Montherlant, Henri de (French, 1896-1972) *Perish in Their Pride*

Newhouse, Edward (American, 1911) *You Can't Sleep Here*

O'Hara, John (American, 1905-1970) *Appointment in Samarra*

Roth, Henry (American, 1907) *Call It Sleep*

Smith, Thorne (American, 1893-1934) *The Glorious Pool*

Stone, Irving (American, 1903) *Lust for Life*

Suckow, Ruth (American, 1892-1960) *The Folks*

Werfel, Franz (Austro-Czechoslovakian, 1890-1945) *The Forty Days of Musa Dagh*

West, Nathanael (American, 1903-1940) *A Cool Million*

Young, Stark (American, 1881-1963) *So Red the Rose*

1934-1935   Laxness, Halldór (Icelandic, 1902) *Independent People*

1934-1937   Fuchs, Daniel (American, 1909) *Williamsburg Trilogy*

1935   Bishop, John Peale (American, 1892-1944) *Act of Darkness*

Briffault, Robert (English, 1876-1948) *Europa*

Cobb, Humphrey (American, 1899-1944) *Paths of Glory*

Davis, H. L. (American, 1896-1960) *Honey in the Horn*

Kromer, Tom (American, 1906) *Waiting for Nothing*

McCoy, Horace (American, 1897-1955) *They Shoot Horses, Don't They?*

Myers, L. H. (English, 1881-1944) *The Root and the Flower*

O'Hara, John (American, 1905-1970) *Butterfield 8*

Ramuz, C. F. (Franco-Swiss, 1878-1947) *When the Mountain Fell*

Read, Herbert (English, 1893-1968) *The Green Child*

Weatherwax, Clara (American, n.d.) *Marching! Marching!*

Williamson, Henry (English, 1897) *Salar the Salmon*

Woodford, Jack (American, 1894-1971) *Four Eves*

Wolfe, Thomas (American, Southern 1900-1938) *Of Time and the River*

1936   Barnes, Djuna (American, 1892) *Nightwood*
        Bowen, Elizabeth (English, 1899–1970) *The House in Paris*
        Canetti, Elias (Bulgarian, 1905) *Auto-da-fé*
        Chevallier, Gabriel (French, 1895) *The Scandals of Clochemerle*
        Farrell, James T. (American, 1904) *A World I Never Made*
        Faulkner, William (American, Southern, 1897–1962) *Absalom, Absalom!*
        Greene, Graham (English, 1904) *This Gun for Hire*
        Gulbranssen, Trygve (Norwegian, 1894) *Beyond Sing the Woods*
        Mitchell, Margaret (American, Southern, 1900–1949) *Gone with the Wind*
        Nin, Anaïs (Spanish-American, 1903–1977) *House of Incest*
        Santayana, George (Spanish, 1863–1952) *The Last Puritan*
        Silone, Ignazio (Italian, 1900) *Bread and Wine*
        Singer, Israel Joshua (Polish, 1893–1944) *The Brothers Ashkenazi*

1937   Appel, Benjamin (American, 1907–1977) *Brain Guy*
        Bernanos, Georges (French, 1888–1948) *The Diary of a Country Priest*
        Cain, James M. (American, 1892–1977) *Serenade*
        Čapek, Karel, (Czechoslovakian, 1890–1938) *War with the Newts*
        Dos Passos, John (American, 1896–1970) *U.S.A.*
        Johnson, Josephine (American, 1910) *Jordanstown*
        Kang, Younghill (Korean-American, 1903–1972) *East Goes West*
        Malraux, André (French, 1901–1976) *Man's Hope*
        Marquand, John P. (American, 1893–1960) *The Late George Apley*
        Prokosch, Frederic (American, 1909) *The Seven Who Fled*
        Raine, William MacLeod (Scots-American, 1871–1954) *Bucky Follows a Cold Trail*
        Roberts, Kenneth (American, 1885–1957) *Northwest Passage*
        Steinbeck, John (American, 1902–1968) *Of Mice and Men*
        Williams, William Carlos (American, 118–1963) *White Mule*

1937–1947 Kawabata, Yasunari (Japanese, 1899–1972) *Snow Country*

1938   Alvaro, Carrado (Italian, 1895–1956) *Man Is Strong*
        Bowen, Elizabeth (English, 1899–1970) *Death of the Heart*

Brand, Max (American, 1900–1944) *Singing Guns*
Du Maurier, Daphne (English, 1907) *Rebecca*
Gombrowicz, Witold (Polish, 1904–1969) *Feryduke*
Greene, Graham (English, 1904) *Brighton Rock*
Lewis, C. S. (English, 1898–1963) *Out of the Silent Planet*
Rao, Raja (South Indian, 1909) *Kanthapura*
Sartre, Jean-Paul (French, 1905) *Nausea*
Tate, Allen (American, Southern, 1899) *The Fathers*

1938–1940   Bacchelli, Riccardo (Italian, 1891) *The Mill on the Po*

1939   Asch, Sholom (Polish, 1880–1957) *The Nazarene*
Chandler, Raymond (American, 1888–1959) *The Big Sleep*
Clarke, Donald Henderson (American, 1887–1958) *Millie's Daughter*
Faulkner, William (American, Southern, 1897–1962) *The Wild Palms*
Joyce, James (Irish, 1882–1941) *Finnegans Wake*
Jünger, Ernst (German, 1895) *On the Marble Cliffs*
Leiris, Michel (French, 1901) *The Age of Man*
Marquand, John P. (American, 1893–1960) *Wickford Point*
Miller, Henry (American, 1891) *The Tropic of Capricorn*
O'Brien, Flann (Irish, 1911–1966) *At Swim-Two-Birds*
Sarraute, Nathalie (French, 1902) *Tropismes*
Steinbeck, John (American, 1902–1968) *The Grapes of Wrath*
Trumbo, Dalton (American, 1905–1976) *Johnny Got His Gun*
Wolfe, Thomas (American, Southern, 1900–1938) *The Web and the Rock*

1940   Bellamann, Henry (American, 1882–1945) *King's Row*
Chandler, Raymond (American, 1888–1959) *Farewell, My Lovely*
Clark, Walter Van Tilburg (American, 1909–1971) *The Ox-Bow Incident*
Costa du Rels, Adolfo (Bolivian, 1891) *Bewitched Lands*
Greene, Graham (English, 1904) *The Power and the Glory*
McCullers, Carson (American, Southern, 1917–1968) *The Heart Is a Lonely Hunter*
Mallea, Eduardo (Argentian, 1903) *The Bay of Silence*
Maltz, Albert (American, 1908) *The Underground Stream*
Nathan, Robert (American, 1894) *Portrait of Jennie*

Richter, Conrad (American, 1890–1968) *The Trees*
Simenon, Georges (French, 1903) *The Patience of Maigret*
Snow, C. P. (English, 1905) *Strangers and Brothers*
Stead, Christina (Australian, 1902) *The Man Who Loved Children*
Still, James (American, Southern, 1906) *River of Earth*
Wright, Richard (Afro-American, 1908–1960) *Native Son*

1941

Alegría, Ciro (Peruvian, 1909–1967) *Broad and Alien Is the World*
Amorim, Enrique (Uruguayian, 1900–1960) *The Horse and His Shadow*
Baldwin, Faith (American, 1893) *The Heart Remembers*
Cary, Joyce (English, 1888–1957) *Herself Surprised*
Goodrich, Marcus (American, 1897) *Delilah*
Gordon, Caroline (American, Southern, 1895) *Green Centuries*
Koestler, Arthur (Anglo-Hungarian, 1905) *Darkness at Noon*
Lewis, Janet (American, 1899) *The Wife of Martin Guerre*
McCullers, Carson (American, Southern, 1917–1967) *Reflections in a Golden Eye*
Patchen, Kenneth (American, 1911–1972) *Journal of Albion Moonlight*
Piovene, Guido (Italian, 1907–1974) *Letters of a Novice*
Schulberg, Budd (American, 1914) *What Makes Sammy Run?*
Werfel, Franz (Austro-Czechoslovakian, 1890–1945) *The Song of Bernadette*
Woolf, Virginia (English, 1882–1941) *Between the Acts*

1942

Camus, Albert (French, 1913–1960) *The Stranger*
Cela, Camilo José (Spanish, 1916) *The Family of Pascual Duarte*
Chase, James Hadley (English, 1906) *No Orchids for Miss Blandish*
Cozzens, James Gould (American, 1903) *The Just and the Unjust*
Douglas, Lloyd C. (American, 1877–1951) *The Robe*
Fast, Howard (American, 1914) *The Unvanquished*
Faulkner, William (American, Southern, 1897–1962) *The Bear*
Haycox, Ernest (American, 1899–1950) *Alder Gulch*
Merritt, Abraham (American, 1882–1943) *Burn, Witch, Burn!*

Short, Luke (American, 1908) *Hardcase*
Waters, Frank (American, 1902) *The Man Who Killed the Deer*
Wright, Austin Tappan (American, 1883–1931) *Islandia*

1943   Asch, Sholem (American, 1880–1957) *The Apostle*
Freeman, Joseph (American, 1897–1965) *Never Call Retreat*
Genet, Jean (French, 1910) *Our Lady of the Flowers*
Greene, Graham (English, 1904) *The Ministry of Fear*
Lins do Rêgo, José (Brazilian, 1901–1957) *Dead Fires*
McKenney, Ruth (American, 1911–1971) *Jake Home*
Rand, Ayn (Russo-American, 1905) *The Fountainhead*
Saroyan, William (American, 1908) *The Human Comedy*
Smith, Betty (American, 1904–1972) *A Tree Grows in Brooklyn*
Stegner, Wallace (American, 1909) *Big Rock Candy Mountain*
Stuart, Jesse (American, Southern, 1907) *Taps for Private Tussie*
Verissimo, Erico (Brazilian, 1905) *The Rest Is Silence*

1944   Bellow, Saul (Canadian-American, 1915) *Dangling Man*
Busch, Niven (American, 1903) *Duel in the Sun*
Cary, Joyce (English, 1888–1957) *The Horse's Mouth*
Dali, Salvador (Spanish, 1904) *Hidden Faces*
Jackson, Charles (American, 1903–1968) *The Lost Weekend*
Joyce, James (Irish, 1882–1941) *Stephen Hero*
Kossak, Zofia (Polish, 1890–1968) *Blessed Are the Meek*
Maugham, Somerset (English, 1874–1965) *The Razor's Edge*
Shute, Nevil (English, 1899–1960) *Pastoral*
Smith, Lillian (American, Southern, 1897–1966) *Strange Fruit*
Williams, Ben Ames (American, 1889–1953) *Leave Her to Heaven*
Winsor, Kathleen (American, 1919) *Forever Amber*

1945   Andric, Ivo (Yugoslavian, 1892–1975) *The Bridge on the Drina*
Broch, Hermann (German, 1886–1951) *The Death of Virgil*
Green, Henry (English, 1905) *Loving*
Hilton, James (English, 1900–1955) *So Well Remembered*
Isherwood, Christoper (English, 1904) *The Berlin Stories*
Laforet, Carmen (Spanish, 1921) *Nada*

Manfred, Frederick F. (American, 1912) *Boy Almighty*
Orwell, George (English, 1903-1950) *Animal Farm*
Sylvester, Harry (American, 1908) *Dayspring*
Williams, Charles (English, 1886-1945) *All Hallow's Eve*

1945-1949 Sartre, Jean Paul (French, 1905) *Roads to Freedom*

1946 Asturias, Miguel Angel (Guatemalan, 1899-1974) *El Senor Presidente*
Gide, André (French, 1869-1951) *Theseus*
Green, Henry (English, 1905-1974) *Back*
Heggen, Thomas (American, 1919-1949) *Mister Roberts*
Kazantzakis, Nikos (Greek, 1883-1957) *Zorba, the Greek*
McCullers, Carson (American, Southern, 1917-1967) *A Member of the Wedding*
Peake, Mervyn (English, 1911) *Titus Groan*
Vittorini, Elio (Italian, 1908-1966) *In Sicily*
Warren, Robert Penn (American, Southern, 1905) *All the King's Men*
Welty, Eudora (American, Southern, 1909) *Delta Wedding*
Yerby, Frank (Afro-American, 1916) *The Foxes of Harrow*

1947 Bellow, Saul (Canadian-American, 1915) *The Victim*
Camus, Albert (French, 1913-1960) *The Plague*
Curtis, Jean-Louis (French, 1917) *The Forests of the Night*
Davis, H. L. (American, 1896) *Harp of a Thousand Strings*
Ehrenburg, Ilya (Russian, 1891-1967) *The Storm*
Guthrie, A. B. (American, 1901) *The Big Sky*
Hartley, L. P. (English, 1895) *Eustace and Hilda*
Heard, Gerald (English, 1889-1971) *Dopplegängers*
Hobson, Laura Zanetkin (American, 1900) *Gentleman's Agreement*
Lewisohn, Ludwig, (German-American, 1882-1955) *The Case of Mr. Crump*
Lowry, Malcolm (Canadian, 1909-1952) *Under the Volcano*
Mann, Thomas (German, 1875-1955) *Doctor Faustus*
Moravia, Alberto (Italian, 1907) *Woman of Rome*
Motley, Willard (Afro-American, 1912-1965) *Knock on Any Door*
Schneider, Isidor (Polish-American, 1896) *The Judas Time*
Spillane, Mickey (American, 1918) *I, The Jury*
Trilling, Lionel (American, 1905-1975) *The Middle of the Journey*

Unamuno y Jugo, Miguel de (Spanish, 1864–1936) *Abel Sanchez*
Willingham, Calder (American, 1922) *End as a Man*
Yáñez, Agustín (Mexican, 1904) *The Edge of the Storm*

1948

Bhattacharya, Bhabani (Indian, 1906) *So Many Hungers*
Capote, Truman (American, Southern, 1925) *Other Voices, Other Rooms*
Dazai Osamu (Japanese, 1909–1948) *No Longer Human*
Desani, G. V. (Indian, 1909) *All About H. Hatter*
Fedin, Konstantin (Russian, 1892) *No Ordinary Summers*
Greene, Graham (English, 1904) *The Heart of the Matter*
Lockridge, Ross, Jr. (American, 1914–1948) *Raintree County*
Mailer, Norman (American, 1923) *The Naked and the Dead*
Morris, Wright (American, 1910) *The World in the Attic*
Paton, Alan (South African, 1903) *Cry, the Beloved Country*
Sender, Ramon (Spanish, 1902) *The King and the Queen*
Shaw, Irwin (American, 1913) *The Young Lions*
Skinner, B. F. (American, 1904) *Walden Two*
Vidal, Gore (American, 1925) *The City and the Pillar*
Vittorini, Elio (Italian, 1908–1966) *The Red Carnation*
Waugh, Evelyn (English, 1903–1966) *The Loved One*

1949

Algren, Nelson (American, 1909) *The Man with the Golden Arm*
Aragon, Louis (French, 1897) *Les Communistes*
Arnow, Harriette (American, 1908) *Hunter's Horn*
Bates, H. E. (English, 1905–1974) *Jacaranda Tree*
Carpentier, Alejo (Cuban-Venezuelan, 1904) *The Kingdom of This World*
Clark, Walter Van Tilburg (American, 1909–1971) *Track of the Cat*
Hawkes, John (American, 1925) *The Cannibal*
Lagerkvist, Pär Fabian (Sweden, 1891–1974) *Barabbas*
Morris, Wright (American, 1910) *The World in the Attic*
Orwell, George (English, 1903–1950) *1984*
Pavese, Cesare (Italian, 1908–1950) *The Moon and the Bonfires*
Pratolini, Vasco (Italian, 1913) *A Hero of Our Time*
Sansom, William (English, 1912–1976) *The Body*
Schaefer, Jack (American, 1907) *Shane*

1950   Bradbury, Ray (American, 1920) *Martian Chronicles*
Buechner, Frederick (American, 1926) *A Long Day's Dying*
Goyen, William (American, 1915) *House of Breath*
Hemingway, Ernest (American, 1899–1961) *Across the River and into the Trees*
Hersey, John (American, 1914) *The Wall*
Simenon, Georges (French, 1903) *The Snow Was Black*
Spillane, Mickey (American, 1918) *My Gun Is Quick*
Subercaseaux, Benjamin (Chilean, 1902) *Jemmy Button*
Warren, Robert Penn (American, 1905) *World Enough and Time*
Williams, Tennessee (American, Southern, 1914) *The Roman Spring of Mrs. Stone*

1951   Beckett, Samuel (Irish, 1906) *Malone Dies*
Cela, Camilo José (Spanish, 1916) *The Hive*
Diáz Lozano, Argentina (Honduran, 1909) *Mayapán*
Giono, Jean (French, 1895–1970) *Horseman on the Roof*
Jones, James (American, 1921–1977) *From Here to Eternity*
Mailer, Norman (American, 1923) *Barbary Shore*
Morante, Elsa (Italian, 1916) *House of Liars*
Morris, Wright (American, 1910) *Man and Boy*
Ooka, Shohei (Japanese, 1909) *Fires on the Plain*
Salinger, J. D. (American, 1919) *The Catcher in the Rye*
Spillane, Mickey (American, 1918) *The Big Kill*
Styron, William (American, Southern, 1925) *Lie Down in Darkness*
Wouk, Herman (American, 1915) *The Caine Mutiny*
Yourcenar, Marguerite (French, 1913) *Hadrian's Memoirs*

1951–1955   Powell, Anthony (English, 1905) *A Dance to the Music of Time*

1952   Boulle, Pierre (French, 1912) *The Bridge Over the River Kwai*
Ellison, Ralph (Afro-American, 1914) *Invisible Man*
Griffin, John Howard (American, Southern, 1920) *The Devil Rides Outside*
Hemingway, Ernest (American, 1879–1961) *The Old Man and the Sea*
McCarthy, Mary (American, 1912) *The Groves of Academe*
MacDonald, John D. (American, 1916) *The Damned*
Malamud, Bernard (American, 1914) *The Natural*

Malaparte, Curzio (Italian, 1898–1957) *The Skin*
Morris, Wright (American, 1910) *Works of Love*
Stafford, Jean (American, 1915) *The Catherine Wheel*
Steinbeck, John (American, 1902–1968) *East of Eden*
Thompson, Jim (American, n.d.) *The Killer Inside Me*
Tutuola, Amos (African, 1920) *The Palm-Wine Drinkard*

1953 Amis, Kingsley (English, 1922) *Lucky Jim*
Baldwin, James (American, 1924) *Go Tell It on the Mountain*
Basso, Hamilton (American, Southern, 1904–1964) *The View from Pompey's Head*
Bellow, Saul (American, 1915) *The Adventures of Augie March*
Gironella, José María (Spanish, 1917) *The Cypresses Believe in God*
Grubb, Davis (American, Southern, 1919) *Night of the Hunter*
Hyman, Mac (American, Southern, 1923–1963) *No Time for Sergeants*
Morris, Wright (American, 1910) *The Deep Sleep*
Oldenbourg, Zoë (French, 1916) *The Cornerstone*
Wain, John (English, 1925) *Hurry on Down*

1954 Arnow, Harriette (American, Southern, 1908) *The Dollmaker*
Beauvoir, Simone de (French, 1908) *Les Mandarins*
Bhattacharya, Bhabani (Indian, 1906) *He Who Rides the Tiger*
Bowles, Paul (American, 1910) *The Sheltering Sky*
De Vries, Peter (American, 1910) *The Tunnel of Love*
Duggan, Alfred (English, 1903–1964) *Leopards and Lilies*
Faulkner, William (American, Southern, 1897–1962) *A Fable*
Frisch, Max (Swiss, 1911) *I'm Not Stiller*
Galván, Manuel de Jesus (Dominican Republican, 1834–1911) *The Cross and the Sword*
Golding, William (English, 1911) *Lord of the Flies*
Jackson, Shirley (American, 1919–1965) *The Bird's Nest*
Jarrell, Randall (American, 1914–1965) *Pictures from an Institution*
Mann, Thomas (German, 1875–1955) *Confessions of Felix Krull*
March, William (American, 1894–1954) *The Bad Seed*
Markandaya, Kamala (Indian, 1924) *Nectar in a Sieve*

Menen, Aubrey (Indian, 1912) *The Ramayana*
Morris, Wright (American, 1910) *The Huge Season*
Nin, Anaïs (Spanish-American, 1903–1977) *A Spy in the House of Love*
Sagan, Françoise (French, 1935) *Bonjour Tristesse*
Thompson, Morton (American, n.d.) *Not As A Stranger*

1954–1955   Tolkien, J. R. R. (English, 1892–1973) *The Lord of the Rin*

1955   Bowles, Paul (American, 1911) *The Spider's House*
Dennis, Nigel (English, 1912) *Cards of Identity*
Donleavy, J. P. (American, 1926) *The Ginger Man*
Dratler, Jay (American, 1911) *The Judas Kiss*
Fülop-Miller, René (German, 1891) *The Night of Time*
Gaddis, William (American, 1922) *The Recognitions*
Millar, Margaret (Canadian, 1915) *Beast in View*
Pasolini, Pier Paolo (Italian, 1922) *The Ragozzi*
Robbe-Grillet, Alain (French, 1922) *The Voyeur*
Rulfo, Juan (Mexican, 1918) *Pedro Páramo*
Singh, Khushwant (Indian, 1915) *Train to Pakistan*
Warren, Robert Penn (American, Southern, 1905) *Band Angels*
West, Anthony (English, 1914) *Heritage*

1956   Barth, John (American, 1930) *The Floating Opera*
Bastide, François-Régis (French, 1926) *Les Adieux*
Beckett, Samuel (Irish, 1906) *Malone Dies*
Bellow, Saul (American, 1915) *Seize the Day*
Camus, Albert (French, 1913–1960) *The Fall*
Gary, Romain (French, 1914) *The Roots of Heaven*
Heinrich, Willi (German, 1920) *The Cross of Iron*
Jhabvala, R. Prawer (Indian, 1927) *Amrita*
Kawabata, Yasunari (Japanese, 1899) *Snow Country*
Kirst, Hans Hellmut (German, 1914) *The Revolt of Gunner Asch*
Metalious, Grace (American, 1924–1964) *Peyton Place*
Moore, Brian (Canadian, 1921) *The Lonely Passion of Judith Hearne*
Morris, Wright (American, 1910) *The Field of Vision*
Renault, Mary (British, 1905) *The Last of the Wine*
Tanizaki, Jun-ichiro (Japanese, 1886–1965) *The Key*
Tracy, Honor (English, 1913) *The Straight and Narrow Path*
Wilson, Angus (English, 1913) *Anglo-Saxon Attitudes*

1957   Agee, James (American, Southern, 1909-1955) *A Death in
                  the Family*
              Bataille, George (French, 1897-1963) *The Blue Sky*
              Bjarnhof, Karl (Danish, 1898) *The Good Light*
              Braine, John (English, 1922) *Room at the Top*
              Butor, Michel (French, 1927-1959) *A Change of Heart*
              Cheever, John (American, 1912) *The Wapshot Chronicle*
              Green, Gerald (American, 1922) *The Last Angry Man*
              Hedyat, Sadegh (Persian, 1903-1951) *The Blind Owl*
              Kerouac, Jack (American, 1922-1970) *On the Road*
              Lytle, Andrew (American, Southern, 1903) *The Velvet
                  Horn*
              Macaulay, Rose (English, 1889?-1958) *The Towers of Tre-
                  bizond*
              Mishima, Yukio (Japanese, 1925-1970) *The Sound of
                  Waves*
              Morris, Wright (American, 1910) *Love Among the Canni-
                  bals*
              Rand, Ayn (Russian-American, 1905) *Atlas Shrugged*
              Robbe-Grillet, Alain (French, 1922) *Jealousy*
              Simon, Claude (French, 1913) *The Wind*
              Vailland, Roger (French, 1907-1965) *The Law*
              White, Patrick (English, 1912) *Voss*

1957-1960   Durrell, Lawrence (Irish, 1912) *Alexandria Quartet*

1958   Amado, Jorge (Brazilian, 1912) *Gabriela, Clove, and Cin-
                  namon*
              Barth, John (American, 1930) *End of the Road*
              Beckett, Samuel (Irish, 1906) *The Unnamable*
              Burdick, Eugene (American, 1918-1965) and Lederer,
                  William (American, 1912) *The Ugly American*
              Gordimer, Nadine (S. African, 1923) *A World of Strangers*
              Humphrey, William (American, Southern, 1924) *Home
                  from the Hill*
              L'Amour, Louis (American, 1908) *Radigan*
              Lampedusa, Giuseppe di (Sicilian, 1896-1957) *The
                  Leopard*
              Mishima, Yukio (Japanese, 1925-1970) *Confessions of a
                  Mask*
              Nabokov, Vladimir (Russian, 1899-1977) *Lolita*
              Narayan, R. K. (S. Indian, 1907) *The Guide*
              Pasternak, Boris (Russian, 1890-1960) *Doctor Zhivago*
              Sillitoe, Alan (English, 1928) *Saturday Night and Sunday
                  Morning*

Traver, Robert (American, 1903) *Anatomy of a Murder*
Uris, Leon (American, 1924) *Exodus*
Wain, John (English, 1925) *The Contenders*
White, T. H. (English, 1906-1964) *The Once and Future King*

1958-1959   Bellow, Saul (American, 1915) *Henderson the Rain King*

1959   Böll, Heinrich (German, 1917) *Billiards at Half-Past Nine*
Burroughs, William (American, 1914) *Naked Lunch*
Castillo, Michel del (French, 1933) *A Child of Our Time*
Connell, Evan S., Jr. (American, 1924) *Mrs. Bridge*
Drury, Allen (American, 1918) *Advise and Consent*
Dürrenmatt, Friedrich (Swiss, 1921) *The Pledge*
Goodman, Paul (American, 1911-1972) *The Empire City*
Grass, Günter (Polish, 1927) *The Tin Drum*
Harris, Mark (American, 1922) *Wake Up, Stupid*
Humes, H. L. (American, 1926) *Men Die*
Johnson, Uwe (German, 1934) *Speculations About Jacob*
Kerouac, Jack (American, 1922-1969) *The Subterraneans*
Knowles, John (American, 1926) *A Separate Peace*
Lafourcade, Enrique (Chilean, 1927) *King Ahalis Feast*
Mauriac, Claude (French, 1910-1970) *The Dinner Party*
Menen, Aubrey (Indian, 1912) *The Fig Tree*
Michener, James (American, 1907) *Hawaii*
Purdy, James (American, 1923) *Malcolm*
Queneau, Raymond (French, 1903-1976) *Zazie in the Metro*
Southern, Terry (American, 1926) *Candy; The Magic Christian*
Stewart, Mary (English, 1916) *Nine Coaches Waiting*
Vale, Eugene (Swiss-American, 1917) *The Thirteenth Apostle*
Waterhouse, Keith (English, 1929) *Billy Liar*
Wilson, Edmund (American, 1895-1972) *Memoirs of Hecate County*
Woolf, Douglas (American, 1922) *Fade Out*

1960   Barth, John (American, 1930) *The Sot-Weed Factor*
Bazin, Hervé (French, 1911) *In the Name of the Son*
Duggan, Alfred (English, 1903-1964) *The Cunning of the Dove*
Ferlinghetti, Lawrence (American, 1919) *Her*
Lee, Harper (American, Southern, 1926) *To Kill a Mockingbird*

Morris, Wright (American, 1910) *Ceremony in Lone Tree*
O'Connor, Flannery (American, Southern, 1925–1964) *The Violent Bear It Away*
Ousmane, Sembène (Senegalian, 1923) *God's Bits of Wood*
Stacton, David (American, 1925–1968) *A Dancer in Darkness*
Thériault, Yves (French-Canadian, 1916) *Ashini*
Trocchi, Alexander (British, 1925) *Cain's Book*
Updike, John (American, 1932) *Rabbit, Run*

1961   Gover, Robert (American, 1929) *One Hundred Dollar Misunderstanding*
Hawkes, John (American, 1925) *The Lime Twig*
Heinlein, Robert (American, 1907) *Stranger in a Strange Land*
Heller, Joseph (American, 1923) *Catch-22*
Madden, David (American, Southern, 1933) *The Beautiful Greed*
Mauriac, Claude (French, 1914) *The Marquise Went Out at Five*
Murdoch, Iris (English, 1919) *A Severed Head*
Ngugi, James (S. African, 1938) *Chocolates for My Wife, Slices of My Life*
Osaragi, Jiro (Japanese, 1898–1973) *The Journey*
Percy, Walker (American, Southern, 1916) *The Moviegoer*
Pirajno, Alberto Denti Di (Italian, 1886) *Ippolita*
Robbins, Harold (American, 1912) *The Carpetbaggers*
Stone, Irving (American, 1903) *The Agony and the Ecstasy*
Yates, Richard (American, 1926) *Revolutionary Road*

1962   Baker, Dorothy (American, 1907–1968) *Cassandra at the Wedding*
Burgess, Anthony (English, 1917) *A Clockwork Orange*
Dumitriu, Petru (Rumanian, 1924) *Incognito*
Duras, Marguerite (French, 1914) *10:30 on a Summer Night*
Friedman, Bruce J. (American, 1930) *Stern*
Fuentes, Carlos (Mexican, 1929) *The Death of Artemio Cruz*
Goytisolo, Juan (Spanish, 1931) *The Party's Over*
Kelly, William Melvin (Afro-American, 1937) *A Different Drummer*

Kesey, Ken (American, 1935) *One Flew Over the Cuckoo's Nest*
La Guma, Alex (Nigerian, 1925) *A Walk in the Night*
Lessing, Doris (English, 1919) *The Golden Notebook*
Newby, P. H. (English, 1918) *The Barbary Light*
Pinget, Robert (French, 1919) *The Inquisitory*
Porter, Katherine Anne (American, 1894) *Ship of Fools*
Singer, Isaac Bashevis (Polish, 1904) *The Slave*
Vonnegut, Kurt (American, 1922) *Mother Night*
Berger, Yves (French, 1936) *The Garden*

1963

Brophy, Brigid (English, 1929) *The Finishing Touch*
Cortazar, Julio (Argentinian, 1914) *Hopskotch*
Dayan, Yael (Israeli, 1939) *Dust*
Donoso, José (Chilean, 1924) *Coronation*
Ekwensi, Cyprian (Lagosian, 1921) *People of the City*
Holt, Victoria (English, 1906) *Bride of Pendorric*
Klein-Haparash, J. (German, 1897) *He Who Flees the Lion*
McCarthy, Mary (American, 1912) *The Group*
McMurtry, Larry (American, Southern, 1936) *Leaving Cheyenne*
Mandiargues, André Pieryre de (French, 1919) *The Motorcycle*
Modisane, Bloke (African, 1923) *Blame Me on History*
Morris, Wright (American, 1910) *Cause for Wonder*
Pynchon, Thomas (American, 1937) *V.*
Rechy, John (American, 1934) *City of Night*
Semprun, Jorge (French, 1923) *The Long Voyage*
Sontag, Susan (American, 1933) *The Benefactor*
Spark, Muriel (English, 1918) *The Girls of Slender Means*
Tevis, Walter (American, n.d.) *Man Who Fell to Earth*
Vonnegut, Kurt (American, 1922) *Cat's Cradle*
Wallant, Edward Lewis (American, 1926–1962) *The Tenants of Moonbloom*
West, Morris L. (Australian, 1916) *The Shoes of the Fisherman*

1964

Abe, Kobo (Japanese, 1924) *The Woman in the Dunes*
Auchincloss, Louis (American, 1917) *The Rector of Justin*
Bellow, Saul (Canadian-American, 1915) *Herzog*
Berger, Thomas (American, 1924) *Little Big Man*
Compton-Burnett, Ivy (English, 1892–1969) *A God and His Gifts*
Friedman, Bruce Jay (American, 1930) *A Mother's Kisses*

Grau, Shirley Ann (American, Southern, 1929) *The Keepers of the House*
Kesey, Ken (American, 1935) *Sometimes a Great Notion*
Larner, Jeremy (American, 1937) *Drive, He Said*
Oates, Joyce Carol (American, 1938) *With Shuddering Fall*
Purdy, James (American, 1923) *Cabot Wright Begins*
Rawicz, Piotr (French, 1919) *Blood from the Sky*
Sarraute, Nathalie (French, 1902) *The Golden Fruits*

1965
Abrahams, Peter (S. African, 1919) *A Night of Their Own*
Calisher, Hortense (American, 1911) *Journal from Ellipsia*
Calvino, Italo (Italian, 1923) *Cosmicomics*
Fleming, Ian (English, 1908–1964) *Thunderball*
Ford, Jesse Hill (American, Southern, 1928) *The Liberation of Lord Byron Jones*
Fowles, John (English, 1926) *Magus*
Herbert, Frank (American, 1920) *Dune*
Herlihy, James Leo (American, 1927) *Midnight Cowboy*
Jones, LeRoi (American, 1934) *The System of Dante's Hell*
Lurie, Allison (American, 1926) *The Nowhere City*
Morris, Wright (American, 1910) *One Day*
Schneck, Stephen (American, 1933) *The Nightclerk*
Williams, John Edward (American, 1922) *Stoner*
Young, Marguerite (American, 1909) *Miss MacIntosh, My Darling*

1966
Achebe, Chinua (Nigerian, 1930) *A Man of the People*
Barth, John (American, 1930) *Giles Goat-Boy*
Capote, Truman (American, 1924) *In Cold Blood*
Farina, Richard (American, 1937–1966) *Been Down So Long It Looks Like Up To Me*
Faust, Irvin (American, 1924) *The Steagle*
Feibleman, Peter S. (American, 1930) *Strangers and Graves*
Gass, William H. (American, 1924) *Omensetter's Luck*
Handke, Peter (German, 1942) *The Hornets*
Holland, Cecelia (American, 1943) *Rokóssy*
Keyes, Daniel (American, 1927) *Flowers for Algernon*
Kŏs, Erih (Yugoslavian, 1913) *Names*
Nozaka, Akiyuki (Japanese, 1930) *Pornographers*
Rexroth, Kenneth (American, 1905) *An Autobiographical Novel*
Singer, Isaac Bashevis (Polish, 1904) *The Family Moskat*
Susann, Jacqueline (American, n.d.–1974) *Valley of the Dolls*

1966–1967   Bulgakov, Milhail (Russian, 1891–1940) *The Master and Margarita*

1967   Barthelme, Donald (American, 1931) *Snow White*
Callado, Antônio (Brazilian, 1917) *Quarup*
Gold, Herbert (American, 1924) *Fathers*
Kazan, Elia (Turkish-American, 1909) *The Arrangement*
Levin, Ira (American, 1929) *Rosemary's Baby*
Macken, Walter (Irish, 1915–1967) *Lord of the Mountain*
Mailer, Norman (American, 1923) *Why Are We in Vietnam*
Matthews, Jack (American, 1925) *Hanger Stout, Awake!*
Molinaro, Ursule (French-American, n.d.) *Green Lights Are Blue: A Pornosophic Novel*
Morris, Wright (American, 1910) *In Orbit*
Oates, Joyce Carol (American, 1938) *A Garden of Earthly Delights*
Salas, Floyd (Spanish-American, 1931) *Tattoo the Wicked Cross*
Sinclair, Andrew (British, 1935) *Gog*
Sontag, Susan (American, 1933) *Death Kit*
Stone, Robert (American, 1937?) *A Hall of Mirrors*
Styron, William (American, 1925) *Confessions of Nat Turner*
Williams, John A. (Afro-American, 1925) *The Man Who Cried I Am*

1968   Armah, Ayi Kwei (Ghanan, 1939) *The Beautiful Ones Are Not Yet Born*
Beagle, Peter S. (American, 1939) *The Last Unicorn*
Coover, Robert (American, 1932) *The Universal Baseball Association, Inc. J. Henry Waugh, Prop.*
Hailey, Arthur (English-Canadian, 1947) *Airport*
Katz, Steven (American, 1935) *The Exaggerations of Peter Prince*
Kosinski, Jerzy (Polish-American, 1933) *Steps*
Momaday, N. Scott (American Indian, 1934) *House Made of Dawn*
Oates, Joyce Carol (American, 1938) *Expensive People*
Puig, Manuel (Argentinian, 1932) *Betrayed by Rita Hayworth*
Richler, Mordecai (Canadian, 1931) *Cocksure*
Solzhenitsyn, Aleksandi I. (Russian, 1918) *The Cancer Ward*
Vargas Llosa, Mario (Peruvian, 1936) *The Green House*
Vidal, Gore (American, 1925) *Myra Breckenridge*

Williams, Thomas (American, 1926) *Whipple's Castle*

1969   Angelou, Maya (American, n.d.) *I Know Why the Caged
                Bird Sings*
            Davis, L. J. (American, 1940) *Cowboys Don't Cry*
            Fowles, John (English, 1926) *The French Lieutenant's
                Woman*
            García Márquez, Gabriel (Brazilian, 1928) *One Hundred
                Years of Solitude*
            Gardner, Leonard (American, n.d.) *Fat City*
            LeGuin, Ursula (American, 1929) *The Left Hand of Dark-
                ness*
            Madden, David (American, Southern, 1933) *Cassandra
                Singing*
            Nabokov, Vladimir (Russian-American, 1899–1977) *Ada*
            Oates, Joyce Carol (American, 1938) *them*
            Puzo, Mario (American, 1920) *The Godfather*
            Reed, Ishmael (Afro-American, 1938) *Yellow Back Radio
                Broke Down*
            Roth, Philip (American, 1932) *The Death of the Novel*
            Woiwode, L. (American, 1942) *What I'm Going to Do, I
                Think*

1970   Bach, Richard (American, 1936) *Jonathan Livingston Sea-
                gull*
            Bellow, Saul (American, 1915) *Mr. Sammler's Planet*
            Brautigan, Richard (American, 1935) *The Abortion: An
                Historical Romance 1966*
            Dickey, James (American, 1923) *Deliverance*
            Didion, Joan (American, 1934) *Play It as It Lays*
            Sanders, Ed (American, 1939) *The Shards of God*
            Seelye, John (American, 1913) *The True Adventures of
                Huckleberry Finn*
            Segal, Erich (American, 1937) *Love Story*
            Shaw, Irwin (American, 1913) *Rich Man, Poor Man*
            Sheed, Wilfrid (American, 1930) *Max Jamison*
            Vasquez, Richard (Mexican-American) *Chicano*
            Vonnegut, Kurt (American, 1922) *Slaughterhouse Five*

1971   Anaya, Rudolpho A. (Mexican-American, 1937) *Bless Me,
                Ultima*
            Blatty, William (American, 1928) *The Exorcist*
            Elkin, Stanley (American, 1930) *The Dick Gibson Show*
            Gaines, Ernest J. (American, 1933) *Autobiography of Miss
                Jane Pittman*

Garrett, George (American, Southern, 1929) *Death of the Fox*

Jones, Madison (American, Southern, 1925) *A Cry of Absence*

Macdonald, Ross (American, 1915) *The Underground Man*

Percy, Walker (American, Southern, 1916) *Love in the Ruins*

Plath, Sylvia (American, 1932–1963) *The Bell Jar*

Raucher, Herman (American, 1928) *Summer of '42*

Stone, Irving (American, 1903) *The Passions of the Mind*

Tryon, Thomas (American, 1926) *The Other*

1972

Barrio, Raymond (Mexican-American, 1921) *The Plum, Plum Pickers*

Camus, Albert (French, 1913–1960) *A Happy Death*

Elliott, George P. (American, 1918) *Muriel*

Hannah, Barry (American, Southern, 1943) *Geronimo Rex*

Millhauser, Stephen (American, 1943) *Edwin Mullhouse: The Life and Death of an American Writer, 1943–1954 by Jeffrey Cartwright*

Rogers, Thomas (American, 1927) *The Confessions of a Child of the Century*

Tournier, Michel (French, 1924) *The Ogre*

1973

Atwood, Margaret (Canadian, 1939) *Surfacing*

Faulkner, William (American, Southern, 1897–1962) *Flags in the Dust*

Glaze, Eleanor (American, Southern, 1930) *Fear and Tenderness*

Jong, Erica (American, 1942) *Fear of Flying*

McGuane, Thomas (American, 1939) *Ninety-two in the Shade*

Pynchon, Thomas (American, 1937) *Gravity's Rainbow*

Sanchez, Thomas (Mexican-American, 1944) *Rabbit Boss*

Sheldon, Sidney (American, 1917) *The Other Side of Midnight*

Sukenick, Ronald (American, 1932) *Out*

Villasenor, Edmund (Mexican-American, 1940) *Macho!*

Vonnegut, Kurt (American, 1922) *Breakfast of Champions*

1974

Adams, Richard (English, 1920) *Watership Down*

Benchley, Peter (American, 1940) *Jaws*

Godwin, Gail (American, 1937) *The Odd Woman*

Jakes, John (American, 1932) *The Bastards*

King, Stephen (American, 1947) *Carrie*

Madden, David (American, Southern, 1933) *Bijou*
Welch, James (American Indian, 1940) *Winter in the Blood*

1975   Clavell, James (English, 1924) *Shogun*
Doctorow, E. L. (American, 1931) *Ragtime*
Drabble, Margaret (English, 1939) *The Realms of Gold*
Gaddis, William (American, 1922) *J R*
McElroy, Joseph (American, 1930) *Lookout Cartridge*
Williams, Tennessee (American, Southern, 1914) *Moise and the World of Reason*

1976   Adler, Renata (American, 1938) *Speedboat*
Alther, Lisa (American, Southern, 1944) *Kinflicks*
Beattie, Ann (American) *Chilly Scenes of Winter*
DeLillo, Don (American) *Ratner's Star*
Fuentes, Carlos (Mexican, 1928) *Terra Nostra*
Gardner, John (American, 1933) *October Light*
Guest, Judith (American, n.d.) *Ordinary People*
Theroux, Paul (American, 1941) *The Family Arsenal*
Walker, Alice (American, 1944) *Meridian*

1977   Bainbridge, Beryle, (English, n.d.) *A Quiet Life*
Cheever, John (American, 1912) *Falconer*
French, Marilyn (American, n.d.) *The Women's Room*
Handke, Peter (German, 1942) *A Moment of True Feeling*
Humphreys, J. R. (American, n.d.) *Subway to Samarkand*
McCullough, Colleen (Australian, n.d.) *The Thorn Birds*
Mayer, Robert (American) *Superfolk*
Morrison, Toni (Afro-American, 1931) *Song of Solomon*
Nin, Anaïs (Spanish-American, 1903–1977) *Delta of Venus*
Rossner, Judith (American, n.d.) *Attachments*
Tyler, Anne (American, 1941) *Earthly Possessions*
Voinovich, Vladimir (Russian, n.d.) *The Life and Extraordinary Adventures of Private Ivan Chonkin*
Wolitzer, Hilma, (American, n.d.) *In the Flesh*

1978   Adams, Alice (American, n.d.) *Listening to Billie*
Apple, Max (American, n.d.) *Zip*
Barthes, Roland (French, 1915) *Lover's Discourse: Fragments*
Carroll, James (American, n.d.) *Mortal Friends*
Chih-yen, Hsia (Chinese, n.d.) *The Coldest Winter in Peking*
Gordon, Mary (American, n.d.) *Final Payments*
Irving, John (American, 1942) *The World According to Garp*

Johnson, Diane (American, n.d.) *Lying Low*
Just, Ward (American, n.d.) *A Family Trust*
Lelchuk, Alan (American, n.d.) *Shrinking, The Beginning of My Own Ending*
Madden, David (American, Southern, 1933) *The Suicide's Wife*
O'Brien, Tim (American) *Going After Cacciato*
Piercy, Marge (American, n.d.) *The High Cost of Living*
Price, Richard (American, n.d.) *Ladies Man*
Ribeiro, Ubaldo Joao (n.d.) *Sergeant Getúlio*
Schulz, Bruno (Polish, 1892–1942) *Sanatorium Under the Sign of the Hour Glass*
Selby, Hubert, Jr. (American, 1928) *Requiem for a Dream*
Simmons, Charles (American, 1924) *Wrinkles*
Stern, Richard (American, 1928) *Natural Shocks*
Wier, Allen (American, 1946) *Blanco*
Yehosha, A. B. (Israeli, n.d.) *The Lover*

1979   Barth, John (American, 1930) *Letters*
Blaise, Clark (American, n.d.) *Lunar Attractions*
Charyn, Jerome (American, 1937) *The Seventh Babe*
Flanagan, Thomas (American, 1923) *The Year of the French*
Grumbach, Doris (American, n.d.) *Chamber Music*
Hardwick, Elizabeth (American, 1916) *Sleepless Nights*
Harnack, Curtis (American, n.d.) *Limits of the Land*
McCarthy, Cormac (American, 1933) *Suttree*
McConkey, James (American, n.d.) *The Tree House Confessions*
Madden, David (American, 1933) *Pleasure-Dome*
O'Conner, Philip (American, n.d.) *Stealing Home*
Sorrentino, Gilbert (American, 1929) *Mulligan Stew*
Styron, William (American, 1925) *Sophie's Choice*

SELECTIVE BIBLIOGRAPHY OF CRITICISM OF THE NOVEL

The following partial list of possible critical approaches may suggest the scope and complexity of literary criticism and the uses of this bibliography. For each approach, at least one of the major critics is listed, though it is very seldom that an individual critic may be characterized by a single approach. Implicitly or explicitly, all critics attempt to define the functions or purposes, aims or ends of literature: to instruct, to delight, produce knowledge, insight, and criticism of men and events, showing causes and effects, or to produce an aesthetic object of the imagination.

Tradition, the influence of: Eliot

Value: Fuller

Norms and criteria, providing means of evaluation: Daiches

Appreciation (taste and discrimination): Pater

Aristotelian precepts from drama (unities, etc.): Crane

Origins: Scholes and Kellogg

Definitions: Beckson

Genetic (the genesis or development of a work): Steegmuller

Genre or category (generic), or modes (epic, heroic, comedy, satire, tragedy, lyric): Frye, Scholes

Kinds (realistic, naturalistic, surrealistic): Levin, Zola, Fowlie, Becker

Types: Ehrenpreis

Mimetic (imitation of reality, Stendhal's concept of the writer as a mirror in the roadway imitating whatever shows up in his mirror): Auerbach

Autonomy (the work of art as a beautiful object, art for art's sake): Rogers, Croce

Nationalism (portrayals of national types and characteristics and great moments in a nation's history or culture): Chase

Periods (in which a work is produced) or *Zeitgeist* (spirit of the times) or eras (Classic, Romantic): Hulme, Praz, Hansen, Bradbury

Historical, sense of the past: Kettle, Watt, Edmund Wilson, Trilling

Biographical (the author's life and literary career): Krutch

Author's moral outlook or vision of life: Gide, Hough

Moral, society's point of view: Winters, Elliott, May, Trilling, Gardner

Nonliterary approaches:

   Philosophical: Glicksberg, Barrett

   Psychological; Freudian, aspects such as stream-of-consciousness; Jungian, the collective unconscious: Hoffman, Friedman

   Scientific: Snow

   Sociological: Fiedler, Duncan

   Political: Howe (Marxian: Fox; radical: Aaron; proletarian: Madden, Rideout)

   Mythological: Frye

   Folk: Rourke

   Archetypal: Bodkin

Impressionistic: D. H. Lawrence, Wright Morris

Aspects of fiction:

   Character: Max Schultz, Bayley, Gillie, Harvey

   Point-of-view: Lubbock, Booth

   Plot: Crane, O'Grady

   Narrative: Hardy, Scholes, Todorov

Setting (time and place): Poulet, Mendilow, Frank

Context: Harvey

Imagination: Levi

Formalistic approaches (New Criticism: Tate, Ransom)

Form and structure (dialectics of form): Burke, Hardy, Rickword

Structure: Muir; structuralism: Barthes

Techniques: Schorer, Macauley

Rhetoric: Booth

Style, language: Lodge, Harris, Martin

Semantic, linguistic, philological: Empson, Richards

Imagery: Ullmann

Symbolism: Tindall, Symons

Allegory: Honig

Comparative, with other literature, other fictional forms, other media, other countries and times: Levin, Bluestone

Eclectic (combinations of the above approaches) or pluralistic (tolerance of all approaches): Hyman, Elliott, Zabell

Experimental: Barthes, Gras

Popular: Cawelti, Madden

Creative process: Allott, Mann, Hildick, McCormack

Audience (study of reader's responses): Slatoff, Leavis, Richards

Relations between writer and reader: Gerould, Gordon, Gibson

Some fiction lends itself more to one kind of critical approach and interpretation than another.

Many of these approaches have been called fallacious or comparatively ineffectual, sometimes implying inadequacies in certain types of novels. Among the fallacies sometimes discussed are the historicist, the formalist, the didactic, the intentional (assuming the author's intentions), communication (claiming that the purpose of literature is to communicate a message), pathetic, and fallacy of expressive form.

A knowledge of literary norms, and their parallels with other arts and areas of knowledge, enables us to experience ways in which the best novels depart or deviate from them. The historical development of the novel is marked by the influence of other forms (drama, poetry, epic, cinema) and other arts (painting, sculpture, music, architecture) and other kinds of knowledge (science, philosophy, history, psychology, religion). On the other hand, other forms and media claim as their primary concern certain aspects of fiction: theme or thought is the province of philosophy; dialog, of drama; fact, of nonfiction; pure narrative, of history; lives, of biography; image, of poetry and the fine arts.

The most comprehensive volume of criticism about the novel as a form is *The Theory of the Novel,* edited by Philip Stevick. It contains seminal essays, key chapters from classical critical works, and a detailed annotated bibliography of almost every other noteworthy essay and book in the field as of 1967. Stevick's bibliography has provided the basis for my own. Another collection that is valuable for its essays and bibliography is *Critiques and Essays on Modern Fiction 1920-1951,* edited by John W. Aldridge (it provides a topical checklist: Problems of the Artist and His Society; Writers on their Craft; the Artist and the Creative Process; the Craft of Fiction: Technique and Style; Realism and Naturalism; and Symbol and Myth, with bibliographies for major authors). *The Modern Tradition: Backgrounds of Modern Literature,* edited by Richard Ellmann and Charles Feidelson, Jr., offers a rich and thorough selection of readings that help to provide an understanding of modern literature in general; concepts and terms in that work have been very suggestive in the writing of this book.

Most of the entries in this bibliography are single works of criticism or collections of critical essays dealing with all the types and techniques discussed in this book and demonstrating all the critical approaches alluded to in the book and outlined above. Some entries cite works dealing with related arts. Fiction writers, mostly novelists, writing about their own works or fiction in general are indicated with an asterisk. Reference volumes are indicated with a double asterisk.

Very few periodicals deal exclusively with fiction. Here is a list of those that do.

The International Fiction Review, University of New Brunswick, New Brunswick, Canada

Journal of Narrative Technique, English Department, Eastern Michigan University, Ypsilanti, Michigan, 48197

Modern Fiction Studies, Department of English, Purdue University, Lafayette, Indiana, 47907

Novel: A Forum on Fiction, Box 1984, Brown University, Providence, Rhode Island, 02912

Studies in American Fiction, Department of English, Northeastern University, Boston, Mass., 02115

Studies in the Novel, P. O. Box 13706, N. T. Station, North Texas State University, Denton, Texas, 76203

Studies in Short Fiction, Newberry College, Newberry, South Carolina, 29108 (see the summer bibliography issues).

Style, University of Arkansas, Fayetteville, Arkansas, 72701 (deals with all genres, including film, but as style is a neglected subject, this publication deserves special notice).

THE BIBLIOGRAPHY

*= author is a writer of fiction   **= reference book

Aaron, Daniel. *Writers on the Left*. N.Y.: Harcourt, Brace, 1961.

Adams, Ken. "Notes on Concretization," *British Journal of Aesthetics*, IV (1964), 115–125.

Adams, Robert M. *Strains of Discord: Studies in Literary Openness*. Ithaca, N.Y.: Cornell Univ. Press, 1958.

Aldridge, John W. *After the Lost Generation*. N.Y.: Noonday Press, 1951, 1958.

———, ed. *Critiques and Essays on Modern Fiction: 1920–1951*. N.Y.: Ronald Press, 1952.

———. *In Search of Heresy*. N.Y.: McGraw-Hill, 1956.

———. *Time to Murder and Create: The Contemporary Novel in Crisis*. N.Y.: David McKay, 1966.

Allen, Dick. *Science Fiction: The Future*. N.Y.: Harcourt, Brace, 1971.

Allen, Dick and Chacko, David. *Detective Fiction: Crime and Compromise*. N.Y.: Harcourt, Brace, 1974.

Allen, Walter. *The English Novel: A Short Critical History*. London: Phoenix House, 1954; N.Y.: Dutton, 1955.

———. *The Modern Novel in Britain and the United States*. N.Y.: Dutton, 1964.

———. "Narrative Distance, Tone, and Character," *The Theory of the Novel, New Essays*. Edited by John Halperin. N.Y.: Oxford Univ. Press, 1974.

———. *Reading a Novel*. London: Phoenix House, 1949; Denver: Swallow Press, 1949.

———. *Writers on Writing.* London: Phoenix House, 1948.

*Allott, Miriam. *Novelists on the Novel.* N.Y. and London: Columbia Univ. Press, 1959.

———. "The Temporal Mode: Four Kinds of Fiction," *Essays in Criticism,* VIII (1958), 214–216.

Alter, Robert, *Rogue's Progress.* Cambridge, Mass: Harvard Univ. Press, 1964.

Ames, Van Meter. *Aesthetics of the Novel.* Chicago: Univ. of Chicago Press, 1928.

———. "Butor and the Book," *Journal of Aesthetics and Art Criticism,* XXIII (1964), 159–165.

———. "The New in the Novel," *Journal of Aesthetics and Art Criticism,* XXI (1963), 243–250.

———. "The Novel: Between Art and Science," *Kenyon Review,* V (1943), 34–48.

*Amis, Kingsley. *New Maps of Hell: A Survey of Science Fiction.* N.Y.: Arno Press, 1975 [c 1960].

*Anderson, Sherwood. *A Storyteller's Story.* N.Y.: Viking Press, 1924.

Aristotle. *The Poetics.* Translated by S. H. Butcher, in *The Great Critics.* Edited by James Harry Smith and Edd Winfield Parks. N.Y.: W. W. Norton, 1932, 1951.

Arnold, Aerol. "Why Structure in Fiction: A Note to Social Scientists," *American Quarterly,* X (1958), 325–337.

Auerbach, Erich. *Mimesis: The Representation of Reality in Western Literature.* Princeton: Princeton Univ. Press, 1953.

Bagehot, Walter. *Literary Studies.* London: Longmans, Green, 1879.

Baker, Ernest A. *A History of the English Novel.* 10 vols. London: H. F. & G. Witherby, 1924–1939.

Baker, Joseph E. "Aesthetic Surface in the Novel," *The Trollopian,* II (1947), 91–106.

Barnes, Hazel E. "Modes of Aesthetic Consciousness in Fiction," *Bucknell Review*, XII (1964), 82–93.

Barrett, William. *Irrational Man, A Study in Existential Philosophy*. Garden City, N.Y.: Doubleday, 1958.

Barthes, Roland. *Writing Degree Zero*. N.Y.: Hill and Wang, 1968.

Bateson, F. W. and Shahevitch, B. "Katherine Mansfield's 'The Fly': A Critical Exercise," *Essays in Criticism*, XII (1962), 39–53.

Bayley, John. *The Characters of Love: A Study in the Literature of Personality*. London: Constable, 1962.

Beach, Joseph Warren. *American Fiction 1920–1940*. N.Y.: Macmillan, 1941, 1960.

————. *The Twentieth Century Novel: Studies in Technique*. N.Y.: Appleton-Century-Crofts, 1932.

Beardsley, Monroe C. *Aesthetics: Problems in the Philosophy of Criticism*. N.Y.: Harcourt, Brace, 1958.

Beck, Warren. "Conception and Technique," *College English*, XI (1950), 308–317.

Becker, George J. *Documents of Modern Literary Realism*. Princeton: Princeton Univ. Press, 1963.

————. "Realism: An Essay in Definition," *Modern Language Quarterly*, X (1949), 184–197.

**Beckson, Karl and Ganz, Arthur. *A Reader's Guide to Literary Terms, A Dictionary*. N.Y.: The Noonday Press, 1960.

Belgion, Montgomery. "The Testimony of Fiction," *Southern Review*, IV (1938), 143–155.

**Bell, Inglis Freeman and Baird, Freeman. *English Novel, 1578–1956: A Checklist of Twentieth-Century Criticisms*. Denver: Swallow Press, 1958.

*Bellamy, Joe David, ed. *The New Fiction: Interviews with Innovative American Writers*. Urbana, Illinois: Univ. of Illinois Press, 1974.

*Bellow, Saul. "Deep Readers of the World, Beware," and "Facts That Put Fancy to Flight," in *Opinions and Perspectives from The New York Times Book Review*. Edited by Francis Brown. Boston: Houghton Mifflin, 1964.

*Bennett, Arnold. *Books and Persons*. N.Y.: G. H. Doran, 1917.

Bentley, Phyllis. *Some Observations on the Art of Narrative*. N.Y.: Macmillan, 1948.

Bergson, Henri. "Laughter," *Comedy*. N.Y.: Anchor Books, 1956.

Besant, Walter. *The Art of Fiction*. London: Brentano's, 1902.

Blackmur, R. P. "Between the Numen and the Moha: Notes Toward a Theory of the Novel," *Sewanee Review*, LXII (1954), 1–23.

_____. *Eleven Essays in the European Novel*. N.Y.: Harcourt, Brace, & World, 1964.

_____. "Notes on Four Categories," *Sewanee Review*, LIV (1946), 576–590.

_____. "Notes on the Novel: 1936," in *The Expense of Greatness*. N.Y.: Arrow Editions, 1940.

Bland, D. S. "Endangering the Reader's Neck: Background Description in the Novel," *Criticism*, III (1961), 121–139.

Bluestone, George. *Novels into Film*. Baltimore, Md.: The Johns Hopkins Univ. Press, 1957.

_____. "Time in Film and Fiction," *Journal of Aesthetics and Art Criticism*, XIX (1961), 311–315.

Bodkin, Maud. *Archetypal Patterns in Poetry: Psychological Studies of Imagination*. N.Y.: Oxford Univ. Press, 1934.

Booth, Bradford A. "Form and Technique in the Novel," in *The Reinterpretation of Victorian Literature*. Edited by Joseph E. Baker. Princeton: Princeton University Press, 1950.

_____. "The Novel," in *Contemporary Literary Scholarship, A Critical Review*. Edited by Lewis Leary. N.Y.: Appleton-Century-Crofts, 1958.

Booth, Wayne C. "Distance and Point-of-View: An Essay in Classification," *Essays in Criticism*, XI. Chicago: Univ. of Chicago Press (1961), 60–79.

_____. *The Rhetoric of Fiction*. Chicago: Univ. of Chicago Press, 1961.

Boulton, Marjorie. *The Anatomy of Prose*. London: Routledge & Paul, 1954.

*Bowen, Elizabeth. "Notes on Writing a Novel," in *Myth and Method: Modern Theories of Fiction*. Edited by James E. Miller. Lincoln, Nebraska: Univ. of Nebraska Press, 1960.

*_____. "Rx for a Story Worth Telling," in *Opinions and Perspectives from The New York Times Book Review*, ed. Francis Brown. Boston: Houghton Mifflin, 1964.

*_____. "The Search for a Story to Tell," in *Highlights of Modern Literature: A Permanent Collection of Memorable Essays from The New York Times Book Review*, ed., Francis Brown. N.Y.: New American Library, 1954.

*_____. "The Writer's Peculiar World," in *Highlights of Modern Literature: A Permanent Collection of Memorable Essays from The New York Times Book Review*, ed., Francis Brown. N.Y.: New American Library, 1954.

Bowling, L. E. "What is the Stream of Consciousness Technique?" *PMLA*, LXV, (1950), 333–345.

Brace, Gerald Warner. "The Essential Novel," *Texas Quarterly*, VIII (1965), 28–38.

Brace, Marjorie. "Thematic Problems of the American Novelist," *Accent*, VI (1945), 44–54.

Bradbury, John M. *Renaissance in the South: A Critical History of the Literature 1920–1960*. Chapel Hill, North Carolina: Univ. of North Carolina Press, 1963.

Bradbury, Malcolm. "Towards a Poetics of Fiction: 1) An Approach Through Structure," *Novel: A Forum on Fiction*. Vol. 1, Fall 1967, 45–52.

*Braine, John. *Writing a Novel*. N.Y.: McGraw-Hill, 1974.

*Breit, Harvey. *The Writer Observed*. Cleveland: World, 1956.

Brooks, Cleanth and Warren, Robert Penn. *Understanding Fiction*. N.Y.: Appleton-Century-Crofts, 1943.

Brooks, Peter. "In the Laboratory of the Novel," *Daedalus*, XCII (1963), 265–280.

*Brooks, Van Wyck. *Writers at Work*, Second Series. N.Y.: Viking Press, 1963.

Brower, R. A. *The Fields of Light: An Experiment in Critical Reading*. N.Y.: Oxford University Press, 1951.

Brown, E. K. *Rhythm in the Novel*. Toronto: Univ. of Toronto Press, 1950.

_____. "Two Formulas for Fiction: Henry James and H. G. Wells," *College English*, VIII (1946), 7–17.

Brown, Huntington. *Prose Styles: Five Primary Types*. Minneapolis: Univ. of Minnesota Press, 1966.

Brown, Rollo Walter, ed. *The Writer's Art*. Cambridge, Mass.: Harvard Univ. Press, 1921.

Brownell, William Crary. *American Prose Masters*. N.Y.: Scribner's, 1909.

Brumm, Ursula. "Symbolism and the Novel," *Partisan Review*, XXV (1958), 329–342.

Bruner, Jerome S. *On Knowing: Essays for the Left Hand*. Cambridge, Mass.: Harvard Univ. Press, 1962.

Buchan, John. *The Novel and the Fairy Tale*. Oxford: Oxford Univ. Press, 1931.

Buchen, Irving H. "The Aesthetics of the Supra-Novel," *The Theory of the Novel, New Essays*. N.Y.: Oxford Univ. Press, 1974.

*Buckler, William E. *Novels in the Making*. Boston: Houghton Mifflin, 1961.

Bullough, Edward. "Psychical Distance as a Factor in Art and an Aesthetic Principle." Edited by Melvin Rader. *A Modern Book of Esthetics,* 3rd ed. N.Y.: Holt, Rinehart & Winston, 1960.

*Burgess, Anthony. *The Novel Now.* N.Y.: W. W. Norton, 1967.

Burgum, Edwin Berry. *The Novel and the World's Dilemma.* N.Y.: Oxford Univ. Press, 1963.

Burke, Kenneth. *The Philosophy of Literary Form.* Baton Rouge, Louisiana: Louisiana State Univ. Press, 1941.

Burns, Wayne. "The Novelist as Revolutionary," *Arizona Quarterly,* VII (1951), 13-27.

Burton, Richard. *Forces in Fiction and Other Essays.* Indianapolis: Bobbs-Merrill, 1902.

Butor, Michel. "Intervention at Royaumont," *Odyssey Review,* I (1961), 176-179.

_____. "Thoughts on the Novel," *Encounter,* XX (June, 1963), 17-24.

*Calisher, Hortense. *Herself, An Autobiographical Work.* N.Y.: Arbor House, 1972.

Campbell, Joseph. *Hero With a Thousand Faces.* N.Y.: Pantheon Books, 1949.

*Camus, Albert. *Notebooks 1935-1942* and *Notebooks 1942-1951.* N.Y.: Knopf, 1963, 1965.

Cannavo, Salvator and Hyman, Lawrence W. "Literary Uniqueness and Critical Communication," *British Journal of Aesthetics,* V (1965), 144-158.

Cartey, Wilfred. *Whispers from a Continent: The Literature of Contemporary Black Africa.* N.Y.: Random House, 1969.

*Cary, Joyce. *Art and Reality: Ways of the Creative Process.* N.Y.: Harper & Row, 1958.

*_____. "On the Function of the Novelist," in *Highlights of Modern Literature: A Permanent Collection of Memorable Essays from The New*

York Times Book Review, ed., Francis Brown. N.Y.: New American Library, 1954.

*_____. "The Way a Novel Gets Written," *Harper's*, CC (February, 1950), 87–93.

Cassirer, Ernest. *Language and Myth*. Translated and edited by Susanne K. Langer. N.Y.: Harper & Brothers, 1946.

*Cather, Willa. *On Writing: Critical Studies on Writing as an Art*. N.Y.: Knopf, 1949.

Caudwell, Christopher. *Illusions and Reality*. N.Y.: Macmillan, 1937.

Cawelti, John. *Adventure, Mystery, and Romance*. Chicago: Univ. of Chicago Press, 1976.

_____. *The Six-Gun Mystique*. Bowling Green, Ohio: Popular Press, 1970.

Cazamian, Louis. "The Method of Discontinuity in Modern Art and Literature," *Criticism in the Making*. N.Y.: Macmillan, 1929.

Cecil, David. *Victorian Novelists: Essays in Revaluation*. Chicago: Univ. of Chicago Press, 1958.

Chase, Richard. *The American Novel and Its Tradition*. N.Y.: Doubleday, 1957.

_____. *Quest for Myth*. Baton Rouge, La.: Louisiana State Univ. Press, 1949.

*Chekhov, Anton. *Notebooks of Anton Chekhov*. London: Huebsch, 1921.

*_____. *The Personal Papers of Anton Chekhov*. N.Y.: Lear Publications, 1948.

Cheney, Sheldon. *Expressionism in Art*. N.Y.: Liveright, 1934.

Church, Margaret. *Time and Reality: Studies in Contemporary Fiction*. Chapel Hill, N.C.: Univ. of North Carolina Press, 1963.

Cockshut, A. O. J. "Sentimentality in Fiction," *Twentieth Century*, CLXI (April, 1957), 354–364.

*Coleridge, Samuel Taylor. *Biographia Literaria*. London: J. M. Dent & Sons, 1906, 1975.

Collins, Norman. *The Facts of Fiction*. N.Y.: E. P. Dutton, 1933.

Colum, Mary. *From These Roots: The Ideas That Have Made Modern Literature*. N.Y.: Scribner's, 1937.

*Comfort, Alex. *The Novel and Our Time*. London: Dent, 1948.

*Conrad, Joseph. *Joseph Conrad on Fiction*. Edited by Walter F. Wright. Lincoln, Nebraska: Univ. of Nebraska Press.

*_____. *Last Essays*. London: J. M. Dent & Sons, 1921.

*_____. *Notes on Life and Letters*. Garden City, N.Y.: Doubleday, 1921.

Cook, Albert. *The Meaning of Fiction*. Detroit: Wayne State Univ. Press, 1960.

Cooper, William. "Reflections on Some Aspects of the Experimental Novel," *International Literary Annual*, II (1959), 29–36.

Cowie, Alexander. *The Rise of the American Novel*. N.Y.: American Book, 1948.

Cowley, Malcolm. *The Literary Situation*. N.Y.: Viking Press, 1954.

_____. "A Natural History of Naturalism," *Critiques and Essays on Modern Fiction, 1920–1951*. Edited by John W. Aldridge. N.Y.: Ronald Press, 1972.

_____. *A Second Flowering: Works and Days of the Lost Generation*. N.Y.: Viking, 1973.

Crane, R. S. "The Concept of Plot and the Plot of Tom Jones," *Critics and Criticism, Ancient and Modern*. Edited by R. S. Crane. Chicago: Chicago Univ. Press, 1952.

_____. *The Language of Criticism and the Structure of Poetry*. Toronto: Univ. of Toronto Press, 1953.

Croce, Benedetto. *Aesthetics*. N.Y.: Macmillan, 1919.

Crothers, George D. *An Invitation to Learning: English and American Novels*. N.Y.: Basic Books, 1966.

Crutwell, Patrick. "Makers and Persons," *Hudson Review*, XII (1959-60), 487-507.

*Dahlberg, Edward and Read, Herbert. *Truth Is More Sacred*. N.Y.: Horizon Press, n.d.

Daiches, David. "The Criticism of Fiction: Some Second Thoughts," *Literary Essays*. Edinburgh: Oliver and Boyd, 1956.

————. *Literature and Society*. London: Gollancz Ltd., 1938.

————. "The Nature of Fiction," *A Study of Literature: For Readers and Critics*. Ithaca, Cornell Univ. Press, 1948.

————. *The Novel and the Modern World*. Chicago: Univ. of Chicago Press, 1960.

————. *A Study of Literature*. Ithaca: Cornell Univ. Press, 1948.

————. "Time and Sensibility," *Modern Language Quarterly*, XXV (1964), 486-492.

Davis, Robert Gorham. "Fiction and Thinking," *Epoch*, I (1948), 87-96.

————. "The Sense of the Real in English Fiction," *Comparative Literature*, III (1951), 200-217.

Davis, Robert Murray, ed. *The Novel: Modern Essays in Criticism*. Englewood Cliffs, N.J.: Prentice-Hall, 1969.

DeVoto, Bernard. *The World of Fiction*. Boston: Houghton Mifflin, 1950.

Dickie, George. "Bullough and the Concept of Psychical Distance," *Philosophy and Phenomenological Research*, XXII (1961), 233-238.

Dillard, R. H. W., Garrett, George, and Moore, John Rees, eds. *The Sounder Few*. Athens, Ga.: Univ. of Georgia Press, 1971.

Dobreé, Bonamy. *Modern Prose Style*. N.Y.: Oxford Univ. Press, 1946.

Dodsworth, Martin. "'The Truth of Fiction?'" *Essays in Criticism*, IX (1959), 443-446.

Dostoevsky, F. M. *The Diary of a Writer.* N.Y.: Scribner's, 1949.

Douglas, Wallace W. "The Meanings of 'Myth' in Modern Criticism," *Modern Philology,* L (1953), 232–242.

Drew, Elizabeth A. *The Modern Novel: Some Aspects of Contemporary Fiction.* N.Y.: Harcourt, Brace, 1926.

_____. The Novel: A Modern Guide to Fifteen English Masterpieces. N.Y.: Dell Publishing, 1963.

Dubois, Arthur E. "The Art of Fiction," *South Atlantic Quarterly,* XL (1941), 112–122.

Duncan, Hugh Dalziel. *Language and Literature in Society.* Chicago: Univ. of Chicago Press, 1953.

Durham, Philip and Jones, Everett L. *The Western Story, Fact, Fiction, and Myth.* N.Y.: Harcourt, Brace, 1975.

Eastman, Richard M. "The Open Parable: Demonstration and Definition," *College English,* XXII (1960), 15–18.

Edel, Leon. "Novel and Camera," *The Theory of the Novel, New Essays.* Ed. by John Halperin. N.Y.: Oxford Univ. Press, 1974.

Edel, Leon and Ray, Gordon. *Henry James and H. G. Wells: A Record of their Friendship, their Debate on the Art of Fiction, and their Quarrel.* Urbana: Univ. of Ill. Press, 1958; Rev. ed. 1964.

_____. *The Modern Psychological Novel.* N.Y.: Grosset's Universal Library, 1955.

Edgar, Pelham. *The Art of the Novel: from 1700 to the Present Time.* N.Y.: Macmillan, 1933.

Ehrenpreis, Irvin. *The "Types" Approach to Literature.* N.Y.: King's Crown Press, 1945.

Eisenstein, Sergei. *Film Form.* N.Y.: Harcourt, Brace, 1949.

Eisinger, Charles. *Fiction of the Forties.* Chicago: Univ. of Chicago Press, 1963.

Eliot, T. S. "Tradition and the Individual Talent," *The Sacred Wood: Essays on Poetry and Criticism.* N.Y.: Knopf, 1921.

*Elliott, George P. "A Defense of Fiction," *Hudson Review*, XVI (1963), 9-48.

*_____. "The Novelist as Meddler," *Virginia Quarterly Review*, XL (1964), 96-113.

*Ellison, Ralph. *Shadow and Act.* N.Y.: Random House, 1953, 1964.

Ellmann, Richard and Feidelson, Charles. *The Modern Tradition.* New York: Oxford Univ. Press, 1965.

Embler, Weller B. "The Novel as Metaphor," *Etc.*, X (1953), 3-11.

Empson, William. *Seven Types of Ambiguity.* New York: New Directions, 1930.

Erlich, Victor. "Some Uses of Monologue in Prose Fiction: Narrative Manner and World-View," in *Stil- Und Formprobleme in Der Literatur.* Ed. by Paul Bockman. Heidelberg: C. Winter, 1959.

Ethridge, James and Kopala, Barbara, eds. *Contemporary Authors: A Bio-Bibliographical Guide to Current Authors and their Works.* Detroit, Mich.: Gale Research, 1962-1979.

Farber, Marjorie. "Subjectivity in Modern Fiction," *Kenyon Review*, VII (1945), 645-652.

*Farrell, James T. *Literature and Morality.* N.Y.: Vanguard Press, 1947.

*_____. "Some Observations on Naturalism, So Called, in Fiction," *Antioch Review*, X (1950), 247-264.

*Faulkner, William. *Faulkner in the University: Class Conferences at the University of Virginia 1957-58.* Ed. by Frederick L. Gwynn and Joseph L. Blotner. New York: Vintage Books, 1965.

Fergusson, Francis. "Myth and the Literary Scruple," *Sewanee Review*, LXIV (1956), 171-185.

Fernandez, Ramon. *Messages.* Trans. by Montgomery Belgion. New York: Harcourt, Brace, 1927.

*Feuchtwanger, Lion. *The House of Desdemona, or The Laurels and Limitations of Historical Fiction*. Trans. by Harold A. Basilius. Detroit: Wayne State Univ. Press, 1963.

Fiedler, Leslie A. *Love and Death in the American Novel*. N.Y.: Stein and Day, 1960, 1966.

_____. *No! in Thunder*. Boston: Beacon Press, 1960.

*Fitzgerald, F. Scott. *The Crack-up*. N.Y.: New Directions, 1945.

*Flaubert, Gustave. *Selected Letters*. Trans. and ed. by Francis Steegmuller. N.Y.: Books for Libraries Press, 1971.

Fleming, William. "The Newer Concepts of Time and Their Relation to the Temporal Arts," *Journal of Aesthetics and Art Criticism*, IV (1945), 101–106.

Flint, F. Cudworth. "Remarks on the Novel," *Symposium*, I (1930), 84–96.

Fogle, Richard Harter. "Illusion, Point of View, and Modern Novel Criticism," *The Theory of the Novel, New Essays*. N.Y.: Oxford Univ. Press, 1974.

Follett, Wilson. *The Modern Novel: A Study of the Purpose and Meaning of Fiction*. N.Y.: Knopf, 1918; rev. ed., 1923.

*Ford, Ford Madox. *The English Novel: From the Earliest Days to the Death of Joseph Conrad*. Philadelphia & London: J. B. Lippincott, 1929.

*_____. *Joseph Conrad: A Personal Remembrance*. London: Duckworth & Co., 1924.

*_____. "Techniques," *Southern Review*, 1 (July, 1935), 20–35.

*Forster, E. M. *Aspects of the Novel*. N.Y.: Harcourt, Brace, 1927.

Fowlie, Wallace. *Age of Surrealism*. N.Y.: Swallow & Morrow, 1951.

_____. *A Guide to Contemporary French Literature, From Valery to Sartre*. N.Y.: Meridian Books, 1957.

Fox, Ralph. *The Novel and the People*. N.Y.: Lawrence & Wishart, 1937; International, 1945.

Frank, Joseph. "Spatial Form in Modern Literature," *Sewanee Review*, LIII (1945), 221–240; 433–456; 643–653.

Frederick, John. "New Techniques in the Novel," *English Journal*, 24 (May, 1935), 355–363.

Freedman, Ralph. *The Lyrical Novel: Studies in Hermann Hesse, Andre Gide, and Virginia Woolf.* Princeton, N.J.: Princeton Univ. Press, 1963.

Frey, John R. "Past or Present Tense? A Note on the Technique of Narration," *JEGP*, XLVI (1947), 205–208.

Friedman, Alan Warren. "The Modern Multivalent Novel: Form and Function," *The Theory of the Novel, New Essays*. Ed. by John Halperin. N.Y.: Oxford Univ. Press, 1974.

––––––. "The Stream of Conscience as a Form in Fiction," *Hudson Review*, XVII (1965), 537–546.

––––––. *The Turn of the Novel: Transitions to Modern Fiction*. N.Y.: Oxford Univ. Press, 1966.

Friedman, Melvin. *Stream of Consciousness: A Study in Literary Method.* New Haven: Yale Univ. Press, 1955.

Friedman, Norman. "Criticism and the Novel," *Antioch Review*, XVIII (1958), 343–370.

––––––. "Forms of the Plot," *Journal of General Education*, VIII (1955), 241–253.

––––––. "Point of View in Fiction: The Development of a Critical Concept," *PMLA*, LXX (1955), 1160–1184.

––––––. "What Makes a Short Story Short?" *Modern Fiction Studies*, IV (1958), 103–117.

Frohock, W. M. *The Novel of Violence*. Dallas Texas: Southern Methodist Univ. Press, 1950, sec. ed.; revised and enlarged, 1957.

Frye, Northrop. *Anatomy of Criticism.* Princeton: Princeton Univ. Press, 1957.

_____. "The Archetypes of Literature," *Fables of Identity: Studies in Poetic Mythology.* N.Y.: Harcourt, Brace, 1963.

_____. "The Four Forms of Prose Fiction," *Modern Literary Criticism 1900–1970.* Ed. by Lawrence I. Lipking and A. Walton Litz. N.Y.: Atheneum, 1972.

Fuller Edmund. *Man in Modern Fiction: Some Minority Opinions on Contemporary American Writing.* N.Y.: Random House, 1949, 1957, 1958.

Gardiner, Dorothy and Walker, Kathrine Sorley. *Raymond Chandler Speaking.* Boston: Houghton Mifflin, 1962.

*Gardner, John. *On Moral Fiction.* N.Y.: Basic Books, 1978.

Garnett, David. "Some Tendencies of the Novel," *Symposium;* I (1930), 96–105.

Garvin, Paul L., ed. and trans. *A Prague School Reader on Esthetics, Literary Structure, and Style.* Washington, D.C.: Washington Linguistic Club, 1955.

*Gass, William. *Fiction and the Figures of Life. Essays & Reviews.* N.Y.: Knopf, 1971.

Geismar, Maxwell. *American Moderns: From Rebellion to Conformity.* N.Y.: Viking Press, 1946.

_____. *The Last of the Provincials: The American Novel, 1915–1925.* Boston: Houghton Mifflin, 1943, 1947, 1949.

_____. *Rebels and Ancestors: The American Novel, 1890–1915.* Boston: Houghton Mifflin, 1953.

_____. *Writers in Crisis: The American Novel, 1925–1940.* Boston: Houghton Mifflin, 1947.

*George, W. L. *A Novelist on Novels.* London: W. Collins & Sons, 1918.

Gerould, Gordon Hall. *How to Read Fiction.* Princeton: Princeton Univ. Press, 1937.

**Gerstenberger, Donna and Hendrick, George. *The American Novel, 1789–1959, A Checklist of Twentieth Century Criticism.* Denver, Swallow Press, 1961.

**_____. *The American Novel, Vol II: Criticism Written 1960–1968, A Checklist of Twentieth Century Criticism on Novels Written Since 1960–1968.* Chicago, Ill.: Swallow Press, 1970.

Ghiselin, Brewster. "Automatism, Intention, and Autonomy in the Novelist's Production," *Daedalus,* XCII (1963), 297–312.

_____. *The Creative Process.* Berkeley, Ca.: Univ. of Ca. Press, 1952.

Gibbon, F. P. "The Truth of Fiction," *Essays in Criticism,* X (1960), 480–483.

Gibson, Walker. "Authors, Speakers, Readers, and Mock Readers," *College English,* XI (1950), 265–269.

*Gide, André. *The Journals of André Gide,* Vols. I, II. Trans., selected, and ed. by Justin O'Brien. N.Y.: Knopf, 1947, 1948, 1949, 1951.

*_____. *Pretexts: Reflections on Literature and Morality.* Ed. by Justin O'Brien. N.Y.: Meridian 1959.

Gillie, Christopher. *Character in English Literature.* London: Chatto & Windus, 1965.

*Glasgow, Ellen. *A Certain Measure: An Interpretation of Prose Fiction.* N.Y.: Harcourt, Brace 1943.

_____. "One Way to Write Novels," *Saturday Review of Literature* II (Dec. 8, 1934), 335, 344, 350.

Glicksberg, Charles I. "Fiction and Philosophy," *Arizona Quarterly,* XIII (1957), 5–17.

_____. "The Numinous in Fiction," *Arizona Quarterly,* XV (1959), 305–313.

_____. *The Self in Modern Literature.* Univ. Park, Penna.: Penna. State Univ. Press, 1963.

*Gold, Herbert. "The Lesson of Balzac's Stupidity," *Hudson Review,* VII (1954), 7–18.

*_____. "The Mystery of Personality in the Novel," *Partisan Review*, XXIV (1957), 453–462.

*_____. "Truth and Falsity in the Novel," *Hudson Review*, VIII (1955), 410–422.

Goldberg, M. A. "Chronology, Character, and the Human Condition: A Reappraisal of the Modern Novel," *Criticism*, V (1963), 1–12.

*Goodman, Paul. *The Structure of Literature*. Chicago: Univ. of Chicago Press, 1954.

Goodman, Theodore. *The Techniques of Fiction*. N.Y.: Liveright, 1955.

Goodstone, Tony, ed. *The Pulps, Fifty Years of American Pop Culture*. N.Y.: Chelsea House, 1970.

*Gordon, Caroline. *How to Read a Novel*. N.Y.: Viking, 1958.

_____. "Some Readings and Misreadings," *Sewanee Review*, LXI (1953), 384–407.

*Gordon, Caroline and Tate, Allen. *The House of Fiction*. N.Y.: Scribner's, 1950.

Grabo, C. H. *The Technique of the Novel*. N.Y.: Scribner's, 1928.

Graham, Kenneth. *English Criticism of the Novel, 1885–1900*. Oxford: Clarendon, 1965.

Gransden, K. W. "Thoughts on Contemporary Fiction," *Review of English Literature*, I (April, 1960), 7–17.

Grant, Douglas. "The Novel and Its Critical Terms," *Essays in Criticism*, I (1951), 421–429.

Gras, Vernon W. *European Literary Theory and Practice, from Existential Phenomenology to Structuralism*. N.Y.: Dell, 1973.

*Graves, Robert. *Occupation: Writer*. N.Y.: Creative Age Press, 1950.

*Graves, Robert and Hodge, Allen, eds. *The Reader Over Your Shoulder, a Handbook for Writers of English Prose*. N.Y.: Macmillan, 1943.

Gray, James. *On Second Thought*. Minneapolis: Univ. of Minn. Press, 1948.

Green, F. C. "Some Observations on Technique and Form in the French Seventeenth and Eighteenth Century Novel," *Stil- Und Formprobleme in Der Literatur*. Ed. by Paul Bockman. Heidelberg: C. Winter, 1959.

Greenberg, Alvin. "The Novel of Disintegration: Paradoxical Impossibility in Contemporary Fiction," *Wisconsin Studies in Contemporary Literature*, VII (1966), 103–124.

*Greene, Graham. "Fiction," *The Spectator*, 1933.

*Greene, Graham, Bowen, Elizabeth, and Pritchett, V. S. *Why Do I Write? An Exchange of Views*. London: Chatto & Windus, 1948.

Greene, Theodore M. *The Arts and the Art of Criticism*. Princeton: Princeton Univ. Press, 1940.

Gregor, Ian and Nichols, Brian. *The Moral and the Story*. London: Faber & Faber, 1962.

Gross, Beverly and Giannone, Richard, eds. *The Shapes of Fiction*. N.Y.: Holt, Rinehart & Winston, 1971.

Grossman, Manuel. *Dada, Paradox, Mystification, and Ambiguity in European Literature*. N.Y.: Bobbs-Merrill, 1971.

Grundy, Joan and James, G. Ingli. "The Mode of the Novel," *Essays in Criticism*, IX (1959), 201–209.

**Guerin, Wilfred L. *A Handbook of Critical Approaches to Literature*. Ed by G. Labor, Lee Morgan, and John R. Willingham. N.Y.: Harper and Row, 1966.

**Hackett, Alice Payne. *Eighty Years of Best Sellers, 1895–1975*. N.Y.: R. R. Bowker, 1977.

Haines, George. "Forms of Imaginative Prose: 1900–1940," *Southern Review* (Spring, 1942), 755–775.

Haines, Helen E. *What's in a Novel*. N.Y.: Columbia Univ. Press, 1942.

*Hale, Nancy. *The Realities of Fiction*. Boston: Little, Brown, 1962.

*Hall, James B. *The Lunatic in the Lumber Room. The British and American Novel Since 1930.* Bloomington, Ind.: Ind. Univ. Press, 1968.

Halperin, John. "Approaches to Fiction: A Select Descriptive Bibliography," *The Theory of the Novel, New Essays.* N.Y.: Oxford Univ. Press, 1974.

———. "The Theory of the Novel: A Critical Introduction," *The Theory of the Novel, New Essays.* N.Y.: Oxford Univ. Press, 1974.

———. "Twentieth-Century Trends in Continental Novel-Theory," *The Theory of the Novel, New Essays.* N.Y.: Oxford Univ. Press, 1974.

Hamilton, Clayton. *Materials and Methods of Fiction.* N.Y.: Baker & Taylor, 1908.

Handy, William. "Toward a Formalist Criticism of Fiction," *Texas Studies in Language and Literature,* III (1961), 81–88.

Hansen, Agnes. *Twentieth Century Forces in European Fiction.* Chicago: American Literary Association, 1934.

Harding, R. M. *An Anatomy of Inspiration.* Cambridge, Mass.: Harvard Univ. Press, 1940.

Hardison, O. B., Jr. "Criticism and the Search for Pattern," *Thought,* XXXVI (1961), 215–230.

Hardy, Barbara. *The Appropriate Form: An Essay on the Novel.* London: Univ. of London, Athlone Press, 1964.

———. "Formal Analysis and Common Sense," *Essays in Criticism,* XI (1961), 112–115.

———. "Towards a Poetics of Fiction 3) An Approach Through Narrative," *Novel: A Forum On Fiction,* II (Fall, 1968), 5–14.

**Harmon, Gary T. and Harmon, Susanna M. *Scholars Market: An International Directory of Periodicals Publishing Literary Scholarship.* Columbus, Ohio: OSU Libraries Publications Committee, 1974.

Harrah, David. "Explication of 'Depth', 'Level', and 'Unity'," *Journal of Philosophy,* LV (1958), 781–785.

Harris, Robert T. "Plausibility in Fiction," *Journal of Philosophy*, XLIX (1952), 5–10.

Harris, Wendell V. "Style and the Twentieth-Century Novel," *Western Humanities Review*, XVIII (1964), 127–140.

Hart, James D. *The Popular Book: A History of America's Literary Taste*. N.Y.: Oxford Univ. Press, 1950.

*Hartley, L. P. "The Novelist's Responsibility," *Essays and Studies*, XV n.s. (1962), 88–100.

Hartt, Julian N. *The Lost Image of Man*. Baton Rouge, La.: La. State Univ. Press, 1963.

Harvey, W. J. *Character and the Novel*. Ithaca, N.Y.: Cornell Univ. Press, 1965.

———. "Character and the Context of Things," in *The Novel. Modern Essays in Criticism*. Ed. by Robert Murray Davis. N.Y.: Prentice Hall, 1969.

Hassan, Ihab. *A Radical Innocence, Studies in the Contemporary American Novel*. Princeton, N.J.: Princeton Univ. Press, 1961.

Hatcher, Anna Granville. "Voir as a Modern Novelistic Device," *Philological Quarterly*, XXIII (1944), 354–374.

Hatcher, Harlan. *Creating the Modern American Novel*. N.Y.: Farrar & Rinehart, 1935.

Hauser, Arnold. "The Conceptions of Time in Modern Art and Art and Science," *Partisan Review*, XXIII (1956), 320–333.

Heilman, Robert B. "Two-Tone Fiction: Nineteenth-Century Types and Eighteenth-Century Problems," *The Theory of the Novel, New Essays*. Ed. by John Halperin. N.Y.: Oxford Univ. Press, 1974.

Henderson, Philip. *The Novel Today*. London: Bodley Head, 1936.

*Hersey, John, ed. *The Writer's Craft*. N.Y.: Knopf, 1974.

Hicks, Granville, ed. *The Living Novel*. N.Y.: Macmillan, 1957.

Hildick, Wallace. *Thirteen Types of Narrative*. N.Y.: Clarkson N. Potter, 1970.

_____. *Word for Word.* N.Y.: W. W. Norton, 1965.

_____. *Writing with Care.* N.Y.: David White, 1967.

*Hills, Rust, ed. *Writer's Choice.* N.Y.: David McKay, 1974.

Hirsch, David. "Reality, Manners, and Mr. Trilling," *Sewanee Review*, LXXII (1964), 420–432.

Hoffman, Frederick J. *The Art of Southern Fiction.* Carbondale, Ill.: Southern Ill. Univ. Press, 1967.

_____. *Freudianism and the Literary Mind.* Baton Rouge, La.: La. State Univ. Press, 1945.

_____. *The Modern Novel in America, 1900–1950.* Chicago: Regnery, 1951.

_____. "The Self in Time," *Chicago Review*, XV (1961) 59–75.

Holloway, John. *The Victorian Sage.* London: Macmillan, 1953.

Honig, Edwin. *Dark Conceit: The Making of Allegory.* Evanston, Ill.: Northwestern Univ. Press, 1959.

_____. "In Defense of Allegory," *Kenyon Review*, XX (1958), 1–19.

Horne, Charles F. *The Technique of the Novel.* N.Y.: Harper & Bros., 1908.

**Hornstein, Lillian Herlands, ed. *The Reader's Companion to World Literature.* N.Y.: Dryden Press, 1956.

Hough, Graham. "Morality and the Novel," *The Dream and the Task.* N.Y.: W. W. Norton, 1964.

Howe, Irving. "The Fiction of Anti-Utopia," *A World More Attractive: A View of Modern Literature and Politics.* N.Y.: Horizon Press, 1963.

_____. "Mass Society and Post-Modern Fiction," *A World More Attractive.* N.Y.: Horizon Press, 1963.

_____. *Politics and the Novel.* N.Y.: Horizon Press, 1957.

Hughes, Helen Sard. "The Middle-Class Reader and the English Novel," *JEGP*, XXV (1926), 362–378.

Hulme, T. E. *Speculations: Essays on Humanism and the Philosophy of Art.* N.Y.: Harcourt, Brace, 1924.

Humphrey, Robert. *Stream of Consciousness in the Modern Novel.* Berkeley: Univ. of Ca. Press, 1954.

_____. "'Stream of Consciousness': Technique or Genre?" *Philological Quarterly*, XXX (1951), 434–437.

Huneker, James Gibbons. "The Great American Novel," *Literary Opinions in America.* Rev. and ed. by Morton Dauwen Zabel. N.Y.: Harper & Brothers, 1937, 1951.

Hyman, Stanley Edgar. *The Armed Vision: A Study in the Methods of Modern Literary Criticism.* N.Y.: Knopf, 1947, 1948.

*James, Henry. *The Art of the Novel*, with intro. by R. P. Blackmur. N.Y.: Scribner's, 1934.

*_____. *The Future of the Novel: Essays on the Art of Fiction.* Ed. with intro. by Leon Edel. N.Y.: Vintage Press, 1956.

_____. *Literary Reviews and Essays.* Ed. by Albert Mordell. N.Y.: Twayne, 1957.

Jameson, Frederick. *The Prison House of Language: A Critical Account of Structuralism and Russian Formalism.* Princeton, N.J.: Princeton Univ. Press, 1972.

*Jameson, Storm. "The Craft of the Novelist," *English Review*, LVIII (1934), 28–43.

*_____. *The Novel in Contemporary Life.* Boston: The Writer, 1938.

*_____. *The Writer's Situation.* N.Y.: Macmillan, 1937.

*Janeway, Elizabeth. "Fiction's Place in a World Awry," in *Opinions and Perspectives from the New York Times Book Review.* Ed. by Francis Brown. Boston: Houghton Mifflin, 1964.

*_____. "What's American and What's British in the Modern Novel," in *Highlights of Modern Literature: A Permanent Collection of Memorable Essays from The New York Times Book Review.* Ed. by Francis Brown. N.Y.: New American Library, 1954.

Jelly, Oliver. "Fiction and Illness," *Review of English Literature*, III (January, 1962), 80–89.

Jessup, Bertram E. "Aesthetic Size," *Journal of Aesthetics and Art Criticism*, IX (1950), 31–38.

———. "On Fictional Expressions of Cognitive Meaning," *Journal of Aesthetics and Art Criticism*, XXIII (1965), 481–486.

*Johnson, Pamela Hansford. "The Genealogy of the Novel," *The New Hungarian Quarterly*, V (1964), 97–107.

Johnson, R. Brimley, ed. *Novelists on Novels*. London: N. Douglas, 1928.

Jolly, R. A., Copland, R. H., and Greenwood, E. B. "Katherine Mansfield's 'The Fly'," *Essays in Criticism*, XII (1962), 335–347.

Jordan, Robert M. "The Limits of Illusion: Faulkner, Fielding, and Chaucer," *Criticism*, II (1960), 278–305.

Kahler, Erich. "The Forms of Form," *Centennial Review*, VII (1963), 131–143.

———. *Out of the Labyrinth, Essays in Clarification*. N.Y.: George Braziller, 1967.

———. "Transformations of Modern Fiction," *Comparative Literature*, VII (1955), 121–128.

Kaminsky, Alice R. "On Literary Realism," *The Theory of the Novel, New Essays*. Ed. by John Halperin. N.Y.: Oxford Univ. Press, 1974.

Karl, Frederick and Hamalian, Leo, eds. *The Naked i*. N.Y.: Fawcett, 1971.

Kaufmann, Walter A., ed. *Existentialism from Dostoevsky to Sartre*. N.Y.: Meridian Press, 1956.

Kayser, Wolfgang. *The Grotesque in Art and Literature*. Trans. by Ulrich Weisstein. Bloomington, Ind.: Univ. of Ind. Press, 1963.

Kazin, Alfred. *Bright Book of Life*. Boston: Atlantic-Little Brown, 1971, 1973.

———. *On Native Grounds*. N.Y.: Reynal & Hitchcock, 1942.

Kennedy, Margaret. *The Outlaws on Parnassus*. London: Cresset, 1958.

Kermode, Frank. "Novel and Narrative," *The Theory of the Novel, New Essays*. Ed. by John Halperin. N.Y.: Oxford Univ. Press, 1974.

_____. *The Sense of an Ending, Studies in the Theory of Fiction*. N.Y.: Oxford Univ. Press, 1966, 1967.

Kettle, Arnold. *An Introduction to the English Novel*, 2 vols. London, N.Y.: Hutchinson's Universal Library, 1951–53.

Kiely, Robert. "The Craft of Despondency—The Traditional Novelists," *Daedalus*, XCII (1963), 220–237.

Killham, John. "The Use of 'Concreteness' as an Evaluative Term in F. R. Leavis's 'The Great Tradition'," *British Journal of Aesthetics*, V (1965), 14–24.

*Kipling, Rudyard. *Something of Myself*. N.Y.: Macmillan, 1937.

Klinkowitz, Jerry, ed. *Innovative Fiction*. N.Y.: Dell, 1972.

Kohler, Dayton. "Time in the Modern Novel," *College English*, X (October, 1948), 15–24.

Kolnai, Aurel. "On the Concept of the Interesting," *British Journal of Aesthetics*, IV (1964), 22–39.

Kostelanetz, Richard, ed. *Breakthrough Fictions*. West Glover, Vt.: Something Else Press, 1973.

_____. *On Contemporary Literature*. N.Y.: Avon Books, 1964, expanded, 1969.

_____. *Twelve from the Sixties*. N.Y.: Dell, 1967.

Krey, Laura. "Time and the English Novel," in *Twentieth Century English*. Ed. by W. S. Knickerbocker, N.Y., 1946.

Krieger, Murray. *The Tragic Vision: Variations on a Theme in Literary Interpretation*. N.Y.: Holt, Rinehart & Winston, 1960.

Kris, Ernst. *Psychoanalytic Explorations in Art*. N.Y.: International Universities Press, 1952.

*Kronenberger, Louis, ed. *Novelists on Novelists: An Anthology.* Garden City N.Y.: Anchor Books, 1962.

Krook, Dorothea. "Intentions and Intentions: The Problem of Intention and Henry James's The Turn of the Screw," *The Theory of the Novel, New Essays.* Ed. by John Halperin. N.Y.: Oxford Univ. Press, 1974.

Krutch, Joseph Wood. *Five Masters: A Study in the Mutations of the Novel.* N.Y.: Cape & Smith, 1930.

*Kuehl, John. *Creative Writing and Rewriting, Contemporary American Novelists at Work.* N.Y.: Appleton-Century-Crofts, 1967.

**Kunitz, Stanley J. *Authors Today and Yesterday.* N.Y.: H. W. Wilson, 1933–1934.

**Kunitz, Stanley, J. and Haycraft, Howard, eds. *Twentieth Century Authors, A Biographical Dictionary of Modern Literature.* N.Y.: H. W. Wilson, 1942.

Langer, Susanne K. *Feeling and Form.* N.Y.: Scribners, 1953.

_____. *Philosophy in a New Key.* Cambridge, Mass.: Harvard Univ. Press, 1942.

Lathrop, Henry Burrows. *The Art of the Novelist.* London: Dodd, Mead, 1919.

Lawall, Sarah N. *Critics and Consciousness, The Existential Structure of Literature.* Cambridge, Mass.: Harvard Univ. Press, 1968.

*Lawrence, D. H. "Morality and the Novel," *Selected Literary Criticism.* Ed. by Anthony Beal. N.Y.: Viking Press, 1956.

*_____. *Selected Letters of D. H. Lawrence.* Ed. by Diana Trilling. N.Y.: Farrar, Straus & Cudahy, 1961.

*_____. *Studies in Classic American Literature.* N.Y.: Viking Press, 1923, 1950, 1961.

*_____. "Why the Novel Matters," *Selected Literary Criticism.* Ed. by Anthony Beal. N.Y.: Viking Press, 1956.

Leavis, F. R. "The Novel as Dramatic Poem (I): 'Hard Times,'" *Scrutiny*, XIV (1947), 185–203.

———. *The Great Tradition*. London: George Stewart, 1949.

Leavis, Q. D. *Fiction and the Reading Public*. London: Chatto & Windus, 1932.

Lee, Vernon (Violet Paget). *The Handling of Words, and Other Studies in Literary Psychology*. N.Y.: Dodd, Mead, 1923.

———. *Laurus Nobilis: Chapters on Art and Life*. London and N.Y.: J. Lane, 1909.

Lees, F. N. "Identification and Emotion in the Novel: A Feature of Narrative Method," *British Journal of Aesthetics*, IV (1964), 109–113.

Leggett, H. W. *The Idea in Fiction*. London: G. Allen & Unwin, 1934.

Leisy, Ernest E. *The American Historical Novel*. Norman, Ok.: Univ. of Ok. Press, 1950.

Lemon, Lee T. "The Illusion of Life: A Modern Version of an Old Heresy," *Western Humanities Reveiw*, XVII, (1963), 65–74.

Lemon, Lee T. and Reis, Marion J., trans. and ed. *Russian Formalist Criticism: Four Essays*. Lincoln, Neb.: Univ. of Neb. Press, 1965.

Lerner, Laurence. *The Truest Poetry: An Essay on the Question What is Literature?* London: H. Hamilton, 1960.

Lesser, Simon O. "The Attitude of Fiction," *Modern Fiction Studies*, II (1956), 47–55.

———. *Fiction and the Unconscious*. Boston: Beacon Press, 1957.

———. "The Functions of Form in Narrative Art," *Psychiatry*, XVIII (1955), 51–63.

Levi, Albert William. *Literature, Philosophy and the Imagination*. Bloomington, Ind.: Univ. of Ind. Press, 1962.

Levin, Harry. *Contexts of Criticism*. Cambridge, Mass.: Harvard Univ. Press, 1957.

_____. "Montage," *James Joyce*. N.Y.: New Directions, 1941, rev. 1960.

_____. "The Novel," *Dictionary of World Literature*. Ed. by Joseph Shipley, rev. ed. N.Y.: Philosophical Library, 1953.

_____. "Toward a Sociology of the Novel," *Journal of the History of Ideas*, XXVI (1965), 148–154.

Levine, George. "Realism Reconsidered," *The Theory of the Novel, New Essays*. N.Y.: Oxford Univ. Press, 1974.

Lévy, Julian. *Surrealism*. N.Y.: Black Sun, 1936.

Lewis, R. W. B. *The Picaresque Saint: Representative Figures in Contemporary Fiction*. Philadelphia: Lippincott, 1959.

*Lewis, Wyndham. *Men Without Art*. London: Cassell, Harcourt, 1934.

*_____. *Time and Western Man*. N.Y.: Harcourt, Brace, 1928.

*Liddell, Robert. *Some Principles of Fiction*. London: Jonathan Cape, 1953.

*_____. *A Treatise on the Novel*. London: Jonathan Cape, 1947.

Littlejohn, David. "The Anti-realists," *Daedalus*, XCII (1963), 250–264.

Litz, A. Walton. "The Genre of *Ulysses*." *The Theory of the Novel, New Essays*. Ed. by John Halperin. N.Y.: Oxford Univ. Press, 1974.

Lodge, David. *Language of Fiction: Essays in Criticism and Verbal Analysis of the English Novel*. London, N.Y.: Columbia Univ. Press, 1966.

_____. "Towards a Poetics of Fiction, 2) An Approach through Language," *Novel, A Forum on Fiction*, V1, (Winter, 1968) 158–169.

Loofbourow, John W. "Realism in the Anglo-American Novel: The Pastoral Myth," *The Theory of the Novel, New Essays*. Ed. by John Halperin. N.Y.: Oxford Univ. Press, 1974.

Lord, Albert B. *The Singer of Tales*. Cambridge: Harvard Univ. Press, 1960.

Lord, Catherine. "Aesthetic Unity," *Journal of Philosophy*, LVIII (1961), 321–327.

Lowenthal, Leo. *Literature and the Image of Man: Sociological Studies of the European Drama and Novel, 1600–1900*. Boston: Beacon Press, 1957.

Lubbock, Percy. *The Craft of Fiction*. N.Y.: Viking Press, 1957.

Lukács, George. "Essay on the Novel," *International Literature*, 5 (1936), 68–74.

————. *The Historical Novel*. Trans. by H. and S. Mitchell. London: Merlin, 1962.

————. "The Intellectual Physiognomy of Literary Characters," *International Literature*, 8 (1936), 55–83.

————. *Studies in European Realism: A Sociological Survey of the Writings of Balzac, Stendhal, Zola, Tolstoy, Gorki, and Others*. Trans. by Edith Bone. London: Hillway, 1950.

————. *The Theory of the Novel*. Cambridge, Mass.: Harvard Univ. Press, 1971.

Lutwack, Leonard. "Mixed and Uniform Prose Styles in the Novel," *Journal of Aesthetics and Art Criticism*, XVIII (1960), 350–357.

*Lytle, Andrew Nelson. "The Image as Guide to Meaning in the Historical Novel," *Sewanee Review*, LXI (1953), 408–426.

*————. "Impressionism, the Ego, and the First Person," *Daedalus*, XCII (1963), 281–296.

*————. "The Working Novelist and the Mythmaking Process," *Daedalus*, LXXXVIII (1959), 326–338.

*Macauley, Robie and Lanning, George. *Technique in Fiction*. N.Y.: Harper & Row, 1964.

*McCarthy, Mary. "Characters in Fiction," *On the Contrary*. New York: Noonday Press, 1961.

*_____. "The Fact in Fiction," *Partisan Review*, XXVII (1960), 438–458; reprinted in *On the Contrary*, New York: Noonday Press, 1961.

*McCormack, Thomas, ed. *Afterwords, Novelists on Their Novels*. N.Y.: Harper & Row, 1969.

*McCormick, John. *Catastrophe and Imagination. An Interpretation of the Recent English and American Novel*. London: Longmans, Green, 1957.

Macdonald, Dwight. *Against the American Grain*. N.Y.: Random House, 1962.

*McHugh, Vincent. *Primer of the Novel*. N.Y.: Random House, 1950.

McKillop, Alan Dugald. *The Early Masters of English Fiction*. Lawrence, Kan.: Univ. of Kan. Press, 1956.

McQuade, Donald and Atwan, Robert, eds. *Popular Writing in America: The Interaction of Style and Audience*. N.Y.: Oxford Univ. Press, 1974.

MacShane, Frank, ed. *Critical Writings of Ford Madox Ford*. Lincoln, Neb.: Univ. of Neb. Press, 1964.

Madden, David, ed. *American Dreams, American Nightmares*. Carbondale, Ill.: Southern Ill. Univ. Press, 1970.

*_____. *Creative Choices*. Glenview, Ill.: Scott, Foresman, 1975.

*_____. *The Poetic Image in Six Genres*. Carbondale, Ill.: Southern Ill. Univ. Press, 1969.

_____. *Proletarian Writers of the Thirties*. Carbondale, Ill.: Southern Ill. Univ. Press, 1968.

*_____. *Rediscoveries*. N.Y.: Crown, 1971.

_____. *Tough Guy Writers of the Thirties*. Carbondale, Ill.: Southern Ill. Univ. Press, 1968.

**Magill, Frank, ed. *Cyclopedia of World Authors*. Englewood Cliffs, N.J., 1974.

**Magill, Frank and Madden, David, eds. *Survey of Contemporary Literature*. Englewood Cliffs, N.J., 1977.

Malin, Irving, ed. *New American Gothic*. Carbondale, Ill.: Southern Ill. Univ. Press, 1962.

_____. *Psychoanalysis and American Fiction*. N.Y.: E. P. Dutton, 1965.

Man, Paul de. *Blindness and Insight: Essays in the Rhetoric of Contemporary Criticism*. N.Y.: Oxford Univ. Press, 1971.

*Mann, Thomas. "The Art of the Novel," *The Creative Vision: Modern European Writers on Their Art*. Ed. by Haskell M. Block and Herman Salinger. N.Y.: Grove Press, 1960.

*_____. *The Genesis of a Novel*. Trans. by Richard and Clara Winston. London: Secker & Warburg, 1961.

*Mansfield, Katherine. *The Journal of Katherine Mansfield*. Ed. by John Middleton Murry. N.Y.: Knopf, 1930.

Marcus, Steven. "The Novel Again," *Partisan Review*, XXIX (1962), 171–195.

Martin, Harold C., ed. *Style in Prose Fiction: English Institute Essays*. N.Y.: Columbia Univ. Press, 1959.

Martin, Robert Bernard. "Notes Toward a Comic Fiction," *The Theory of the Novel, New Essays*. Ed. by John Halperin. N.Y.: Oxford Univ. Press, 1974.

Masson, David. *British Novelists and Their Styles*. Boston: Gould & Lincoln, 1859.

Matthews, J. H. *Surrealism and the Novel*. Ann Arbor: Univ. of Mich. Press, 1966.

*Maugham, W. Somerset. *The Summing Up*. N.Y.: Literary Guild, 1938.

*_____. *A Writer's Notebook*. Garden City, N.Y.: Doubleday, 1949.

*de Maupassant, Guy. "Essays on the Novel," *The Portable Maupassant*. N.Y.: Viking Press, 1947.

*Mauriac, Claude. "The 'New Novel' in France," *Opinions and Perspectives from the New York Times Book Review*. Ed. by Francis Brown. Boston: Houghton Mifflin, 1964.

Maurois, André. *The Art of Writing*. Trans. by Gerard Hopkins. N.Y.: Dutton, 1960.

May, Derwent. "The Novelist as Moralist and the Moralist as Critic," *Essays in Criticism*, X (1960), 320–328.

Mayhead, Robin. *Understanding Literature*. Cambridge: Cambridge Univ. Press, 1965.

Melchiori, Giorgio. *The Tightrope Walkers: Studies in Mannerism in Modern English Literature*. London: Routledge & Paul, 1956.

Mendilow, A. A. *Time and the Novel*. London: Nevill, 1952.

Mercier, Vivian. *The New Novel: From Queneau to Pinget*. N.Y.: Farrar, Straus, & Giroux, 1971.

*Meredith, George. "An Essay on Comedy," *Comedy*. N.Y.: Anchor Books, 1956.

Meyerhoff, Hans. *Time in Literature*. Berkeley: Univ. of Ca. Press, 1955.

*Miller, Henry. *Henry Miller on Writing*. N.Y.: New Directions, 1957, 1964.

Miller, J. Hillis. *The Form of Victorian Fiction*. Notre Dame: Univ. of Notre Dame Press, 1968.

Miller, James E., ed. *Myth and Method, Modern Theories of Fiction*. Lincoln: Univ. of Neb. Press, 1960.

Millett, Fred B. *Contemporary American Authors: A Critical Survey and 219 Bio-Bibliographies*. N.Y.: Harcourt, Brace, 1943.

Mizener, Arthur. *The Sense of Life in the Modern Novel*. Boston: Houghton Mifflin, 1964.

Moffatt, James and McElheny, Kenneth R. *Points of View.* N.Y.: New American Library, 1966.

Monroe, N. Elizabeth. *The Novel and Society.* Chapel Hill: Univ. of N.C. Press, 1941.

*Montague, C. E. *A Writer's Notes on His Trade.* London: Chatto & Windus, 1930.

Moore, Patrick. *Science and Fiction.* London: G. G. Harrap, 1957.

*Morris, Wright. *About Fiction.* N.Y.: Harper & Row, 1975.

*_____. *Earthly Delights, Unearthly Adornments:* N.Y.: Harper & Row: 1978.

*_____. *The Territory Ahead.* N.Y.: Harcourt, Brace, 1958.

Morris-Jones, H. U. W. "The Language of Feelings," *British Journal of Aesthetics,* II (1962), 17–25.

Moscowitz, Sam. *Seekers of Tomorrow, Masters of Modern Science Fiction.* Cleveland and N.Y.: World Publishing Co., 1965.

*Moss, Howard. "Notes on Fiction," *Wisconsin Studies in Contemporary Literature,* VII (1966), 1–11.

Mothersill, Mary. "'Unique' as an Aesthetic Predicate," *Journal of Philosophy,* LVIII (1961), 421–437.

Mudrick, Marvin. "Character and Event in Fiction," *Yale Review,* L (1960), 202–218.

_____. "Looking for Kellerman; or, Fiction and the Facts of Life," *The Theory of the Novel, New Essays.* Ed. by John Halperin. N.Y.: Oxford Univ. Press, 1974.

Mueller, William R. *The Prophetic Voice in Modern Fiction.* N.Y.: Association Press, 1959.

Muir, Edwin. *The Structure of the Novel.* N.Y.: Hogarth Press, 1929.

Muller, H. J. "Impressionism in Fiction," *American Scholar,* VII (1938), 355–367.

_____. *Modern Fiction: A Study of Values.* N.Y.: Funk & Wagnalls, 1937.

Murry, John Middleton. *The Problem of Style.* Oxford: Oxford Univ. Press, 1922.

Myers, Walter L. *The Later Realism: A Study of Characterization in the British Novel.* Chicago: Univ. of Chicago Press, 1927.

*Nabokov, Vladimir. *Speak, Memory, the Conclusive Evidence, an Autobiography Revisited.* N.Y.: G. P. Putnam's Sons, 1951, 1966.

Nicholson, Norman. *Man and Literature.* London: Macmillan, 1943.

Nevins, Francis M. *The Mystery Writer's Craft.* Bowling Green, Ohio: Bowling Green Popular Press, 1970.

*Nin, Anaïs. *The Novel of the Future.* N.Y.: Macmillan, 1968.

Noon, William T. "Modern Literature and the Sense of Time," *Thought,* XXXIII (1958), 571–603.

*Norris, Frank. "The Novel with a Purpose," *The World's Work,* 4 (May, 1902), 2117–2119.

*_____. *The Responsibilities of the Novelist.* N.Y.: Doubleday, 1903.

Nye, Russel. *The Unembarrassed Muse, The Popular Arts in America.* N.Y.: Dial Press, 1970.

*Oates, Joyce Carol. *The Edge of Possiblity: Tragic Forms in Literature.* N.Y.: Vanguard Press, 1972.

*O'Connor, Flannery. *Mystery and Manners, Occasional Prose.* N.Y.: Farrar, Straus & Giroux, 1969.

*O'Connor, Frank. *The Mirror in the Roadway: A Study of the Modern Novel.* N.Y.: Knopf, 1956.

O'Connor, William Van, ed. *Forms of Modern Fiction.* Minneapolis: Univ. of Minn. Press, 1948.

_____. *The Grotesque: An American Genre and Other Essays.* Carbondale, Ill.: Southern Ill. Univ. Press, 1962.

_____. "The Novel as a Social Document," *American Quarterly*, IV (1952), 169–175.

_____. "The Novel of Experience," *Critique*, I (1956), 37–44.

_____. *Seven Modern American Novelists*. Minneapolis: Univ. of Minn. Press, 1964.

*O'Faoláin, Seán. *The Short Story*. N.Y.: Devin-Adair, 1951.

*_____. *The Vanishing Hero: Studies of the Hero in the Modern Novel*. N.Y.: Atlantic Little Brown, 1956.

O'Grady, Walter. "On Plot in Modern Fiction: Hardy, James, and Conrad," *Modern Fiction Studies*, XI (1965), 107–115.

O'Hare, Charles B. "Myth or Plot? A Study in Ways of Ordering Narrative," *Arizona Quarterly*, XIII (1957), 238–250.

Opel, Harold. "The Double Symbol," *American Literature*, XXIII (1951), 1–6.

Ortega y Gasset, José. "Notes on the Novel," in *The Dehumanization of Art and Other Writings on Art and Culture*. Princeton: Princeton Univ. Press, 1948.

Orvis, Mary Burchard. *The Art of Writing Fiction*. N.Y.: Prentice-Hall, 1948.

Overton, Grant. *The Philosophy of Fiction*. N.Y.: Appleton, 1928.

Pacifici, Sergio. *A Guide to Contemporary Italian Literature*. Cleveland, Ohio: The World Publishing Co., 1962.

Parkinson, Thomas, ed. *A Casebook on the Beat*. N.Y.: Thomas Y. Crowell, 1961.

Pascal, Roy. "The Autobiographical Novel and the Autobiography," *Essays in Criticism*, IX (1959), 134–150.

_____. "Tense and Novel," *Modern Language Review*, LVII (1962), 1–11.

*Pasternak, Boris. *Safe Conduct, An Autobiography and Other Writings*. N.Y.: New Directions, 1949, 1958.

Pater, Walter. *Appreciations: With an Essay on Style.* N.Y.: Macmillan, 1927.

Paul, David. "The Novel Art," *Twentieth Century,* CLIII (June, 1953), 436–442.

———. "The Novel Art: II," *Twentieth Century,* CLIV (October, 1953), 294–301.

———. "Time and the Novelist," *Partisan Review,* XXI (1954), 636–649.

Penzoldt, Peter. *The Supernatural in Fiction.* London: P. Nevill, 1952.

Perry, Bliss. *A Study of Prose Fiction.* Boston: Houghton Mifflin, 1902.

Peter, John. "Joyce and the Novel," *Kenyon Review,* XVIII (1956), 619–632.

Peyre, Henri. *Literature and Sincerity.* New Haven: Yale Univ. Press, 1963.

———. *French Novelists of Today.* N.Y.: Oxford Univ. Press, 1967.

Piper, Warrene. "Sources and Processes in the Writing of Fiction," *American Journal of Psychology,* XLIII (1931), 188–201.

*Plimpton, George, ed. *Writers at Work: The Paris Review Interviews.* N.Y.: Third series, 1968, Fourth series, 1976.

Podhoretz, Norman. "The Article as Art," *Doings and Undoings.* N.Y.: Noonday Press, 1964.

Poirier, Richard. *A World Elsewhere.* N.Y.: Oxford Univ. Press, 1966.

*Porter, Katherine Anne. *The Collected Essays and Occasional Writings of Katherine Anne Porter.* N.Y.: Delacorte Press, 1970.

Poulet, Georges. *The Interior Distance.* Baltimore: Johns Hopkins Univ. Press, 1959.

———. *Studies in Human Time.* Baltimore: Johns Hopkins Univ. Press, 1956.

Praz, Mario. *The Romantic Agony.* N.Y.: Oxford Univ. Press, 1933.

*Priestley, J. B. "Some Reflections of a Popular Novelist," *Essays and Studies*, XVIII (1932), 149–159.

Pritchett, V. S. "The Future of English Fiction," *Partisan Review*, XV (1948), 1063–1070.

————. *The Living Novel*. London: Chatto & Windus, 1946.

*Proust, Marcel. *On Art and Literature, 1896–1919*. Trans. by Sylvia Townsend Warner. N.Y.: Meridian, 1958.

Rahv, Philip. "The Cult of Experience in American Writing," *Image and Idea*. N.Y.: New Directions, 1949.

————. "Fiction and the Criticism of Fiction," *Kenyon Review*, XVIII (1956), 276–299.

Raleigh, John Henry. "The English Novel and the Three Kinds of Time," *The Novel, Modern Essays in Criticism*. Ed. by Robert Murray David. N.Y.: Prentice-Hall, 1969.

*Ransom, John Crowe. "Characters and Character," *American Review*, VI (January, 1936), 271–288.

*————. "The Content of the Novel," *American Review*, VII (1936), 301–318.

*————. "The Understanding of Fiction," *Kenyon Review*, XII (1950), 189–218.

Rathburn, Robert C. and Steinmann, Martin Jr., eds. *From Jane Austen to Joseph Conrad*. Minneapolis: Univ. of Minn. Press, 1958.

*Read, Herbert. *English Prose Style*. N.Y.: Pantheon Books, 1952.

Reiss, H. S. "Style and Structure in Modern Experimental Fiction," *Stil- Und Formprobleme in Der Literatur*. Ed. by Paul Bockman. Heidelberg: C. Winter, 159.

Richards, I. A. *The Philosophy of Rhetoric*. N.Y.: Oxford Univ. Press, 1936.

————. *Practical Criticism, A Study of Literary Judgment*. N.Y.: Harcourt, Brace, n. d. (First Published, 1929).

Rickword, C. H. "A Note on Fiction," *Forms of Modern Fiction*. Ed. by William Van O'Connor. Minneapolis: Univ. of Minn., 1948.

Rideout, Walter. *The Radical Novel in the United States, 1900–1954*. Cambridge: Harvard Univ. Press, 1965.

**Riley, Caroline and Mendelson, Phyllis Carmel, eds. *Contemporary Literary Criticism: Excerpts from Criticism of the Works of Novelists, Poets, Playwrights and Other Creative Writers*. Detroit, Mich.: Gale Research, 1974–79.

*Robbe-Grillet, Alain. *For a New Novel, Essays on Fiction*. N.Y.: Grove Press, 1965.

*_____. "From Realism to Reality," *Evergreen Review*, X (1966), 50–53, 83.

*_____. "Reflections on Some Aspects of the Traditional Novel," *International Literary Annual*, I (1958), 114–121.

Roditi, Edouard. "Trick Perspectives," *Virginia Quarterly Review*, XX (Oct, 1944), 545–549.

Rodway, A. E. "The Truth of Fiction: A Critical Dialogue," *Essays in Criticism*, VIII (1958), 405–417.

Rogers, W. H. "Form in the Art-Novel," *Helicon*, II (1939), 1–17.

Romberg, Bertil. *Studies in the Narrative Technique of the First-Person Novel*. Stockholm: Almquist & Wiksell, 1962.

**Rosenheim, E. W., Jr. *What Happens in Literature: A Student's Guide to Poetry, Drama and Fiction*. Chicago: Univ. of Chicago Press, 1960.

*Roth, Philip. *Reading Myself and Others*. N.Y.: Farrar, Straus and Giroux, 1975.

Rourke, Constance. *The Roots of American Culture*. N.Y.: Harcourt, Brace, 1942.

*Rovit, Earl H. "The Ambiguous Modern Novel," *Yale Review*, XLIX (1960), 413–424.

**Rubin, Louis, D. ed., *A Bibliographical Guide to the Study of Southern Literature*. Baton Rouge: La. State Univ. Press, 1969.

*————. *The Curious Death of the Novel, Essays in American Literature*. Baton Rouge, La.: La. State Univ. Press, 1967.

*Rubin, Louis D. and Moore, John Rees, eds. *The Idea of an American Novel*. N.Y.: Thomas Y. Crowell, 1961.

Saintsbury, George. "Technique," *Dial*, LXXX (April, 1926), 273-278.

Sale, Roger, ed. *Discussions of the Novel*. Boston: Heath, 1960.

*Sarraute, Nathalie. *The Age of Suspicion: Essays on the Novel*. Trans. by Maria Jolas. N.Y.: George Braziller, 1963.

*Sartre, Jean-Paul. *What is Literature?* Trans. by Bernard Frechtman. N.Y.: Philosophical Library, 1949.

*————. *The Words*. N.Y.: George Braziller, 1964.

Savage, D. S. *The Withered Branch*. London: Eyre & Spottisworde, 1950.

Schlauch, Margaret. *Antecedents of the English Novel, 1400-1600*. Warsaw and London: PWN-Polish Scientific Publishers, 1963.

Scholes, Robert. *Approaches to the Novel*. San Francisco: Chandler, 1961.

————. "Towards a Poetics of Fiction: An Approach Through Genre," *Novel: A Forum on the Novel*. II (Winter, 1969), 101-110.

Scholes, Robert and Kellogg, Robert. *The Nature of Narrative*. N.Y.: Oxford Univ. Press, 1966.

*Schorer, Mark. *Society and Self in the Novel: English Institute Essays, 1955*. N.Y.: Columbia Univ. Press, 1956.

————. "Fiction and the 'Analogical Matrix'," *The World We Imagine*. N.Y.: Farrar, Strauss, and Giroux, 1968.

*————. "Technique as Discovery," *The World We Imagine*. N.Y.: Farrar, Straus, and Giroux, 1968.

Schulz, Max F. "Character (Contra Characterization) in the Contemporary Novel," *The Theory of the Novel, New Essays*. Ed. by John Halperin. N.Y.: Oxford Univ. Press, 1974.

Scott, Nathan A., Jr. *Forms of Extremity in the Modern Novel*. Richmond, Va.: John Knox, 1965.

Scrutton, Mary. "Addiction to Fiction," *Twentieth Century*, CLIX (April, 1956), 363–373.

Sears, Sallie and Lord, Georgianna W. eds. *The Discontinuous Universe: Selected Writings in Contemporary Consciousness*. N.Y.: Basic Books, 1972.

Shapiro, Charles, ed. *Contemporary British Novelists*. Carbondale, Ill.: Southern Ill. Univ. Press, 1965.

Sherman, Caroline B. "A Brief for Fiction," *South Atlantic Quarterly*, XXXVI (1937), 335–347.

Sherwood, Irma Z. "The Novelists as Commentators," *The Age of Johnson: Essays Presented to Chauncey Brewster Tinker*. Edited by F. W. Hilles. New Haven: Yale Univ. Press, 1949.

Shroder, Maurice Z. "The Novel as a Genre," *Massachusetts Review*, IV (1963), 291–308.

Shumaker, Wayne. *Literature and the Irrational*. Englewood Cliffs, N.J.: Prentice-Hall, 1960.

*Simenon, Georges. *The Novel of Man*. N.Y.: Harcourt, Brace, 1964.

Singer, Godfrey Frank. *The Epistolary Novel*. Philadelphia: Univ. of Penn. Press, 1933.

Slatoff, Walter. *With Respect to Readers*. Ithaca, N.Y.: Cornell Univ. Press, 1970.

Smart, Charles A. "On the Road to Page One," *Yale Review*, XXXVII (1947), 242–256.

Smith, Janet Adam, ed. *Henry James and Robert Louis Stevenson: A Record of Friendship and Criticism*. London: R. Hart-Davis, 1948.

Snell, George. *Shapers of American Fiction*. N.Y.: Dutton, 1947.

*Snow, C. P. "Science, Politics, and the Novelist," *Kenyon Review*, XXIII (1961), 1–17.

Solotaroff, Theodore. *The Red Hot Vacuum, and Other Pieces on the Writing of the Sixties*. N.Y.: Atheneum, 1970.

*Sontag, Susan. "On Style," "Notes on 'Camp,'" *Against Interpretation*. N.Y.: Farrar, Straus & Giroux, 1966.

Sorenson, Virginia. "Is it True?—The Novelist and His Materials," *Western Humanities Review*, VII (1953), 283–292.

Southern, Terry, ed. *Writers in Revolt*. N.Y.: Frederick Fell, 1963.

Spencer, John. "A Note on the 'Steady Monologue of the Interiors,'" *Review of English Literature*, VI (April, 1965), 32–41.

**Spiller, Robert E., et al. *Literary History of the United States*. N.Y.: Macmillan, rev., 1974.

*Stafford, Jean. "The Psychological Novel," *Kenyon Review*, X (1948), 214–227.

Stallman, Robert Wooster, ed. *The Critic's Notebook*. Minneapolis: Univ. of Minn., 1950.

———. "Fiction and Its Critics: A Reply to Mr. Rahv," *Kenyon Review*, XIX (1957), 290–299.

Stamm, James R. *A Short History of Spanish Literature*. N.Y.: Anchor Books, 1967.

Stang, Richard. *The Theory of the Novel in England, 1850–1870*. N.Y.: Columbia Univ. Press, 1959.

*Steegmuller, Francis. *Flaubert and Madame Bovary, A Double Portrait*, Revised. Chicago: Univ. of Chicago Press, 1977.

*Stegner, Wallace. "A Problem in Fiction," *Pacific Spectator*, III (1949), 368–375.

*Stein, Gertrude. *Narration*. Introduction by Thornton Wilder. Chicago: Univ. of Chicago Press, 1935.

*Steinbeck, John. *Journal of a Novel*. N.Y.: Viking Press, 1969, 1972.

*Stephen, Leslie. *Hours in a Library*. N.Y.: 1904.

Stern, Madeline B. "Counterclockwise: Flux of Time in Literature," *Sewanee Review*, XLIV (1936), 338–365.

Sternberg, Meir. "What Is Exposition? An Essay in Temporal Delimitation," *The Theory of the Novel, New Essays*. Ed. by John Halperin. N.Y.: Oxford Univ. Press, 1974.

Stevenson, David L. "The Activists," *Daedalus*, XCII (1963), 238–249.

Stevenson, Lionel. *The English Novel: A Panorama*. Boston: Houghton Mifflin, 1960.

*Stevenson, Robert Louis. "A Gossip on Romance," "A Humble Remonstrance," *Works*, XIII. N.Y., 1895.

Stevick, Philip, ed. *Anti-Story, An Anthology of Experimental Fiction*. N.Y.: The Free Press, 1971.

_____. "Fictional Chapters and Open Ends," *Journal of General Education*, XVII (1966), 261–272.

_____. "The Theory of Fictional Chapters," *Western Humanities Review*, XX (1966), 231–241.

_____. *The Theory of the Novel*. N.Y.: The Free Press, 1967.

Struve, Gleb. "*Monologue Interieur:* The Origins of the Formula and the First Statement of its Possibilities," *PMLA*, LXIX (1954), 1101–1111.

*Sukenick, Ronald. *The Death of the Novel*. N.Y.: Dial Press, 1969.

*_____. Interview in *The Falcon*. Spring, 1971, 5–25.

*_____. "The New Tradition," *Partisan Review*, XXXIX (1972), 580–588.

Sutton, Walter. "The Literary Image and the Reader: A Consideration of the Theory of Spatial Form," *Journal of Aesthetics and Art Criticism*, XVI (1957), 112–123.

Svoboda, Karel. "Content, Subject and Material of a Work of Literature," *Journal of Aesthetics and Art Criticism*, IX (1950), 39–45.

*Swinnerton, Frank. "Variations of Form in the Novel," *Essays and Studies*, XXIII (1937), 79–92.

Symons, Arthur. *The Symbolist Movement in Literature.* N.Y.: Dutton. 1919, 1947, 1958.

Symons, Julian. "Politics and the Novel," *Twentieth Century,* CLXX (Winter, 1962), 147–154.

Sypher, Wylie. "Appendix: The Meaning of Comedy," *Comedy.* N.Y.: Anchor Books, 1956.

———. *Loss of the Self in Modern Literature and Art.* N.Y.: Random House, 1962.

Tante, Dilly (Stanley J. Kunitz), ed. *Living Authors: A Book of Biographies.* N.Y.: H. W. Wilson, 1935.

*Tate, Allen. "The Post of Observation in Fiction," *Maryland Quarterly,* 2 (1944), 61–64.

*———. "Techniques of Fiction," *Sewanee Review,* LII (1944), 210–225.

*Tate, Allen and Gordon, Caroline. *House of Fiction,* 2nd ed. N.Y.: Scribner's, 1950, 1960.

Taylor, H. W. "Modern Fiction and the Doctrine of Uniformity," *Philological Quarterly,* XIX (1940), 226–236.

———. "'Particular Character': an Early Phase of a Literary Evolution," *PMLA,* LX (1945), 161–174.

Thompson, Denys. *Reading and Discrimination.* London: Chatto & Windus, 1949.

Tilford, John E. "Point of View in the Novel," *Emory University Quarterly,* XX (1964), 121–130.

———. "Some Changes in the Technique of the Novel," *Emory University Quarterly,* IX (1953), 167–174.

Tillotson, Kathleen. *The Tale and the Teller.* London: R. Hart-Davis, 1959.

Tillyard, E. M. W. *The Epic Strain in the English Novel.* London: Chatto & Windus, 1958.

———. "The Novel as Literary Kind," *Essays and Studies,* IX (1956), 78–86.

Tindall, William York. *Forces in Modern British Literature, 1885–1946*. N.Y.: Knopf, 1947.

_____. *The Literary Symbol*. N.Y.: Columbia Univ. Press, 1955.

Todorov, Tzvetan. "Structural Analysis of Narrative," *Novel: A Forum on Fiction*. (Fall, 1969), 70–76.

Toynbee, Philip. "Experiment and the Future of the Novel," *The Craft of Letters in England*. Edited by John Lehmann. London: Cresset Press, 1956.

*Trilling, Lionel. *The Liberal Imagination*. N.Y.: Scribner, 1976 [1950].

_____. *The Opposing Self*. N.Y.: Viking Press, 1955.

Turnell, Martin. *The Novel in France*. N.Y.: New Directions, 1951.

Ullman, Stephen. *The Image in the Modern French Novel*. London: Cambridge Univ. Press, 1960.

_____. "Style and Personality," *Review of English Literature*, VI (April, 1965), 21–31.

_____. *Style in the French Novel*. Oxford, England: B. Blackwell, 1964.

_____. "The Uses of Comic Vision," *The British Imagination: A Critical Survey from The Times Literary Supplement*. N.Y., 1961.

Uzzell. Thomas H. *The Technique of the Novel*. N.Y., 1959.

Van Doren, Carl. *The American Novel, 1789–1939*. N.Y.: Macmillan, 1921, rev. 1940.

_____. *Contemporary American Novelists 1900–1920*. N.Y.: Macmillan, 1922, 1931.

Van Ghent, Dorothy. *The English Novel, Form and Function*. N.Y.: Rinehart, 1953.

Van Nostrand, Albert. *The Denatured Novel*. Indianapolis and N.Y.: Bobbs-Merrill, 1960.

**Vinson, James and Kirkpatrick, D. L. eds., *Contemporary Novelists*. N.Y.: St. Martin's Press, 2nd ed., 1976.

Vivas, Eliseo. *The Artistic Transaction and Essays on Theory of Literature*. Columbus, Ohio: Ohio State Univ. Press, 1963.

———. "The Self and its Masks," *Southern Review*, I (1965), 317–336.

Wagenknecht, Edward. *Cavalcade of the English Novel*. N.Y.: Holt, 1943.

Wagner, Geoffrey. "Sociology and Fiction," *Twentieth Century*, CLXVII (February, 1960), 108–114.

*Wain, John. "The Conflict of Forms in Contemporary English Literature," *Essays on Literature and Ideas*. London: Macmillan; N.Y.: St. Martin's Press, 1963.

Walcutt, Charles Child. "From Scientific Theory to Aesthetic Fact: The 'Naturalistic' Novel," *Quarterly Review of Literature*, III (1946), 167–179.

———. "Interpreting the Symbol," *College English*, XIV (1953), 446–454.

Warburg, Jeremy. "Idiosyncratic Style," *Review of English Literature*, VI (April, 1965), 56–65.

**Warfel, Harry R. *American Novelists of Today*. N.Y.: American Book Company, 1951.

Watt, Ian. *The Rise of the Novel*. London: Chatto & Windus; Berkeley: Univ. of Ca., 1957.

**Weber, J. Sherwood. *Good Reading: Guide for Serious Readers*. N.Y.: New American Library, 1935, 1969.

Webster, Harvey Curtis. *After the Trauma, Contemporary British Novelists Since 1920*. Lexington: The Univ. Press of Ky., 1970.

Welleck, René and Warren, Austin. *Theory of Literature*. N.Y.: Harcourt, Brace, & World, 1949.

*Welty, Eudora. "Words into Fiction," *Southern Review*, I (1965) 543–553.

Wenger, J. "Speed as Technique in the Novels of Balzac," *PMLA*, 55 (1940), 241–252.

*Wescott, Glenway. *Images of Truth: Remembrances and Criticism.* N.Y.: Harper & Row, 1962.

*West, Paul *The Modern Novel.* London: Hutchinson, 1963.

_____. "The Nature of Fiction," *Essays in Criticism,* XIII (1963), 95–100.

West, Ray B. *The Writer in the Room.* East Lansing, Mich.: Mich. State Univ. Press, 1968.

*West, Rebecca. *The Strange Necessity.* Garden City, N.Y., 1928.

Westbrook, Max, ed. *The Modern American Novel: Essays in Criticism.* N.Y.: Random House, 1966.

Weston, Harold. *Form in Literature.* London: Rich & Cowan, 1934.

*Wharton, Edith, *A Backward Glance.* N.Y.: Appleton Century, 1934.

_____. *The Writing of Fiction.* N.Y.: Scribner's, 1925.

Wheelwright, Philip. *The Burning Fountain.* Bloomington, Ind.: Univ. of Ind. Press, 1954.

Williams, Raymond. *Culture and Society, 1780–1950.* London: Chatto & Windus, 1958.

_____. *Reading and Criticism.* London: Muller, 1950.

_____. "Realism and the Contemporary Novel," *Partisan Review,* XXVI (1959), 200–213.

*Wilson, Angus. "The Novelist and the Narrator," *English Studies Today: Second Series; . . . Fourth Conf., Internat'l Assn. of Univ. Professors of English . . . Lausanne and Berne, August, 1959.* Berne: Francke Verlag, 1961.

*Wilson, Colin. *The Outsider.* Boston: Houghton Mifflin, 1956.

*Wilson, Edmund. *Axel's Castle: A Study of Imaginative Literature of 1870–1930.* N.Y.: Scribner's, 1931.

_____. "The Historical Interpretation of Literature," *The Triple Thinkers.* N.Y.: Oxford Univ. Press, 1948.

Wimsatt, W. K. *The Verbal Icon*. Lexington: The Univ. Press of Ky., 1954.

Wimsatt, W. K. and Brooks, Cleanth. *Literary Criticism, A Short History*. N.Y.: Knopf, 1957.

Winters, Yvor. *Maule's Curse*. N.Y.: New Directions, 1938.

*Wolfe, Thomas. "The Story of a Novel," *The Thomas Wolfe Reader*. Ed. by C. Hugh Holman. N.Y.: Scribner's, 1962.

Woodman, Roos. "Literature and Life," *Queens Quarterly*, LXVII (1962), 621–631.

Woodress, James, ed. *American Literary Scholarship, An Annual* (begins, 1963). Durham, N.C.: Duke Univ. Press.

*Woolf, Virginia. *The Common Reader*. N.Y.: Harcourt, Brace, 1925.

*_____. *Granite & Rainbow*. N.Y.: Harcourt, Brace, 1958.

*_____. *The Second Common Reader*. N.Y.: Harcourt, Brace, 1932.

*_____. "The Workaday World that the Novelist Never Enters," *The British Imagination: A Critical Survey from the Times Supplement*. N.Y., 1961.

*_____. *A Writer's Diary*. N.Y.: Harcourt, Brace, 1953, 1954.

Wright, Andrew. "Irony and Fiction," *Journal of Aesthetics and Art Criticism*, XII (1953), 111–118.

Wright, Walter Francis, ed. *Joseph Conrad on Fiction*. Lincoln, Neb.: Univ. of Neb. Press, 1964.

_____. "Tone in Fiction," *The Theory of the Novel, New Essays*. Ed. by John Halperin. N.Y.: Oxford Univ. Press, 1974.

Wyndham, Francis. "Twenty-five Years of the Novel," *The Craft of Letters in England*. Ed. by John Lehmann. London: Cresset Press, 1956.

Zabel, Morton Dauwen. *Craft and Character: Texts, Method, and Vocation in Modern Fiction*. N.Y.: Viking Press, 1957.

_____. *Literary Opinion in America,* revised. N.Y.: Harper & Brothers, 1937, 1951.

**Zitner, Sheldon P., et. al. *The Practice of Criticism.* Chicago: Scott, Foresman, 1966.

Zola, Emile. *The Experimental Novel and Other Essays.* Translated by Belle M. Sherman. N.Y.: Cassell, 1893.

INDEX A: AUTHORS AND TITLES

This index does not cover the Chronology or the Bibliography. A "C" precedes the final page number in the entries for most of the authors to indicate the page in the Chronology on which the reader will find the birth and death dates of the authors. Authors and titles in the text are cited or discussed because of their effectiveness as examples of types or techniques; among the more than two hundred authors cited in the chronology but not in the text, and thus not in this index, are some of the finest writers in the history of fiction.

INDEX B: TYPES AND TECHNIQUES, AND OTHER TERMS

Note: To encourage their use, and to stress their importance, some terms are included in this index that are often used in literary discussions, but that are seldom given the status of literary terms, and are thus often omitted from indexes

Absolute, 6, 93, 99, 167; art as a modern, 100

Abstract expressionist painting, 204

Abstraction, 8, 74, 125, 204, 206, 263; in descriptions, 171; embodied in images, 206; in style, 171; in symbols, 190

Absurd: concept of, 202

Accessibility: of popular fiction, 46, 210

Accidental, the, 183

Action, 3, 14–15, 35, 72, 74, 90, 105, 107, 113, 116, 119, 121, 125, 127, 142, 149–50, 152, 159–60, 171–72, 207, 229, 244, 253, 283, 289, 291, 294, 299–300, 302; emotional, 133; enveloping, 142; extreme, 165; falling, 143; hero's, 190; mental, 133; narrative, 158; overt, 158; physical, 133, 158; psychological, 121; setting and character in, 133; style as, 52, 58, 160; superficial, 158

Actuality, 61, 179

Adjectives: 171, 219, 221; de Maupassant on, 167

Adolescent perception: novel of, 26, 47

Adventure, 1, 3, 10, 12, 36–37, 41, 46, 158, 303

Advertising, 2; mass, 46; study of, 188

Aesthetes, 99

Aesthetic, 16, 27, 30, 201; anti- 199; achievements, 81; constants, 102; conventional notions of, 200; (psychic) distance, defined, 105, 108; effect, 189; elements, 102; emotion, 98; experience, 100, 156; experience, qualities of, 72, 102; form, 102; harmony, 184; ideals, 34; mysticism, 99; norms, 102; object, 186, 208; pattern, 144; pleasure, 48; qualities, 53, 100; rules, 102; term, honorific, 64; theorizing, 156;

traditional concept of, 184; trap, 63; truths, 135; values, 102; works, 183; writers, 65, 186. *See also* art; distance

Aesthetician, 36

Aim: of fiction, 15, 60, 99, 154, 190, 192; of satire, 15

Air novels, 158

Alienation, 122, 208; effect, 105

Aliterature, 203

Allegorical novel, 91–92, discussed; autobiography, 21; figure, 31

Allegory, 3, 8, 11–12, 21, 30–32, 37, 121, 265; fantasy, 42; of love, 3–4; moral, 32; pastoral, 5; pseudo-classical heroic, 5

Allusion, 148, 248; defined, 108; literary, 108

Amalgam, 185

Ambience, 38, 183; emotional, 133

Ambiguity, 117, 140, 208; defined, 107; uncontrolled, 107; unintentional, 107

American Indian (Native American) novels, 71

Amplification, 181

Anachronism, 102

Analogy, 98, 173, 255; matrix of, 173; musical, 184

Analysis, 60, 102, 159–60, 197; close, xi–xii, 213–308; intellectual, 207; over-emphasis on, 186

Anarchic: artist, 34; novel, 137

Anecdote, 2

Anovel, 203

Antagonist, 92, 301; defined, 121; writer as reader's, 93

Anticipation, 127, 144, 174, 188–89, 229–30

Anti-hero, 92, 125, 300; discussed, 203–08; novel 92–95

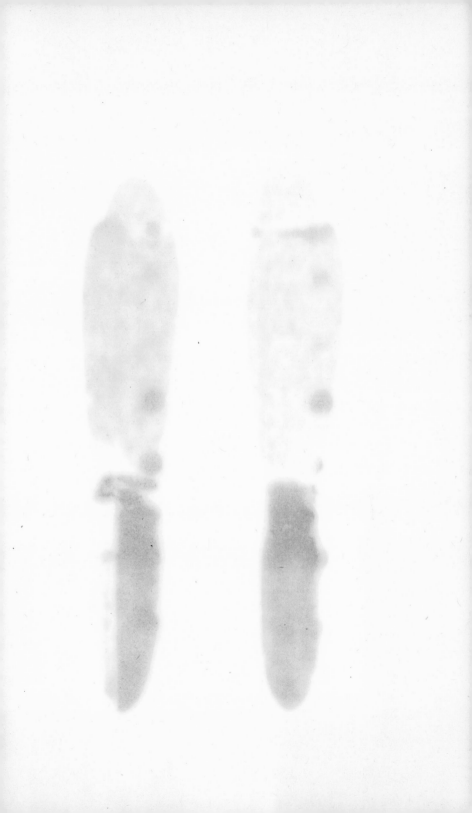